KNOWING, THINKING, AND BELIEVING

KNOWING, THINKING, AND BELIEVING

Festschrift for Professor David Krech

Edited by

Lewis Petrinovich
University of California, Riverside

and

James L. McGaugh
University of California, Irvine

PLENUM PRESS · NEW YORK AND LONDON

Library of Congress Cataloging in Publication Data

Main entry under title:

Knowing, thinking, and believing.

Includes bibliographies and index.

CONTENTS: Petrinovich, L. and McGaugh, J. Introduction.—Historical and methodological issues: Petrinovich, L. Molar reductionism. Wyers, E. J. Learning and evolution. Garcia, J. I. Krechevsky and I. Zolman, J. F. Developmental constraints on conditioning. [etc.]

1. Krech, David, 2. Cognition—Addresses, essays, lectures. I. Krech, David. II. Petrinovich, Lewis F. III. McGaugh, James L. IV. Title.

BF311.K6384 153.4 76-40273

ISBN 0-306-30928-9

A Division of Plenum Publishing Corporation
227 West 17th Street, New York, N.Y. 10011

Printed in the United States of America

CONTRIBUTORS

Edward L. Bennett • Lawrence Berkeley Laboratory, University of California, Berkeley, California

Marian Cleeves Diamond • Department of Physiology-Anatomy, University of California, Berkeley, California

John Garcia • Departments of Psychology and Psychiatry, University of California, Los Angeles, California

Kenneth R. Hammond • Institute of Behavioral Science, University of Colorado, Boulder, Colorado

James L. McGaugh • Department of Psychobiology, School of Biological Sciences, University of California, Irvine, California

Lewis Petrinovich • Department of Psychology, University of California, Riverside, California

Thomas H. Roderick • The Jackson Laboratory, Bar Harbor, Maine

Mark R. Rosenzweig • Department of Psychology, University of California, Berkeley, California

George Stone • Langley Porter Neuropsychiatric Institute, University of California, San Francisco, California

Jane W. Torrey • Department of Psychology, Connecticut College, New London, Connecticut

Cynthia C. Wimer • Division of Neurosciences, City of Hope National Medical Center, Duarte, California

Richard E. Wimer • Division of Neurosciences, City of Hope National Medical Center, Duarte, California

Everett J. Wyers • Department of Psychology, State University of New York, Stony Brook, New York

James F. Zolman • Department of Physiology and Biophysics, University of Kentucky Medical Center, Lexington, Kentucky

CONTENTS

Physiological Mediation

Social and Cognitive Issues

INTRODUCTION

The impetus for this volume is provided by a feeling common to several of us who took Ph.D.s in psychology at Berkeley between the end of World War II and the early 1960s. As many people do, we talk of the "good old days" when psychology progressed without the elaborate technology which characterizes much of today's research. You know the line, "iron men with T-mazes, stopwatches, and *F* scale." Through the years, however, we have come to realize that the climate at Berkeley during that period was more than just intellectually stimulating for the participants. It was a period during which many of us acquired (perhaps without understanding it at the time) a general view of psychological inquiry. This view is not tied to a specific subject field and requires no commitment to a specific research problem, apparatus, or technique. It is, rather, a dedication to one's own special research field tempered by an historically based appreciation of overriding general psychological issues and their ramifications. For those of us who grew up at Berkeley, it has been difficult to step into our laboratories and to immerse ourselves in a research problem without being concerned about the implications of our mode of inquiry and the meaning of our experimental results in a broad perspective.

As Hammond has pointed out in this volume, this overriding concern was produced by the individual influence of members of the "Berkeley Group," David Krech, Edward Chace Tolman, and Egon Brunswik. "These psychologists will be praised . . . not only for their academic contributions, but for their efforts to relate their scientific work to the world outside the laboratory."

This influence was instilled by these three psychologists primarily in two formal settings. Brunswik was encountered in his graduate course, The Conceptual Framework of Psychology, and Tolman and Krech in Tolman's

Seminar in Animal Psychology. Tolman's seminar was attended by most of the Berkeley faculty in experimental and physiological psychology, a visiting professor or two, and a few hardy graduate students thrown in for seasoning.

The typical seminar meeting was presided over by Tolman. Those attending included several Berkeley faculty—Krech, Leo Postman, Mark Rosenzweig, D. A. Riley, Benbow Ritchie, and six or seven graduate students. The topic usually (in those good old days) revolved around some theoretical question concerning the Berkeley-Yale-Iowa conflict—with one of the faculty or graduate students presenting a theoretical paper, the results of some recently completed research, or a discussion of some of the latest experiments by the Neo-Hullians on a topic such as latent learning or place learning. The seminar would be convened at 7 p.m. and would continue until 10 or 11—often until the building custodians started making conspicuous their desire to clean the room and finish their work. Then, for us, a young faculty member or two, and maybe a visiting professor, it was off to a local beer hall for more talk.

The discussion in the seminars was always active. The loud and heated arguments—quite often between Krech and some hapless adversary—were punctuated by Tolman's gentle ministrations and goadings to get on with the proceedings. The times were exciting, we were all involved, and the weekly animal seminar meetings fueled everyone for a week of hard work and thought. The reverberations were felt over coffee in the graduate student–faculty commons twice a day and we prepared to pursue the issues with renewed vigor "as soon as the results of my new experiment are in—but it looks good and will settle things once and for all."

All these "Tolmaniac" sessions were prodded by Krech from two directions. From one direction he would always insist that we not become enmeshed in the details of our research designs or encapsulated in statistical analysis, but that we focus always on the relevance of our results to the "Big Question," and consider why our answer was better than any other that was current.

Tom Roderick has captured this spirit as follows:

> For any number of complex reasons, the psychological make-up of most young scientists inclines them to ask the question, "Why?" when exposed to new sets of experiences or facts. And it is not surprising that during the course of graduate studies, this propensity would be reinforced by mentors, peers, and the general academic environment. Krech encouraged this approach to new experience, but he nourished something else that in my opinion was enormously important; he framed discussions of hypotheses with the question, "Why not?" This attitude toward hypotheses was part of Krech's facility to juggle several hypotheses simultaneously, to bounce them off each other, and to reveal their interplay. This attitude, furthermore, guarded against a premature commitment to an inflexible research approach. Krech's attitude is

> characteristic of a liberal intellect, and essential for creativity. It was also good medicine for the generally sheltered and somewhat conservative group of graduate students of the '50s.

While maintaining a focus on "big questions," Krech also stressed the need to identify mediational mechanisms—and would continually probe from that direction as well. This concern for molecular mechanism simultaneously with insistence on careful attention to molar explanatory systems is perhaps the dominant theme of Krech's career. He took his Ph.D. with Tolman, and Tolman's emphasis on a dynamic, purposive view of behavior is a major influence on Krech's thinking. The balance of these views was nurtured by Lashley, with whom Krech worked early in his postdoctoral career, inquiring into relationships between "hypotheses" and brain function.

Following this early period, Krech turned his attention to social psychology. He was one of the founders of the Society for the Psychological Study of Social Issues (SPSSI) and wrote, with Richard Crutchfield, *Theory and Problems of Social Psychology*, which was published in 1948. The book represented a major step toward organizing the subject matter and theory of social psychology and was widely recognized as a major achievement. As Krech has phrased it, "we had done well by doing good."

During his social psychology period, he testified as an expert witness in the historic 1951 desegregation decision, the first time a federal court allowed social psychologists to testify as expert witnesses. After these years as one of the world's preeminent social psychologists, Krech was led again to these same two themes in his studies of kinesthetic aftereffects in humans. This led him to develop the concept of "cortical conductivity," which, in turn, led him to look for the "stuff" of cortical conductivity in the enzymes and transmitters of the central nervous system of the rat.

At the risk of oversimplifying (but to characterize Krech *at all* is to oversimplify!), we suggest that there are four major threads running through all Krech's work. The first is a primary concern for the meaning of individual differences. His early studies of hypotheses in rats were based on an analysis of what each individual rat was doing on each trial. From this base, he constructed overall schema to characterize the nature of problem solving. This attention to individual differences was coupled with a healthy disrespect for those analytic statistics which, essentially, reduce individual differences to an error term against which to evaluate mean differences.

A second characteristic, as we have noted, is an insistence on the primary importance of the "Big Question." The concern was with what all of these results meant. After that has been settled with all the clarity that can be achieved, then and only then is it appropriate to do an experiment, to invoke statistical safeguards, and to proceed with caution to explore a network of hypotheses. Krech never lost sight of the importance of events to the larger scheme of things. These larger schemata invariably involved the application of psychological knowledge to the problems of human functioning.

This leads us to the third characteristic of Krech's science—a search for the mechanisms responsible for molar behavioral processes. His molar view of behavior is always accompanied by attention to molecular reduction. Thus throughout his career Krech served two mistresses: one molecular and mechanistic, and the other molar and humanistic. While much of Krech's research involved the rat, his psychology is always the psychology of humans, and animal preparations are used only to cast light on the human condition. His remarks as discussant at the symposium on the Chemistry of Mood, Motivation, and Memory reveal his attitude quite clearly. "We dare not encapsulate ourselves in the goldfish, or mouse, or rat, or even the human *laboratory*. We must look at people—raw, living unyoked people" (p. 221). Although he firmly believes that the smaller the unit of analysis, the greater the generality of the findings, all of this molecular analysis is of value primarily to help us to understand human brain functioning. All else, to him, is beside the point as far as psychology is concerned. "Take your laboratory findings and bring them out, and test them on people, and return refreshed to wrestle with renewed zest with your pigeons and rats and mice" (p. 223). Thus what we are attempting to build is a psychology of people. "Go constantly to look at . . . people. Know what you are studying, and whence came your question, and before whom your work will be judged" (p. 223).

Finally, we must emphasize Krech's overriding concern for and commitment to the essential views of Gestalt psychology. He accepted the essential organized unity of human behavior and resisted those who would fractionate this unity into static, molecular pieces. Instead of compartmentalizing behavior into components such as perception, feeling, and thinking and then studying each of these three as separate entities, Krech believed that the processes represented by those three must be considered to be an organized whole. Thus perception, feeling, and thinking are to be replaced by a superordinate "perfink." The textbook *Theory and Problems in Social Psychology*, coauthored with Professor Crutchfield, stands as one of the most comprehensive and systematic treatises of social psychology, and its strength is due in large measure to this overriding Gestalt orientation. The first edition of Krech and Crutchfield's introductory textbook in psychology, *Elements of Psychology*, reflected even more clearly Krech's construal of psychological knowledge. Its treatment of each psychological "subject" begins with phenomenology, considers the experimental data which can be brought to bear on these phenomenological issues, and then proceeds to a physiological reductionistic analysis of the subject. Throughout this process, the original phenomenological focus is never lost—set aside briefly, perhaps, but always at stage left, ready for its next entrance.

As there was no Tolmanian school of psychology so there is no Krechian school. Krech is dismayed by simplistic thinking and has low regard for models which draw attention away from psychological phenomena and direct it, instead, toward the formalism of a model. He quotes, with favor, Brewster Ghiselin, who wrote, "The crudest approximation, if it provides hints for the solution of a broad range of problems, has every advantage over the most elegant mathematical law which asserts nothing of interest."

His catholicism in terms of explanatory constructs and the data on which they should be based has influenced psychologists from a wide variety of disciplines. The essays in this volume attest to the diversity of interests and approaches of those influenced by Krech. The subjects represented here run the gamut from genetics to general issues in the history and philosophy of science. This diversity has led some of us to concentrate on molecular and reductionistic approaches to the complex issues of organismic behavior. Some of us, on the other hand, have been led to adopt molar approaches to settle the same issues. From this apparent diversity the editors are impressed by an overriding strong communality: a refusal to ignore or to define away the richness of behavior. This refusal to sidestep "messy" complexity was incubated both by Krech's own example and by his almost ruthless treatment of the culprit who was caught in attempted murder of behavior in all its beautiful ramifications.

Instead of "Krechians," we find, among his students and colleagues, a diverse group of behavioral scientists, all of whom were taught to value honest scientific endeavor of all kinds and to be somewhat skeptical of their own attempts to unravel behavioral mysteries. However, the historical perspective instilled by Krech helped us all to achieve some degree of satisfaction from our efforts since we were taught a perspective from which to appreciate the nature of scientific progress and development and are still able to savor the pleasure that comes from knowing we have not ignored the complexity of behavior in our attempts to subject it to scientific scrutiny.

Krech obviously had an influence on the intellectual peregrinations of those represented here. In addition, he demonstrated to all of us that he could operate in a creative capacity in any of these subject disciplines. This quickly discouraged any tendencies we might have developed toward being well-rounded dilettantes. He takes a strong interest in the intellectual development of those of us who worked with him and demands that we send him reprints of our current research in order that he might keep in touch with our progress. The most flattering aspect is that he reads them, and the useful aspect is that he often writes a critique regarding their goodness and their weakness—and, sometimes, raises an eyebrow at us over their triviality.

One aspect of Krech's academic prowess that we wish to emphasize is his extraordinary ability to teach. He is a brilliant and exciting seminar leader and teacher of advanced psychology classes. In addition, he is an inspired teacher of introductory psychology. He achieves this, not only by being histrionic (which he is), and by having a strong intellectual grasp of the subject matter (which he has), but also by spending long hours to prepare each lecture, to study how to present the ideas in just the right way, with the proper example from the literature, and the proper slide to add to the presentation. His introductory lecture course in psychology was always scheduled in Wheeler Auditorium—the largest on the Berkeley campus. Enrollment in the course was generally large. When Krech taught it, however, there was a heavy sprinkling of auditors who were there because they enjoyed a good, informative lecture, because they wanted to know something about the topic to be covered, or because they were about to leave the nest to teach their own introductory psychology classes and were studying the master at work.

Enough of academic analysis and moralizing. There are many characteristics of Krech which have profoundly influenced those of us who cherish the time we have spent and will yet spend with him. These are subtle, intangible influences which perhaps can be communicated to some extent by a page or so of sentimental reminiscence.

Krech treated all graduate students with respect and (with a little teasing added in) as equals. When passing a graduate student in the hall, his typical greeting was "Good morning, professor," accompanied by a waggle of the eyebrows and a broad grin. This often startled one, especially a beginning student, because the greeting could well have been tendered in mockery by some. It became obvious that the tone was not mockery, but one which communicated an expectation and, even, an admonition that one would damned well behave in a "professorial" manner. On our part it would not have occurred to us to call him by his first name or to refer to him as Doctor Krech —he was, and always will be, Professor Krech or, more informally, just Krech.

As a beginning graduate student one approached Krech with awe and respect, and, as the acquaintance with him broadened, a mixture of love and fear developed. The awe and respect were the result of his sharp wit, incisive criticism, and the incredible range of information he could bring to bear on a question. The fear was occasioned by the possibility that his scorching critical ability might be directed to expose one in the act of *the* cardinal sin—thinking simplistically. The love grew with the realization that he cared for our intellectual development enough to spend hours with us, and that he cared that we grow to be able to enjoy the excitement of our academic labors as much as he did.

We, in turn, came to expect acerbic criticism and to accept the fact that this was part of the *rites de passage* which we were experiencing and for which we would be grateful throughout our careers. The possibility of withering assault led us to consider our ideas and to plan our experiments carefully before exposing them to the light of day. Yet it wasn't permissible to withdraw into the refuge of the safe statement. Any new idea presented to Krech would be received with cheerful scorn and a spirited explanation of how it was all "nonsense." However, this barrage would be accompanied by a careful explication of how it was *almost* a good idea if only this were added and that were changed: "You see how it could be done—and how important the question is that you were asking. You didn't realize that, did you?" So, at the same time your idea was being rejected as inadequate to resolve the issue you were commended for understanding the importance of the issue, and the electrical excitement of posing such questions was communicated.

After having decided on the experimental procedures appropriate to the task, and having received Krech's skeptical benediction to try it because you were young and had plenty of time for such nonsense, you became aware that whenever the latest data from the experiment were being examined Krech would be hovering over the numbers and showing you "what it *really* means—don't you see that this is much more important than you thought it was when you started. Just two more groups and . . . ."

The one big event in our graduate student days was the annual Psi Chi Show at the end of the academic year, just after the Ph.D. preliminary examination, and usually just before the results were known. The show was an elaborate affair in those days. We had some musicians, some singers, some fearless hams, and some writers with deep psychological insights into the nature of humor (mainly run on phasic hostility and a neat turn of a dirty phrase). Of course, the major topic of the show revolved around the real and imagined insults and injustices endured by the students at the hands of the faculty. And, of course, since Krech was one of the more flamboyant and critical members of the faculty and would most likely have deflated our pretensions and damaged our egos, he was one of the characters molested most in our skits. His response was one of delight. In a particularly intensive skit characterizing the animal seminar in full swing, Krech was quite broadly portrayed—shouting, arguing, ignoring the other "seminar" members, pacing back and forth on the table top while the student-portrayed Tolman murmured "boys, boys." If his feelings were wounded, he managed to conceal the feelings quite effectively. At the end of the show, Krech bestowed the ever-present tea rose from his lapel on his impersonator with a muttered "You play Krech better than I do."

No discussion of Krech would be complete without a strong emphasis on the influence of Hilda Krech. We first met her at the evening proseminar for first-year graduate students in their home—a stressful time for hoping-to-be psychologists. Midway in the tense proceedings, a pleasant Hilda would call us for coffee and cookies, and would distract us all with urbane conversation. Through the years we have come to appreciate her influence as a constant source of understanding, imagination, and support, and as a gentle critic. We have spent many hours on many occasions in spirited discussions with "Hildy" and Krech, and are enriched by the memories of those splendid times.

Krech's autobiographical statement (1974) deals with many aspects of his personal and professional life and there is little point in repeating it here. The essays presented here do more than we, the editors, can to capture the breadth of Krech's influence, and this breadth, in the last analysis, will be more meaningful than any paeons of praise.

Perhaps one of the best summaries of our feelings can be reflected by the last paragraph of the autobiography. "In my forty-odd years of wandering in and out of academia and psychology I have found ill will, nastiness, and fraud; I have also found warmth, companionship, friendship, integrity, excitement, intellectual wonder, and fulfillment. On balance, I am satisfied."

We, as students and colleagues, conclude that we have even more to cherish than does he. We were privileged to have a close association with Krech. On balance, we are satisfied.

Lewis Petrinovich
James L. McGaugh

HISTORICAL AND METHODOLOGICAL ISSUES

1

Lewis Petrinovich

MOLAR REDUCTIONISM

In the past few years, I have been concerned about the state of psychology as a science. I have been expressing this concern in a series of papers concerned with such things as the psychobiology of language development (Petrinovich, 1972), the evolution of language (Petrinovich, 1976), the methodological traditions and shortcomings of psychology as a science (Petrinovich, 1973*a*), and these principles as examined in the context of a research problem (Petrinovich, 1973*b*). This series of papers has led me to a series of questions. Have we progressed toward an understanding of the behavior of organisms? Do we know much more now than we did 50 years ago about what organisms are likely to do in the environmental contexts that are representative of their life space? Are we approaching a better understanding of why organisms adapt to certain situations in the way they do, and why they do not adapt in an adequate manner to other situations? I have come to the awareness that we have not made a great deal of progress toward finding the answers to these questions, and that it is time for us to confront these issues full face and to stop merely casting sideways glances at them. After all, they do comprise the major tasks for psychology as a science.

What I will outline in this chapter is a methodological strategy based on a unifying theme: an evolutionary molar reductionism. This theme is based on the assumption that psychology as a reductionistic science has moved in the wrong direction. Instead of seeking to reduce behavioral functioning to a more molecular level, it should seek to reduce it to a unifying set of molar principles.

Lewis Petrinovich • Department of Psychology, University of California, Riverside, California.

But first a word on behalf of the sponsoring occasion. My belief that we should continually subject our research questions, our research strategies, and our methodological niceties to the test of logical, historical, and practical scrutiny was nurtured under the sometimes withering tutelage of Professor Krech. On at least two occasions after I had fledged from the Berkeley nest I had to step back and question whether the research path I was following was one which could possibly lead to the ends I had sought at the outset. The answer was no on each occasion, and I modified my research program accordingly. I feel that the ability to entertain such a question was due, in large measure, to my professional initiation, enriched by the sharply critical acumen of Professor Krech. The possibility of undergoing his critical appraisal led one to maintain an alert attitude of self-critical awareness rather than risk the mortification which would result from having overlooked the obvious. At the present time, I believe that the nonexperimental and nontraditional positions I espouse in this chapter are the product of that initiation. Professor Krech might not approve of certain aspects of my thesis since I will disagree with him in at least one major regard—on the value of molecular reductionism in psychological explanation. With these preliminaries out of the way, let me sketch my argument, and then proceed to its development.

The basic argument runs as follows: (1) The behavioral sciences in general, and psychology in particular, have tended to emulate the research models of the older physical sciences. (2) These research models are not appropriate to the study of complex biological systems, especially at the level of behavior. (3) This is because the traditional experimental models do not allow the variability inherent in behavioral systems to express itself. (4) The statistical models which emphasize the testing for significant differences between groups constrict the research enterprise, and lead to a self-fulfilling reductionism. (5) The appropriate functional question is directed toward identifying those variables which control "meaningful" proportions of the total variance in behavior. (6) An acceptance of those research methods adequate to allow the expression of the inherent probabilism in behavioral systems will result in a paradigmatic revolution of the type discussed by Kuhn (1970). (7) The successful completion of this revolution is essential if behavioral science is to move toward a molar functionalism adequate to achieve an understanding of the behavior of complex organisms interacting with their environment.

Views Regarding Psychology as a Science

Psychology has had a long and checkered past in its search for *the* proper data and methods to further its development as a scientific discipline. Concern has often been expressed regarding the propriety of using subjective data to speak to what might seem the inherently subjective nature of psychology. Some have insisted that psychology as a science is properly conceived of as the study of objective behavior (Hull, 1943*a*; Skinner, 1938; Watson, 1924), some have insisted that this view is much too narrow and confining (Allport, 1947; Maslow, 1966), while others have accepted the fact that there is a need to objectify psychology but believe we should retain as much of the richness of the subjectivist view as possible (Hebb, 1949; Tolman, 1932).

Still others have avoided definitional issues by attending to the methods used to gather data and to the coordination of theoretical constructs and objective data (Bergmann and Spence, 1941; Stevens, 1939). The preoccupation with objectivity (often accompanied by a lack of concern with maintaining an adequate scope) has resulted in what Brunswick (1952) calls a "misconception of exactitude" in psychology. This misconception of exactitude is the consequence of slavishly adopting the research designs and experimental procedures which have proved useful to the physical sciences—"to do for 'mind' what physics has done for 'matter' . . ." (Brunswik, 1952, pp. 694–695). The focus of such a science becomes elementistic since it seeks to break "mind" down to the basic units of which it is thought to be composed—the S-R unit becomes the basic element. It also becomes nomothetic with its interest in discovering the general and universal laws which govern behavior—associationism becomes the basic principle. Brunswik considers this "overawed 'me-too' attitude" of psychology to have led to the rather uncritical acceptance of an outdated image of the older natural sciences—especially those sciences which deal with macrophysical events. This same concern has been expressed by Esper (1964), who writes: "the history of psychology reveals over and over again the pathetic eagerness of psychologists to adopt *analogically* the current fashion in physics or chemistry" (p. 9).

Psychology has wholeheartedly adopted methods which are satisfactory to deal with relatively static events and has applied these methods to the study of dynamic processes. The ideal, according to the classic experimental tradition, is to use procedures which embody the virtues of the single-variable experiment—hold all independent variables constant but one, vary that one systematically, and observe the consequent changes in the dependent variable (e.g., Underwood, 1957, p. 34–36; 1966, p. 10). Variants of this method exist which allow the experimenter to vary two or more independent variables simultaneously and to observe not only the independent simple effects but the interactions as well (i.e., complex analysis of variance). (See Brunswik, 1955, for a general discussion of the inherent limitations of such systematic designs.)

The major difficulty with this manner of proceeding stems from two sources: (1) it distorts the structure of natural events, and (2) it embodies a misleading conception of the meaning of individual differences. The first point refers to the fact that to use techniques such as analysis of variance one must select a range of stimulus values in some arbitrary fashion, must choose a dependent variable to measure which is an arbitrary, and often limiting, operational translation of the conceptual variables in which the experimenter is interested, and must abstract the entire experimental operation out of the complex of variables in which the behavior is usually embedded.

The systematic experimental method separates the variables controlling behavior from the fabric in which they are embedded and, in this way, destroys the pattern of correlations between variables as it exits in natural situations. The utilization of this approach has serious limiting consequences if the behavioral system under study is one which has multiple and intersubstitutable determiners and involves vicarious and hierarchical modes of response. If we wish to generalize the behavior under study to the contexts in which it normally occurs, we should not destroy the pattern of correlations that exists in such contexts. Only if such correlations are maintained intact can we assess the probable importance of any given variable or combination of variables since it is important that the variables appear, both separately and in interaction, with a natural distribution density (Petrinovich, 1976). Thus if we wish to determine the proportion of the total variance which can be attributed to the different variables involved in behavior we must abandon strict reliance on traditional experimental methods.

Let us examine some of the strengths of systematic experimentation that have led to its widespread utilization in science. In order to control variables other than the one (or ones) of major interest, the experimenter isolates the organism from the action of uncontrolled variables. This is done by performing the experiment in a controlled laboratory environment which permits a maximum degree of control of extraneous variables. In addition, subject differences are reduced by drawing subjects from a relatively homogeneous pool. Random assignment of individuals to the different treatment groups is used to eliminate differences due to uncontrolled and unwanted differences among individual subjects. In this way, the average value of these variables should approximate the values found in the population at large, and their influence should be the same for each of the groups. Against this homogeneous background, the influence of changes in the critical variable under study can be seen since no other influences have been permitted to enter the experimental situation. Since we cannot rule out all unwanted variability, we employ a method of significance testing that evaluates the magnitude of differences between the means of the treatment groups relative to the amount of variability found within the groups. This within-group variance is called the "error variance" since it is the result of uncontrolled factors that have kept the experiment from attaining a perfect expression of the influence of the treatment variable on each and every subject. As Kerlinger (1973) has pointed out, the purpose of such research designs is to control variance, to "maximize systematic variance, control extraneous systematic variance, and minimize error variance" (p. 306). The true experiment, in which one can randomly assign subjects to experimental treatments, is a powerful way to maximize the effectiveness of experimental variance.

This view usually involves acceptance of the principle of determinism: that general laws exist which would allow complete predictability of behavior if measurement were precise and if all relevant variables could be controlled. Thus Underwood (1957) writes: "Every natural event (phenomenon) is assumed to have a cause, and if that causal situation could be exactly reconstituted, the event would be duplicated" (p. 4). Hull develops this same view in more detail: "That this lack of perfect correlation is due to the difficulty of measurement of the conditions rather than to the capriciousness of the alleged law is suggested by the fact that as measurements are improved, repeated, and pooled, the verification of the formula becomes increasingly exact, i.e., the correlation becomes progressively higher" (1943*b*, p. 275).

In this view, prediction would be exact if the general laws of behavior could be freed from the constraints of intrinsic and extrinsic masking and modulating variables. The variability in the behavior of individuals, say from trial to trial, is a factor which is, itself, lawful and in principle predictable. In spite of this belief in determinacy, Hull found it necessary to introduce a systematic construct, behavioral oscillation, to acknowledge that there would always be a standard error of prediction at the level of molar behavior. He believed this variability was due to "the variability in the molecular constituents of the nervous system, the neurons" (Hull, 1943*a*, p. 309).

Systematic experimentation is a method designed to detect whether or not a particular variable has *any* systematic effect on behavior. It has been successfully used to identify the nature of those variables which potentially influence behavior—and the result has been what I have called a species-possible science (Petrinovich, 1973*b*, 1976). The experimental method is useful, then, in the initial stage of inquiry to identify those variables potentially involved in the causation of behavior at the functional level. Postman (1955), an exponent of the virtues of the experimental method, expresses this quite nicely: "we can proceed . . . only if we have (a) knowledge of what the universe to be sampled is, particularly what the units are of which it is composed, and (b) if we have identified the dimensions or features with respect to which the sampling is to be representative" (p. 223). Thus systematic experimentation might be considered to be a prolegomena to the development of a molar functional psychology.

Another step in the justification of the laboratory method is to issue a declaration similar to the following by Hilgard (1948) in the first edition of his classic *Theories of Learning*: "Ultimately the same constants begin to crop up in different equations. When that happens within the equations of two or more miniature systems, these systems can be integrated into a more comprehensive system" (p. 356). Hilgard tells us in the second edition that "A principle once discovered in a better controlled situation can be validated in a less-well-controlled one" (1956, p. 490). Apparently, by 1956, his faith in the former statement of 1948 had diminished somewhat—perhaps in view of the lack of success of such miniature systems as the one proposed by Hull (1943*a*)—since the statement does not appear in the 1956 edition.

Postman (1955) is explicit in his adherence to the position that miniature systems research eventually leads to general and more comprehensive theories. "The systematic experimenter may be content for the time being to restrict his generalizations to the conditions studied, to build "miniature systems" preliminary to the attack on the large-scale problems" (p. 223).

I suggest that this fond hope is much less justified than it was when Postman proposed it—at least if we consider the arena of the learning theories of the 1950s and 1960s, which were among the most highly developed miniature systems in psychology.

An examination of a recent collection, *Essays in Neobehaviorism* (Kendler and Spence, 1971), supports the view that these miniature systems have not led to an attack on the "large-scale problems." The editors of the volume observe that there is "a definite backtracking from the goal of general behavior theory to the development of more specific formulations" (p. 30). No longer do they seek to "establish a theory of all the behavioral (social) sciences," as did Hull. Nor do they even seek the integration of data to "show how the theory may be extended to more complex types of behavioral phenomena such as selective and paired-associate learning," as did Spence. Rather, they write: "as the following essays suggest, most of the current theoretical attempts within the neobehavioristic tradition have been concerned with an even more restricted range of phenomena" (p. 30).

The miniature systems approach is based on an acceptance of the principle of *extensional analysis*, whereby a full explanation of a small region is sought with the aim of extending the complete explanation of the restricted region to adjoining regions, each of which has been explained in the same manner by other investigators. This approach seems to have been relatively unsatisfactory in the sense that it never appears to attain the level of molar behavioral analysis. The explication of the restricted region never seems to end, and the exploration tends to become more and more miniature instead.

Greater progress in the attack on the large-scale problems has come about through the efforts of those using *intensional analysis*, whereby a partial analysis of a whole region is made more and more adequate by way of filling in critical details here and there. This intensional analysis might well be followed by the development of miniature systems in crucial regions whose identity will have been established in terms of their *probable* importance in the entire explanatory fabric. This difference in methodological strategy, although it would seem to be minor, exerts a profound influence on the direction and fabric of the scientific system. All of my preceding remarks presume that one of the major tasks for psychologists is to understand the molar behavior of organisms interacting with their environments. This need not be the only task of psychologists, but it certainly should occupy the attention of a meaningful number of basic researchers. We should move away from modes of study which permit us to see only the strongest possible expression of variables against a background contrived to be neutral and should seek research modes which allow us to determine the relative proportion of variance that can be attributed to the variables involved in the control of the behavior of organisms in their environmental context. Brunswik (1955) expresses this concern quite elegantly: "The main function both of art and of systematic experimentation, then, is to . . . mold us by exaggeration and extreme correlation or absence of correlation. But exaggeration is distortion, and this distortion must in science eventually be resolved by allowing the more palatable systematic design to mature into, and to be superseded by, the more truthful representative design" (p. 215).

Thus a major difference between systematic, molecular analysis and a molar functional one is in the meaning of behavioral variability. Variability of behavior becomes a mere annoyance to the molecular analyst who utilizes the systematic laboratory approach—an annoyance which "is to a large extent responsible for the relatively backward condition of the social, as compared with the physical, sciences" (Hull, 1943*a*, p. 317). Again, we see psychology laboring under the burden of an imprecision that keeps it from being the equal of the "more advanced sciences, such as chemistry and physics," as Hilgard (1956) phrased it. Best (1972) has expressed the view I am developing here as follows: "The name of the game is to ascertain which of the factors yield associated deterministic component estimates that are improbably different from zero, i.e., 'significant,' in the light of the error variance found in the experiment. . . . Error variance, in this scheme of things, is what separates men from the gods. It is not considered an intrinsic part of the behavior, but a measure of the imperfection of the experimenter" (p. 74).

Rather than accept the classic point of view, why not question whether the model of reality satisfactory for the physical sciences is an appropriate one for functional psychology?

Inherent Variability of Biological Processes

It seems apparent, at least to me, that the subject matter of psychology is such that it will not yield its secrets to the questioning of a science utilizing the methods which have been found to be satisfactory to the "older" sciences. Brunswik (1952, 1955, 1956) pointed this out repeatedly, and it has been suggested by many other philosophers and scientists as well.

For example, Polanyi (1958) suggests that the psychological domain is different from that of the "exact sciences," which can rely on what he calls a mathematical formalism. The pattern of science must, he believes, change radically when experience is brought in as a part of the scientific enterprise—it is no longer possible to approximate the methods of a "completely detached natural science."

Ernst Mayr is more explicit when discussing a statement by the physicist Bunge regarding causality. Bunge had written that "A theory can predict to the extent to which it can describe and explain." Mayr's comment is that "It is evident that Bunge is a physicist; no biologist would have made such a statement. The theory of natural selection can describe and explain phenomena with considerable precision, but it cannot make reliable predictions . . ." (Mayr, 1965, p. 43). This point has been developed in some detail by Scriven (1959), who develops the argument that evolutionary biology constitutes a powerful explanatory scientific system, which does not have the ability to *predict.*

Since psychology deals with the behavior of organisms interacting with their environments, it has many problems in common with functional biology. For this reason, the model of the biological sciences will be more appropriate for psychology than that of the physical sciences. Psychology not only shares common problems with biology but also can reap the benefits that biology enjoys as the largesse of an overriding organizing principle which operates at a molar functional level—the principle of evolution.

The subject matters of biology and of psychology differ from those of the physical sciences in at least two major regards: (1) individual variability is the essence of organic life; (2) vicariousness of action is a basic organizing principle of all organic systems which are involved in information exchange with their environment. These two facts make it necessary to develop teleological explanations in order to understand organic systems—and evolutionary theory provides a satisfactory teleological system on which to base and to develop a science with adequate explanatory power.

Variability is a general characteristic of behaving organisms at all levels. This variability comes about as a function of differences among individual organisms: "The uniqueness of biological entities and phenomena is one of the major differences between biological and the physical sciences" (Mayr, 1965, p. 46). Thus, in the molar physical world with which many physicists and chemists deal, homogeneity of samples from the same population tends to be the rule, while in the organic world "all individuals are unique, all stages in the life cycle are unique, all populations are unique, all species and higher categories are unique, all interindividual contacts are unique, all natural associations of species are unique, and all evolutionary events are unique" (Mayr, 1965, p. 47). Best (1972) not only has emphasized this uniqueness but also has drawn attention to the fact that in many instances behavior is "designed" to be random by evolutionary selection in order to make the behavior unpredictable. This unpredictability is especially important if members of a species have to cope with such things as pressures from a predator, and it is essential if the species is to be protected against the vagaries of changing environmental conditions. A residue of randomness in the behavioral potential of a species allows some individual members of the species to respond in a satisfactory fashion to sudden environmental changes and promotes the continuation of the species. If such variability and randomness are lacking, extinction of the species is often the alternative.

Thus biology and psychology must be conceived, in a functional sense, as being historical disciplines. "Physics ignores history. Biology is a branch of it. Physics traditionally has sought to derive general laws that leave out the peculiarities of the things being generalized about. Biology concerns itself with diversity as such, and it is of fundamental theoretical significance that each organism is unique. Hence a physicist's general point of view may predispose him to overlook that which is most basic to our understanding of anything that evolves" (Ghiselin, 1971, pp. 117–118).

The suggestion that the organizing principle of organic life is vicariousness of action is based on the fact that the mediating processes in organisms (in terms of both information utilization and action patterns) are not completely determined. This is because organisms must operate in a semichaotic environmental medium and must make adaptations on the basis of cues, each of which taken individually is of limited trustworthiness. The world is not a stable, orderly, and completely predictable medium for a cell any more than it is for a human being who is interacting with a complex world composed of other human beings.

An Argument for Teleology

Another fundamental difference between the physical and biological sciences is that teleological explanations are not only useful for the latter but are also often the order of the day if we are to attain a satisfactory explanatory system. Teleological conceptions have been "outlawed" from polite science for most of this century because of overtones that persist from the nineteenth-century controversy in which the issue was one of mechanism vs. teleological vitalism. As Kaplan (1964) has pointed out, it is possible to analyze natural phenomena using teleological concepts which satisfy the most stringent criteria of the mechanists, and "teleological phenomena themselves can be adduced in such a way as to have explanatory force" (p. 154).

Nagel (1965) writes that "teleological explanations are more frequent in the biological than in the physical sciences, not because the former are less advanced than are the latter, but simply because living organisms are teleonomic [continue to operate in certain specified ways despite adverse environmental changes, because they are provided with identifiable mechanisms that can compensate within limits for such changes] with respect to some of their attributes while most physical systems are not" (p. 25). Teleological explanations cannot be dispensed with in biology since they constitute one of the distinguishing features of biology as a natural science. In this context, Ayala (1972) considers one of Darwin's greatest accomplishments to have been the substitution of scientific teleological mechanisms for a theological one.

These teleological principles are admissible because the physical mechanisms which regulate the action of the systems can be identified. These mechanisms are the familiar ones involved in maintaining physiological and developmental homeostasis. This homeostatic teleology does not require any external agent to direct the process or any conscious tendency on the part of the adapting system. The guiding principle at the level of organism–environment interaction is the principle of natural selection—a principle which can be mechanistically stated in genetic and statistical terms. The driving force of this evolutionary process is differential reproduction. Thus the *proximal* features of organisms—their functional and morphological characteristics—can be understood only with reference to the *ultimate* goal to which all of the proximate aspects contribute. That goal is reproductive success. "The only nonrandom process in evolution is natural selection understood as differential reproduction. Natural selection is a purely mechanistic process and it is opportunistic" (Ayala, 1972, p. 11). Thus if we adopt this evolutionary model we can utilize teleological modes of thinking which acknowledge the fact that means-end relationships characterize the behavior of organic systems and can do it in such a way that we do not have to abandon mechanistic causal principles. We merely must state these principles in such a way that variability and vicariousness of function are acknowledged as they contribute to the reproductive fitness of organisms coping with their environment.

Ernst Mayr argues that it is legitimate to speak of teleological purposiveness in the same way we consider a "programmed" computer to act purposively. This program of the computer constitutes its historically determined purposiveness, just as the genetic program of an individual organism constitutes its historically determined purposiveness. "The purposive action of an individual, as far as it is based on the properties of its genetic program, therefore, is no more nor less purposive than the actions of a computer that has been programmed to respond appropriately to various inputs. It is a purely mechanistic purposiveness" (Mayr, 1965, p. 4). Just as computer programs can be steadily improved through the selection of more efficient subroutines built to meet the needs of various demands of the data field, so genetic programs can be improved by evolutionary adaptations controlled by natural selection in response to the demands of the environment.

Thus this teleological purposiveness neither requires any vitalistic goal seeking nor demands any natural design in nature beyond the well-established principle of natural selection. This mechanistically based view of teleology leads us to a dynamic and molar view of organismic adaptation. "In view of the high number of multiple pathways possible for most biological processes . . . and in view of the randomness of many of the biological processes, particularly on the molecular level . . . , causality in biological systems is not predictive, or at best is only statistically predictive" (Mayr, 1965, p. 48).

Probabilism

Since environmental influences are complex and the causes of behavior are manifold, we must employ a research strategy commensurate with such manifold complexity. The idealized single-variable models of the physical sciences simply will not do.

These considerations have led me to the realization that the necessity for a probabilistically based behavioral science is not merely a function of an imperfect functional expression of a set of underlying general laws. Such a "uniformity" point of view has been expressed both by such nomotheticists as Hull (1943*b*, p. 206) and by such probabilists as Brunswik (1955). For example, although Brunswik believes that uncertainty is a feature of the relationship between organisms and distal environment, he states that "uncertainty is not seen as a necessary feature of intraorganismic processes" (1955, p. 210). Brunswik points out, quite correctly, that being a probabilist does not necessarily rule out a belief in the existence of general laws applicable to behavior.

I am suggesting, here, that the probabilism does not reside merely in the functional expression of behavior, but that it is inherent in the biological processes themselves on which the behavior depends. Thus probabilism is the result of a series of processes beginning at the level of the gene, which is subject to spontaneous mutation caused by errors in DNA replication. "The occurrence of a given mutation is in no way related to the evolutionary needs of the particular organism or of the population to which it belongs. The precise results of a given selection pressure are unpredictable because mutation, recombination, and developmental homeostasis are making indeterminate contributions to the response to this pressure" (Mayr, 1965, p. 46).

This probabilism is further enhanced by the very means by which organisms propagate themselves. "We now know that organisms have sex because it generates variability; an idea virtually unknown outside the circle of professional biologists, the notion that sex is a means of increasing the quality, rather than the quantity of life . . ." (Ghiselin, 1971, p. 127).

Elsewhere, I have discussed the importance of probabilistic mechanisms in the process of evolution (Petrinovich, 1976). The adaptations of organisms are complexly and multiply determined. These adaptations range from the level of gene action, through the phenotypic expression of the genotype, to the processes determining speciation. This same point of view can be extended to understand the action of the nervous system when this action is embedded in the context of behaviors of evolutionary significance. It may be possible to understand the isolated nerve cell, to trace the neural wiring, and to explicate the physical principles by which the nerve cells operate. However, the questions with which a functional psychology must deal require us to understand these operations in the context of the environment—an environment to which the organism has been adapted through the evolutionary history of the species and to which the organism must relate if the species is to perpetuate itself.

It would be unwise to construct an organism for which any single unit is essential to its survival. We see, therefore, that large dynamic entities, such as the brain, are constructed so that an initial equipotentiality exists for most complex functions, and the eventual functional organization involves a good deal of vicarious functioning (what Lashley, 1949, considered to be the result of mass action). In addition, the functioning organism is constructed so that it can operate quite satisfactorily with large tissue deficits. This is due both to the multiple and diffuse organization of neural systems and to the fact that there is a vicarious sensory and motor mediation of complex responses. Hammond has shown how systems of vicariously mediated and hierarchically organized cues are involved in human social judgments (Hammond *et al.*, 1975), and has summarized this view in Chapter 9 of the present volume.

Reductionism

All of these considerations have led me to take issue with the molecular reductionism usually espoused. Before I outline the meaning of this statement, let us examine some of the formal tenets of reductionism. Nagel (1961) formulates two formal conditions that must be satisfied in order for one science to be reduced to another. The first is the *condition of connectability*, which requires that connections must be established between the terms of the reducing and the reduced sciences. This is usually done by a redefinition of the terms of the reduced science to those of the reducing science or by some sort of coordinating definitions. The second is the *condition of derivability*, which requires that the laws and theories of the reduced science must be shown to be logical consequences of the reducing science.

In addition to these essential aspects, the sciences are usually considered to be hierarchically ordered. Usually this hierarchy runs from physics upward to chemistry, physiology, through psychology, the social sciences, and on to the historical disciplines. The suggested manner of proceeding is in a molecular direction; i.e., psychology is to be reduced to some aspect of physiology, and physiology, in turn, to the level of chemistry and physics. A corollary, as Jessor (1958) has pointed out, is that the terms of the reducing science are usually considered to provide a more fundamental or basic level of explanation than those of the reduced science.

Krech (1950*a*, *b*) has been one of the staunchest advocates of the use of molecular reductionism in psychology—from the purely psychological level to that of neurology. "It seems to me that the most fruitful thing to do would be to take the plunge and announce that henceforth our hypothetical constructs (through the use of which we hope to understand all behavior and experience) are to be conceived of as molar neurological events—that and nothing more. Such a step amounts to accepting the universe . . ." (Krech, 1950*a*, p. 288).

Twenty-five years later, we still wait to collect on the promissory notes Krech and the other neuroscientists have issued. We await forlornly the more basic molecular explanations that will illuminate our molar existence.

At the present, some argue that a majority of biological problems cannot be as yet approached at the molecular level. This makes it even more likely that such a reduction will be difficult at the psychological level since we have not progressed far beyond the state of affairs which prevailed in 1936, when Tolman wrote: "A psychology cannot be explained by a physiology until one has a psychology to explain" (p. 90). In fact, I must agree with Ayala (1972), who writes that "laws discovered at a higher level of organization have more frequently contributed to guide research at the lower level than *vice versa*" (Ayala, 1972, p. 6).

Thus molecular reductionism has not led to a breathtaking understanding of molar behavior. This lack of progress might well be due to an overemphasis on molecular reductionism and to not enough emphasis on the search for unifying functional principles at a molar level.

This same concern is shared by Nagel (1961), who quotes Woodger as follows: "an entity having the hierarchical type of organization such as we find in the organism requires investigation at all levels, and investigation of one level cannot replace the necessity for investigation of levels higher up in the hierarchy" (p. 440).

The reason for the lack of success of this reductionist hope may be that the reductionism was taken exclusively in one direction. Instead of attempting a molecular reduction for psychology, perhaps we should follow the example that biology has found so rewarding. Those biologists who seek to understand organismic adjustment (the evolutionary and population biologists and the population ecologists) have been developing a set of *molar reductionist* principles. This reductionism seeks to reduce explanation to the general historical principles involved in biological adaptation at the molar functional level. It embodies the realization that behavioral adaptations (and natural selection) occur at the behavioral level and not at the level of internal circuitry. As the psychologist Neisser (1967) has phrased it, "it would not help the psychologist to know that memory is carried by RNA as opposed to some other medium. He wants to understand its utilization, and not its incarnation" (p. 6).

The difference between approaches emphasizing these two fundamentally different levels of discourse has long been accepted within the science of biology. A clear distinction is appreciated between questions which have to do with "how" things function—the level of functional biology—and those which have to do with "why" or "how come"—the level of evolutionary biology (Mayr, 1965). The former discipline is molecular and experimental, and nourishes itself on the single-variable ideal in its search for *proximate causes*. The latter is historical, takes as its subject matter the diversity of the organic world, and attempts to construct the causal sequences involved in the diversity of adaptations to the environment in its search for *ultimate causes*.

This reorientation has the potential—and here I issue a promissory note—to place psychology solidly in the domain of the natural sciences since it will allow us to operate at a level of complexity adequate to understand behavioral adaptations at all levels of complexity. In this way "normal science" from the field of evolutionary biology should lead to revolutionary science in psychology. Ghiselin (1971) has argued that this is the normal manner of progress for scientific paradigmatic revolutions, a view which modifies that of Kuhn (1970), who concentrates mainly on the paradigmatic shifts within a single discipline. Ghiselin argues that for biology the revolutionary paradigm shifts have come from without the science (e.g., from economics) rather than from within the discipline.

Thus, given the occasion, I must somewhat ungraciously take exception to the statement recently made by Krech: "the same kind of proteins and enzymes operate pretty much in the same way in the cell body, or the dendritic, axonic, and synaptic zones of a bird's neuron as they do in a person's.

My guiding principle can be stated as follows: The smaller (or simpler, or 'more basic') the unit of analysis, the greater the generality of the findings across species" (1974, p. 249).

It might well be true, as Krech (1955) would have it, that uniform laws exist in the microscopic world. However, these similarities of structure and function are of trivial significance if we are to understand the uniquely species-typical behaviors of organisms of different species. The basic molecular similarities cannot account for the tremendous diversity of functional adaptations which are found among living species. The *differences* in adaptive strategies and the general classes of those strategies which hold across different species in similar environments are what is intriguing, and they overwhelm the molecular reductionist hypothesis.

If we are to understand the functioning of organisms in an environmental context, we will be stopped short unless we include that context in our formal system principles. It is for these reasons that I suggest we have taken our reductionism in the wrong direction. Instead of searching for *molecular* reductionistic principles, we should develop *molar* reductionistic principles, and those principles will be found if we look to the principles of evolutionary theory and to the methods of population ecology. The principles that lead to reproductive fitness, and hence that are involved in natural selection, are at a level of complexity sufficient to unify behavioral adaptations at all levels.

Once Krech (1955) wrote in a pejorative tone "My most general (and perhaps least fair) reaction to Brunswik's position may be summarized by saying that he has taken a methodological *criticism* and made of it a *cosmology* (p. 229). I suggest that, with the addition of the molar reductionistic principles provided by the modern synthetic theory of evolution, we might, indeed, be able to turn this methodological criticism into a fruitful cosmology. Instead of casting our hypothetical constructs as molar neurological events, as Krech would have us do, I believe it will profit us more to conceive of them as molar evolutionary events—that and nothing more. In taking this step we accept a set of universal principles of extraordinary generality. These same principles will provide us with the unifying power we seek at the molar functional level. As Brunswik has written, "I would like to place reductionism in a marginal position to psychology unless it is executed in firm contact with . . . functional aims. . . . In contrast with most previous movements in psychology, probabilistic functionalism thus does not exclude anything; rather, its scope is encompassing enough to allow us to envisage a system to end all systems" (1955, p. 237).

In this same section, Brunswik states what is my own major concern with the science of psychology as a formal, systematic discipline: "The nomothetic-reductionist-systematic type of approach has in the past been overstressed at the expense of the probabilistic-functional-representative approach, notwithstanding all the epoch-making discoveries. . . . We have had all of the former and nothing of the latter for too long. Now we must balance psychology in the molar and molecular realm (1955, p. 237).

If we follow this path, we may realize the ideal Krech (1950*b*) expressed in the following quotation: "As we go from the data of one scientific field to another in our search for unity, we should not seek to *reduce* the data, but we should seek to *redefine* the principles so that borderlines begin to disappear" (p. 346). He continues: "the more inclusive field must enlarge the concepts of the less inclusive if we are ever to achieve a genuine unity of science" (p. 346). Perhaps the methods and data from a rigorous functional analysis at the molar level will provide the inclusive concepts we have all been seeking for so long—and move us toward that "system to end all systems."

References

Allport, G. W. 1947. Scientific models and human morals. *Psychological Review*, *54*, 182–192.

Ayala, F. J. 1972. The autonomy of biology as a natural science. In: *Biology*, *History*, *and Natural Philosophy*. A. D. Breck and W. Yourgrau (Eds.). Plenum Press, New York, pp. 1–16.

Bergmann, G., and Spence, K. W. 1941. Operationism and theory in psychology. *Psychological Review*, *48*, 1–14.

Best, J. B. 1972. The evolution and organization of sentient biological behavior systems. In: *Biology*, *History*, *and Natural Philosophy*. A. D. Breck and W. Yourgrau (Eds.). Plenum Press, New York, pp. 37–78.

Brunswik, E. 1952. The conceptual framework of psychology. In: *International Encyclopedia of Unified Science*, Vol. 1, No. 10. University of Chicago Press, Chicago.

Brunswik, E. 1955. Representative design and probabilistic theory in a functional psychology. *Psychological Review*, *62*, 193–217.

Brunswik, E. 1956. *Perception and the Representative Design of Psychological Experiments* (2nd ed.). University of California Press, Berkeley.

Esper, E. A. 1964. *A History of Psychology*. Saunders, Philadelphia.

Ghiselin, M. T. 1971. The individual in the Darwinian revolution. *New Literary History*, *3*, 113–134.

Hammond, K. R., Stewart, T. R., Brehmer, B., and Steinmann, D. O. 1975. Social judgment theory. In: *Human Judgment and Decision Processes: Formal and Mathematical Approaches*. M. F. Kaplan and S. Schwartz (Eds.). Academic Press, New York.

Hebb, D. O. 1949. *The Organization of Behavior*. Wiley, New York.

Hilgard, E. R. 1948. *Theories of Learning*. Appleton-Century-Crofts, New York.

Hilgard, E. R. 1956. *Theories of Learning* (2nd ed.). Appleton-Century-Crofts, New York.

Hull, C. L. 1943*a*. *Principles of Behavior*. Appleton-Century-Crofts, New York.

Hull, C. L. 1943*b*. The problem of intervening variables in molar behavior theory. *Psychological Review*, *50*, 273–291.

Jessor, R. 1958. The problem of reductionism in psychology. *Psychological Review*, *65*, 170–178.

Kaplan, A. 1964. *The Conduct of Inquiry*. Chandler, San Francisco.

Kendler, H. H., and Spence, J. T. 1971. Tenets of neobehaviorism. In: *Essays in Neobehaviorism*. H. H. Kendler and J. T. Spence (Eds.). Appleton-Century-Crofts, New York, pp. 11–40.

Kerlinger, F. N. 1973. *Foundations of Behavioral Research* (2nd ed.). Holt, Rinehart and Winston, New York.

Krech, D. 1950*a*. Dynamic systems, psychological fields, and hypothetical constructs. *Psychological Review, 57*, 283–290.

Krech, D. 1950*b*. Dynamic systems as open neurological systems. *Psychological Review, 57*, 345–361.

Krech, D. 1955. Discussion: Theory and reductionism. *Psychological Review, 62*, 226–228.

Krech, D. 1974. David Krech. In: *History of Psychology in Autobiography*, Vol. 6. Prentice-Hall, New York, pp. 219–250.

Kuhn, T. S. 1970. *The Structure of Scientific Revolutions* (2nd ed.). University of Chicago Press, Chicago.

Lashley, K. S. 1949. In search of the engram. In: *Symposium of the Society for Experimental Biology*, No. 4. Cambridge University Press, Cambridge, pp. 454–482.

Maslow, A. H. 1966. *The Psychology of Science*. Harper and Row, New York.

Mayr, E. 1965. Cause and effect in biology. In: *Cause and Effect*. D. Lerner (Ed.). Free Press, New York, pp. 33–50.

Nagel, E. 1961. *The Structure of Science*. Harcourt, Brace and World, New York.

Nagel, E. 1965. Types of causal explanation in science. In: *Cause and Effect*. D. Learner (Ed.). Free Press, New York, pp. 11–26.

Neisser, U. 1967. *Cognitive Psychology*. Appleton-Century-Crofts, New York.

Petrinovich, L. 1972. Psychobiological mechanisms in language development. In: *Advances in Psychobiology*, Vol. 1. G. Newton and A. H. Riesen (Eds.). Wiley, New York, pp. 259–285.

Petrinovich, L. 1973*a*. Darwin and the representative expression of reality. In: *Darwin and Facial Expression*. P. Ekman (Ed.). Academic Press, New York, pp. 223–256.

Petrinovich, L. 1973*b*. A species-meaningful analysis of habituation. In: *Habituation: Behavioral Studies*, Vol. 1. H. V. S. Peeke and M. J. Herz (Eds.). Academic Press, New York, pp. 141–162.

Petrinovich, L. 1976. Communication and Language: An evolutionary view. In: *Biology and Language*. S. K. Ghosh (Ed.). University Park Press, Baltimore.

Polanyi, M. 1958. *Personal Knowledge*. University of Chicago Press, Chicago.

Postman, L. 1955. The probability approach and nomothetic theory. *Psychological Review, 62*, 218–225.

Scriven, M. 1959. Explanation and prediction in evolutionary theory. *Science, 130*, 477–482.

Skinner, B. F. 1938. *The Behavior of Organisms*. Appleton, New York.

Stevens, S. S. 1939. Psychology and the science of science. *Psychological Bulletin, 36*, 221–263.

Tolman, E. C. 1932. *Purposive Behavior in Animals and Men*. Appleton, New York.

Tolman, E. C. 1936. Operational behaviorism and current trends in psychology. In: *Proceedings of the 25th Anniversary Celebration of the Inauguration of Graduate Studies*. University of Southern California Press, Los Angeles, pp. 89–103.

Underwood, B. J. 1957. *Psychological Research*. Appleton-Century-Crofts, New York.

Underwood, B. J. 1966. *Experimental Psychology* (2nd ed.). Appleton-Century-Crofts, New York.

Watson, J. B. 1924. *Psychology from the Standpoint of a Behaviorist* (2nd ed.). Lippincott, Philadelphia.

2

Everett J. Wyers

LEARNING AND EVOLUTION

The basic ideas that I will expound in this chapter are old ones. They are clearly expressed in the following quotations taken from the writings of William James and David Krech:

> Mental facts cannot be properly studied apart from the physical environment of which they take cognizance . . . our inner faculties are adapted in advance to the features of the world in which we dwell, . . . not only our capacities for forming new habits, for remembering sequences, and for abstracting general properties from things and associating their usual consequences with them, . . . but our emotions and instincts . . . if a phenomenon is important for our welfare, it interests us and excites us the first time we come into its presence. Dangerous things fill us with involuntary fear; poisonous things with distaste; indispensable things with appetite. Mind and world in short have been evolved together, and in consequence are something of a mutual fit. (James, 1893, p. 4)

The idea that all things in this world evolved together is now generally accepted. The implication that mind is rooted in physical events controlling "mindful" organisms is far from generally accepted. That implication is here noted:

> The animal, placed in a new situation and confronted with new obstacles which are to be overcome, does not rush about on mere chance urgings, but his very first response is a meaningful, intelligent one; meaningful in that it betrays some plan, some *unifying* aspect. With learning, the animal substitutes one unified series of responses for another until he eventually adopts the "correct" one. (Krechevsky, 1932*a*, p. 518)

Everett J. Wyers • Department of Psychology, State University of New York, Stony Brook, New York.

Animals approach novel situations systematically and "mindfully," it is said. But from where does such *unified* behavior come?

> The environment is an essential part to consider when describing the animal's behavior, but to assume that the environment is of primary importance and that the immediately presented stimuli are responsible for the *initiation* of behavior is, we believe, inaccurate . . . . The environment determines which, of all the behavior-units the animal *can* apply (a priori to experiencing this environment), he shall apply. This is giving to the environment a *limiting* function and not an initiating function. (Krechevsky, 1932*b*, pp. 56–57)

The environment limits and restricts behavior, it does not initiate behavior. The "mindful" animal does that. But how does that animal do so?

> The factors within the rat which initiated "hypotheses" could not be assigned to effects of training alone, but rather, in some degree, to hereditary differences among the rats . . . the kind of "hypothesis" which an animal can bring with him to a problem-situation is to some extent hereditarily determined. (Krechevsky, 1933, p. 109)

Heredity contributes to the initiation of behavior in novel situations and that behavior is organized and systematic. The *existing* environment simply filters and selects from behaviors potentially available those that "work." One systematic series of responses replaces another until the "correct" one appears. That one is fixed and retained, until again novelty (change) intrudes.

It is our intention here to examine the *past* environmental context (the shifting manifestations of selection pressure) in which genetic predisposition to learn appears. In keeping with the dictum that all things evolved together, emphasis is placed throughout on environmental context and that context is seen as containing the essence of what learning is and must be, even the more complex and abstract manifestations of learning.

The necessity of a concept of associative learning and the possible origins of such a capacity are first considered. Association is seen as a matter of environmental circumstance to which evolving organisms must adapt. Next the nature of associations as dictated by the environment is considered. Analysis and conclusion regarding this consideration are deferred, however, pending a review of abstractions of current views concerned with the evolution of learning. From this review, a position consistent with the synthetic theory of evolution is reached and thereafter analysis proceeds. The principle of natural selection in terms of the criterion of reproductive success is rigidly adhered to throughout the analysis. It is concluded that sensitivity to association of events by environmental constraint (contingency) is the primordial basis of learning capacity, and that such sensitivity is reflected in genetically influenced predispositions to systematic reactivity and subsequent learning in the face of any novel situation. Finally, more complex manifestations of learning are derived in a manner consistent with the synthetic theory.

A Problem: Associative Learning

The twin problems of the nature of learning and the nature of knowledge, i.e., memory, are undergoing a resurgence of interest. Not since the years surrounding the turn of the century has interest in these problems been so high. Demonstrations of learning in the phenomena of animal behavior have proliferated almost beyond count. Phenomena as diverse as the development of basic feeding patterns (Rozin and Kalat, 1971; Teitelbaum, 1971), celestial navigation (Emlen, 1970), species and individual recognition (Hailman, 1967), predation of carnivorous animals (Krebs, 1973), and entrainment of circadian rhythms (Renner, 1960), to name a few, now provide a variety of opportunities, in a variety of animals to characterize the nature and variety of learning.

The characterization of learning must take cognizance of species differences in sensitivity to events in space and time and of species differences in capacity to use such events. Both the animal *and* its investigator must appreciate the variety of associative relationships in which environmental events can occur. In other words, both must take cognizance of how the resources of the environment are used. Because these are distributed in time and space, comparative study of the behavior and of the evolution of species is necessary. To understand its use of time and space, consideration must be given to how a species got to be what it is. Thus the evolution of learning remains a matter of critical concern. Many have so argued (e.g., Garcia and Ervin, 1968; Petrinovich, 1973*a*, *b*; Seligman and Hager, 1972).

Overall, no one questions that superior ability to learn increases the probability of individual survival. No one doubts that his own abilities to learn exceed those of any horseshoe crab, any ant, bee, or wasp, any fish, any dog, and indeed any specimen of any nonhuman species. Moreover, despite the absence of a possibility of direct test, it seems that different animal species can be ranked, or ordered, in terms of their ability to learn. These three beliefs are widespread. That they are in reality untested (and perhaps untestable) assumptions is seldom attended to.

These assumptions are of concern in considering the evolution of learning. Harlow (1958) said that the evolution of learning problem is one of the most difficult of problems to solve. In considering the problem, he accepted the three assumptions as valid. A different approach to the problem is offered if the three assumptions are rejected. In that case, it is assumed that all animals are equally adept at learning. The question immediately arises of how then to take into account the evident differences in animals: if animals do not differ in learning, in what do they differ? Certainly *performance* in so-called learning situations differs.

There are difficulties in following the approach suggested above. One difficulty is the absence of precise scaling of learning problems in terms of difficulty and complexity. In part, this difficulty is related to the more fundamental one of defining learning at all. It has not been possible for all investigators to agree on the definition of even the simplest forms of learning. For example, some include habituation and sensitization, and others do not. All agree that classical conditioning and instrumental conditioning are forms of learning. This stems from respect for tradition and conviction that evidence of associative learning represents a more positive criterion of an instance of learning. Hence Miller (1967) refers to "grade-A certified learning" in attempting to collectivize opinion. Nevertheless, it should not be forgotten (or ignored) that as a defining characteristic even "associative learning" is known only by a process of exclusion of alternatives. There is no universal indicator signifying the presence of learning, whether associative or not. We may then ask whether inquiry into the evolution of learning requires a concept of association as a necessary one.

In psychological research, learning is considered to be the formation of associations. Associations of what: of ideas, of stimulus and response, of stimulus, or response and reward? Associations are then inside the animal: in its central nervous system or somewhere. Traditional methods of putting them there are classical conditioning, instrumental conditioning, and operant conditioning together with their various elaborations. These need not be described here. All ensure the controlled occurrence of at least two events in the environment of the animal subject. These events are dubbed stimuli, responses, and rewards (reinforcers). Each has an internal representation inside the animal, and, if control of their occurrence is appropriate, associations are formed between the internal representations. From knowledge of these associations, an animal's use of the resources of time and space are to be reconstructed. Can this reveal how an animal gets around in space, how it organizes and integrates its temporal scheme of things? In other words, can we do without internalized associations in understanding the organization of behavior in space and time?

The methodology of conditioning research reminds us that indeed "associations" are real: we cannot do without them. In the real world, an association *is* an environmentally constrained relationship between two (or more) events—physically describable events whose relationship is also physically describable. The events and their relationship are indeed *represented* inside the animal. It is the nature of their representation that is at question: need it be isomorphic with the methodological constraints of the conditioning situation? Such a conception of internal associations suggests sequential ordering of the representations of real events and their relationships. Does memory work in that manner? Does perception?—are space and the location of objects a matter of sequential run-off of stored associative processes at various brain loci?—can behavior, or learning, be understood in such terms?

Associative Sensitization

M. J. Wells (1967) has provided an interesting and plausible account of the evolution of associative learning. He points out that experience can lead to adaptive change apart from the precise sequence of events, i.e., "regardless of the precise sequence of action and reward." This will be so if the occurrence of a harmful (predatory) stimulus sensitizes withdrawal and the occurrence of a beneficial (prey) stimulus sensitizes approach to *any* succeeding stimulus for a period of time: predators and prey do not often depart immediately after their initial stimulation of an animal. Thus a subsequent stimulus is apt to derive from the continued presence of a predator or prey (as the case may be) and such sensitization will enhance the probability of survival and well-being of the animal.

Associative learning presumably evolved through several stages. First, sensitization of *innate* approach and withdrawal responses evolved, followed, with increasing sensory sensitivity, by central neural differentiation (classification) of sensory input. This allowed for development of a second stage. Differential sensitizability to different stimuli permitting short-term discrimination "learning" characterized the second stage. The animal was able to reduce (suppress) response to a harmful stimulus at this stage, while maintaining or increasing (enhancing) the same response to a beneficial stimulus. As central neural precision in differentiating sensory input continued to evolve, memory (synaptic lability) developed to accommodate more permanent response changes of survival value. This ushered in the third stage, ensuring that the consequences of response influenced only the organization of that response.

We need not consider the specific models proposed as possible means by which the three stages are achieved (Wells, 1967). It is clear that already in the first stage differentiation of the locus of stimulation in space and of the nature of that stimulation is present. The hypothetical ancestor of all associatively educated animals moves toward one kind of stimulus and away from another kind of stimulus. Even if the distinction is based on a response to stimulus intensity which is generalized to all stimulus sources in the ancestral *Umwelt*, as Schneirla (1959) has suggested, classification of those stimulus sources into two sorts is already present. Our associatively inclined ancestor approaches weak stimuli and withdraws from strong stimuli. Which class a particular stimulus is sorted into depends on a threshold process demarcating the boundary of the classes. All sensitization does is to shift this boundary; but note that it can be shifted in two directions. In this Schneirla case, weak stimuli (especially if repeated frequently enough) can be reacted to as strong stimuli, or strong stimuli (if repeated at appropriate intervals) can be reacted to as weak stimuli. In the Wells case, classification of some stimulus as either a "good event" (food and feeding) or a "bad event" (predator and escape) must also precede and guide the direction of sensitization (approach or withdrawal) to stimuli not yet encountered. The fact that the to-be-encountered stimuli (whether food or predator related), such as a sudden shadowing or vibration, cannot be distinguished as "feeding" or "injury" stimuli without closer contact does not help. Two separate events are associated in time by environmental circumstance and that association is reflected and preserved inside our hypothetical ancestor by the kind of sensitized state it is in. The second stimulus event is classified in accordance (associated) with the nature of the first stimulus event. Thus we may say that sensitization in itself is an associative process the function of which is to bridge a time interval.

So also with the habituation phenomenon so ubiquitous in the animal kingdom (Thorpe, 1963). Here again an earlier environmentally prescribed stimulus event, or series thereof, determines the nature of our associatively inclined ancestor's reactivity to a succeeding stimulus event. That stimulus may be approached, withdrawn from, or not reacted to at all, depending on its physical relation to the preceding stimulus, or stimulus series. The habituation phenomenon simply indicates that our primordial ancestor has a minimum of three ways of classifying stimulus events. A subsequent stimulus may be classified as the same as (associated with) the preceding stimulus, or stimuli, or it may be classified as different from (not associated with) that stimulus, or those stimuli. In the former case (same as), no reaction occurs. In the latter case (different from), as we have seen, two different reactions are possible. The subsequent stimulus may be classified as an approach stimulus or as a withdrawal stimulus. Thus, at a minimum, three ways of classifying stimulus events must have existed in our primeval ancestor.

The important point is that associations are of and between environmentally determined events and these associations can be represented inside animals only at the dictates of natural selection. It matters not that these associations can be represented in different ways and for differing periods of time according to the animal, the species, and other circumstance. What matters is that we cannot do without a concept of association in inquiring into the evolution of learning. The question becomes one of whether more than one concept of association is needed. Harlow (1958, and elsewhere) clearly recognized this in his habituation theory of the evolution of learning. But what of "grade-A certified learning" (Miller, 1967)? In the view of Miller, it can be said that our usage of association here is a misusage, that habituation, sensitization, and certified associative learning are distinguishable and no purpose is served in calling them all by the same name.

In a sense this criticism has its point. It is true that the detection of habituation and sensitization requires different operations. It is true that "grade-A certified" associative learning requires operations distinct from these, and is dependent on appropriate pairing of at least two stimulus events. In fact, its existence is certified by demonstration of the absence of simple habituation and/or sensitization. However, all three—sensitization, habituation, and "grade-A certified" associative learning—involve an internalized representation over time of the occurrence of environmentally associated events. As Wells (1967) implies, the evolution of systematic classification and processing of sensory input imposed increasingly complex constraints on the sensitization and habituation of primordial approach and withdrawal. In such a view, "grade-A certified" associative learning depends as much on constrained and complex forms of sensitization and/or habituation as on appropriate pairing of events.

An Example: Coelenterate Learning

All three forms of associative representation appear in representatives of all modern-day animal phyla possessing a central nervous system. The occurrence of sensitization and habituation in coelenterates and platyhelminths has long been accepted (Thorpe, 1963; Rushforth, 1973; Corning and Kelly, 1973). However, the occurrence of "grade-A certified" associative learning in coelenterate species has been controversial (Rushforth, 1973). Although little research has been done, the evidence for such learning in coelenterates has at least been suggestive (Rushforth, 1973). More recently, Haralson *et al.* (1971, 1974, 1975) have provided convincing evidence.

The Haralsons and their colleagues performed a variety of experiments using the sea anemone, *Cribrina xanthogrammica.* They recorded responses electrically via electrodes placed on opposite sides of the column, and visually via a camera placed over the animal. Reactions, such as central tentacle erection, mouth opening, bending, and folding were observed. Classical conditioning was obtained using either light or shrimp extract as CS and either electrical shock or a water jet as US. The electrical response provided the more convincing results. Control conditions indicated that the results were not attributable to sensitization or pseudoconditioning. Random pairing of light and shock (Rescorla, 1967) did not enhance response to light alone (as presentation of light alone and shock alone did not). However, when light and shock were randomly paired prior to the conditioning procedure, conditioning was facilitated. Extinction and spontaneous recovery (24 hr later) were also observed. Similar results were found using a water jet as US or a shrimp extract as CS.

These results are certainly indicative of "grade-A certified" associative learning in this species of sea anemone. However, in another experiment the Haralsons and their colleagues went a step further. Eight animals were trained in a successive discrimination task. Four animals with light-shock paired and shrimp extract unpaired plus four animals with the shrimp extract-shock paired and light unpaired provided evidence of efficient differential conditioning. In sum, the results indicated discrimination of light, shrimp extract, and shock or water jet stimulation in these animals. Pairing of CS and US was necessary for conditioning to occur, but their simultaneous occurrence was not.

Unfortunately, the precise nature of the conditioned behavioral reactions under the various procedures is not clear in all cases. This is of some import *à propos* the possibility of some form of constraint of sensitization. For example, an apparent case of pure "simple" sensitization occurred when shrimp extract as a CS was paired with shock as a US. Prior to pairing, the original mouth-opening response to presentation of the shrimp extract alone quickly habituated. After pairing began, only mouth opening and not bending or folding (the response elicited by shock) was recorded as occurring during the CS. However, the electrically recorded response to shock was clearly present during the CS and it could not be attributed to sensitization. Apparently "bending" or "folding" occurred, but at a level not detectable by the camera. Did mouth opening inhibit, suppress, or somehow mask the overt expression of bending and folding? One cannot be certain. In this instance, the precise nature of the conditioned change in the anemone cannot be assayed.

However, in most instances conditioned behavioral reactions resembling *both* the original response to the CS and the response elicited by the US occurred during CS-US pairing. This result was clearly evident when light was used as a CS. The light originally elicited extension of the central tentacles, a response which habituated very quickly prior to the pairing procedure. When the light was paired with either shock or a water jet, both of which elicited bending or folding, central tentacle extension as well as bending or folding (and the electrical response) occurred as a conditioned response. The pairing procedure was necessary for this to occur, the responses could be extinguished, and spontaneous recovery occurred 24 hr later.

From these results, it appears that the pairing procedure (and only this) could cause both an approach response (mouth opening, central tentacle extension) characteristic of the CS and a withdrawal response (partial folding, bending) characteristic of the US to occur. One must conclude that although "grade-A certified" associative learning is here demonstrated (as in the electrical response), further analysis of the descriptive character of the CRs and URs involved is needed. If two approach stimuli characterized by different original responses were used, one as CS and the other as US, what would the CR be like? A "simple" sensitization might well be indicated (as Wells, 1967, implies), if both of the original responses occurred to the CS in CS-US pairing. However, if the CS and US are drawn from distinct and opposed stimulus realms (approach and withdrawal) and the original responses to both occur to the CS in CS-US pairing (as Wells, 1967, also implies), then a "simple" sensitization effect is rejected. A more complex and differentiated control of response to the CS, contingent not just on how the CS is "classified" by the organism but also on how the organism "classifies" the succeeding stimulus (the US), is indicated. This is the finding of the Haralsons' experiments. At such a level of complexity, one need not yet refer to the consequences of response as influencing the organization of future responses in accordance with the "precise sequence of action and reward" (Wells, 1967, p. 391). One need only refer to the organization of future responses in accordance with a discriminated sensitization of both response to the CS and response to the US. In short, the pairing operation provides a bridge between stimuli normally eliciting either approach or withdrawal when presented alone and all other succeeding stimuli presented alone (and at sufficient strength).

Why should this be? Why should true blue "grade-A certified" associative learning in even so simple a creature as a sea anemone depend on organismic classification of stimuli as weak or strong (Schneirla, 1959), or beneficial or harmful (Wells, 1967)? It would appear that environmentally determined associations of events occurring to the anemone's ancestors were internally represented in their temporal dimension (as sensitization) and in their qualitative dimension (as approach or withdrawal). Approach and withdrawal imply sensitivity to directionality in space. Thus three factors must have weighed nearly equally in the evolution of learning: (1) the qualitative nature of stimulation, i.e., whether it resulted in death or survival; (2) the temporal nature of stimulation, i.e., whether a succeeding stimulus occurred sooner or later; (3) where the origin of the stimulation was located in space, i.e., proximally or distally. The assumption that learning could not have evolved without developing capacity to register internally (and preserve) the occurrence of environmental events associated as to kind, time, and place seems a necessary one.

Evolution of Learning

No form of life could evolve without appreciation of the kind, place, and time of occurrence of environmental events happening to it. At some level, appreciation of the kind of event (life facilitating or life debilitating), the place of its occurrence (relative to bodily structure: in terms of direction and distance), and the time of its occurrence (immediate, recent, or past) is necessary. If one accepts such a premise, the question nevertheless remains of how such appreciation could evolve.

Whatever the answer, modern animals in their behavior indicate that the evolution of learning figures importantly in the evolution of appreciation of the kind, place, and time of occurrence of environmental events in their ancestral history. When one considers modern points of view regarding the evolution of learning, it is evident that all either accept explicitly, accept implicitly, or disregard two basic concepts fundamental to their various positions. One is the concept of the reflex (S-R connectionism) and the other is the concept of variation (individual difference). Both in this day and age bear a heavy vesture of acceptance in tradition. The former, the reflex concept, traces its modern vestments back through Sherrington, Pavlov, and Sechenov to Descartes. The latter, the variation concept, does so through Fisher, Haldane, and Wright to Darwin. In addition, both concepts stand foursquare on a solid empirical base: reflexlike connectivities do exist and individuals do vary therein. Thus evolution from a general condition of irritability to discrete approach and withdrawal responses to specific stimuli prior to the appearance of learning capacity is generally assumed. The directionality of response (approach or withdrawal) presumably evolved through dependence on the intensity and bodily distribution of stimulation relative to time without such stimulation and the consequences of response. Learning capacity, then, presumably evolved from a base in a coordinated and temporally organized concatenation of specific reactions to specific stimuli.

Thus far, an attractive answer to our question seems indicated. It is an answer in the Cartesian tradition consistent with our present connectionistic, stimulus-response, neurological, and behavioral formulations. It reduces consideration to specific stimulation and its consequent response. Surely consistent response to specific stimulation is critical to survival and such conceptualizations may yet fully account for the intricacies of organic, physiological, and behavioral adaptation in the plant and animal world. Even so, the question remains: how has the exquisitely adjusted stimulus-response connectionism seen in modern forms of life evolved?

The modern synthetic theory of evolution completes the answer in a manner consistent with the Cartesian reflex concept. During development, genetic and environmental influences produce variation in the response of individual species members to stimulation. It is wholly in how the individual (given the vagaries of recently past environmental and physiological circumstance) reacts to a given stimulus relative to how other individuals react that the course of evolution is determined. This, again, is an attractive answer. It relies wholly on individual difference in reactivity to environmental circumstance at the moment of occurrence. It speaks only of "response now" to "present stimulation" and requires only that individual species representatives differ in such response *as individuals*. They need not differ from instance to instance. Given individual consistency, natural selection takes its course and evolution proceeds.

Nothing in the synthetic theory speaks to the importance of *intraindividual* variation, as contrasted with *interindividual* variation. It matters only that one individual of a species differs from another at the moment (or in the period) of application of a specific selective pressure. Logically there is no incumbence within the theory that demands recognition of intraindividual variation; it is enough for individuals to differ for natural selection to have its course. If capacity for intraindividual variation is to be recognized, it must be as any other character differentiating individuals. As such, systematic, rather than haphazard, trends in intraindividual variation gain importance; i.e., the individual who varies from instance to instance in a manner predictive of regularities underlying environmental events is favored over one who varies in a random haphazard manner with respect to such regularities. It is, after all, individuals who are favored or not favored; and natural selection must have its raw material.

The connectionistic, stimulus-response, answer to our question is attractive. Nevertheless, the innumerable demonstrations of intraindividual variation in responsiveness to recurrent stimulation extant in all modern ways of animal life demand recognition. When it is seen that differences in such intraindividual responsiveness can promote long-term adaptiveness (i.e., promote life continuance), then a concept such as "learning" must be recognized. To be able to change response to recurrent events so as to continue and prolong life must confer selective advantage in the evolution of species variants. Yet interindividual stability of responsiveness to recurrent stimulation seems more parsimonious and basic. Derivation of systematic variation within individuals (learning) from within individual consistency and stability (stereotypy) seems required. This may simply be because we are so imbued with ("stuck with") the connectionistic, stimulus-response, dogma. Nowadays, if the question is addressed at all, one speaks of how variable responsiveness to recurrent stimulation evolved from consistent responsiveness.

In considering the evolution of learning, most modern writers either implicitly or explicitly accept one of four alternative viewpoints. Others are possible and subvarieties of the four are distinguishable, but they will not be discussed here. Attention will be paid only to the most abstract and idealistic statement of the four points of view. These are demarcated by their positions along two dimensions of concern. The dimensions are "continuity-discontinuity" and "independence-dependence" in the evolution of learning capacity. Note that the points of view discussed are simplified and idealized ones. The publications referenced often contain other variants, qualifications, and complexities of view than are represented here.

The four points of view may be briefly stated as follows: (1) Learning capacity evolved in a continuous gradual fashion as an independent and general character from an obscure origin in genetic reassortment, recombination, and, perhaps, mutation. (2) Learning capacity evolved repeatedly within the confines of different bioecological systems but was limited to those systems as needed or possible. (3) Learning capacity evolved as an independent and general character, but was made use of or not (was excluded or not) within different bioecological systems as needed. (4) Learning capacity evolved in a discontinuous saltatory fashion as an independent and general character, but only as the evolution of other more basic characters and systems made qualitative jumps in learning capacity possible.

The first view is perhaps the one most commonly expressed (e.g., Thorndike, 1901; Harlow, 1958). According to it, capacity to learn was selected for in and of itself. Presumably differences in level of learning capacity through the ancestral sequence were quantitative and relatively small rather than qualitative and large in nature. Since increased learning capacity is seemingly just more of the same, this view is frequently linked to brain size, or to size or proportion of some portion of brain (Rensch, 1967; Jerison, 1973). This is an attractive view and it has stirred up considerable activity in a variety of fields over the years (see Jerison, 1973, for a recent accounting).

However, the idea that increased capacity to learn, in and of itself, was of such importance as to be specifically selected is difficult to reconcile with the synthetic theory. It is difficult to envision how increasing learning capacity would result in the requisite increase in number of offspring. Other forms of adaptation would appear more effective in this regard, i.e., structural and physiological adaptations to habitat conditions, particularly changes within essential embryological and developmental relations with the environment. Such conditions and relations frequently remain stable for long periods in species history. During such periods, two things can and do happen. The species "norm" shifts to a "better fit" within a particular ecological niche, and subpopulations are formed as some species members move (shift) into other available niches (radiation). Frequently, if not invariably, both things involve a change in behavior (Mayr, 1970). Thus learning capacity could play a part. However, once initiated both of these results involve alterations in structure and/or physiology. These changes in turn tend to constrain (to limit) the expression of whatever general learning capacity there may be. If this were not so, if selection for general learning capacity were favored over structural and physiological adaptations, i.e., resulted in disproportionately more offspring, all modern animals would closely resemble each other in learning ability.

The second view is expressed with increasing frequency these days (e.g., Garcia *et al.*, 1972; Seligman and Hager, 1972; Manning, 1975), although it was implicit or explicit in much earlier writing (e.g., Tinbergen, 1951; Krechevsky, 1932*a*, *b*; 1933). According to this view, increased learning capacity was selected for only where developmental and environmental stabilities made it possible to increase the efficiency of other adaptive modes. In this case, the evolution of learning capacity is specific and dependent. It fits with and into the evolution of other forms of adaptation selected for in the course of ancestral history. If this is so, all modern animals would vary greatly in learning capacity over the spectrum of their ecological relationships. Where such relationships are held in common, learning capacity would be functionally similar regardless of species form and nature.*

For example, many animals maintain a shelter in which they hold and care for their offspring, and the adult animal ranges far and wide in hunting for provisions to sustain its young. In these cases, a remarkable capacity to learn and orient to the specific location of the shelter is common. Digger wasps have been especially noted for this capacity (Tinbergen, 1951; Thorpe, 1963). One species (*Bembix rostrata*), a fly-hunting specialist, not only rivals man in quickness of learning and efficiency of orientation to shelter location but also uses similar cues in a similar way (van Iersel and van den Assem, 1965). Despite this remarkable capacity to learn, it is unlikely that *Bembix* rivals man in learning related to hunting and provisioning. A related digger wasp (*Philanthus triangulum*), a bee hunter, modifies its hunting behavior little, if at all, with experience and changing circumstance (Tinbergen, 1972). Another relative (*Ammophila campestris*), a caterpillar hunter, is similarly inflexible in its provisioning behavior (Baerends, 1941) (see later, pp. 54–55). Nevertheless, both *Philanthus* and *Ammophila* apparently rival *Bembix* and man in shelter location learning and orientation. Learning capacity may not be absent in the hunting and provisioning activities of these digger wasps; it may simply be different, and thus far have gone undetected. The fact that each of the wasps is a specialist in hunting for provisions for its offspring and that man is a generalist in this regard is of interest. According to the second point of view, analysis of what man learns and orients to when hunting flies, when hunting bees, and when hunting caterpillars would produce the com-

* Ecology is involved with the body of principles relating the survival of an animal to varying (or different) facets of its habitat. Thus ecological relations are aspects of an animal's life style and place which have been molded by intensive selection pressure. Where learning capacity in such a relation provides reproductive advantage, it would be expected to develop in any species whose gene pool still contained the potentiality. Note that while capacity to learn is specific to specific ecological relations in the second view it is not necessary that the underlying mechanisms also be specific.

parisons of interest; not that similarities to the wasp would emerge, but that situational specificity or generality within man would emerge.

The third point of view is rarely expressed explicitly. However, there are Lorenz's conception of the intercalation of learning and fixed-responses (e.g., Lorenz, 1965) and the implicit assumptions of reinforcement-based learning theory (e.g., Hull, 1943). This point of view can be said (like the first view) to hold that learning capacity evolved in and of itself as an independent and general character but (like the second view) its application in specific bioecological systems was constrained and limited as selective advantage demanded. To distinguish this view from the second one, it could be described as "constraint within associative capacity" and the second view as "associative capacity within constraint." Thus the specific uses and applications of a superordinate general learning capacity were limited and controlled. In effect, barriers to its expression were erected where its expression would be deleterious. Skinner (1969), in essence, speaks of "genetic assimilation" of learning (see Waddington, 1953). This point of view, although difficult to separate from the second one, should find support in cases where learning occurs in unnatural "laboratory" situations but not in their naturalistic analogues. If learning capacity evolved only within separate and specific bioecological relationships (the second view), a correspondence should be found between the naturalistic and nonnaturalistic expression of such relationships.

Consideration of offspring recognition in gulls and a hypothetical experiment illustrates the distinction between the third and the second points of view. Social birds normally provide only for their own young, even in crowded rookeries. Herring gulls learn to recognize their own young, Kittiwakes do not (Cullen, 1957). Kittiwakes nest in relative isolation on cliff ledges. They presumably evolved from an ancestor with herring gull nesting characteristics. In the kittiwakes' evolution from rookery to cliff one of two things must have happened. Either a specific parent-young learning capacity was lost from lack of need (positive selection pressure) or a specific block to use of a general learning ability in parent-young recognition evolved due to need (negative selection pressure). It is not conceivable that parent-young recognition would have been lost in the presence of an unfettered general learning ability (either saltatorily or gradually evolved) without there having been a need for its loss. It also is not conceivable how parent-young recognition on the cliff could be detrimental to reproductive success. However, one can conceive that a specific parent-young learning capacity could be lost through dissipation and displacement of the necessary gene complex in the absence of positive selection pressure. Thus parent-young learning was lost either by disuse (the second view) or by destruction (the third view). A simple experiment can rule out one or the other of these alternatives. What is to be expected if kittiwake young are used as cues in a discrimination test? In nature, adult kittiwakes feed all young kittiwakes indiscriminately: they do not recognize their own. Suppose the feeding of only one of two or more young kittiwakes was permitted. Would the adult learn to feed only that one? According to the second view (plasticity within constraint—but recalling that the plasticity is now gone), the adult would continue to attempt to feed whichever one was first at hand. According to the third view (constraint within plasticity—recalling that a general learning capacity is present), the adult would soon come to approach and feed only that one. This would have to be so because restriction of reward (feeding) to only one of several discriminative stimuli (the selected young one) artificially creates a situation in which a general learning capacity, if present, can be effective. According to the second view, such a capacity is not present; animals can learn only in naturalistic situations, or their artificial analogues, and in the naturalistic situation described natural selection has deprived our animal of opportunity to do so. It follows that in the artificial analogue to the naturalistic situation here hypothetically created the animal should likewise be deprived of opportunity to do so.

The fourth point of view has had varied and frequent expression (e.g., Schneirla, 1949; Bateson, 1972; Razran, 1971; Bitterman, 1965). According to it, increased learning capacity was not selected for in and of itself, nor was it selected for or against within the confines of different bioecological adaptive systems. Rather, selective pressures exerted on more basic structural and physiological characters resulted in increased organismic complexity. Learning capacity appeared as an offshoot of this (as an epiphenomenon—albeit a useful one). In general, adherents of this view envision the evolution of increasingly complex levels of learning capacity. The more advanced learning emerged from, is superordinate to, and includes the more primitive. This again is an attractive proposition and it is frequently linked to complexity of nervous system and/or brain organization (e.g., Dethier and Stellar, 1970; Jerison, 1973; Razran, 1971).

According to this last view, then, a general independent learning capacity evolved as an incidental by-product of increasing refinement and differentiation within established bioecological relationships. As the organism became better able to exploit its niche, sensory, motor, and central processing of information became more efficient. The range and precision of possible discriminations within the reproductive, defensive, nutritional, and spatial aspects of adaptation increased. As selection thus continually refined the adaptation of the organism to the stable features of its habitat and development (redefining and shifting its ecology), the capacity to learn as a correlated by-product of such selection shifted and changed. Along some lines of evolutionary change, the shift resulted in the emergence of a qualitative saltatory jump in that capacity (e.g., abstraction, reasoning, conceptual power). If the emergent capacity increased the precision and refinement of the organism's adaptation to its ecology, it was preserved, but not advanced. Its advance awaited the occurrence of structural and physiological conditions permitting the emergence of a new level of dealing with environmental fluctuations.

Environment, Probability, and Learning

Apart from the question of its evolution, learning must have something to work with. Avenues of communication with the environment (points of input and output contact) must exist. As the fourth viewpoint suggests, evolution may rest in the selective alteration and refinement of organismic-environmental contact points with little or no advantage resting in increased associative learning capacity of the central connectivities involved. It may indeed take a quantum jump in refinement of organismic-environmental interactions for advantage to accrue. Often the opposite effect, a disadvantage, would be expected through increased capability to shift reproductive, defense, nutritional, and spatial adaptive coordinations away from their appropriate inputs to others dependent on the vagaries of individual experience. Thus, before a quantum jump in learning (the emergence of a new capacity to associate events, to organize, abstract, and conceptualize them) can appear, a newly won supporting base for it in some realm of life offering reproductive advantage must already be in existence. If this is so, and danger can exist in unlimited ability to form internalized representations of associations, one must ask why associative capacity has not been rigidly and invariably subjected to selective exclusion. Clearly many if not all animal species have a degree of associative ability. The answer appears to lie in the second view presented: i.e., the conception of learning evolving as "associative capacity within constraint." According to this view, learning capacity evolved only within bioecological relations where it was useful: i.e., where it could enhance the efficiency of adaptation. Under what conditions would this be so?

In the normal course of events, some stimulus-response-stimulus (S-R-S) sequences exist whose occurrence assures reproductive success. They consist of events necessary but not sufficient to reproductive success; i.e., the probability that they will have preceded reproductive success can be said to be 1.0. For example, an animal must eat. These events, which must in every instance occur if an animal is to reproduce, are those critically involved in the bioecological relationships essentially delineating the life style of the species. It is in accordance with those relationships that selective shift and refinement of adaptation have occurred. The goal and terminus, then, of selective adaptation is to maximize the probability that any given event will come to ensure (lead to) reproductive success, i.e., lead to an event necessary to reproductive success. Such a terminus event must occur. Associative learning must not shift or otherwise alter the S-R-S sequence involved (or, at the least, the sequence of antecedent and consequent stimulus events associated with the response). Here indeed associative capacity must be subjected to selective control.

It is also the case in the normal course of events that many events exist for which the probability of ensuring reproductive success is less than 1.0. In such cases, associative learning capacity is of some value. It can provide refinement and attunement of adaptation (increase the efficiency and perfection of bioecological relationships). It can do so by chaining sequences of events along continua of increasing probability of occurrence of a terminus event that does certify the possibility of reproductive success. To do so would provide reproductive advantage and hence selective pressure (a positive feedback through the gene pool) to enhance such associative capacity.

However, the enhancement of associative capacity must be constrained, as we have seen, if selection is to be effective. Response leading into a terminus event must be appropriate, if a response is required to complete the transition into that event. Chaining of events, for example, by intervening response must be appropriate to a specific terminus event, i.e., provide for increasing the probability of occurrence of that event to 1.0. If the events in every possible sequence were equally associable without regard for the occurrence of an event assuring reproductive success, it appears that confusion and disorganization of behavior of a simple trial-and-error sort would result. This result would provide pressure for selective exclusion of associative capacity. In other words, association by simple temporal contiguity of events alone cannot provide for learning. An additional principle is required. For psychologists, a favorite has been the reinforcement principle (the so-called law of effect).

We are not suggesting here that the terminus events guiding adaptation and selection are the reinforcers of psychology. Some, perhaps all, reinforcers may be terminus events, but it is not necessary that all terminus events be reinforcers. (They would be expected to lack the transsituational generality attributed to reinforcers.) Rather, we are suggesting simply that through the evolutionary process some stimulus situations, or elements therein, are predisposed to be selectively associated with specific terminus events; i.e., they have a predictive utility. This view may be seen as an attempt to specify the origin of Seligman's "preparedness" (Seligman, 1970) or Mayr's "open programs" (Mayr, 1974). Reinforcement is quite another matter. Garcia, in three theoretical contributions (Garcia and Ervin, 1968; Garcia *et al.*, 1972, 1973), has clearly elucidated the distinction between the traditional view of "reinforcement" and the consequences of evolution in learned behavior.

There are three problems with the present view: (1) Any stimulus situation can be decomposed into constituent elements. How do we know to fractionate out the relevant elements for a given species and terminus event?

(2) Events of increasing probability stand out as islands in a temporal and spatial sea of events of lesser, zero, and negative probability. How do we know to recognize such events for species and terminus event? (3) Animals only sometimes seek out specific terminus events. This is in large part influenced by internal organismic conditions. How do we know to predict the effects of selective attention and perception (of state of the organism) on learning?.

A prerequisite to answers to these questions is examination of the species ecology. What does it consume? How does it obtain its food? Where does it find shelter? How does it find, orient to, and court its mate? What are its predators? How does it defend itself? How does it use space? The answers to such questions are essential to delineating the variables critical to our view. Petrinovich (1973*b*), in "A Species-Meaningful Analysis of Habituation," has emphasized the value of representative design (Brunswik, 1956) as the methodology of choice in the delineation of ecologically relevant variables. The application of representative design and other probabilistic methods, within the conceptual framework of Brunswik's "probabilistic functionalism" (Brunswik, 1955), could supply the answers to our questions. At the least, useful estimates of the variables cutting through event sequences that organize and "chain" such sequences should be provided. In so doing, specific terminus events will be "pointed out." Thereafter the organization of learning within "terminus-event sequences" can be examined in detail.

For example, by gathering a representative sample of events when an animal moves through space, one may, by noting similarities and differences, detect those stimulus elements of greatest "functional validity" to the animal. In delineating stimulus elements in events as used by the animal, one not only defines or determines their functional validity but also obtains an estimate of their "ecological validity" (environmental significance). Shifts in ecological validity among stimulus elements through a sequence of events should indicate not only terminus events but also those elements predisposed to, or constrained from, being associated with the terminus event.

Space and Memory

The use of space is a critical factor in the evolution of species. For most, if not all, animal forms, orientation and movement in space are critical to survival and reproductive success. This is of such importance that ability to locomote must have appeared early on. To orient directionally in space requires but a single event. However, to move directionally in space requires a sequence of at least two events. Such associations of events are environmentally controlled insofar as the organism is concerned. They can be bound together in the environment (associated) by a bridging stimulus as in following a sensory gradient. Moving down-gradient involves a different sequence of at least two events than moving up-gradient with the same event as the common starting point.

The evolution of greater sensitivity to small differences along such a gradient (as suggested earlier) may constitute the beginning of "grade-A certified" associative learning ability. Increased sensitization, or its refined control, is implied. For the organism, a smaller displacement in space would then constitute the demarcation between two successive events, the intensitive nature of their common elements providing the basis for their discrimination. The correlation of one intensity change (increase or decrease) with ultimate assurance of reproductive success could then provide a basis for selection for further increases in sensitivity. With increased sensitivity to sensory gradients comes increased ability to discriminate directional orientations in space and presumably with that an increased variety of potential locomotory directions in space. In such manner must an animal's apprehension of physical space and its localities evolve.

Consider the *Umwelt* of Jakob von Uexkull's wood tick lying in wait over an animal path (in Schiller, 1957). The world of the tick, von Uexkull says, is dominated only by the presence or absence of butyric acid. As a sweaty animal passes beneath, the air bears upward particles of the acid. They reach the tick's buytric acid receptors and the tick releases its hold and drops; a terminus event has occurred. If fortunate, it lands amidst warmth and hair, and dominated now by temperature, or some other sensory gradient, it bores down and then into the skin. A second terminus event now occurs; it engorges itself with warm mammalian blood. If the sequence of events is to occur as described, what must the tick do? Certainly it cannot release at the first hint of butyric acid in the air. Instead, it must wait and desist through a series of events. The first two events (passage of one JND's change in butyric acid intensity at a minimum) may be sufficient to provide directional orientation (whether the prey animal is withdrawing or approaching and in what direction). If not, the next few events will do so (note that it is not necessary for the tick to move, although it may—detection of stimulus change defines an event). Having oriented properly, the tick must now await the critical event, or series of events, indicating that the prey is directly beneath it (a prolonged period without intensity change in butyric acid or following a series of successive events containing intensity increases of diminishing order). Once this occurs, it releases its hold and falls.

It is not suggested that von Uexkull's tick actually does all the things noted. The example points to the reproductive advantage a tick would have if it did do all those things. It also shows that if those things were done the tick's *Umwelt* would in fact be spatially differentiated. In fact it must be, for the tick does not spend its entire life in trees prior to its triumphant fall. It moves over the ground, it climbs, it courts and copulates, and it locates a place to leave its eggs. Whether the sensory gradients used in doing these things are centrally integrated in representing events inside the tick is not critical. It may be that "space" is defined in terms of a series of successive events involving only one sensory gradient (say moisture) and ending in a terminus event (say appropriate dryness and upward surface). Thereafter another sensory gradient may become critical (say gravity, or light, or both) until another terminus event occurs, and so on.

If central integration of two or more sensory gradients does in fact occur in an animal, one may characterize the sequence of events as representing "space" in a more humanlike frame. That is, continuity of one gradient would provide a "spatial" framework through event sequences in which another gradient varies. The second could even be present at first, then be absent, and then reappear again. Even in such a case, ability to orient directionally and to locomote directionally would be potentially present if an impression of the "grade" of the temporarily absent sensory experience were held over the interval of its absence. If actually present, this ability could provide for reproductive advantage. Ability to orient and locomote directionally is tantamount to ability to represent internally the association of two events in space. Retention of an impression of a former sensory event in a particular place (spatial association) over a time period implies "associative learning."

How may an impression of a past sensory input be retained? Earlier we attributed just this function to sensitization. Note that it was an impression of the "nature" of an initial stimulus which at that time was said to be retained until a succeeding stimulus occurred (in both sensitization and habituation). There may be other means of retaining an impression of a past sensory input, but at the moment let us consider what "sensitization" means in the present context. It means a persisting activation of a response orientation or direction in the absence of immediately exciting stimulation of the originally activating sort. After detection of a stimulus element in an event which leads ultimately to a terminus event, and given that appropriate response is made, response orientation in terms of that element persists. It persists over temporal sequences of events in which because of the vagaries of environmental circumstance the relevant element is attenuated and even totally absent. Given that the sensory element provides guidance through a series of events to a terminus event (predicts its occurrence), it follows that persistence of response orientation or direction can ultimately lead to a reproductive advantage. In short, the ability to persist in an initially excited response orientation during the absence of the exciting cue can provide a reproductive advantage and therefore be subject to selective pressure. This ability despite the many possible forms of its bodily-mechanistic enactment is conventionally stylized under the rubric of memory. Memory is then, in psychological terms, a form of sensitization, a state of the organism. That sensitized state may persist either until it decays through time or until it is disrupted (altered) by other sensory inputs or until it is removed in some other manner. Again, persistence of sensitization through "distraction" and "prolonged delay" could gain a reproductive advantage. But how, and at what cost? The "how" rests in being able to refine and differentiate peripheral and central sensory input channels so that only a portion contain the persisting sensitization (memory) while others remain free for controlling response to "distractive" and "irrelevant" stimulation. If activity (sensitization-memory) persisted in such a subchannel long enough, a bridge to the terminus event would be provided. In the history of a species, it is the capacity of an earlier event to predict that a terminus event will occur that determines terminus event selectivity in learning, provided that appropriate intervening events (which may or may not depend on response) occur. Communality of physical elements in both events is not necessary, although the presence of such may help. (It may be that the evolution of terminus-event selectivity is the basis of perceived similarity between events in present-day representatives of a species.)

The cost rests in the necessity of committing genetic "energy" to somatic "form." Reproductive success provides the only possible basis for the operation of natural selection, i.e., for the forms of evolutionary adaptation, including learning capacity. This is a simple point, but one frequently overlooked or ignored. When it is so treated, two forms of adaptation are usually recognized—that relating to the existence of the individual (somatic survival) and that relating to the existence of the species (reproductive survival). However, it is clear that individual survival can be selected for only when bodily survival is necessary for reproductive survival.

Basically all adaptation must relate to reproduction. The cost then is in terms of individual somatic survival. By utilizing a portion of its limited capabilities to store information about past events (sensory inputs), rather than holding all in readiness for possible present danger, the individual's chances of survival are somewhat diminished. The tradeoff occurs where the animal who "runs the risk" also reproduces more of its kind compared to the animal who does not.

The "risk" is minimized where environmental stability exists (where the occurrence of one event reliably predicts the occurrence of another). The genetic influence in the development of somatic capability to respond to "present danger" is also minimized in such cases. For example, a predisposition to associate *any* stimulus event that reliably precedes the "bite-of-a-snake" requires less specification in the genome than full specification of all *specific* "snake-related" sensory inputs. Again, familiar tastes do not (by definition) result in illness and possible death. It requires less of the genome to specify distinctive (usually novel) tastes as predictors of such an event than to specify all the particular tastes related to such events in the history of the species (Garcia *et al.*, 1972; Rozin and Kalat, 1971).

Spatial Contiguity and Similarity

An ability to form associations (to learn) based on spatial contiguity exists which is orthogonal to that based on temporal contiguity. This is indicated by results obtained in research on many behavioral phenomena (Seligman and Hager, 1972; Hinde and Stevenson-Hinde, 1973; Garcia *et al.*, 1973). In bait-shyness research, for example, if an animal eats a bit of toxic food and becomes ill sometime later, its ability to reproduce its kind is seriously affected. If it repeatedly eats the same food, becoming ill each time, its reproductive potential is further reduced. If it eats too much of it, and dies, its reproductive potential is reduced to zero. In such circumstances, the animal that samples the food once, becomes ill, and henceforth does not eat that food has a marked reproductive advantage.

Such an animal associates its malaise with novel tastes over the time intervals required for the illness to develop. Garcia suggests that in the rat this is possible because the nucleus solitarius in the brain stem acts as an "and-gate." This nucleus receives both taste and visceral afferents, and, Garcia suggests, it will transmit neural impulses to higher centers only when activated by both. That is, it transmits information "integrating taste and visceral information." The arrival of taste information changes the "state" of the nucleus solitarius. It then remains in this "state" for a prolonged period (sensitization-memory). When illness information arrives via the visceral afferents, a further change in "state" occurs which involves excitation of exit pathways to higher centers. This event sets, or helps to set, the association of taste with illness and thereafter the animal refuses food of that specific taste. That is, the association of taste-illness in the stream of events constituting the animal's environmental experience is now represented inside the animal. Other evidence indicates that for a sick (malnourished) animal the association of taste events and eventual beneficial effects of specific foods can also gain internal representation. Food preferences so ordained disappear once the sick animal is well again. Here again the advantage in individual reproductive potential is evident. Healthy animals produce more offspring than unhealthy ones, as a general rule.

In both cases, the time intervals involved are bridged by mechanisms (states) other than those based on temporal contiguity. Intervening taste or other events do not interfere with sensitivity to the association of taste–illness, or taste–well-being, in the stream of events constituting the animal's experience of its *Umwelt* (Garcia *et al.*, 1969; Rozin, 1969; Borer, 1968). Two novel events located in the same "spatial" milieu, the internal milieu, involving "similar" sensory inputs, are associated because the one is necessary to and predicts the other; and both relate directly to reproductive success.

In these examples, the selection of associated events in the animal's experience to be learned is in part a function of the state of the animal. State-dependent learning has been delineated precisely in other studies (Girden, 1940; Overton, 1968). What is meant by state of the animal? Cyclically altering behavior under constant environmental exposure is the essential meaning. The environmental exposure may involve either sequentially changing or unchanging conditions. It is a commonplace observation that behavior comes in sequential "chunks" of greater or lesser duration. The chunks are composed of behaviors related in the sense that they contribute to a given change in the animal's immediate environment or in its behavior: predation, courting, nest building, escape, etc. Events terminating such behavior sequences are frequently referred to as consummatory events. The occurrence of a consummatory event changes the state of an animal. The term "consummatory" implies the consumption (the using up) of something, i.e., "drive." The term "terminus event" is more neutral, implying only an alteration in the descriptive content of behavior.

A terminus event is the final event in a stream (chunk) of behavior which brings about a state of affairs necessary (but not sufficient) to ensure reproductive success. Note that this state of affairs may be as innocuous as assuming a certain position (i.e., as in hunting, fishing, or the triumphant fall of von Uexkull's tick). Note again that this state of affairs need not be followed by success, i.e., it need not result in actual reproduction of kind in more than a minority of instances. It is favorably selected only because whenever reproductive success has in fact occurred the state of affairs itself has also in fact already occurred. Finally, note also that this favored state of affairs need not include a particular stimulus that "releases" another and different behavioral reaction (Tinbergen, 1951; Thorpe, 1963). It is a transition point in the stream of events. Through its occurrence, it makes possible the occurrence of other events (see later, pp. 58–59).

In terms of the evolution of species characteristics, a terminus event can be said to have a probability of 1.0 of ensuring reproductive success, even if accidental death intervenes. Other events can be said to have probabilities of less than 1.0 of ensuring reproductive success. Some may be totally unrelated (probability of 0.0) and others negatively related, as approaching stimuli signifying predation (probability of −1.0). At any one time, an animal can be said to be in some degree separated in time and space from a terminus event.

In moving from the one to the other, the animal moves through a universe of *potentially* possible events. Each member of this universe of events can be characterized as affecting the probability that the animal will actually experience a terminus event. Modern members of an animal species tend to move through sequences of events along continua of increasing probability of occurrence of a terminus event. In past generations, the chain of environmental events selectively eliminated those who did not tend to do so.

Considering the vagaries of environmental circumstance in moving through space and time, how could the evolution of behavior sequences along such continua be mediated? One factor is selection for variations in organismic state controlling attention to stimulus sources within the *Umwelt* of the animal. Another is selection for variations in behavioral reactivity to attended stimuli facilitating occurrence of a succeeding event of greater probability. A third factor is selection for variations in learning promoting the efficiency of the other two factors. In the case of the second factor, ability to bridge environmentally imposed gaps in the sequence of events would be especially valuable as a selective influence.

An environmental event registers and thus is represented inside the experiencing animal. An event may contain a variable number of the primary stimulus elements contributing to the animal's *Umwelt*. Their internal inputs (representations) interact to organize a relatively unitary process (the biologically relevant stimulus). Two forms of learning are possible, if such a unitary process leaves an internal aftereffect when its initiating event is over. One is based on the temporal contiguity of events (one form of environmentally prescribed association of events). The other is based on the spatial contiguity of events (another form of environmental prescription of association). Neither is more basic than the other. Both can in essence be seen as one and the same (Kohler, 1941).

Given that an organized unitary after effect of a past event persists inside the animal and is present when a later event occurs, two things can happen. Either the later event contains some or all of the primary stimulus elements present in the past event or it does not. Even if it contains only one such primary element, the internal representation of that element *may*, as an organized component of a unit, reactivate the whole of that unit. This kind of process is what psychologists have assumed to underlie "recall," "redintegration," and "reactivation." It is, in some sense, "association by similarity" (Kohler, 1947). However, reference to internal coding of an association has not been made. What is there in a process of recollection that permits internal coding of associated environmental events? Why are the events, which may be widely separated in time and space, said to be associated at all? There can only be two reasons. Either a past event predicts (is necessary to) the occurrence of a future one, or they both contain common elements of the animal's *Umwelt*.

Reactivity to the common elements within each event defines the probability of each leading to a terminus event. A pathway is defined leading from one event to another (just as the sensory gradient defined a pathway for von Uexkull's tick). As the predictability of terminus event occurrence increases, so reactivity to common elements increases. As long as this potentiality exists, recall of the occurrence of a past event in the presence of another constitutes raw material for the operation of selection. Selection operates to narrow the range of reactivity (the orientation of reactivity) within each event. "Reactivity" includes the "doing-of-nothing" behaviorally, if a sequence of environmentally prescribed events so ordains. The tendency for reactivity to an event may be selected to enhance the probability of occurrence of an ensuing event. This ensuing event is even more predictive of a terminus event. It is on this sequence that the internal coding of the association is based.

We have asserted that recollection involves associative learning through spatial contiguity of the associated events. There are two reasons for making this assertion:

1. The organization of primary stimulus elements in the *Umwelt* into a unitary process represents the physical world as "objects" or "things" in the *Umwelt* of any animal. No matter how different for different animals, the primary elements defining their *Umwelt* arise from the presence of environmental objects or things in the physical world: objects or things which must be traversed, withdrawn from, approached, captured, eaten, etc. Such objects or things occupy space and collectively stand in spatially defined relations to each other. Where relevant to the individual's survival, the apperception of those relations is especially critical. Thus when we say two events are associated spatially we mean either that one or more common objects or things are present in the physical environment comprising those events or that spatial relations between objects or things in the two events are the same. Note that in the latter case the physically present objects or things need not be the same in the two events. They need only define the same (physical) pattern of spatial relations (e.g., Gibson, 1966; Testa, 1974). In both cases, perception of the events involved as the same or similar is not required—hence the use of the term "apperception."
2. In both of the above cases, we assume that activity in spatially discrete loci within the animal will occur. If events contain common elements (objects, things, or otheir spatial interrelationships), activity at the same loci not only will be doubly supported but also will occur in the presence of activity at loci not directly activated by the present event. Activity at such other loci is conditioned by recall of the unitary process stemming from the past event. Thus one might say with

Hebb (1949) that unitary processes representative of both the past and the present event are active simultaneously (temporal contiguity), with an alteration of internal structure of the animal being the consequence.

In essence, then, association of environmental events depends in part on the degree to which they are physically alike, recognizing that dimensions of physical description relevant to different species differ. The internal representation of an association is in essence an apperception of both events. Now, of course, the events cannot be identical either physically or apperceptively. Each event is to a greater or lesser extent unique. However, selection has built animals in such a way that they can approximate the identicalness of objects and things as arranged and moving in space from one event to another. A present sensory input is influenced by past experience. Thus, apperceptively, two quite dissimilar events can be interpreted as alike. For example, two events need have only "movement-to-the-right" to be apperceived as alike, but if one predicts the probable occurrence of the other they will become so linked in the history of the species, provided only that ultimately reproductive success eventuates. Contiguity in time is important only in permitting the integrative (reorganizational) process described to occur, and the more integrative time required the less associated the events to be learned are.

A Burrowing Wasp

The digger wasp (*Ammophila campestris*) brings caterpillars to its burrow as food for its larvae. It drops the caterpillar in front of the entrance before opening the burrow. After entering and inspecting the interior, it returns to the entrance and pulls the caterpillar inside. If the caterpillar is removed to some distance during the inspection, the wasp searches for it, finds it, returns to the burrow, puts it down at the entrance, and again inspects the interior. The caterpillar can be removed some 30 or 40 times before the wasp enters the nest directly with it, foregoing the inspection (Baerends, 1941). The wasp requires considerable "integrative time" before the association of the event "open-entrance" with the event "interior-clear" is internally represented, even though the two events are nearly adjacent in time. Where two terminus events occur successively in time, or near successively, by environmental constraint alone, selection pressure for alternative associatively predisposed "event pathways" is absent, or nearly so (however, see later, pp. 61–62).

In this case, to open the entrance and inspect the burrow the wasp must face into the burrow. However, to pull the caterpillar inside it must face out of the burrow; i.e., it must "back in," dragging the caterpillar after it. Thus the events "caterpillar-at-entrance," "open-entrance," "clear-burrow," and "caterpillar-in-burrow" necessarily occur in that order and in quick succession. These are all terminus events (with the possible exception of "open-entrance") in that each terminates a brief but nevertheless related sequence of behaviors, e.g., "sand-removal."

In such a case, the animal needs little or no capacity to learn. The sequence of events is almost entirely environmentally prescribed. Yet there is here a strong associative predisposition, for opening the burrow entrance almost invariably results in sand particles falling down the vertical shaft and into the burrow's small chamber. The removal of these particles provides a reproductive advantage. Thus a series of events involving "sand-in-burrow" (the wasp carries the sand away in short flights) intervenes between the terminus events "open-entrance" and "clear-burrow." The associative predisposition here is between "sand-in-burrow" and "clear-burrow," not between "open-entrance" and "clear-burrow." By environmental constraint, the latter two events are less associated than the former two.

In related species of digger wasps, the burrow-opening maneuvers entail little chance of sand falling into the burrow. In such species, direct entrance should occur after fewer prey removal "trials." Where burrow inspection does not occur, direct entrance should require only one "trial."

What of cases where the sequence of events is not so rigidly constrained by environmental circumstances? Learning capacity should here be more readily evident. Consider nest building in some birds.

Nest-Building Birds

For many bird species, the sequence of events involved in constructing their species-typical nest is critical to reproductive success. Those individuals who most efficiently build the most effective nest accrue a reproductive advantage. Of course, many factors influence reproductive success and under appropriate circumstances a less effective nest may provide as well as a more effective one. Nevertheless, there is a degree of ineffectiveness which will militate against reproductive success in even the best of circumstances. The norm of nest effectiveness for the species will not be the least degree of effectiveness. Rather, over the span of evolutionary time, i.e., over the range of changing environmental circumstance, the norm will come to rest between that permissible under the worst of circumstances and that tolerable under the best of circumstances. This must mean that many, if not most, individual members of the species build nests of a degree of effectiveness greater than that required for reproductive success under most circumstances typical of the species history.

The effectiveness of a nest depends on the structure of the whole, i.e., where the nest is placed relative to other features of the environment and how its own component parts are fitted together. The structure of the whole is species typical; it characterizes all members of the species. Therefore, the critical difference must lie in the selection of component parts and how they are fitted together. The "selection" and "fitting" have been said to be appetitive acts, and consummatory acts (fixed-action patterns) have been said to guide discrimination between and selective usage of such acts (Lorenz, 1965; Thorpe, 1963). Sitting in a completed nest presumably is the final consummatory act. During nest construction, successive approximations to fuller expression of this consummatory act guide discrimination and usage of the appetitive acts (however, see Hinde and Steel, 1972). In short, the members of the species all learn to recognize appropriate component parts and to desist from attempts to fit inappropriate parts (e.g., ravens and jackdaws, Thorpe, 1963).

We have referred to certain events as terminus events. The consummatory nest-sitting act would seem to constitute such an event. Its occurrence (nest completion) is accompanied by a shift from nest-building behavior to other behaviors. However, it is not strictly accurate to refer to *the* "consummatory act" or *the* "terminus event." As the nest is completed, nest-building activities decline in frequency and other behaviors increase in frequency. A uniquely typical behavior does not occur once and only once at the end of a sequence of behavior. A terminus event refers to a descriptive change (a transition state) in the ongoing sequence of behavior. Such a shift of state is always with reference to the animal's interactions with its environment.

Individual members of a species learn to build nests in accordance with evolutionarily selected specifications. What is the behavioral embodiment of those specifications in the individual? Selective reaction to objects among the components of an environmental event, i.e., to a perceptual pattern, is more important than the specific actions of behavior (Mayr, 1970). The nest is completed when a specific perceptual pattern results from ongoing construction. But what is this perceptual pattern?

The releasing stimuli of ethology are very specific perceptual elements uniquely potent in directing attendance of specific behavioral actions. A bit of reddish fluff leads an English robin to attack (Lack, 1943). The lateral movement of a contrasting area at the tip of a parent gull's bill leads the neonate gull chick to grasp (Hailman, 1967). Such simple perceptual elements can quickly become incorporated into a perceptual pattern which then conditions occurrence of the behavioral reaction. After only a few experiences, the young gull reacts only to a pattern characterizing its own species; i.e., a form of learning occurs (Hailman, 1967). The perceptual pattern attending nest completion requires more than a releasing stimulus. Perhaps the participation of sensory input through several modalities, e.g., visual, tactual, warmth, is required. Indeed, the pattern may itself be learned. Evolutionary specification of a species nest need not overlook consistency in developmental experience. In some cases (e.g., cowbird, cuckoo), a form of imprinting could well serve. In any case, it is unlikely that genetically influenced internal constraints are at all stages absent (Thorpe, 1963).

Considering only visual inputs and their relations, what must be incorporated in the perceptual pattern attending nest completion? The roominess of the nest could be one element, e.g., the distance between the walls and top, if any, and the sitting bird. The level of the upper edge of the nest, or the position and size of the entrance hole, as the case may be, with respect to the sitting bird could be another critical element. Apart from internal features, the relations of external objects to the nest as a whole must be critical. These all involve objects in space (position of a branch over the nest) and their relations to each other and the nest (size of angle between branchlets supporting the nest). The perceptual pattern must involve a variety of such spatial arrangements and relations.

So also with nest site selection. Species-typical sites for construction must be selected in terms of the spatial arrangements of environmental objects. As noted, the prescription need not be entirely genetic. Nevertheless, it is there and requires the apperception of objects and their interrelations in space. Once the appropriate situation is found, nest building begins. The animal now proceeds to fill its selected hole in space with a new object, its nest. This involves the manipulation of objects in space. As noted, for efficient, effective construction, those objects must fit. Ravens and jackdaws, for example, bring twigs to their nest site. The twig newly arrived at the nest site must find its way into the nest. It must fit into an appropriate hole in the nest. For the animal, here again is a perceptual pattern. To understand this perceptual pattern, we can only observe the behavior of a variety of twigs in relation to an available hole. So again, to understand the perceptual pattern which initiates and terminates nest building, we can only look to the behavior of the nest as a whole: i.e., just what kinds of holes in space does it seek, and how does it grow to fill the selected hole?

Where to initiate nest construction may be controlled by a visual perceptual pattern alone and termination of nest construction by participation of inputs from other sensory modalities in a more integrative perceptual pattern. However, the evolutionary thesis remains the same. Natural selection provides for a perceptual pattern, all of whose components provide for maximization of reproductive success. The filling-in of this pattern is the business of the individual species member. At each stage of the process, the event most predictive of reproductive success is brought into being. Interim actions may appear controlled by a final goal state maximally conducive to reproductive success, but this is not the case. At each and every moment in nest construction, behavioral actions are controlled by events in the immediate past of the individual and in the remote past of the species.

How are the effects of individual and species past experience embodied in the behavior of the individual? In the course of building a nest, the bird encounters events incorporating features "similar" to features of previously experienced events. The "similar" features are those with appropriate spatial configuration. A hole in the nest having been experienced, recognition of an appropriately shaped twig would provide a reproductive advantage. An event containing a twig of a specific shape having been experienced, recognition of a hole in the nest into which it would fit would also do so.

Terminus Events and Reproductive Success

This nest-building example illustrates the relative nature of the concept of terminus event. "Nest-completion" is a terminus event, but so is "the-fitted-twig." Both bring a characteristic sequence of actions to a close. Both are necessary to successful reproduction. To understand what an animal is predisposed to learn and hence the nature of its *Umwelt*, both the fine-grain and the molar aspects of its behavior need to be studied. This does not render the concept any the less useful. It simply points the way to discovery of the natural units of behavior and the context of circumstances in which they occur.

Natural units of behavior involve a variety of actions and events. To take nest building as an example again, the three-spined stickleback (*Gasterosteus aculeatus*) uses a variety of actions in bringing about successive terminus events while constructing its nest. It may "glue," "push," "sand-carry," etc., in fixing a bit of vegetation in place. The occurrence of one of these actions does not designate a terminus event. It is the "fixing" that does, and this is indicated by a shift of behavior away from the bit of vegetation. A shift, perhaps, to "hovering," "looking," "swimming-to," "material-testing," etc., involves another series of events leading again to a terminus event indicated by a further shift in behavior to "biting," "carrying," or "nest-visit." There are things the stickleback has to learn because environmental determination of the events during nest building was variable in the history of the species. These can be detected only by contextual analysis of the events associated with the transition points in its behavior.

The concept of reproductive success is also a relative one. Selection of variants occurs through their reproductive success. Technically everything an animal does which is necessary for reproduction, or which provides a reproductive advantage, should be subject to selection. Ultimately the concept must be defined in terms of the number of offspring produced that in turn reproduce. This does not provide for a convenient measure. It means that everything from fertilization (release of gametes) through attainment of independence at maturity (separation from parents) is relevant. Thus any earlier event (prior to fertilization) that enhances the occurrence of any postfertilization event facilitating survival of offspring to maturity could be selectively important.

Animals differ in their mode of reproduction. Some simply shed their gametes into the surrounding medium. Others utilize internal fertilization. Some, like many invertebrates and the salmon, have only one crack at reproduction. Others have seasonal opportunities, and still others have shorter periodicities, or are continuously in a reproductive condition. Terminus events, by definition, are selected as necessary to reproductive success. Terminus events guide the occurrence and nature of learning. Some terminus events, in particular those related to somatic survival, may exist regardless of mode of reproduction. Others must be specific to the mode of reproduction. What is needed is an analysis of learning in relation to mode of reproduction. Systematic differences may well appear.

The Pacific salmon (*Oncorpymchus* spp.), among other species of fish, travels long distances over a period of years. It has only one chance to reproduce. For such an animal, the ability to return to the region of its birth offers a marked reproductive advantage. Successful reproduction is more probable where it has previously occurred. During its return journey, the salmon's digestive system atrophies and the conformation of its mouth alters in a manner precluding efficient eating but conducive to efficient fighting. Once "home," it exceeds any other fish of similar size in competitive fighting for territory and female. Once it spawns, the fish dies almost immediately (Williams, 1966; Wynne-Edwards, 1962). Care of the eggs and young and complex nest-construction activities are totally absent. Is learning based on the types of spatial apprehension necessary in nest construction, as seen in other fish, also absent? Comparison with other fish, e.g., many Salmonidae which do breed more than once, is possible.

Terminus Events, Releasers, and Reinforcers

How does a "terminus event" differ from a "releasing stimulus"? Both have evolved in the interests of reproductive survival, and consummatory responses involve not only releasing stimuli but also terminate sequences of behavior. What then is the import of the distinction? A releasing stimulus does not necessarily involve a change in behavioral state; a terminus event does. A releasing stimulus elicits a fixed response; a terminus event may not involve a response at all (in the sense of a behavioral reaction occurring in the event itself). A releasing stimulus and fixed response are selected for only where their appearance renders a sequence of events of increasing probability of reproductive success more likely. A releasing stimulus and fixed response need not necessarily occur prior to reproductive success. A terminus event must. A terminus event is selected for as necessary for reproductive success. Thus some terminus events may involve releasing stimuli, but not all releasing stimuli appear in terminus events.

How does a "terminus event" differ from a "reinforcer"? Reinforcement frequently terminates a behavior sequence and often contributes to somatic and/or reproductive survival. However, in a proper sense a reinforcing event can be very brief and a long succession of such events can be necessary to terminate a behavioral sequence. It takes many food pellets to sate the bar-pressing rat (and terminate bar-pressing). Many "escapes" from shock are required before the rat gets off the grid (and terminates its "mincing" gait) efficiently—at least initially. A terminus event heralds a shift in behavior each time it occurs. Reinforcement does not. Terminus events guide learning (at least associative learning). Their occurrence makes possible the action of reinforcers..

Reinforcement guides performance. Its occurrence is said to increase the probability of a response again occurring in similar circumstances. This appears to be so in some circumstances. The thirsty mammal may well return to the site where it last found water (Petrinovich and Bolles, 1954; Oatley, 1970). A water source is a consistent feature of its *Umwelt*. For a predatory carnivore, food sources are much less so. The carnivore is predisposed to attend to quite different aspects of its *Umwelt* in a search for food. Like the bar-pressing rat and the key-pecking pigeon, the carnivore has difficulty learning that food once depleted at a particular spatial locus can be automatically replenished. Water and food reinforcers, as terminus events, call upon predispositions to learn quite different "event sequences" in their service. However, at the same time, water consumption and food consumption may serve quite the same function in a variety of animals as they do in carnivores. They are necessary to reproductive success, but they are not necessarily reinforcers as in the carnivore's way of life. They terminate sequences of behavior, but they may not necessarily call upon particular predispositions to learn particular "event sequences." The insect, or other animal, that takes its water from whatever leaf it may stand upon each morning need not be predisposed to learn particular sequences of events carrying it through space to a fixed pond or other body of water. It may well be predisposed to learn, considering the consistency of the environmentally constrained events governing its life, but only to move from the event of moisture upon its lower appendages to the event of drinking, and that only when its organismic state so dictates.

Primacy of Associative Learning

It is well to recognize the primacy of associative learning in the evolution of learning capacity, but what of the higher, more complex forms of learning? What of abstraction, conceptualization, insight, and reasoning, those forms of individual adaptive modification of behavior so tantalizingly "self-evident" in the primate division of the mammalian heritage? Thus far we have been discussing the "primordial aspect" of the evolution of learning capacity, i.e., the conditions existing in the ancestral history of every modern species that had to be met if there were to be modern representatives of the species. We have concluded that the evolution of learning capacity must have been (and is) constrained within the limits of bioecological relationships necessary to the survival of the individual (somatic survival) and survival of its genes (reproductive survival). Both we have seen to be subject to the criterion of reproductive success. With subjection to this criterion, we have seen that only sensitivity to physically constrained associations of environmentally imposed events can provide a continuing basis for the evolution of learning capacity. This sensitivity we have said to be built into the somatic aspect of genic survival because of developmental processes in the elaboration of an individual life; i.e., the individual is predisposed by its ancestral history to learn in accordance with the environmental events of its developmental history. Thus where developmental and ancestral history coincide learning is easy, and where developmental and ancestral history do not coincide learning is difficult if not impossible.

Against this view we must compare the variety of undoubted learning phenomena evident in modern animals. There can be no doubt that different species of animals do possess different learning capacities. The yucca moth (*Pronuba yuccasella*) is sometimes exemplified as one that possesses none (Stone, 1942; Eibl-Eibesfeldt, 1970). This moth as once described (Morgan, 1896) apparently bursts from its chrysalis case "knowing" what it must do:

> The silvery, straw-colored insects emerge from their chrysalis cases, just when the large, yellowish-white bell-shaped flowers of the yucca open, each for a single night. From the anthers of one of these flowers the female moth collects the golden pollen and kneads the adhesive material into a little pellet, which she holds beneath her head by means of the greatly enlarged bristly palps. Thus laden, she flies off and seeks another flower. Having found one, she pierces with the sharp lancets of her ovipositor the tissue of the pistil, lays her eggs among the ovules, and then, darting to the top of the stigma, stuffs the fertilizing pollen-pellet into its funnel-shaped opening. (p. 14)

The moth apparently "knows" that it must collect pollen prior to laying its eggs, and that after having laid its eggs in one place it must place its burden, the pollen pellet, in another place. This is necessary for the pollination of the flower. No other insect does this and no other method can accomplish the task. It is also necessary for the growth of the yucca moth's larvae, once they emerge from their eggs 4 or 5 days hence. Having eaten of the fertilized ovules around them, the larvae cut holes through the plant's ovary, spin webs, and descend to the ground. Thereafter they burrow in and pass the winter in the pupal condition, from which they emerge the following year, at the time when the yucca is in flower, as adults.

Adaptations of this nature are dependent on precise coordination of developmental and environmental events. Where they exist, an ancestral history of a precise sequence of events of such high reproductive advantage as to virtually exclude alternative sequences of events is indicated. Where such precise coordinations occur, much *must* be left to the environment. Associative learning predispositions are not thereby excluded, but rather facilitated. Like *Ammophila campestris* in moving from "sand-in-burrow" to "clear-burrow," *Pronuba yuccasella* must move from "anther-contact" to "completed-pellet," for one, and from there to "pistil-contact," by way of flying and "yucca-contact-with-pellet," for another. It is a mistake to overemphasize the stylized "species-specific responses" by which the moth molds its pellet, the wasp grasps and removes the sand in its burrow, and the raven or jackdaw fits the twig to its nest using a "trembling" motion. These are fixed responses, and species typical, it is true, but so is that action of the man who swings his hammer to drive a nail. Some may be more efficient at these actions than others, some may gain proficiency in the action more quickly than others, but all are provided opportunity to learn in the course of the action. Limited as the opportunity may be, relative to other cases, the environment still offers *Pronuba yuccasella* alternative event sequences from initiation to termination of "pollen-collection." In the past, as in the present, those predisposed to adopt the event sequences providing reproductive advantage narrow the alternatives available to future generations. Among these, those predisposed to systematically modify their next action in terms of the results of the last (in approximation to a terminus event) must be counted. If alternative ways of making a pollen pellet appear to be limited today and the actions involved are stereotyped and species specific, it is because their alternates were selected against in the competition for genetic survival. The elaboration of structural changes abetting the surviving alternatives is in most cases the result of secondary phases of the competition (Mayr, 1958, 1960).

Terminus Events, Concepts, and Reasoning

Where the coordination of developmental and environmental events is less precise, greater (or, at least, more evident) variation is to be found.

Where a single sequence of events does not offer overwhelming reproductive advantage, associative learning capacity is more evident. Where many alternative event sequences can lead to occurrence of the same terminus event, "higher" forms of learning can be in evidence. Selection for genic predisposition to sensitivity to specific environmental event associations necessarily leads to higher learning in certain cases.

We have emphasized that a variety of events can facilitate reproductive success (provide an advantage) and some must necessarily occur (terminus events). It is the sequencing of these events into alternative event pathways that is of concern here. Consider the case where from event *X* the occurrence of events *a*, *b*, and *c* could lead to the occurrence of terminus event *Y* (i.e., reproductive success) with a probability of 0.20. If event *d* or *e* occurs following *X*, however, this probability is 0.90. Genic influences predisposing *d* or *e* to follow *X* will increase in the population gene pool. The longer such selection goes on, the lower the proportion of genic influences predisposing to occurrence of *a*, *b*, or *c* in that gene pool will become. It is assumed that genic predisposition for *d* or *e* to follow *X* originally developed in separate individuals. The probability of a single genome derived from that gene pool containing predisposing influences to the occurrence of both *d* and *e* must necessarily increase the longer selection goes on.

It follows that where a number of associative predispositions of high and approximately equal selective value exist which lead to a terminus event, many will eventually appear in the same genome. It also follows that such genomes will eventually become the norm for the population. That all such associative predispositions do not eventually appear in all genomes depends on incompatibility among their genic determiners and on incompatibility in their elaboration during individual development. Thus general adaptiveness of behavior in the face of changing environmental circumstance may depend on the kind and number of associative predispositions the individual possesses related to the same terminus event. Where many relate to the same terminus event, a "concept" *may* have evolved.

It must also be that the more different kinds of terminus events that are required for reproductive success, the greater the number of associative predispositions there will be. Thus where shelter and care of offspring must be provided, individual adaptiveness may appear greater. The more different terminus events required and the more different associative predispositions related to the same terminus event, the greater the probability that the same intervening event could appear in different associative predispositions (i.e., event sequences). Particularly in the case where that common ("intersect") event predicts occurrence of its associated terminus events with a high probability (together with succeeding events in each sequence), it may achieve a unique status. Perhaps such multiply associated events could provide a basis for higher learning, e.g., concept formation and reasoning. Two speculative instances are considered below.

An important element in the argument has been that the association of a terminus event with a prior event by similarity also involves association of intervening events with both, provided only that the one predicts the other. Natural selection has marked events as "similar" if their successive occurrence (irrespective of intervening events and time passage) enhances reproductive success. That is, when one occurs it reinstates the other's internal representation. Association by "similarity" is the normal way associations are formed in any species of animal. This occurs in the framework of the species *Umwelt*. Take, for example, an event signaling predation. The prey animal that terminates the succeeding events by entering an appropriate refuge (a hole, or perhaps a tree) will survive to reproduce its kind. The prey animal that is "reminded" of a previously seen nearby refuge by occurrence of the predation-signaling event will then be at a reproductive advantage, particularly so the more efficiently it gains the refuge. Efficiency is gained if the multiply associated signs of predation can be recognized more specifically. So also with signs of a refuge. Thus a concept of "predation," or of "danger," goes with the evolution of a concept of "refuge," of "security," or of "safety." This predisposed pairing of events, of actions, or of developing concepts suggests a law of opposites in associative learning.

Reproductive success occurs in an *Umwelt* imposed by the interaction of the "nature of the beast" with "reality." For most if not all animals, the *Umwelt* is a spatial one. There are three aspects or features, of space. First, there is a coordinate framework defining sectors of space. For a bilaterally symmetrical animal, as for others, these must relate to the body. There are a front sector and a back sector, a right and a left, and an above and a below. Second, these six sectors are divisible into regions of space. The regions relate to behavior, as the sectors relate to bodily posture. Provisionally, for the example of visual space, we may recognize a "contact" region bordered in extension from the organism by a "reachable" region. Beyond this is a "leapable," "jumpable," or "chargeable" region. Still further distant from the animal, an "approachable," "stalkable" region may be distinguished, bordered finally by an "unattainable," "too far away" region. The third feature of space is the presence of "objects" and "areas" (figure and ground) in the various regions. These relate also to behavior, but in a different sense. They provide the elements of an event associating it with other events, including terminus events. Presumably a variety of event sequences contain common ("intersect") events defining "contactableness," "reachableness," "leapableness," etc. Thus space for the animal is defined in terms of the representation in its *Umwelt* of the objects and their interrelations in the physical world.

There are things related to space that have to be learned. For example, to reproduce their kind certain birds must build nests of a sort appropriate to their somatic characteristics. However, two nests cannot be built in the exact same physical locus. To build a nest and raise its young, a bird must be able to learn its nest locus and return to it in an efficient manner from a distance. Many birds on returning to their nest with food for their mate or young do so in a manner deceptive to human and apparently other predatorial eyes. They land at a distance and follow a changing diversified course on final approach. They apparently have learned not only the locus of their own individual nest but also the relations to it of surrounding and distant loci of a varied botanical and geographic character. Such learning, or at least its expression in behavior, can be said to be a function of the parental state of the bird. In this sense, it may be that a state-specific learning is involved, a learning specifically selected for in the history of the species to augment the efficiency of parental care in the interests of reproductive success.

But what of the state of the male bird prior to the acquisition of a mate, the advent of courtship, and the building of a nest? Many birds establish territories which are defended against the incursion of other males and which are important in the attraction of a female conspecific. In this process, they move around the territory and frequently adopt favorite vantage points. Is the learning of intraterritorial loci specific to the state of the male bird at that time? What does the bird learn about its territorial characteristics at that time? Is this learning transferable to the parental state *en toto*?

The characteristics of a given territory reacted to, and learned, could be quite different in the two states. The question of who chooses the nest locus is relevant. The male may well know the boundary marks of its territory, i.e., those characteristics associated with the withdrawal of an intruder or a stand-off with a neighboring rival. At the same time, the interrelation of geobotanical internal features of the territory may well have "passed notice" until the female has selected the nest site and building proceeds. To the extent that multiply associated (intersect) events are held in common between "territorial boundary" and "territorial internal differentiation" learning, a basis for inter-state transfer might be provided. However, the specific aspects of the commonly held features utilized could be quite different, i.e., opportunities for visibility in the territorial phase and opportunities for hideability in the parental phase. As terminus events, differential physical characteristics of the same territorial feature could well be involved.

If, on the other hand, common intersect events underlie the learning of spatial features and relationships relevant to different behavioral states, the utilization of these could provide a basis for the evolution of reasoning. In other words, the more diversified the aspects of the environment necessarily interacted with in the interests of genic survival the more learning and reasoning capacity would be expected to develop. This generalization should hold without regard for phylogenetic relationship or the presence of underlying homologous structures. This should be so even though in all modern animal species capacity to represent critical associations of environmental events is equal, i.e., associative learning ability is equal.

Concluding Statement

Neither a dichotomy nor a polarization of instinct vs. learning appeared in our analysis of the evolution of learning. Instead, learning and instinct were found to be one and the same. Once genes and nervous systems are recognized as being physical components of physical events and as necessary to "mind," no other conclusion is possible. It is, rather, that the environment ordains that living organisms adapt to contingent relations between events. The adaptation, like the contingency, is probabilistic in character. The more certainly one happening predicts the occurrence of another, the more likely the organism is to use that relationship in its way of life. In all cases, using a relationship implies changing behavior as opportunity repeats itself. Behavioral adaptations, like structural and other adaptations, provide varied means of realizing probabilistic relationships. Where the probability of realization of relationships necessary to reproductive success is enhanced by one of a variety of means rather than another, it gains in favor. Where reproductive success is not enhanced, the variety of means remains unaltered. No matter how favored by environmental circumstance, no matter how restricted the variety of means may become in the interests of reproductive success, a variety still remains. From this remaining variety of means, repetitive opportunity selects in accordance with changing circumstance. If reproductive success is not affected, behavior will be altered idiosyncratically, i.e., to fit the limitations of bodily structure, as in swinging a hammer. If reproductive success is affected, behavior will be altered in accordance with those circumstances which facilitate genic survival. The point is that living organisms are a series of physical events in time consisting of a variety of physical components. To survive through time, those physical events and their components must fit into, and mesh with, the context of extraorganismic physical events within which they exist. Without variety at each step along the way, survival is jeopardized. All evolution can do is impose constraint through favorable selection of those variants that meet the test. The point has been repeatedly made by others in emphasizing the determination of life and change by physicochemical laws of nature, e.g., Kohler (1960) through his principle of invariance and von Bertalanffy (1968) through open-systems analysis of living organismic processes.

The principle of invariance (that physicochemical law remains invariant in all evolutionary expressions of life) has taken us *through* the synthetic theory of evolution (Simpson, 1958) to the realization that (1) "associative learning capacity," i.e., sensitivity to contingencies necessary to genic survival, in one form or another, is basic to life; (2) analysis of "true-blue certified" associative learning and all other more complex forms of learning should be cast in terms of what is required for reproductive success in each instance; (3) the characteristics of modern animals which are necessary to reproductive success reflect the course of events which occurred in their ancestral history and intimately bind their capacity to modify the course of future events in their own lifetimes.

References

Baerends, G. P. 1941. Fortpflanzungsverhalten und Orientierung der Grabwespe, *Ammophila campestris. Tijdschrift für Entomologie*, *84*, 68–275. (Discussed in: Eibl-Eibesfeldt, I. 1970. *Ethology: The Biology of Behavior.* Holt, Rinehart and Winston, New York, p. 218.)

Bateson, G. 1972. *Steps to an Ecology of Mind.* Chandler, San Francisco.

Bitterman, M. E. 1965. The evolution of intelligence. *Scientific American*, *212*, 92–100.

Borer, K. T. 1968. Disappearance of preferences and aversions for sapid solutions in rats ingesting untasted fluids. *Journal of Comparative and Physiological Psychology*, *65*, 213–221.

Brunswik, E. 1955. Representative design and probabilistic theory in a functional psychology. *Psychological Review*, *62*, 193–217.

Brunswik, E. 1956. *Perception and the Representative Design of Psychological Experiments.* University of California Press, Berkeley.

Corning, W. C., and Kelly, S. 1973. Platyhelminthes: The Turbellarians. In: *Invertebrate Learning*, Vol. 1. W. C. Corning, J. A. Dyal, and A. O. D. Willows (Eds.). Plenum Press, New York, pp. 171–224.

Cullen, E. 1957. Adaptations in the kittiwake to cliff-nesting. *Ibis*, *99*, 275–302.

Dethier, V. G., and Stellar, E. 1970. *Animal Behavior.* Prentice-Hall, Englewood Cliffs, N.J.

Eibl-Eibesfeldt, I. 1970. *Ethology: The Biology of Behavior.* Holt, Rinehart and Winston, New York.

Emlen, S. T. 1970. Celestial rotation: Its importance in the development of migratory orientation. *Science*, *170*, 1198–1201.

Garcia, J., and Ervin, F. R. 1968. Gustatory-visceral and telereceptor-cutaneous conditioning-adaptation in internal and external milieus. *Communications in Behavioral Biology*, *1*, 389–415.

Garcia J., Green, K. F., and McGowan, B. K. 1969. X-ray as an olfactory stimulus. In: *Olfaction and Taste III: Proceedings of the Third International Symposium.* C. Pfaffmann (Ed.). Rockefeller University Press, New York.

Garcia, J., McGowan, B. K., and Green, K. F. 1972. Biological constraints on conditioning. In: *Classical Conditioning II: Current Research and Theory.* A. H. Black and W. F. Prokasy (Eds.). Appleton-Century-Crofts, New York, pp. 3–27.

Garcia, J., Clarke, J. C., and Hankins, W. G. 1973. Natural responses to scheduled rewards. In: *Perspectives in Ethology.* P. P. G. Bateson and P. H. Klopfer (Eds.). Plenum Press, New York, pp. 1–42.

Gibson, J. J. 1966. *The Senses Considered as Perceptual Systems.* Houghton Mifflin, Boston.
Girden, E. 1940. Cerebral mechanisms in conditioning under curare. *American Journal of Psychology, 53,* 397–406.
Hailman, J. P. 1967. The ontogeny of an instinct: The pecking response in chicks of the laughing gull (*Larus atricilla* L.) and related species. *Behaviour, Supplement 15,* 1–159.
Haralson, J. V., Groff, C. I., and Stewart, R. A. 1971. Conditioned responses in the sea anemone *Cribrina xanthogrammica.* Paper read at the meetings of the Animal Behavior Society, Logan, Utah.
Haralson, J. V., Groff, C. I., and Haralson, S. J. 1975. Classical conditioning in the sea anemone *Cribrina xanthogrammica. Physiology and Behavior, 15,* 455–460.
Haralson, S. J., and Haralson, J. 1974. Cognitive aspects of classical conditioning in the sea anemone, *Cribrina xanthogrammica.* Paper read at the meetings of the Western Psychological Association, San Francisco.
Harlow, H. F. 1958. The evolution of learning. In: *Behavior and Evolution.* A. Roe and G. G. Simpson (Eds.). Yale University Press, New Haven, pp. 269–290.
Hebb, D. O. 1949. *The Organization of Behavior.* Wiley, New York.
Hinde, R. A., and Stevenson-Hinde, J. (Eds.). 1973. *Constraints on Learning.* Academic Press, New York.
Hull, C. L. 1943. *Principles of Behavior.* Appleton-Century-Crofts, New York.
James, W. 1893. *Psychology.* Henry Holt, New York.
Jerison, H. J. 1973. *Evolution of the Brain and Intelligence.* Academic Press, New York.
Kohler, W. 1941. On the nature of associations. *Proceedings of the American Philosophical Society, 84,* 489–502.
Kohler, W. 1947. *Gestalt Psychology.* Liverwright, New York.
Kohler, W. 1960. The mind-body problem. In: *Dimensions of Mind.* S. Hook (Ed.). New York University Press, New York, pp. 3–23.
Krebs, J. R. 1973. Behavioral aspects of predation. In: *Perspectives in Ethology.* P. P. G. Bateson and P. H. Klopfer (Eds.). Plenum Press, New York, pp. 73–112.
Krechevsky, I. 1932*a*. "Hypotheses" in rats. *Psychological Review, 39,* 516–532.
Krechevsky, I. 1932*b*. The genesis of "hypotheses" in rats. *University of California Publications in Psychology, 6,* 45–64.
Krechevsky, I. 1933. Hereditary nature of "hypotheses." *Journal of Comparative Psychology, 16,* 99–116.
Lack, D. 1943. *The Life of the Robin.* Cambridge University Press, London.
Lorenz, K. 1965. *Evolution and Modification of Behavior.* University of Chicago, Press, Chicago.
Manning, A. 1975. Animal learning: Ethological approaches. In: *Neural Mechanics of Learning and Memory.* M. R. Rosenzweig and E. L. Bennet (Eds.). M.I.T. Press, Cambridge, Mass.
Mayr, E. 1958. Behavior and systematics. In: *Behavior and Evolution.* A. Roe and G. G. Simpson (Eds.). Yale University Press, New Haven, pp. 342–362.
Mayr, E. 1960. The emergence of evolutionary novelties. In: *Evolution After Darwin: The Evolution of Life,* Vol. 1. S. Tax (Ed.). University of Chicago Press, Chicago, pp. 349–380.
Mayr, E. 1970. *Population, Species, and Evolution.* Harvard University Press, Cambridge, Mass.
Mayr, E. 1974. Behavior programs and evolutionary strategies. *American Scientist, 62,* 650–659.
Miller, N. E. 1967. Certain facts of learning relevant to the search for its physical basis. In: *The Neurosciences: A Study Program.* G. C. Quarton, T. Melnechuk, and F. O. Schmitt (Eds.). Rockefeller University Press, New York, pp. 643–652.

Morgan, C. L. 1896. *Habit and Instinct*. Edward Arnold, London.

Oatley, K. 1970. Brain mechanisms and motivation. *Nature* (*London*), *225*, 797–801.

Overton, D. A. 1968. Visual cues and shock sensitivity in the control of T maze choice by drug conditions. *Journal of Comparative and Physiological Psychology*, *66*, 216–219.

Petrinovich, L. 1973*a*. Darwin and the representative expression of reality. In: *Darwin and Facial Expression*. P. Ekman (Ed.). Academic Press, New York, pp. 223–256.

Petrinovich, L. 1973*b*. A species-meaningful analysis of habituation. In: *Habituation: Behavioral Studies*, Vol. 1. H. V. S. Peeke and M. J. Herz (Eds.). Academic Press, New York, pp. 141–162.

Petrinovich, L., and Bolles, R. 1954. Deprivation states and behavioral attributes. *Journal of Comparative and Physiological Psychology*, *47*, 450–453.

Petrinovich, L., and Bolles, R. 1957. Delayed alternation: Evidence for symbolic processes in the rat. *Journal of Comparative and Physiological Psychology*, *50*, 363–365.

Razran, G. 1971. *Mind in Evolution: An East-West Synthesis of Learned Behavior and Cognition*. Houghton Mifflin, Boston.

Renner, M. 1960. The contribution of the honey bee to the study of time-sense and astronomical orientation. *Cold Springs Harbor Symposium on Quantitative Biology*, *25*, 361–367.

Rensch, B. 1967. The evolution of brain achievements. In: *Evolutionary Biology*, Vol. 1. T. Dobzhansky, M. K. Hecht, and W. C. Steere (Eds.). Appleton-Century-Crofts, New York, pp. 26–68.

Rescorla, R. A. 1967. Pavlovian conditioning and its proper control procedures. *Psychological Review*, *74*, 71–80.

Rozin, P. 1969. Central or peripheral mediation of learning with long CS-US intervals in the feeding system. *Journal of Comparative and Physiological Psychology*, *67*, 421–429.

Rozin, P., and Kalat, J. W. 1971. Specific hungers and poison avoidance as adaptive specializations of learning. *Psychological Review*, *78*, 459–486.

Rushforth, N. D. 1973. Behavioral modifications in coelenterates. In: *Invertebrate Learning*, Vol. 1. W. C. Corning, J. A. Dyal, and A. O. D. Willows (Eds.). Plenum Press, New York, pp. 123–170.

Schiller, C. H. (Ed.). 1957. *Instinctive Behavior: The Development of a Modern Concept*. International Universities Press, New York.

Schneirla, T. C. 1949. Levels in the psychological capacities of animals. In: *Philosophy for the Future: The Quest of Modern Materialism*. R. W. Sellars, V. J. McGill, and M. Farber (Eds.). Macmillan, New York, pp. 243–286.

Schneirla, T. C. 1959. An evolutionary and developmental theory of biphasic processes underlying approach and withdrawal. In: *Nebraska Symposium on Motivation*. M. R. Jones (Ed.). University of Nebraska Press, Lincoln, pp. 1–42.

Seligman, M. E. P. 1970. On the generality of the laws of learning. *Psychological Review*, *77*, 406–418.

Seligman, M. E. P., and Hager, J. L. 1972. *Biological Boundaries of Learning*. Appleton-Century-Crofts, New York.

Simpson, G. G. 1958. The study of evolution: Methods and present status of theory. In: *Behavior and Evolution*. A. Roe and G. G. Simpson (Eds.). Yale University Press, New Haven, pp. 7–26.

Skinner, B. F. 1969. *Contingencies of Reinforcement*. Appleton-Century-Crofts, New York.

Stone, C. P. 1942. Maturation and "instinctive" functions. In: *Comparative Psychology*. F. A. Moss (Ed.). Prentice-Hall, New York, pp. 32–64.

Teitelbaum, P. 1971. The encephalization of hunger. In: *Progress in Physiological Psychology*, Vol. 4. E. Stellar and J. M. Sprague (Eds.). Academic Press, New York, pp. 319–350.

Testa, T. J. 1974. Causal relationships and the acquisition of avoidance responses. *Psychological Review*, *81*, 491–505.

Thorndike, E. L. 1901. The mental life of the monkeys. *Psychological Review Monograph, Supplement 3*, 1–57.

Thorpe, W. H. 1963. *Learning and Instinct in Animals.* Harvard University Press, Cambridge, Mass.

Tinbergen, N. 1951. *The Study of Instinct.* Oxford University Press, London.

Tinbergen, N. 1972. On the orientation of the digger wasp *Philanthus triangulum* Fabr., 1932. The homing of *Philanthus triangulum*, I, 1932. The hunting behaviour, II, 1935. Selective learning of landmarks, III, 1938. In: *The Animal in Its World*, Vol. 1. Harvard University Press, Cambridge, Mass.

van Iersel, J. J. A., and van den Assem, J. 1964. Aspects of orientation in the digger wasp *Bembix rostrata. Animal Behaviour, Supplement 1*, 145–162.

von Bertalanffy, L. 1968. *General System Theory.* Braziller, New York.

von Uexkull, J. 1957. A stroll through the worlds of animals and men. In: *Instinctive Behavior: The Development of a Modern Concept.* C. H. Schiller (Ed.). International Universities Press, New York, pp. 5–80.

Waddington, C. H. 1953. The evolution of adaptations. *Endeavor*, *12*, 134–139.

Wells, M. J. 1967. Sensitization and evolution of associative learning. In: *Neurobiology of Invertebrates.* J. Salanki (Ed.). Akadémiai Kiado, Budapest, pp. 391–411.

Williams, G. C. 1966. *Adaptation and Natural Selection.* Princeton University Press, Princeton, N.J.

Wynne-Edwards, V. C. 1962. *Animal Dispersion in Relation to Social Behaviour.* Oliver and Boyd, Edinburgh.

3

John Garcia

I. KRECHEVSKY AND I

ONCE UPON A TIME AT BERKELEY

In dim recall, it seems that giants strode the halls of the Department of Psychology when I was a student at Berkeley. Edward Chace Tolman was there, dazzling us with his brilliant meandering lectures. Aided and abetted by Benbow Ritchie, he presided over the intellectual pyrotechnical displays in the learning seminars. Leo Postman restored order and intellectual discipline in human learning seminars. Egon Brunswik burst our brains with his methodological foundations and R. Nevett Sanford and Elsa Frankel-Brunswik made us whole again with soothing Neo-Freudian balm. Donald McKinnon initiated us into the mysteries of Jung, and, for too brief a period, Eric Homberger Erickson enchanted us with dynamic explanations of how children grew up. In that happy time, psychology had not yet congealed into rigid areas. There were old giants like Robert Tryon, Warner Brown, C. W. Brown, and E. Ghiselli and young giants like Al Riley and John McKee, to name a few I encountered in class and seminar.

Even the graduate students stood tall. Tim Leary was tuned in there and had not yet turned on, or dropped out. Richard Christie adroitly juggled social surveys, child problem solving, and rat research all at the same time. Henry Gleitman played poker, starred in little theater, and ran learning experiments at midnight. Julie Hochberg was the teaching assistant in my experimental lab and Joe Greenbaum was the teaching assistant in my learn-

John Garcia • Departments of Psychology and Psychiatry, University of California, Los Angeles, California.

ing lab. Bill Wilson and Bob Rollins were practicing brain lesions with a primitive stereotaxic instrument. Murray Jarvik was probing memory and Jerry Hirsch was behaviorally and genetically separating flies into upward- and downward-bound races. A constant stream of new graduate students (Everett Wyers, Robert Bolles, Lew Petrinovich, Jim McGaugh, Al Parducci, and others) were challenging their elders for lab space.

The shortest and the mightiest of them all was David Krech, known in an earlier existence as I. Krechevsky. It was the animate Professor Krech who guided my faltering graduate career spanning some 15 years, but it was the shadowy student I. Krechevsky who haunted my scientific thoughts in those days. Let me relate some of the seminal contributions of that legendary graduate student at Berkeley.

The Biased Rat in the Insoluble Maze

Although Krechevsky was nurtured in an environmentally biased behaviorism, his research from the beginning was centered on the contribution which the organism brought to the learning situation. Most behaviorists believed that the organism approached its problem with a formless "random" array of responses, which were then hammered into a coherent habit by repetitious collisions with environmental rewards and punishments in the microcosmic mazes and puzzle boxes of that day. The correct path to the goal box was arbitrary, and so the initial responses of a group of animals, classed as correct or erroneous against this capricious criterion, appeared random or unsystematic as some animals took one option and some took another. In one sense, this resembles the Darwinian model requiring only the assumptions of random response variation and the selective pressure of the goal box. However, the behaviorists ignored a greater Darwinian truth: animals are already equipped to deal systematically with their environment because of their long evolutionary history.

Many a behavorist watching a rat's first attempts to cope with a complex problem must have subvocalized, "What is that damned rat trying to do?" Karl Lashley (1929) gave voice to the unspeakable notion that the rats were attempting systematic solutions which apparently defied objective description and measurement. But the 20-year-old Krechevsky (1932) devised a brilliantly simple method to demonstrate the phenomenon objectively in the laboratory situation with the laboratory rat. He presented his rats with clear-cut choices, well marked by salient cues, but these cues and choices were randomly related to the ultimate reward. Since random reward could not impress a pattern in the rat's choices, each rat was free to reveal its inherent tactics toward the distinctive alternatives confronting him. Krechevsky then looked at the effort of an individual rat over a large series of trials and observed its emergent idiosyncratic pattern (a pattern which would have been submerged in the response chaos created by the usual behavioristic practice of pooling the data from a large group of rats).

One version of the Krechevsky maze was a series of four identical discrimination units leading to a goal box. In each unit, the rat was presented with two left-right openings, either of which could be made bright or dark. Behind each opening, the rat encountered a door which was either closed or opened into the next unit. If the door was closed, the rat had to retrace its steps and enter the next unit through the alternative door. Ultimately the animal found its way to food in the goal box. Over a series of trials, each rat behaved systematically to some cue, as if it believed that cue pointed the way to the goal box. Krechevsky (1932) labeled these systematic tendencies "hypotheses," a term which he attributes to Tolman, who denied the allegation (Krech, 1974). To circumvent the heresy of "mentalism," Krechevsky defined a hypothesis as a response tendency falling outside the chance range of 50% ± 3 SD. In other words, a rat would have to choose the left door most of the time before Krechevsky would say that the animal had a hypothesis that left was correct.

Even with the laboratory rat or pigeon as protagonist, it is becoming abundantly clear today that the conception of the organism as a random system is unworkable. But it was in 1932 that Krechevsky demonstrated that the coping rat was hypothetically biased in its attentive focus and that this bias was apt to be maintained over repeated trials without differential reinforcement and ultimately abandoned only in favor of yet another biased hypothesis.

Despite Krechevsky's *experimentus crucis*, the notion of randomness or unsystematic variation in behavior prior to environmental reinforcement was to remain in vogue for decades, reaching its most elegant expression in the Estes (1959) sampling theory. Estes' conceptual organism restlessly scanned the environment during learning and became conditioned to those elements in attentive focus when reinforcement was applied. Any preexisting bias in the scanning process was considered an emprical constant of little theoretical significance. This theory was a prototype, spawning a large number of mathematical and computer simulations of perceptual and learning processes. It is difficult to say that these models were incorrect since they were designed to deal with a constricted data base, but their effect was to incorrectly direct the study of most psychologists away from the inherently structured nature of man and beast.

The same can be said for the operant conditioning system (Skinner, 1959) which came to dominate American behaviorism. Skinner's conceptual organism emitted a hierarchy of responses each with a certain probability of occurrence. Reinforcement was all-important because it altered response probabilities, yet no theories of reinforcement action were permitted. Initial baseline response probabilities were mere empirical matters. Skinner believed that responses and reinforcers could best be specified in terms of external contingencies without recourse to the internal structure of the organism.

Young Krechevsky's notion that patterns of coping behavior stemmed from factors "within the skin of the animal" anticipated the "new look" in learning forced by ethological evidence. The presolution responding was made systematic by biological constraints prior to any reinforcing environmental influences. Moreover, young Krechevsky, displaying his natural flair for teaching, summarized his data in the heuristic and flexible concept of the "hypothesis," predating Lorenz's (1956) "internal schoolmarm" who directs the organism's activities according to a genetically programmed textbook. Lorenz's internal schoolmarm instructs the naive stickleback to defend its watery nesting territory against male rivals marked with red bellies and to accept females with swollen bellies. Like Krechevsky's rats, Lorenz's fish have biased reactions toward environmental stimuli inherent in their neural structure due to natural selection of their species. Unlike Krechevsky, the ethologists originally stressed the rigidity of species-specific behavior, leaving little, if any, role for learning. In their conceptual hydraulic model, the rising levels of internal motivation can be traded off for appropriateness of the environmental stimuli. When motivational levels are low, only the genuine red-bellied male releases the innate attack patterns in Lorenz's stickleback, but as the level rises motivation can produce the patterned attack in an environment devoid of rivals.

In contrast, Krechevsky (1933*a*) stressed the docile nature of the rat's hypothesis. His conceptual organism used its hypothesis in a purposive way, maintaining its bias when it was effective to obtain food, dropping it in favor of another attempted solution when it proved ineffective. Thus learning was a discontinuous information-seeking and testing process, where insight came suddenly by confirmation of hypotheses. This was also a radical notion, for tradition from Edward Thorndike to Clark Hull held that the learning process was a continuous incremental growth of associative strength. Krechevsky (1938) again challenged the establishment with a bold and simple paradigm published in *The Psychological Review*. He trained rats on a simple visual discrimination of two patterns on a Lashley jumping stand. His two experimental groups were rewarded for the "wrong" response the first 2 or 4 days of training, respectively, after which they were rewarded for the "correct" response. His control group had the correct response rewarded from the beginning. His rats were not handicapped by reinforcement of the wrong response, contrary to the notion of continuous accumulation of response strength through reinforcement. Actually, his experimental groups mastered the discrimination with fewer errors and less trials than the control group.

Krechevsky (1938) explained:

> At first the animal goes through a "pre-solution" period during which he responds to various "irrelevant" stimuli and during which he solves a number of subsidiary problems . . . .
>
> In the course of responding with these various "irrelevant" hypotheses during the pre-solution period, the reinforcements and non-reinforcements of the animal's responses have little residual effect in determining the animal's behavior *as far as the relevant discriminanda are concerned.* It is suggested that only when the animal begins to "pay attention to" or "react to" the important stimuli does reinforcement begin to have any effect.

Over 20 years later, in a paper published in the same journal, W. K. Estes (1960) took the same position without mention of Krechevsky. He wrote:

> We noted that in virtually all contemporary learning theories, the concept of strength is assumed to have at least three different empirical manifestations—the habit hierarchy, the growth of associative strength in the sense of response probability as a function of number of reinforcements, and the increase in resistance to forgetting of once established associations with additional reinforcement. We tested for all three of these effects by means of the simplest controlled comparisons we could arrange, doing our utmost to eliminate the confoundings and the layers of statistical processing that shield the behavioral changes occurring on individual learning trials completely from view in conventional experimental designs. And under these presumably favorable circumstances, all three effects mysteriously evaporated, leaving a picture of unitary associations the learning and unlearning of which proceed on an essentially all-or-none basis.

Hypothesis, Heredity, and Brain Action

In spite of its cogency and its potential, Krechevsky's conceptual organism did not meet with instant approval. Behavorial logicians were to criticize "hypothesis" as a circular concept, arguing that it was drawn *ad hoc* from the very behavior it explained; i.e., "A rat is systematic because it has a hypothesis, and we know it has a hypothesis because it is systematic." This criticism ignores the fact that on the descriptive level Krechevsky had effectively disputed random responding, which was equally circular. What is more important, Krechevsky went on to manipulate hereditary differences and brain damage and noted their effects on hypothesis behavior, thus breaking the circularity of behavioral explanations of behavior in the only way that it can be broken.

Young Krechevsky turned to Robert C. Tryon in order to test hereditary influences on the hypothetical bias of the rat. Tryon had initiated one of the earliest behavioral genetic programs, which was already established and productive by 1932. Some 15 years later, when I came to Berkeley, the Tryon maze was still intact, a marvelous complex apparatus filling an experimental room. A revolving "magazine" filled with rats delivered each subject in turn to the starting point of the circuitious maze. Each rat wandered through alleys and *culs-de-sac*, tripping treadles which recorded his score with clicks and clatters, and ultimately entered the final food box, thus activating the mechanism which delivered the next rat to the startbox untouched by human hands. Low-scoring males were mated to low-scoring females and high-scoring males to high-scoring females. After seven generations, a bright race and a dull race of rats evolved whose maze scores could be predicted by examining their lineage before they entered the Tryon maze for the first time.

With characteristic generosity, the good Professor Tryon made his bright and dull races available to the graduate student Krechevsky. Krechevsky (1933*b*) tested both races in his hypothesis apparatus. The very nature of intelligence was at issue. Was the bright race generally more intelligent than the dull race? If general intelligence existed, then the bright race should be more adaptive than the dull race. Krechevsky found no differences between the races in total number of hypotheses generated in the repeated attempts to solve the insoluble maze. There was no difference in the time it took the respective racial types to generate their first hypothesis or to switch to their second hypothesis. He found one difference. The bright rats seemed to prefer spatial hypotheses while the dull rats preferred visual hypotheses. Control rats from the common laboratory stock preferred neither spatial nor visual hypotheses. If anything, the dull rats appeared to be free to select alternative hypotheses, while the brights were more limited to the spatial hypotheses, reflecting the selective pressure of Tryon's spatial maze. Krechevsky concluded that maze brightness was a specific spatial response tendency. Obviously such a response tendency would be advantageous in spatial problems and disadvantageous in nonspatial problems. Subsequent research demonstrated that, for rats, maze ability was not highly correlated with discrimination box ability or problem box ability; thus the notion of general intelligence was not supported (Garcia, 1975). Krechevsky's skepticism toward general abilities was shared by Tryon and by Jerry Hirsch, who was to carry on the tradition of behavioral genetics from Tryon. Ironically, the voices of these investigators who actively researched the hereditary aspects of behavior were to be lost in the popular furor caused by the advocacy of general racial intellectual superiority in humans by "academic intellectoids" who never turned a gene.

Young Krechevsky journeyed to the Chicago laboratories of Karl

Lashley to test brain damage effects on the hypothetical bias of the rat. He found that the main effects of brain damage on the plasticity of the coping rat were clear enough. Brain-damaged animals perseverated longer on a given hypothesis, displayed fewer hypotheses, and did not reverse their hypothetical bias as often as intact animals. The locus of the brain damage did not produce clear-cut effects. Destruction of more than 20% of the visual area tended to increase spatial hypotheses, but damage to the area designated as "spatial" area had an ambiguous effect. Destruction of at least 20% of the "spatial" area and less than 20% of the visual area increased preference for the visual hypotheses. Differential and complex cortical functions were indicated.

Krechevsky (1935) was cautious in his discussion of "Brain Mechanisms and Hypotheses." He attempted to revise Lashley's equipotentiality and mass action principles toward a more differentiated notion of brain action. At one point, he wrote that "There is no correlation with *extent* of lesion, but rather with *locus* of lesion," but at another point he stoutly maintained that "nowhere in Lashley's statements is there the assumption that the brain acts like an undifferentiated mass of jelly, an interpretation of Lashley's statements which has been made by both critics and defenders of the theory."

The differences between the thinking of Lashley and Krechevsky were reflected in their respective appartus. Lashley's III maze was his most sensitive measure of cortical brain damage. It provided a multiplicity of unspecified cues for the rat and could be traversed with various response patterns. However, since the maze yielded a unitary measure of performance it did not test Lashley's hypotheses of mass action and equipotentiality; it merely ensured his conclusions. Given that the brain is an aggregate of related and redundant input-output systems, a rat with one damaged brain system copes with the maze with the remaining systems and shows a decrement in performance. If a second rat has an entirely different system damaged, he can only show a similar decrement on that unitary performance score; thus both systems appear equipotential as far as the Lashly maze is concerned. If a third rat has several systems damaged, then it shows a greater decrement in performance than the other two, thus illustrating mass action. The unitary maze score, like the rectal thermometer, cannot distinguish the causes of the incremental changes it measures.

In contrast, Krechevsky's maze yielded a variety of scores which could be related to environmental information. The rat was free to choose one set of inputs and ignore another, thus revealing more specifically the nature of his deficit. It is interesting to speculate what might have happened if Lashley had adapted and developed a line of Krechevsky mazes. By increasing the number and complexity of the sensory inputs beyond visual and spatial cues, by adding response alternatives, and by offering alternative incentives, he might have developed a marvelously diagnostic instrument which would have revealed the specific effects of his cortical lesions.

It Must Have Been Something I Ate

Quite naturally I came to be skeptical about traditional learning theory and to believe that behavior should only be "explained" in terms of brain mechanisms. So, some 30 years later and with a little help from my friends, I attacked two general premises of learning theory. As we have argued elsewhere (Garcia *et al.*, 1972), these premises have been used by behavioral theorists to avoid dealing with biological structure, or, as Krech (1974) says, to promote their "mindless, brainless" theories of learning.

The first premise, called the equipotentiality rule, stems primarily from Pavlov (1928), who assumed that any stimulus perceived by the organism could be used to signal the animal. For example, any visual stimulus, any odor, any touch, or any sound could be used to signal the animal that food was coming to its mouth or that shock was coming to its paw. Of course, most traditional behaviorists remarked at one time or another that "we all know" animals can learn some things more quickly than others, but they really felt that these differences in learning were due to differences in stimulus intensity, response effectiveness, timing, or task complexity. Certainly not one of them believed that information from one afferent channel would be handled in a completely different way than information from another channel in a simple conditioning situation. Rather, they believed that the signaling potential for all perceptible stimuli was essentially the same, so discussions of different stimulus qualities, their afferent channels, and their central neural integration were of no great import to learning theory. Privately, of course, most theorists agree that a sweet taste signifies something very different from a loud clap, and sharp pain signifies something very different from a belly-ache; but it is apparently considered bad form to say so in the professional learning literature.

Scientific protocol dictates that such notions should be expressed in the experimental idiom, so we set up a Krechevsky paradigm to do so. A thirsty rat licked a water spout with two sets of salient cues: a light flash activated by a clicking relay and a sweet taste induced by saccharin in the water. Both cues were contingent upon a lick of the spout. As in Krechevsky's maze, both cues bore a constant relationship to the reinforcer so the rat was "free" to attribute the consequences of its behavior to either cue, to neither cue, or to both cues. For some rats, this bright-noisy sweet water was immediately followed by a brief shock to the feet during the session. For other rats, drinking the bright-noisy sweet water was punished by an illness induced after the session. On intervening days, animals drank water without cues or punishment. The rats were then tested with each cue on separate occasions without punishment. The response measure was licking at the spout. The rats that had been shocked refused the bright-noisy water but drank the sweet water. The rats that had been sick refused the sweet water but drank the bright-noisy water (Garcia and Koelling, 1966).

This cue-consequence paradigm was critically examined in a number of learning labs with the following logic: Clicks and shocks have abrupt, vibratory properties. Taste and sickness have "steady-state" lingering properties. Therefore, time and intensity patterns of the paired stimuli may be able to account for the differential cue-consequence results without recourse to wet mechanisms within the skin of the animal (Garcia *et al.*, 1973, 1974). Fortunately for all contending parties, our original findings were substantiated. If they had not been supported, we would all face untold difficulties in explaining why it is so easy to obtain conditioning when the steady-state cues of a distinctive avoidance chamber are paired with a sawtooth footshock, or when the snap of a finger calls the dog to dinner.

The second premise of traditional theories is that behavioral events must be contiguous in time for rapid learning to occur. In classical conditioning, the CS must be followed immediately by the US and in operant lore the response must be followed immediately by the reinforcer. Yet in a habituation study or a recognition study a test stimulus can be presented and one-trial learning is apparent when that same test stimulus is presented for a second time several days later. Some people say that habituation occurs because "nothing" happens after the test stimulus is presented, and so the organism ceases to pay attention to it. Does this also explain recognition where subjects attend to the familiar? If reinforcement can be either "something happening" or "nothing happening" immediately after a signal, who needs it?

In any case, our previous work with ionizing radiation had indicated that in taste-illness conditioning the illness could be delayed for hours after the taste was presented. Since sublethal does of the rays produce a delayed illness, the onset of which is difficult to specify, we used apomorphine injections which produce visible gastrointestinal disturbances to examine the delay gradient. We gave rats saccharin water followed by apomorphine injection at varying intervals. Delays up to 30 min had absolutely no effect on the degree of conditional aversion for the saccharin water (Garcia *et al.*, 1966). The flavor–delayed illness paradigm has also been repeated over and over again in may learning labs, with similar effects achieved with delays of many hours (Garcia *et al.* 1974). In Krechevsky's words, the sick rat acts as if it has formed this hypothesis: "It must have been something I ate." Even if it has not eaten for hours, it searches among its food memories for the probable cause of its discomfort.

Brain Mechanisms and the Hypothesis of the Sick Rat

Over 10% of the plants available as potential food sources for animals have toxic alkaloids and glycosides, so the hypothesis "It must have been something I ate" has functional significance in the evolution of animal species (Garcia and Hankins, 1975). As we have pointed out elsewhere, the proof of this functional significance must be found in the structure of the mammalian brain, for we can hardly travel backward through time to observe the evolution of the "sick hypothesis" (Garcia *et al.*, 1972).

Accordingly, my friends and I followed in Krechevsky's footsteps and committed a number of brain laceration experiments. We tested our brain-damaged rats for acquisition of buzzer-shock and flavor-illness conditioning. The response measure was always inhibition of licking. We selected some brain sites where the literature suggested small lesions would be likely to disrupt buzzer-shock learning. Lateral septal and ventral hippocampal lesions had clear-cut differential effects, disrupting buzzer-shock learning but actually enhancing flavor-illness learning. The mechanisms which relate auditory signals to immediate peripheral pain in the external environment are at least partially independent of those mechanisms which adjust the flavor of food commensurate with visceral feedback from ingestion over long delays (McGowan *et al.*, 1969, 1972; Hankins *et al.*, 1974).

We also examined the behavior of rats deprived of their sense of smell, because the central hookups of these sensory channels indicate they have different functions. Olfactory fibers project primarily to the limbic system, while gustatory fibers project to the same relay station which receives feedback afferents from the internal monitors. In some studies, we used apple juice as our fluid because it has a distinctive odor as well as taste. When we followed apple juice with shock, we found that our intact controls which could both smell and taste the fluid were much more effective in avoiding shock than our anosmic rats which could only taste the shock fluid. However, when we followed apple juice with illness we found that the anosmic animals were slightly but consistently *more effective* than the controls in acquiring an aversion for the illness fluid. It seems that gustation has the unique consummatory role of adjusting palatability and olfaction has a different role in appetitive arousal and food selection. Because of its location, the nose very quickly learns a great deal about food from the mouth as it constantly sniffs what the mouth receives. An odor followed by bad taste is probably avoided because of contiguous conditioning, but gustatory-illness pairing directly changes good tastes to bad tastes over long delays. Direct odor-illness aversions are much more difficult to establish (Hankins *et al.*, 1973, 1976).

The Neurology of the Sick Conceptual Organism

It is a paradox that the "Tolmaniacs" from Berkeley who tend to speak of rats as "little furry people" are much more likely to search for central neural mechanisms than S-R theorists who speak of rats as "little furry machines." True to that Berkeley tradition, I will describe my sick conceptual organism in terms of a switchboard, thus parting company with Krechevsky and his dynamic interrelated fields.

Neural fibers from the gustatory analyzers and fibers from the internal monitors converge to the same relay station in the brain stem. Other peripheral sensory systems do not converge so propitiously with the internal monitoring system. Rostrally the tract divides at the pontine level, with some fibers projecting via thalamus to cortex while others appear to be aimed at hypothalamic feeding sites. We have a primitive notion that the incoming gustatory signal is split and that part of it is held at an "and-gate" in the hypothalamus. There it awaits the delayed visceral effects of ingestion. If this feedback is noxious, the and-gate mechanism adjusts the hedonic tone of the gustatory signal in a negative direction. The next time the animal encounters a similar flavor it will taste bad (Garcia *et al.*, 1974). Converse hedonic shifts take place with beneficial feedback from the visceral monitors; in this case, flavors will taste better next time.

The remaining part of the split gustatory signal goes to a "forebrain" mechanism where it serves as a cue which can be used to signal immediate shock if the learning conditions are propitious. However, when saccharin water is followed by immediate shock, the rat does not acquire an aversion for the sweet flavor; it merely learns that the flavor is "associated" with shock. In the home cage, it is apt to drink more deeply of the forbidden sweets (Garcia *et al.*, 1970). Of course, one can arrange shock conditions so that a rat will fear to drink the sweet water under all test conditions and "operationally" the shock appears to mimic the effects of a toxin, which goes to show that in the hands of an expert "operationalism" can be used to confuse concepts as well as to elucidate them.

Let me file another complaint. Readers of the cue-consequence paper often come to the conclusion that we theorized that rats cannot learn to associate external cues with illness, ignoring our early studies where we demonstrated that animals avoided the chambers in which they were exposed to pernicious X-rays (Garcia *et al.*, 1957). With temporal contiguity, repeated trials, and restricted inputs (and with effort and ingenuity on the part of the experimenter), the rat will entertain wondrous hypotheses, including "This place makes me sick." However, we do issue this challenge: "It is impossible in one trial to condition an aversion for a bell which tolls 2 hours before a bout of illness."

From my biased (nonrandom) viewpoint, it seems that the evidence I reviewed should have completely routed the dark forces of the black box, but a glance at the learning literature indicates they thrive to this day in the reaches of the American Midwest. However, a paper emanating from Yale, the Eastern citadel of S-R theory, indicates that cracks are appearing in its grand edifice. In an experiment which resembles the shock portion of the cue-consequence paradigm, a 30-sec drink of either bright-noisy water or saccharin water was followed by a strong footshock at varying intervals of 5, 30, and 210 sec. With bright-noisy water, a traditional steep delay gradient was observed when the rats were returned to the shock apparatus and asked to drink for 240 sec in the presence of the CS without shock. Strong suppression was obtained with 5-sec delay, much less with a 30-sec delay, and none with 210-sec delay. Strikingly different results were obtained with the strong saccharin water. Pseudoconditioning was obvious. The rats were reluctant to drink the strong flavor in a place where they had been shocked, even though they had never experienced saccharin-shock pairing. A curious inverse delay gradient may be discerned above this cloud of pseudoconditioning. Significantly more conditioned suppression appears at the longer intervals (30 and 210 sec) than at the brief (5 sec) delay (Krane and Wagner, 1975).

The authors agree with us in concluding that taste cues are somehow different from audiovisual cues. At one point they comment:

> It should be seen, however, that the results of the present study could be generated by conventional principles of Pavlovian conditioning plus the assumption that the stimulus trace occasioned by saccharin consumption is more persistent than that occasioned by exposure to a light-tone compound.

We are willing to grant the authors this assumption and many more, but here again we feel that while a simple duration assumption may help them in their present explanation, it will cause them trouble when they apply it to all those Pavlovian studies which indicate that the onset and offset of stimuli are most important and that duration matters little. They will be troubled as well by all those flavor–delayed illness studies where interference with the lingering traces of ingestion did not disrupt aversion conditioning. Besides, in our memory, songs last as long as banquets. Therefore, we encourage the authors to make further assumptions about the unique properties of gustatory stimuli, of odor stimuli, of auditory stimuli, of visual stimuli, of pain stimuli, and of illness stimuli as well. We also encourage them to verify their assumptions by observing the trace activity in the afferent channels and in the integrative mechanisms of the brain.

Fortunately, at Berkeley, our data are accepted with alacrity and joy. I still recall when I first showed the cue-consequence results to David Krech. He was sitting at his familiar rolltop desk and took in the results at a glance. "These are Krechevsky rats," he commented with obvious satisfaction. I agreed with obvious pride. Somewhere I. Krechevsky smiled down on us both.

References

Estes, W. K. 1959. The statistical approach to learning theory. In: *Psychology—A Study of a Science*. S. Koch (Ed.). McGraw-Hill, New York, p. 2.

Estes, W. K. 1960. Learning theory and the new "mental chemistry." *Psychological Review*, *67*, 207–223.

Garcia, J. 1975. The futility of comparative I.Q. research. In: *Brain Mechanisms in Mental Retardation*. N. A. Buchwald and M. A. B. Brazier (Eds.). Academic Press, New York

Garcia, J., and Hankins, W. G. 1975. The evolution of bitter and the acquisition of toxiphobia. In: *Olfaction and Taste V*. D. Denton and J. P. Goghlan (Eds.). Academic Press, New York.

Garcia, J., and Koelling, R. 1966. Relation of cue to consequence in avoidance learning. *Psychonomic Science*, *4*, 123–124.

Garcia, J., Kimeldorf, D., and Hunt, E. 1957. Spatial avoidance in the rat as a result of exposure to ionizing radiation. *British Journal of Radiology*, *30*, 318–321.

Garcia, J., Ervin, F., and Koelling, R. 1966. Learning with prolonged delay of reinforcement. *Psychonomic Science*, *5*, 121–122.

Garcia, J., Kovner, R., and Green, K. 1970. Cue properties vs. palatability of flavors in avoidance learning. *Psychonomic Science*, *20*, 313–314.

Garcia, J., McGowan, B., and Green, K. 1972. Biological constraints on conditioning. In: *Classical Conditioning II: Current Research and Theory*. A. Black and W. Prokasy (Eds.). Appleton-Century-Crofts, New York, pp. 3–27.

Garcia, J., Clarke, C., and Hankins, W. G. 1973. Natural responses to scheduled rewards. In: *Perspectives in Ethology*. P. P. G. Bateson and P. Klopfer (Eds.). Plenum Press, New York, pp. 1–41.

Garcia J., Hankins, W. G., and Rusiniak, K. W. 1974. Behavioral regulation of the milieu interne in man and rat. *Science*, *185*, 824–831.

Hankins, W. G., Garcia, J., and Rusiniak, K. W. 1973. Dissociation of odor and taste in baitshyness. *Behavioral Biology*, *8*, 407–419.

Hankins, W. G., Garcia, J., and Rusiniak, K. W. 1974. Cortical lesions: Flavor-illness and noise-shock conditioning. *Behavioral Biology*, *10*, 173–181.

Hankins, W. G., Garcia, J., and Rusiniak, K. W. 1976. Dissociation of odor and taste in shock avoidance learning. *Behavioral Biology*, in press.

Krane, R. V., and Wagner, A. R. 1975. Taste aversion learning with a delayed shock US: Implications for the generality of the laws of learning. *Journal of Comparative and Physiological Psychology*, *88*, 882–889.

Krech, D. 1974. David Krech. In: *History of Psychology in Autobiography*, Vol. 6. Prentice-Hall, New York, pp. 219–250.

Krechevsky, I. 1932. "Hypotheses" in rats. *Psychological Review*, *39*, 516–532.

Krechevsky, I. 1933*a*. The docile nature of "hypotheses." *Journal of Comparative Psychology*, *15*, 429–443.

Krechevsky, I. 1933*b*. Hereditary nature of "hypotheses." *Journal of Comparative Psychology*, *16*, 99–116.

Krechevsky, I. 1935. Brain mechanisms and "hypotheses." *Journal of Comparative Psychology*, *19*, 425–468.

Krechevsky, I. 1938. A study of the continuity of the problem-solving process. *Psychological Review*, *45*, 107–133.

Lashley, K. S. 1929. *Brain Mechanisms and Intelligence*. University of Chicago Press, Chicago.

Lorenz, K. 1965. *Evolution and Modification of Behavior*. University of Chicago Press, Chicago.

McGowan, B., Garcia, J., Ervin, F., and Schwartz, J. 1969. Effects of septal lesions on bait-shyness in the rat. *Physiology and Behavior*, *4*, 907–909.

McGowan, B., Hankins, W. G., and Garcia, J. 1972. Limbic lesions and control of the internal and external environment. *Behavioral Biology*, *7*, 841–852.

Pavlov, I. P. 1928. *Lectures on Conditioned Reflexes*. International Publishers, New York.

Skinner, B. F. 1959. A case history in scientific method. In: *Psychology—A Study of a Science*. S. Koch (Ed.), McGraw-Hill, New York, p. 2.

James F. Zolman

DEVELOPMENTAL CONSTRAINTS ON CONDITIONING

Emphasis on developmental research has been associated historically with the controversy between hereditarians who claimed that most behavioral patterns are preprogrammed genetically and environmentalists who maintained that behavior is the product of experience, both embryonic and postnatal. As history tends to repeat itself, the pendulum of scientific opinion has swung ponderously but predictably from one of these two extreme philosophies of behavior to the other. Whenever this recycling pendulum passed through the middle of its arc, the significance of developmental research increased dramatically, and then it declined slowly as either end of the arc was approached.

As psychology separated gradually from philosophy, instinctual explanations of behavior predominated. The most complex behavioral patterns were assumed to be the overt expressions of underlying instinctive drives or needs (e.g., McDougall, 1921). The advent of radical behaviorism in the 1920s was the environmental counterforce opposing these instinctive explanations (e.g., Kuo, 1924). Although Beach (1955) has noted that this nature-nurture dispute was argued mostly with words and inferential reasoning, developmental research did receive its expected impetus since ontogenetic studies were interpreted and reinterpreted to support either position. Once behaviorism became the predominant scientific movement, however, the importance of developmental research slowly waned. While a few developmentalists continued their age-related analysis of behavior, most psychologists

James F. Zolman • Department of Physiology and Biophysics, University of Kentucky Medical Center, Lexington, Kentucky.

were concerned with the search for and the establishment of universal laws of behavior generalizable to all species and to all developmental ages. Consequently, the nature-nurture controversy was relegated to the periphery of scientific discussion.

In the 1950s, three convergent trends provided a rebirth of developmental research. First, a revived interest in Freudian theory, which postulated that normal infant development could be arrested or fixated at certain stages, provided the impetus for the early experience studies of gentling, handling, depriving, and traumatizing the young of many species (King, 1958). Second, Hebb's (1949) influential neurological theory, which stressed the importance of early perceptual experience for subsequent discrimination ability, resulted in numerous studies which increased and/or restricted sensory stimulation of the young organism. Third, a new nature-nurture dispute, which continues today, was initiated by the translations of the observations and theories of European biologists who were studying the adaptive behavior of a variety of species (Tinbergen, 1951; Lorenz, 1950). Instinct as an explanatory concept was reintroduced in their analysis of these species-specific behaviors and the experiential counterattack was immediate (Lehrman, 1953). Thereafter, numerous review articles appeared, each one supposedly driving the final nail in the coffin of the nature-nurture pseudodichotomy (e.g., Lehrman, 1970; Whalen, 1971). But this genetic-environmental confrontation still continues, for example, between those biologists and psychoanalysts who believe that man, because of his evolutionary history, has inborn aggressive predispositions that must be recognized and then controlled (Lorenz, 1966; Storr, 1968) and those anthropologists and psychologists who believe that man is aggressive because of early exposure to aggressive behavioral models and the reinforcement of aggressive responses (Montagu, 1968).

Therefore, as might be expected, a substantial amount of developmental research is still attempting to differentiate between response patterns that are genetically encoded and those that are produced by environmental stimulation (Thorpe, 1963; Hess, 1973). This research philosophy, of course, endorses a dichotomous classification of complex behavioral patterns which has appeared synonymously as the "nature-nurture," "instinct-learning," "unlearned-learned," "innate-acquired," "performistic-epigenetic" dilemma. To solve this persistent problem, some developmentalists have emphasized the integrative influence of both intraorganic and environmental processes throughout the ontogeny of behavioral patterns (Hinde, 1970; Lehrman, 1970; Schneirla, 1966). Essentially, their position is that behavioral development is a unitary process, and what takes place in one period of development is dependent on the prior developmental history of the organism. This integrative position can be made clearer by comparing it with the other major theoretical position on behavioral development.

Theories of Behavioral Development

In contrast to the integrative developmental position is the view that behavioral development is composed of many different and relatively independent processes which are programmed sequentially by an invariant maturational scheduling of biological processes of growth and differentiation. Consequently, a particular experience may have a profound effect on concurrent and subsequent behavior only during specific limited periods in development. These limited periods are designated "critical periods," and manipulations prior to or after these critical periods are assumed to have very little effect on subsequent behavior. An implicit corollary of this critical period analysis is that if the experience does not occur at the proper time in development subsequent behavioral development will be abnormal. Thus behavioral development is viewed as a sequence of critical periods which are more common early in life, and during which the appropriate stimulation must be provided if normal behavioral development is to occur.

For the integrative developmental position, the developmental history of an organism is the basis of investigation. Since critical periods in development are viewed as outcomes of previous developmental integrations, manipulation of prior developmental events may have profound effects on the duration and on the time of occurrence of these periods. For this reason, "sensitive periods" in development have been suggested during which the probability of a behavior being emitted and the probability of reinforcement by the environment coincide (King, 1968). Since either response emission or environmental reinforcement probabilities may be changed independently by prior developmental events, the synchrony of responses and reinforcement contingencies may be retarded at certain periods or enhanced at other periods and the duration of the period may be increased or decreased. Since sensitive periods can be manipulated, the consequences of stimuli exposed and/or responses emitted during these periods do not necessarily have irreversible consequences on subsequent behavioral development.

This distinction between critical and sensitive periods in development raises the important question of what is meant by "developmental age." Unfortunately, developmental age, or stage, has been used both as a descriptive term and as an explanatory concept. As a descriptive term, age of the organism can be assumed to be either specifically correlated with biological processes of tissue differentiation and organization or correlated with the integrative influences among these biological processes and experiential processes. It appears that the former unidirectional structure-function relation predominates in the earliest stages of embryogenesis, whereas the latter integrative structure-function relation emerges at the latest stages of behavioral embryology (for a review, see Gottlieb, 1973*b*).

While developmental age is useful as a descriptive time marker, it easily becomes an explanatory concept. That is, if a young organism cannot make a particular response whereas an older animal readily exhibits the response, this difference may be explained by the developmental age or stage of the animal. There are, of course, significant functional changes in both neural and endocrine systems during ontogeny which may be highly correlated with the emergence of particular behavioral responses. But to explain the emergence of these responses as due to the age of the animal implies an understanding of their significant developmental processes, e.g., the growth of new processes, functional development of synapses, activation or repression of genes leading to differentiation and subsequent organization, and experiential stimulation. While it is evident that the necessary neural organization must be functional for responses to occur, the use of developmental age as an explanation for the behavior observed negates further study of significant neurogenetic processes. Also, even a complete understanding of neurogenesis will not explain behavioral development, and consequently the degree of differentiation of the nervous system at any given stage only delimits the range of behavioral potentialities (Hamburger, 1973).

Maturational Bases of Behavior

Maturational changes in neural and endocrine processes have been suggested for many age-related behavioral differences observed during development. First, the sensitive period of imprinting has been suggested to be terminated by maturational mechanisms underlying fear (Hess, 1964; Hoffman and Ratner, 1973). Innate eliciting reinforcement cells have been postulated to release the imprinting response (Hoffman and Ratner, 1973), specifically the maturation of movement detectors in the chick's retina (Sackett, 1963). Second, species-specific perceptual preferences have been assumed to be due to the development of selectively filtering oil droplets for color preferences and to innate releasing mechanisms for form preferences (for a review, see Hailman, 1970). Third, the observation that the young organism does not retain information as well as the adult (Campbell and Spears, 1972) has been attributed specifically to neural maturation (Campbell *et al.*, 1974). Fourth, the inability of young animals to inhibit responses as well as older animals (Hinde, 1970) has been suggested to be due to the incomplete functional development of neural inhibitory structures, particularly those in the hippocampus (Altman *et al.*, 1973). The implicit assumption of these neurological maturation suggestions is that the behavior of the young organism is restricted at various periods of development solely because of structural deficits.

It is interesting that now, instead of an instinctual explanation, a maturational explanation of behavior development is being proposed. Thus the sensitive period of imprinting is limited to a particular developmental stage because of the maturation of fear; preferential responsing of the young organism is determined by the maturation of species-specific visual detectors; forgetting in the young animal is due to an immature nervous system; the young organism cannot inhibit responses because forebrain and hippocampal inhibitory structures are not fully functional. If these behaviors are also assumed to be due to an invariant maturational scheduling caused by genetic determinants, then no difference exists between maturational and instinctual explanations of behavior. That is, certain behaviors will be present or not present dependent solely on whether the underlying neural structures are functional or not yet functional. Unfortunately, this sequential correlational analysis leads to rather simplistic explanations of behavioral development and assumes no integrative effects among intraorganic and experiential processes during ontogeny. Furthermore, two additional assumptions must be made with any correlational ontogenetic analysis: (1) that knowledge regarding structural changes is sufficient to determine that no other biological processes are correlated with the same behavior, and (2) that the developing behavior of the organism is also well known. Perhaps it is too evident to note that the biological and behavioral development of the young organism is largely unknown, and both descriptive and experimental studies will be necessary before any speculative maturational explanations can be evaluated seriously. Because of our ignorance, single-factor cause-effect explanations of behavioral development tend to predominate initially, but as analysis continues these first approximations become suspect very quickly, and multifactor interpretations then appear the most reasonable.

Developmental Constraint on Conditioning: Preferential Responding

In the young organism, sensitive period learning, preferences, retention loss, and lack of behavioral inhibition may all be considered as developmental constraints on conditioning. Any proposed developmental constraint on conditioning, however, should be evaluated in a species whose developmental history, both biological and behavioral, has been substantially studied. Preferential responding of the young chick meets this requirement, and therefore the development of preferences in the young chick will be considered as a developmental constraint on conditioning.

Although the developmental history of the young chick is the best understood of any species, substantial disagreement still remains regarding this development (see Bateson, 1973*a*, *b*; Hess, 1973; Gottlieb, 1973*c*). This is true mainly because behavioral studies with newly hatched chicks have been beset with many problems, particularly with the problem of replicability. For example, Gottlieb (1971) has stressed the fact that unknown and uncontrolled variables affect the reliability of imprinting and preference results with domestic chicks. Indeed, since most imprinting studies have found considerable variability in following behavior, a large number of chicks must be used to obtain representative results (Sluckin, 1973, pp. 31–32). Typically, only about 75% of the birds tested will show significant following even during the sensitive period of imprinting (Gottlieb and Klopfer, 1962; Klopfer and Hailman, 1964; Polt and Hess, 1966). Likewise, most of the pecking preference data on color and form are based on a large number of group-tested birds. The necessity of using a large number of birds has been justified because of the tremendous variability in specific pecking preferences of different hatches of the same breed of chicks (Goodwin and Hess, 1969). Also, a group testing procedure has been justified because of the low response rates of individually tested chicks. Supposedly, only when large numbers of chicks are tested socially in batches of 30–75 and many pecks are obtained is consistency of pecking preferences achieved (Goodwin and Hess, 1969). In conditioning studies, the most important problem in testing young chicks has been the lack of an effective reinforcer. Traditional reinforcers, such as food and water, exert little control over newly hatched chicks since they use the absorbed yolk sac for nutrition during the first few days of life (Marley and Morse, 1966). Similarly, since the feet of the 1-day-old chick are almost completely insensitive to shock up to 100 V (Quinta, 1966), instrumental aversive conditioning of the young chick is difficult even when the feet are coated with electrode paste or dipped into water to ensure shock delivery on every trial (Fischer and Campbell, 1964; James and Binks, 1963).

These behavioral testing problems are not insurmountable, however, since recent studies in our laboratory have demonstrated that heat is a potent reinforcer for conditioning either approach or pecking responses in the young chick (Zolman, 1968, 1969; Zolman *et al.*, 1972; Zolman and Lattin, 1972). These thermal reinforcement procedures permit preferential responding to be determined in individually tested chicks with as few as ten chicks in each preference group, and have been used to study the development of brightness and form preferences and their effects on discrimination learning of the young chick. Specifically, approach preferences have been found in both form and brightness simultaneous discrimination learning, and pecking preferences have been observed in successive form discrimination learning. The development of these visual preferences and their effects on learning indicate clearly that preferential responding of the young chick is an important developmental constraint on conditioning.

Preferential responding of the young organism is a general developmental problem as the young of many species, including human infants, show distinct visual preferences (Fantz, 1965). Explanations for the visual preferences of the young organism have included the following: (1) a particular cue may elicit a species-specific behavioral pattern that has some specific adaptive value, (2) preferential responding may channel subsequent behavioral development in one direction or another, and (3) preferential responding may be a useless vestige of some earlier biological adaptive behavioral pattern which now may only appear under restricted experimental conditions. While visual preferences may affect the conditioning of the young organism, their influence on subsequent behavioral development is still not known. It is evident, however, that in many species not all physical stimuli activating the receptors of the adult organism are equally effective in controlling particular behavioral patterns. The classical ethological model of "sign stimuli" and the "innate releasing mechanism" (IRM) explained how certain forms and colors elicit highly selective behavioral patterns (Tinbergen, 1951). But the complexity of preference development has led to an expansion of this classical model by Schleidt (1962) to include not only the IRM but also the "innate releasing mechanism modified by experience" (IRME) and the "acquired releasing mechanism" (ARM). While this model was very useful in focusing attention on species-specific behaviors and their controlling stimuli in a variety of species, its emphasis on a unitary, innate releasing mechanism has been questioned seriously (see Hinde, 1960).

More important, the use of an innate releasing mechanism as either a descriptive or an explanatory concept is misleading because of the implication that preferences do not have developmental histories (Quine and Cullen, 1964). Indeed, a number of alternative possibilities for preference development have been considered: preferences could be completely functional immediately after hatching and remain unchanged throughout the life of the bird; preferences could be maturationally scheduled to emerge at different periods after hatching; preferences could be maturationally specified at hatch but require some diffuse nonspecific stimulation to emerge or remain stable; preferences could be partially maturationally specified but modifiable by experimental stimulation; preferences could depend solely on rapid critical period conditioning during embryological development or immediately after hatching; finally, and most likely, preferential responding in the young organism could be the integrative outcome of both intraorganic and experiential processes during prior ontogeny.

Also, once a preference has been established the modification of the preference, dependent on its development, could be impossible, moderately easy, or very easy. Thus there is no reason to presume that the resistance to modification of preferences that have been established, most likely by different integrative processes, would be the same. The degree of difficulty of preference modification, of course, may depend on the conditioning procedures used. For example, a preference that has not been modified by numerous conditioning procedures may be easily modified by a slight change in the testing procedure. For this reason, it would be more appropriate to consider the degree of difficulty in modifying a preference as correlated with conditioning procedures that significantly affect other response systems but that fail to modify the preference responding of the organism. Hence a preference of an organism that is immutable to most subsequent environmental contingencies but changeable by only a few conditioning procedures would be restricted to unique environmental conditions. Depending on the probability of these contingencies occurring during subsequent development, the likely importance of the preference on subsequent development could be assessed. That is, preferences modified by numerous environmental procedures would not have the same importance as a subsequent constraint on development as preferences whose modification is restricted to unique contingencies.

Because of this complexity in the development and modification of visual preferences, the significance of preferential responding of the young organism depends on the preference being considered. Therefore, preferential responding during the sensitive period of imprinting and the subsequent restriction of preferences following imprinting will be considered first, and then brightness and form preferences of the young chick as developmental constraints on conditioning will be evaluated.

Preferences in Sensitive Period Learning

Sensitive Period Learning

Imprinting has generated much controversy because of the instantaneous and irreversible effects that were postulated to characterize the exposure of various stimuli to some newly hatched birds during a brief and relatively specific period of ontogeny. Some ethologists believe that there is a definite critical period for imprinting and have argued that imprinting is a special process distinct from learning (Lorenz, 1937; Hess, 1973). On the other hand, a few psychologists have sought to reconcile imprinting with universal principles of learning (James, 1959; Moltz, 1963). Most theorists, however, have incorporated some of the unique features of imprinting (i.e., the apparent lack of reinforcement or the reinforcing aspects of eliciting stimuli) into general theories of either perceptual learning (Bateson, 1973*c*; Salzen, 1970) or reinforcement conditioning (Hoffman and Ratner, 1973).

The debate now is whether imprinting can best be understood either as a process distinct from learning, as the establishment of a perceptual neuronal model, or as reinforcement conditioning. As a unique process, the onset of the critical period of imprinting is explained by the maturation of locomotor ability and the termination of this period by the maturation of fear. These two independent maturational phenomena are assumed to be produced by the invariant consequences of cellular differentiation (Lorenz, 1937; Hess, 1959). Imprinting is also explained as the establishment of a neuronal model of a particular source of stimulation simply as a consequence of exposure. Once this gradual learning occurs, response emission is subsequently restricted to those classes of stimuli that match the learned neuronal model. Novel stimulation produces a mismatch and thereby evokes a fear and, if possible, a flight reaction (Bateson, 1973*a*; Salzen, 1970). In the reinforcement conditioning model, innately eliciting cues of the imprinting stimulus have reinforcing properties which classically condition other features of the exposure stimulus. The termination of imprinting is caused by an age-related increase in the tendency of the young bird to react fearfully to stimuli (Hoffman and Ratner, 1973).

The common assumptions in these imprinting models are the following: (1) innate visual preferences elicit the initial approach of the young bird to the exposure stimulus during a restricted period of life, and (2) the termination of the imprinting process is due to the development of fear responses of the young bird to novel stimuli. The differences among these models are whether other cues of the exposure stimulus are neuronally recorded passively by exposure or actively by conditioning, and whether the fear responses of the bird are maturationally scheduled or due to the establishment of a neural model. It is difficult to differentiate between the development of fear and the development of a perceptual neuronal model as the cause of the termination of imprinting. Experimental manipulations which restrict the development of a neuronal model (e.g., dark rearing) may lengthen the sensitive period because of the slower learning of a viable "dark" neuronal model or because reduced sensory stimulation may affect maturational processes. These maturational processes would have to be influenced by experiential variables and, consequently, could not be caused by invariant genetic scheduling. Similarly, injecting young chicks with sodium pentobarbital during the first 4 days after hatching, a procedure which delays the offset of the sensitive period of imprinting (MacDonald, 1968), could reduce the visual experience necessary for a viable neural model (Bateson, 1973*b*) or equally likely could retard maturational processes by slowing necessary metabolic processes.

Whatever the bases for the termination of the sensitive period of imprinting, it is well established that the young chick does decrease its approach to various stimuli as a function of age. But it is also evident that the young chick can be conditioned to approach stimuli after the sensitive period.

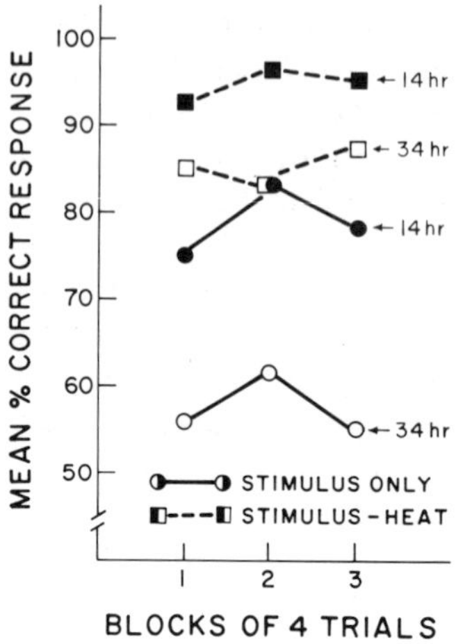

Figure 1. Mean percentage of correct responses for 14- and 34-hr-old chicks. Half of the chicks in each age group were exposed only to a red circle while the other chicks were not only exposed to the circle but also reinforced with heat. From Zolman (1968).

These two findings are illustrated in a study of the approach responses of chicks of two ages (14 and 34 hr old) in which half of the chicks of each age were exposed only to a red circle and the other chicks were reinforced with heat to approach the same circle. In this study, the circle was placed in two sides of a discrimination box in a random sequence, the other side remained empty, and all of the dark-reared chicks were each given 12 discrete trials (Zolman, 1968). As can be seen in Figure 1, for the exposure-only chicks, the 14-hr-old chicks approached the red circle on about 80% of the trials, whereas the older chicks approached on less than 60% of the trials. But by reinforcing approaches to the circle, 34-hr-old chicks could be conditioned to approach on 85% of the trials. Other studies have shown that older chicks will also learn to approach stimuli even if they are merely confined with the stimulus. Gradually the chick stops avoiding and begins to approach and follow the initially frightening stimulus. If older birds, however, are allowed to escape from confinement, they continue to avoid the stimulus (Ratner and Hoffman, 1974).

While birds past the sensitive period of imprinting can be induced to approach or follow a novel stimulus by reinforcement or confinement, an important question is whether there are subsequent differences in behavioral development between imprinted and conditioned chicks. Although there are no studies that have answered this particular question, subsequent learning differences between imprinted and nonimprinted chicks have been found. Imprinted chicks will learn a discrimination quicker than nonimprinted controls whether the prior exposure stimulus is either the rewarded or the nonrewarded cue (Bateson, 1964; Kovach *et al.*, 1966; Polt, 1969; Chantrey, 1972). That is, imprinting facilitates subsequent discrimination when there is a possibility of transfer of training, and under these conditions chicks not exposed during the sensitive period of imprinting show a definite developmental constraint on conditioning.

There are also significant differences in form discrimination learning between chicks tested during the sensitive period and older chicks past this period. One-day-old chicks tested on a simultaneous circle-triangle discrimination have a significant circle preference but 3-day-old chicks do not (Figure 2). Thus, in this study, the emergence of the young chick's circle preference depended on the simultaneous presentation of the two stimuli on the first posthatch day (Zolman, 1969). Exposure only to the circle during the sensitive period also results in a circle preference and, more important, exposure only to the triangle during this time produces a subsequent circle preference. Thus exposure to the triangle during the peak period of imprinting does not result in a triangle preference (Figure 3). Rather, chicks will show a significant circle preference if they have been exposed simultaneously to both cues or to either cue during the sensitive period of imprinting (Zolman, 1969). Therefore, while exposure to most stimuli during the sensitive period will result in a subsequent restriction of approach responses to those classes of stimuli that match the imprinting stimulus (Sluckin, 1973), a specific attachment is not always produced to the form or color of the stimulus presented during the sensitive period. Also, chicks imprinted to a particular stimulus will learn a subsequent discrimination quicker than nonexposed controls even when the imprinted stimulus is the nonrewarded cue (Bateson, 1973*a*). Furthermore, exposure to certain cues during the sensitive period of imprinting apparently activates other subsequent form and color preferences (Klopfer, 1967; Zolman, 1969).

As mentioned, all theories of imprinting assume that the initial approach and following responses of young precocial birds are elicited by *salient*

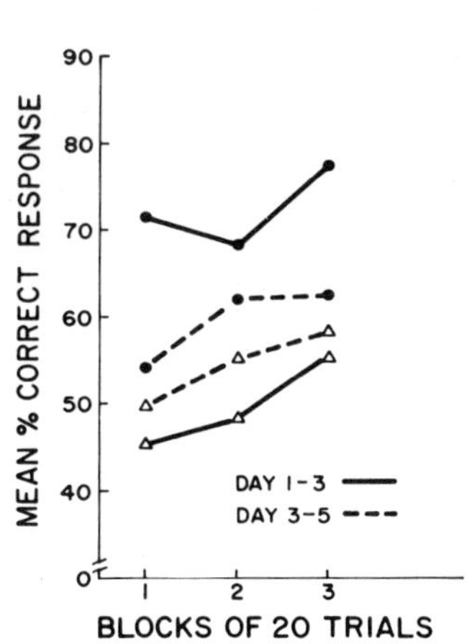

Figure 2. Mean percentage of correct responses for 1- and 3-day-old chicks on a simultaneous circle-triangle discrimination. For half of the chicks in each age group the circle (●) was the S^+, while for the other chicks the triangle (△) was the S^+. From Zolman (1969).

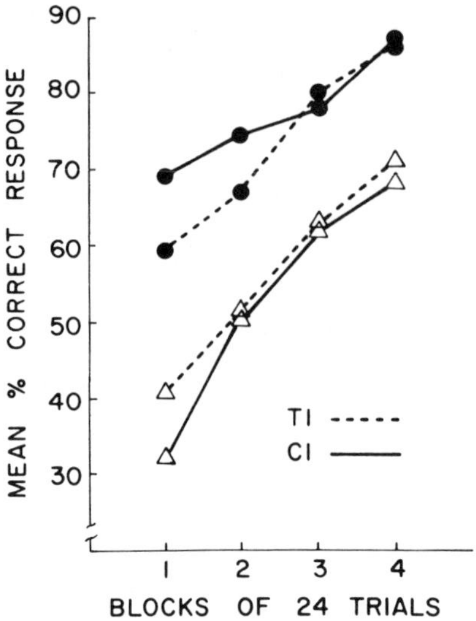

Figure 3. Mean percentage of correct responses for circle-imprinted (CI) and triangle-imprinted (TI) chicks on a simultaneous circle-triangle discrimination. For half of the chicks in each imprinting group the circle (●) was the S^+, while for the other chicks the triangle (△) was the S^+. From Zolman (1969).

releasing cues. Most imprinting stimuli have been bizarre stimulus complexes of sound-emitting colors and forms moving jerkily, intermittently, or smoothly away from or toward the young bird. While these complex stimuli have been used for their combined effectiveness, auditory and movement cues are more potent in eliciting approach behavior than either the color, shape, or size of the exposure stimulus (Bateson, 1966; Sluckin, 1973). Although young birds will selectively respond to the maternal assembly call of their own species (Gottlieb, 1973*a*), there apparently is no single visual cue that selectively elicits approach and following behavior in any young bird. For this reason, young birds will approach and follow most visual cues during the sensitive period of imprinting and, thereafter, restrict their approach behavior to those classes of stimuli that match the previously exposed stimulus. But certain colors and forms are more effective than others in eliciting the initial approach behavior of the young chick. For example, red and blue are the most effective colors and round stimuli are the most effective forms in eliciting following (Hess, 1964). The developmental histories of these auditory and visual preferences of the young chick present an important challenge which, so far, has been neglected in the experimental analysis of sensitive period learning (Gottlieb, 1973*a*).

Sensitive Period Conclusions

Sensitive periods for visual, food, and environmental imprinting (Hess, 1973) and for visual preference activation (Klopfer, 1967; Zolman, 1969) indicate clearly that many important developmental processes remain unknown. Therefore, the only meaningful conclusion regarding sensitive periods in development is as a description of current ignorance. Discovery of sensitive periods should then serve to focus attention and experimentation on the intraorganic and experiential processes contributing to these rather striking behavioral discontinuities found in ontogeny. Unfortunately, sensitive periods drift into explanatory concepts which, like instincts, negate subsequent developmental inquiry. Indeed, much of current developmental research appears to be searching for sensitive periods as explanations for subsequent behavioral deficiences. For this reason, undue emphasis is placed on the apparent behavioral discontinuities observed during development rather than on the developmental history of the organism. Thus experiments are designed to show that the behavior exhibited during a sensitive period is distinctly different from the behavior which emerges after or before the particular sensitive period or, conversely, that the behavior during the sensitive period can be explained by universal principles that have been identified to operate before or after the sensitive period.

Besides determination of the prior developmental history of the organism before a sensitive period, the questions of irreversibility and effects on behavior after the sensitive period would appear to be the most important. Any subsequent behavioral differences between animals exposed to stimuli during sensitive periods and those reinforced after sensitive periods to make the same type of emitted responses would help clarify the significance of sensitive periods in development. At the present time, sensitive periods may be regarded as important developmental constraints on conditioning. That is, during development, unexpected behavioral responses are observed. Being unexpected means, of course, that the important developmental variables remain unknown.

Perhaps the reason the developmental processes underlying sensitive periods are relatively unknown is that the proposed onset and offset mechanisms are exceedingly complex. For example, the onset of the sensitive period of imprinting is probably due to the functional development of locomotor activity, a complex sensory-motor integrative phenomenon. Likewise, the offset of the sensitive period of imprinting has been suggested to be due either to the maturation of fear, a neural-endocrine integration hardly understood, or to the development of a neuronal model, a problem involving the understanding of the physical basis of memory and its retrieval. In addition, the innate eliciting cues which are the supposed basis of imprinting require an understanding of perceptual and motivational integration. That these processes associated with the onset, the active phase, and the termination of the sensitive period of imprinting occur within a few days after hatching indicates quite clearly that simplistic single-factor explanations of developing behavior are doomed from the beginning.

Development and Modification of Brightness and Form Preferences

So far, preferential responding during the sensitive period of imprinting and the subsequent restriction of preferences after imprinting have been discussed. The significance of brightness and form preferences of the young chick as developmental constraints on conditioning will now be considered. General stimulus preferences (preference for stimuli in one modality over another or for particular types of stimuli within one modality) have been the most commonly observed type of preference in the young chick. Response-specific stimulus preferences, in which the chick will respond to a particular cue in one environmental context but not in another, and reinforcement-specific stimuli, where the reinforcement seems to determine which stimuli are associated (Hinde, 1973), have been reviewed recently and therefore will not be discussed (see Hinde and Stevenson-Hinde, 1973; Hess, 1973).

Brightness Preference

Preferential approach responses of the young chick are elicited by flickering stimuli that differ in rate, intensity, and size (Gottlieb and Simner, 1969; Smith, 1960; Smith and Hoyes, 1961). Also, young chicks will learn instrumental responses for light onset (Bateson and Reese, 1969). The emergence of the young chick's brightness preference can be understood only by a consideration of the progressive interaction between the developing chick and its sensory environment. That is, the modification of the young chick's brightness preference by conditioning depends on the age of the chick, its prior rearing condition, the sensory environment between testing sessions, and the length of the interval between testing sessions (Zolman and Lattin, 1972).

For example, 3-day-old light-reared chicks prefer to approach the brighter side of a two-choice discrimination box (Figure 4). In this experiment, half of the chicks were reinforced with heat to approach the bright goal box (18.5 ft-candles) and the rest were reinforced to approach the dim goal box (1.5 ft-candles). But, as can be seen, both the bright S^+ and the dim S^+ chicks approached the bright goal box and heat reinforcement did not change this preferential responding. To determine whether this brightness preference was dependent solely on light experience, 1- and 3-day-old dark-reared chicks were reinforced with heat to approach the dim side (Figure 5). However, even these dark-reared chicks approached the bright side on 60% of the trials and again heat reinforcement did not affect this preferential responding. This brightness preference of the young chick, therefore, is so stable that it cannot be eliminated by incubating, hatching, and rearing in the dark. However, varying the sensory conditions prior to testing can increase this

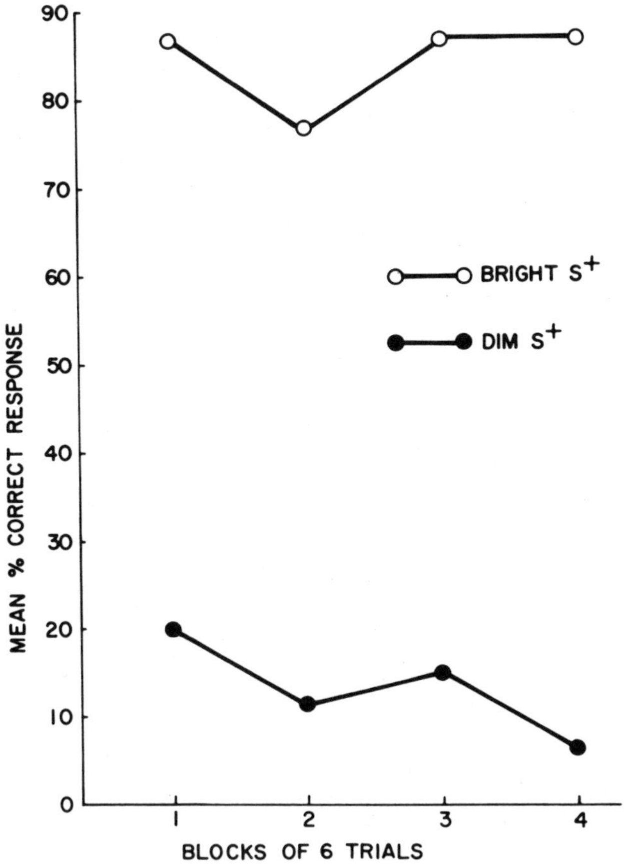

Figure 4. Mean percentage of correct responses for 3-day-old chicks reared socially in a lighted brooder before brightness discrimination testing. For half of the chicks the bright stimulus was the S^+ while for the other chicks the dim stimulus was the S^+. From Zolman and Lattin (1972).

preference since light-reared chicks when 3 days old will approach the bright side on over 80% of the trials whereas dark-reared chicks of the same age will approach this side on only about 60% of the trials (Figures 4 and 5).

In these initial experiments, the brightness preference could not be modified by reinforcing, with heat, approaches of the chick to the dim side. Increasing the number of conditioning trials by fourfold still did not change the brightness preference of 2-day-old chicks that received 24 daily conditioning trials for 4 consecutive days (Zolman and Lattin, 1972). Since form preferences of the young chick can be significantly changed by heat reinforce-

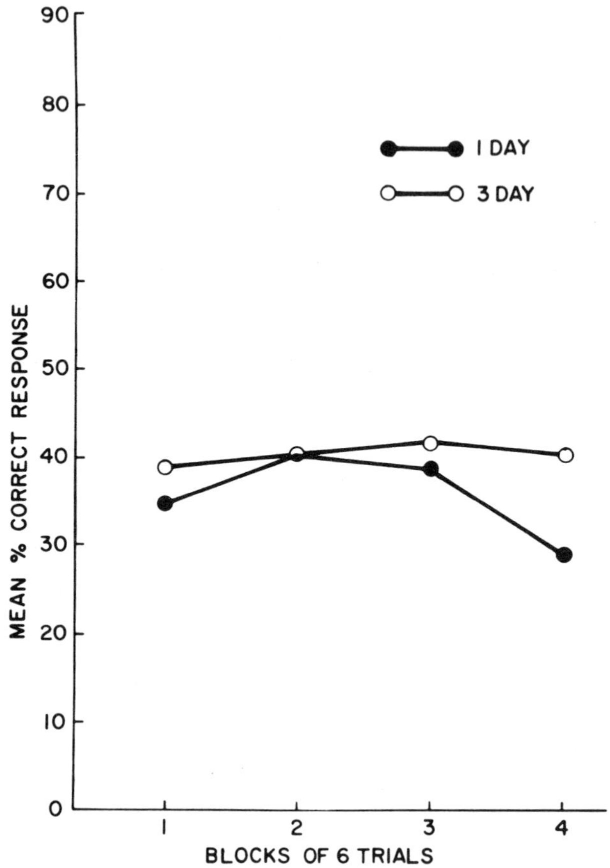

Figure 5. Mean percentage of correct responses for 1- and 3-day-old dark-reared chicks. For both ages, the dim stimulus was the S^+. From Zolman and Lattin (1972).

ment within 96 conditioning trials (Figure 3), our initial interpretation was that the brightness preference of the young chick was very resistant to modification by conditioning. But, rather than accept this conclusion that heat reinforcement was ineffective, massed conditioning trials were used in a subsequent experiment. In this study, 1- and 3-day-old chicks were tested using either short (1 hr) or long (6 hr) intersession intervals and were reinforced to approach the dim side. On the first block of 24 trials, before these intervals were started, 1-day-old chicks made significantly more correct responses than the 3-day-old chicks (Figure 6), indicating that these older chicks had a stronger brightness preference than the younger chicks. But these older chicks did learn to approach the dim side when the intersession interval was short. With the longer 6-hr interval, however, these 3-day-old

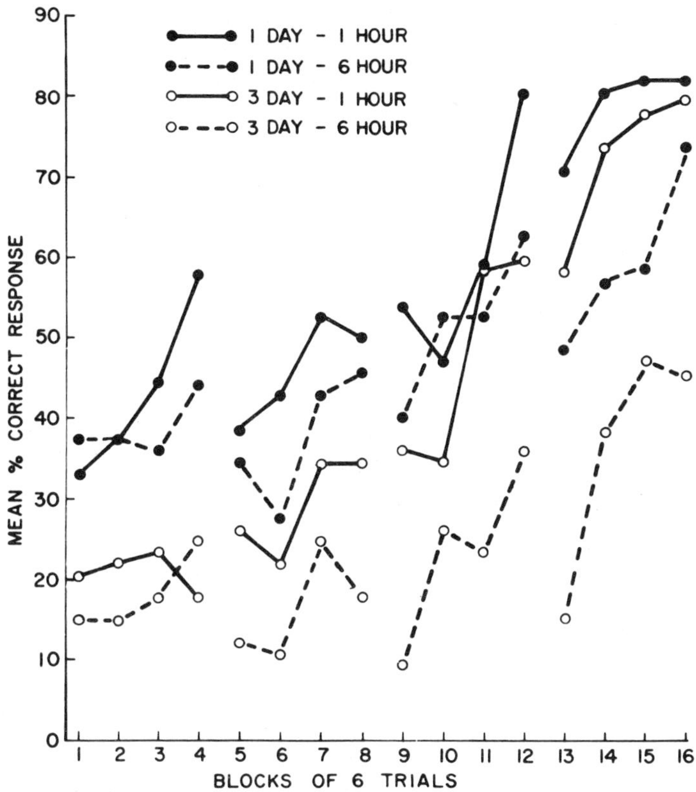

Figure 6. Mean percentage of correct responses for 1- and 3-day-old chicks reared socially in a lighted brooder before brightness discrimination testing. For half of the chicks in each age group the intersession testing interval was less than 1 hr, while for the other chicks this interval was about 6 hr. From Zolman and Lattin (1972).

chicks did not reach 50% correct responding to the dim side. In contrast, the 1-day-old chicks learned to approach the dim side with either short or long intervals.

In subsequent experiments, 3-day-old chicks isolated in either light or dark boxes for 6 hr between testing sessions also learned to approach the dim side, with the dark-held chicks learning quicker. Similarly, 3-day-old chicks isolated in dark boxes for either 1 or 6 hr between sessions learned to approach the dim side, with the shorter-interval chicks learning quicker. Therefore, the brightness preference of the 3-day-old chick can either remain unchanged or be rather easily modified by conditioning depending on the sensory conditions during the intersession testing interval. For these older chicks, it appears that all sensory stimuli associated with communal housing, as well as the time between testing sessions, contribute nonspecifically to the significant differences in modification of the brightness preferences of chicks tested with short or long intersession intervals. It is apparent, therefore, that a multifactor interpretation of the development of the brightness preference of the young chick and its modification by conditioning is the most reasonable.

Pecking Preferences

Form-pecking preferences and their effects on successive discrimination learning of the young chick have also been studied using a thermal reinforcement procedure. Since the young chick is not handled between trials, this key-peck conditioning procedure permits even better stimulus control over its performance than can be obtained in the form- and brightness-approach tests. Also, numerous conditioning trials can be scheduled with this procedure, and with our 3-day testing schedule each chick receives 624 discrete conditioning trials.

While an extensive developmental analysis of the emergence of form preferences has not yet been completed, in five experiments the age of chick, the stimuli used, and the reinforced and nonreinforced cues were varied to determine the effects of form preferences on successive discrimination learning. In these experiments, behavioral testing was performed in four discrimination boxes with each box housed individually in a 16-ft^3 incubator in which the ambient temperature was maintained at 10°C (Figure 7). Another incubator with an auxilliary 2000-W heater was set at 35°C, and plastic tubing (20 and 10 cm) connected each cold incubator with this heat source (Figure 8). A push-pull fan arrangement in the heat incubator was used to maintain a balanced flow of warm air to each discrimination incubator. Heat onset in each discrimination box was controlled by two separate rotary solenoids that when activated displaced two butterfly valves. One valve diverted instantaneously the warm 35°C air up through the discrimination box, whereas the other valve opened to replace in the air flow system the same amount of warm air diverted. A 2-W light bulb located under each discrimination box was also turned on so that reinforcement consisted of both heat and light onset.

Behavioral testing included autoshaping young chicks to peck the single response key and then testing on a successive discrimination. After autoshaping, discrimination sessions of 48 trials were run with the S^+ and S^- stimuli presented successively in a semirandom sequence. Three discrimination sessions of 48 trials each were given on the first day of training and five sessions of 48 trials were given on both the second and third days of training. The sequence of events on a trial during discrimination testing was as follows: (1) key light onset for 16 sec; (2) key light offset followed by a 5-sec interval

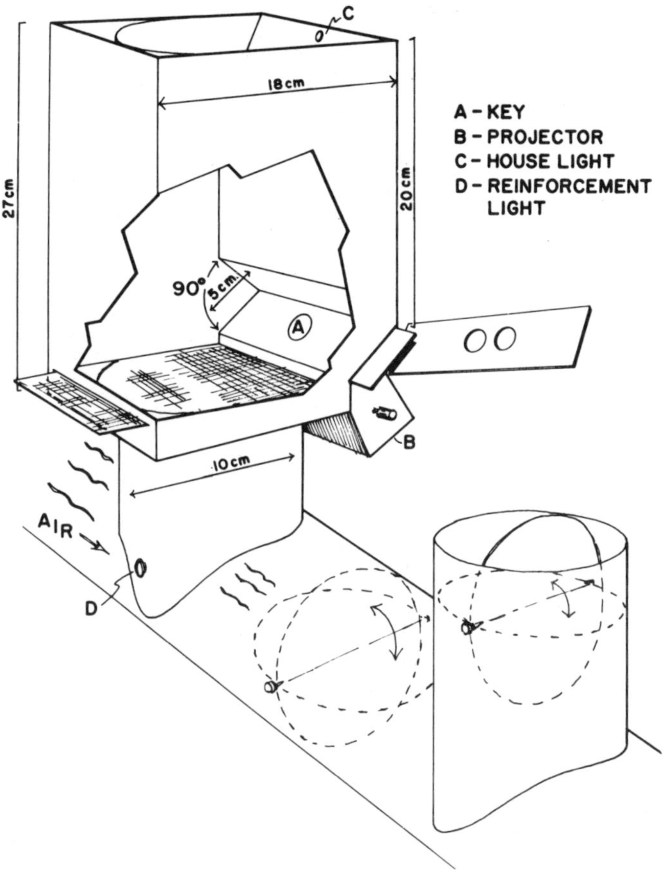

Figure 7. Discrimination box for key-peck conditioning of young chicks using heat reinforcement (from Zolman *et al.*, 1975).

(ITI) with house light on; and (3) key light onset for 16 sec. If the chick pecked the key anytime the S^+ cue was projected, the key light was turned off, reinforcement (8 sec 35°C air and light) was delivered immediately, and a new trial was begun after the 5-sec ITI. Responses on trials in which the S^- was presented were not reinforced; rather, the chick was held in the dark chamber for 8 sec. If the chick failed to respond on any trial, the 5-sec ITI was initiated and 16 sec was recorded for that trial.

Group-tested chicks prefer to peck at round stimuli in nonrewarded situations, and this preference has been reported to remain constant during at least the first posthatch week (Fantz, 1957; Hess, 1964). Therefore, in the first two experiments 1- to 3-day-old and 3- to 5-day-old chicks were tested individually on a successive circle-triangle discrimination to determine whether this circle preference would significantly affect discrimination learn-

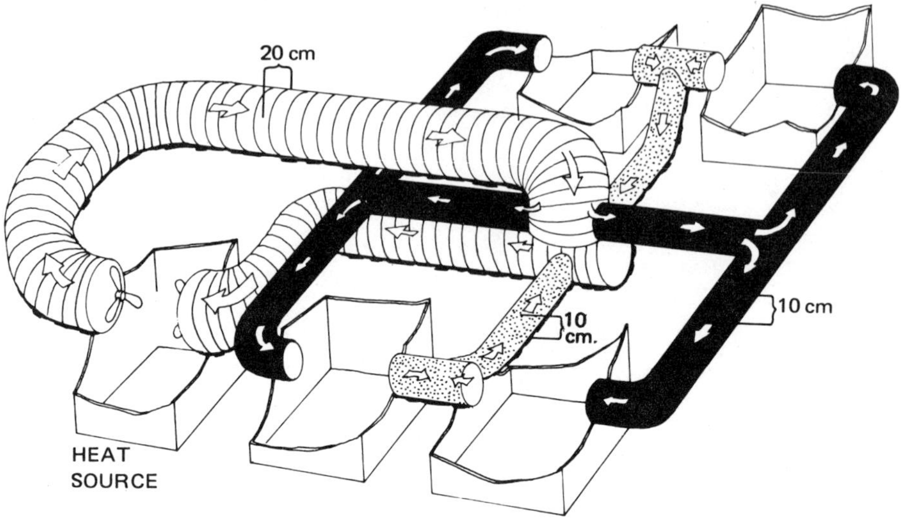

Figure 8. Heat delivery system to the four discrimination incubators (from Zolman *et al.*, 1975).

ing of the young chick. In each experiment, the chicks were randomly assigned to the two preference conditions; e.g., for half of the chicks of each age group the white circle was the S^+ and the white triangle the S^-, and for the other chicks the white triangle was the S^+ and the white circle the S^-. These cues were projected on a red background and 10–12 chicks were used in each preference group.

The results for the 1- to 3-day-old chicks tested on this discrimination are presented in Figure 9. It is quite clear that both groups learned this discrimination, but the circle S^+ group learned quicker than the triangle S^+ group. Since the only difference between these two groups of chicks was which cue was the S^+ during training, it is evident that there is an early preference for young chicks to peck at a circle rather than a triangle. This perference, however, could be modified as the chicks did learn to respond to the triangle for heat reinforcement. Also, a test of retention of the discrimination indicated that young chicks do retain this differential responding to S^+ and S^- for at least 3 days. That is, chicks trained to peck the triangle do not revert to their original circle preference.

The performance of 3- to 5-day-old chicks on the same circle-triangle discrimination is presented in Figure 10. Similar results were obtained with these older chicks in that both groups learned the discrimination, but again the circle S^+ chicks learned quicker than the triangle S^+ chicks. Also, the differential responding to the S^+ and S^- was retained, in this case, for 7 days

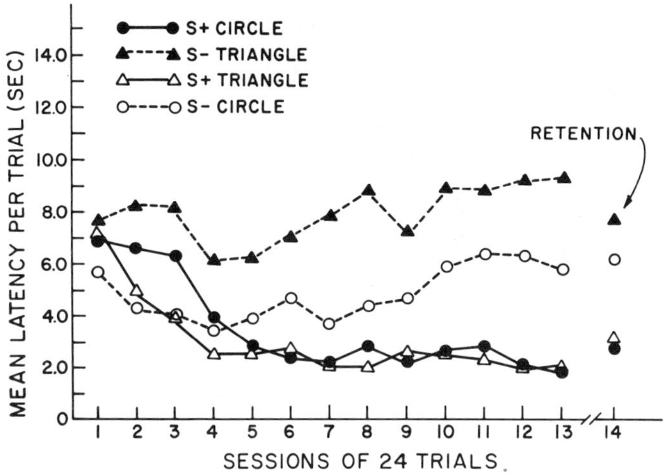

Figure 9. Mean response latencies of 24-trial sessions for chicks that were tested on a circle-triangle successive discrimination when 1–3 days old. For half of these chicks the circle was the S^+, while for the other chicks the triangle was the S^+. A retention test was given 3 days after the thirteenth discrimination session.

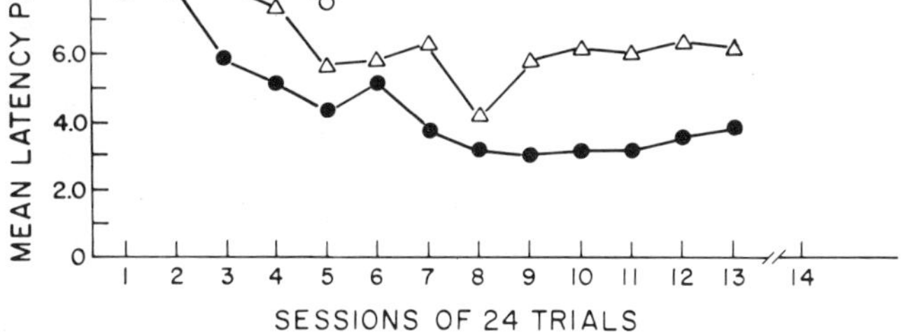

Figure 10. Mean response latencies of 24-trial sessions for chicks that were tested on a circle-triangle successive discrimination when 3–5 days old. For half of these chicks the circle was the S^+, while for the other chicks the triangle was the S^+. A retention test was given 7 days after the thirteenth discrimination session.

after the initial discrimination training. The results of these first two experiments therefore confirm the circle preference reported in 1- to 3-day-old chicks tested in large social groups without any external reinforcement (Fantz, 1957; Hess, 1964; Goodwin and Hess, 1969) and show that this preference has significant effects on discrimination learning of the young chick, particularly during the initial phase of discrimination training. Also, the young chick retains the effects of the conditioned modification of its initial preference.

Preferential responding to the orientation of a cue has also been observed in some young birds. For example, herring gull chicks peck more at vertical- than horizontal-oriented beaks or rods, whereas arctic tern chicks peck slightly more at horizontal- than vertical-oriented rods (Quine and Cullen, 1964). Recently, we have found that the young domestic chick has a striking preference for vertical-oriented stimuli compared to horizontal-oriented stimuli which remains constant for at least the first 3 days posthatch. For example, 1- to 3-day-old chicks tested either with a triplet of dots presented vertically or horizontally or with a white bar presented vertically or horizontally show a striking preference for the vertical-oriented cues. The results from these two experiments are presented in Figures 11 and 12, respectively. This preference for the vertical orientation, unlike the circle preference, was maintained throughout discrimination testing and therefore appears to be a stronger stimulus preference than the circle preference. To determine whether this vertical orientation preference, like the circle preference, is constant during the first few days after hatching, 3- to 5-day-old socially reared chicks were tested on the vertical-horizontal dot discrimination. These results are presented in Figure 13, which shows that these older chicks also have a preference for the vertical orientation.

Therefore, the young chick has both circle and vertical orientation preferences that remain constant during at least the first few days after hatching. When either of these preferred cues is the nonreinforced cue in a successive discrimination task, the young chick has difficulty in learning not to respond to it but learns quickly not to respond to an unpreferred cue (e.g., triangle or horizontal-oriented dots and bar). Similar results have also been found in studies on the effects of color preferences on subsequent learning (Kovach and Hichox, 1971; Bateson and Reese, 1969). In a blue-green simultaneous discrimination, chicks learned quicker when the preferred blue cue was the S^+ than when the unpreferred green cue was the S^+ (Kovach and Hichox, 1971). Similarly, chicks trained to pedal-step to turn on flashing lights learned this instrumental response more quickly when reinforced with a preferred orange light than when reinforced with an unpreferred green light (Bateson and Reese, 1969). In conclusion, brightness, form, and color preferences significantly influence discrimination learning of the young chick specifically

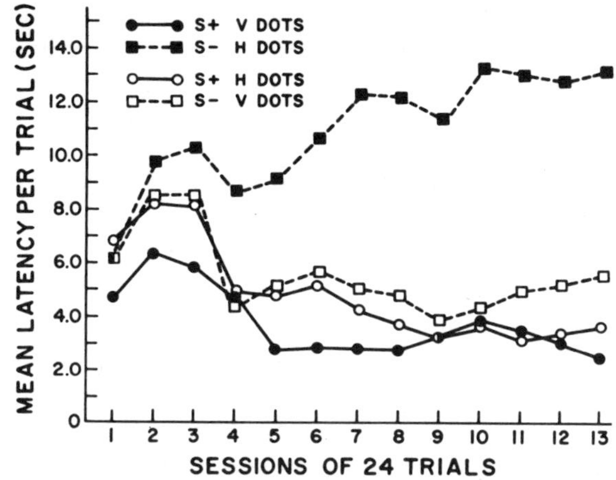

Figure 11. Mean response latencies of 24-trial sessions for chicks that were tested on a vertical-horizontal dots successive discrimination when 1–3 days old. For half of these chicks the vertical cue was the S^+, while for the other chicks the horizontal cue was the S^+.

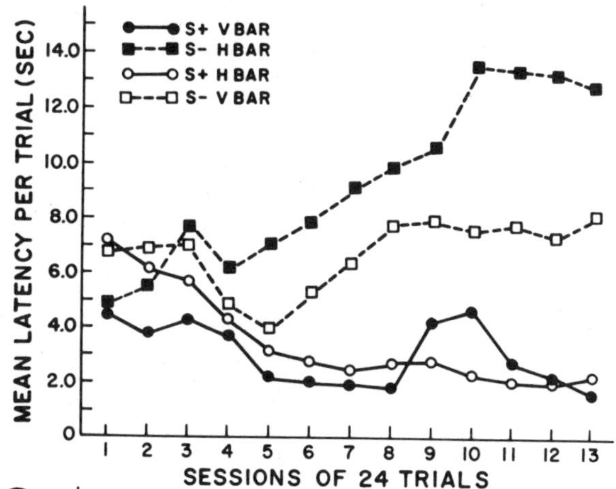

Figure 12. Mean response latencies of 24-trial sessions for chicks that were tested on a vertical-horizontal bar successive discrimination when 1–3 days old. For half of these chicks the vertical bar was the S^+, while for the other chicks the horizontal bar was the S^+.

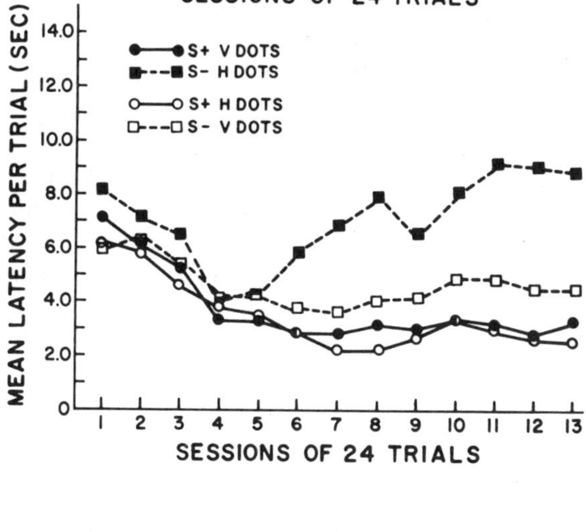

Figure 13. Mean response latencies of 24-trial sessions for chicks that were tested on a vertical-horizontal dots successive discrimination when 3–5 days old. For half of these chicks the vertical cue was the S^+, while for the other chicks the horizontal cue was the S^+.

in that learning is more rapid when the preferred cue is the S^+ than when it is the S^- and therefore these preferences are important developmental constraints on conditioning.

Development and Modification of Preferences

While preferential responding of the young chick is an important developmental constraint on conditioning, no valid generalization can be made regarding preference development in the young chick. For example, brightness-approach preferential responding increases as a function of light rearing and, consequently, the 3-day-old light-reared chick has a stronger brightness preference than the 1-day-old chick (Figure 6). Conversely, for form-approach preferences the 1-day-old chick appears to have a stronger circle preference than the 3-day-old chick (Figure 2). Finally, the circle and vertical orientation pecking preferences of the young chick remain constant during the first few days after hatching. Therefore, with the same breed of chick tested using heat as reinforcement, preferential responding may increase, or decrease, or not change as a function of age.

While both intraorganic and experiential processes have been shown to be important in brightness preference development of the young chick (Zolman and Lattin, 1972), posthatch analysis of form- and color-approach and pecking preferences has not been very extensive (Kovach, 1971). Likewise, prehatch analysis of visual preferences of the young organism has been neglected (Gottlieb, 1973*a*). The integrative influence of both intraorganic and experiential processes on preference development, of course, makes ontogenetic analysis very time consuming. But, because of the complexity of preference development of the young organism, single-factor explanations would appear to be too restrictive and therefore integrative explanations of behavioral ontogeny are necessary.

Apparently the brightness, form, and color preferences of young chicks do not elicit distinct species-specific behavioral patterns, suggesting that their importance would be in channeling the subsequent development of the chick in one direction or another. It is conceivable that exposure to a preferred cue during a particular period of life might produce a significant change in subsequent development (e.g., imprinting), but, what is more likely, a number of interrelated preferences would probably influence the development of any significant behavioral pattern. For example, Hogan (1973) has recently concluded that "neither the behavior of a mother-hen nor the immediate effects of pecking and ingestion nor the delayed effects of ingestion is necessary for the development of food recognition, and all these factors can partially compensate for disturbances that occur where one or more of these factors malfunctions" (p. 136). Similarly, preferential approach and pecking responses of young chicks may play some role in the development of effective food-seeking behavior. This is not to imply, of course, that these numerous developmental buffers would always lead to the completion of an adaptive behavioral pattern since the feeding at specific times of only particular foods, such as mealworms, can result in chicks that will starve amidst an available food supply (Hogan, 1973).

Regarding preference modification, it appears that almost any visual preferential responding of the young chick can be modified by conditioning procedures. Form- and color-approach preferences of chicks can be easily changed by conditioning (Kilham *et al.*, 1968; Taylor *et al.*, 1969; Zolman, 1969) and brightness-approach preferences can also be rather easily modified using massed-trials reinforcement procedures. But whether these modifications in approach preferences are transitory or relatively permanent has not been determined. Only in pecking preference studies has the permanency of the induced changes been tested (Brown and Brown, 1970; Hess, 1973; Meyer and Frank, 1970). Hess (1964) has reported that pecking preferences of the young chick can be quickly changed by reinforcing, with food, pecks to the unpreferred cue. When this reinforcement training is given to 1-, 2-, 7-, or 9-day-old chicks, they quickly revert to their initial preferences during subsequent extinction sessions. When this training is given to chicks that are 3–5 days old, however, over 80% of all pecks during subsequent extinction are to the previously reinforced, normally unpreferred cue (Hess, 1964). Attempts to replicate this permanent modification of the chicks' pecking preference, however, have not been successful. In these studies, chicks given reinforcement training between the ages of 3 and 5 days revert to the normally preferred cue during extinction, stop responding consistently to either cue, or show rapid extinction to the previously reinforced cue (Brown and Brown, 1970; Frank and Meyer, 1970; Meyer and Frank, 1970).

Unfortunately, it has usually been assumed that once response modification of preferences has occurred these learning changes are as permanent as those following conditioning in the mature organism in which significant retention may be found after years of no specific practice. The assumption of the same effect occurring in young organisms appears dubious for at least two reasons: (1) Most preference-modification studies have used both 100% reinforcement and massed-trials procedures. Since the mature animal shows rapid extinction of responses learned with a 100% reinforcement massed-trials paradigm, it would be expected that young animals trained under these procedures would also extinguish quickly any learned response. (2) Based on a series of experiments comparing retention between young and adult rats and guinea pigs, Campbell (1967) has concluded that, if original training conditions are equivalent, the young organism will always have a greater retention loss than the adult animal. If the young animal does indeed have a greater retention deficit than the adult, then it would be expected that following conditioning of the young organism there would be rapid forgetting of the learned response, and any initial preferential responding might reappear. From these considerations, therefore, the conditioned modification of preferences of the young organism may only be transitory. But to assume that learning principles based on adult performance also apply to the young organism in general and to preference modification in particular is, of course, placing one conjecture upon another.

Conclusions

Developmental research has been associated with the persistent nature-nurture controversy. Now, although attempts are being made to understand the integrative influence of both intraorganic and experiential processes on behavioral development, maturational explanations of emerging behaviors are replacing older instinctual explanations. In the young organism, sensitive period learning, perceptual preferences, retention loss, and lack of behavioral inhibition have all been suggested to be due to normal maturational processes. But maturational explanations of these behaviors negate inquiry of prior developmental events and greatly oversimplify the ontogeny of behavior.

Preferential responding of the young organism is observed in many species and, in the young chick, is an important developmental constraint on conditioning. Because of the complexity of preference development and its modification by conditioning, integrative explanations of these processes are necessary. For example, preferential responding may increase, decrease, or not change as a function of the age of the chick. Also, exposing young chicks to different stimuli during the sensitive period of imprinting may result in either the subsequent restriction of responding to those classes of stimuli that match the exposure stimulus or the activation of other preferences. Furthermore, chicks imprinted to a particular stimulus will learn a subsequent discrimination quicker than nonexposed controls even when the imprinted stimulus is the nonrewarded cue. Therefore, a specific attachment is not always produced to the form or color of the stimulus exposed during the sensitive period.

Besides preferential responding during the sensitive period of imprinting and the subsequent restriction of preferences, brightness, color, form, and stimulus orientation preferences have been observed in the young chick. In discrimination learning, when a preferred cue is the nonrewarded cue the young chick has difficulty in learning not to respond to this cue but learns quickly not to respond to an unpreferred cue. While some of these preferences can be rather easily modified by conditioning, the modification of other preferences requires unique massed-trials conditioning procedures. Also, once the preferential responding of the young chick has been modified by reinforcement, it is not known whether this modification is relatively permanent or only transitory.

For these reasons, the significance of general stimulus preferences of the young chick on subsequent behavioral development must still be determined. Since these visual preferences of the young chick do not elicit distinct species-specific behavioral patterns, they probably are but one of many interrelated processes involved in the development of adaptive behavioral patterns. The developmental histories of most of these general preferences and of preferential responding during the sensitive period of imprinting are also unknown. Unfortunately, emphasis has focused on the innateness of these perceptual preferences and on the behavioral discontinuities during sensitive periods rather than on prior developmental integrations. Therefore, while preferential responding of the young organism may be regarded as an important developmental constraint on conditioning, the development and activation of preferences, their modification by conditioning, and their subsequent effects on other emerging behavioral patterns remain significant and intriguing developmental problems.

ACKNOWLEDGMENTS

Support of the studies reported in this chapter was provided by the Human Development Studies Program of the College of Medicine, University of Kentucky, with funds granted by the Foundations' Fund for Research in Psychiatry (T64-205) and by Research Grant MD-24260 from the National Institute of Mental Health.

I am indebted to R. C. Dillehay, A. J. Nonneman, B. Peretz, and J. E. Spivey for their helpful criticisms of this chapter during its preparation.

References

Altman, J., Brunner, R. L., and Bayer, S. A. 1973. The hippocampus and behavioral maturation. *Behavioral Biology*, *8*, 557–596.

Bateson, P. P. G. 1964. An effect of imprinting on the perceptual development of domestic chicks. *Nature* (*London*), *202*, 421–422.

Bateson, P. P. G. 1966. The characteristics and context of imprinting. *Biological Review*, *41*, 177–220.

Bateson, P. P. G. 1973*a*. Imprinting of birds. In: *Ethology and Development*. S. A. Barnett (Ed.). W. Heinemann Ltd., London, pp. 1–15.

Bateson, P. P. G. 1973*b*. Internal influences on early learning in birds. In: *Constraints on Learning*. R. A. Hinde and J. Stevenson-Hinde (Eds.). Academic Press, New York, pp. 101–116.

Bateson, P. P. G., and Reese, E. P. 1969. The reinforcing properties of conspicuous stimuli in the imprinting situation. *Animal Behavior*, *17*, 692–699.
Beach, F. A. 1955. The descent of instinct. *Psychological Review*, *62*, 401–410.
Brown, R. T., and Brown, D. F. 1970. Failure to modify pecking preferences in chicks. Paper presented at the meeting of the Southeastern Psychological Association, Louisville.
Campbell, B. A. 1967. Developmental studies of learning and motivation in infraprimate mammals. In: *Early Behavior: Comparative and Developmental Approaches*. H. W. Stevenson, E. H. Hess, and H. L. Rheingold (Eds.). Wiley, New York, pp. 43–71.
Campbell, B. A., and Spears, N. E. 1972. Ontogeny of memory. *Psychological Review*, *79*, 215–236.
Campbell, B. A., Lytle, L. D., and White, D. C. 1974. Species differences in ontogeny of memory: Indirect support for neural maturation as a determinant of forgetting. *Journal of Comparative and Physiological Psychology*, *87*, 193–202.
Chantrey, D. F. 1972. Enhancement and retardation of discrimination learning in chicks after exposure to the discriminanda. *Journal of Comparative and Physiological Psychology*, *81*, 256–261.
Fantz, R. L. 1957. Form preferences in newly hatched chicks. *Journal of Comparative and Physiological Psychology*, *50*, 422–430.
Fantz, R. L. 1965. Ontogeny of perception. In: *Behavior of Nonhuman Primates*, Vol. II. A. M. Schrier, H. F. Harlow, and F. Stollnitz (Eds.). Academic Press, New York, pp. 365–403.
Fischer, G. J., and Campbell, G. L. 1964. The development of passive avoidance conditioning in Leghorn chicks. *Animal Behavior*, *12*, 268–269.
Frank, L. H., and Meyer, M. E. 1970. Food imprinting in domestic chicks as a function of social contact and number of companions. *Psychonomic Science*, *19*, 293–294.
Goodwin, E. B., and Hess, E. H. 1969. Innate visual form preferences in the pecking behavior of young chicks. *Behaviour*, *34*, 223–237.
Gottlieb, G. 1971. *Development of Species Identification in Birds: An Inquiry into the Prenatal Determinations of Perception*, University of Chicago Press, Chicago.
Gottlieb, G. 1973*a*. Neglected developmental variables in the study of species identification in birds. *Psychological Bulletin*, *79*, 362–372.
Gottlieb, G. 1973*b*. Introduction of behavioral embryology. In: *Behavioral Embryology*. G. Gottlieb (Ed.). Academic Press, New York, pp. 3–48.
Gottlieb, G. (Ed.) 1973*c*. *Behavioral Embryology*. Academic Press, New York.
Gottlieb, G., and Klopfer, P. 1962. The relation of developmental age to auditory and visual imprinting. *Journal of Comparative and Physiological Psychology*, *55*, 821–826.
Gottlieb, G., and Simner, M. L. 1969. Auditory versus visual flicker in directing the approach response of domestic chicks. *Journal of Comparative and Physiological Psychology*, *67*, 58–63.
Hailman, J. P. 1970. Comments on the coding of releasing stimuli. In: *Development and Evolution of Behavior*. L. R. Aronson, E. Tobach, D. S. Lehrman, and J. S. Rosenblatt (Eds.). Freeman, San Francisco, pp. 138–147.
Hamburger, V. 1973. Anatomical and physiological basis of embryonic motility in birds and mammals. In: *Behavioral Embryology*. G. Gottlieb (Ed.). Academic Press, New York, pp. 52–76.
Hebb, D. O. 1949. *The Organization of Behavior: A Neuropsychological Theory*. Wiley, New York.
Hess, E. H. 1959. Two conditions limiting critical age for imprinting. *Journal of Comparative and Physiological Psychology*, *52*, 515–518.

Hess, E. H. 1964. Imprinting in birds. *Science*, *146*, 1128–1139.

Hess, E. H. 1973. *Imprinting: Early Experience and the Developmental Psychobiology of Attachment*. Van Nostrand Reinhold, New York.

Hinde, R. A. 1960. Energy models of motivation. *Symposium of the Society for Experimental Biology*, *14*, 199–213.

Hinde, R. A. 1970. *Animal Behaviour: A Synthesis of Ethology and Comparative Psychology* (2nd ed.). McGraw-Hill, New York.

Hinde, R. A. 1973. Constraints on learning—An introduction to the problem. In: *Constraints on Learning*. R. A. Hinde and J. Stevenson-Hinde (Eds.). Academic Press, New York, pp. 1–19.

Hinde, R. A., and Stevenson-Hinde, J. (Eds). 1973. *Constraints on Learning*. Academic Press, New York.

Hoffman, H. S. and Ratner, A. M. 1973. A reinforcement model of imprinting: Implications for socialization in monkeys and men. *Psychological Review*, *80*, 527–544.

Hogan, J. A. 1973. How young chicks learn to recognize food. In: *Constraints on Learning* R. A. Hinde and J. Stevenson-Hinde (Eds.). Academic Press, New York, pp. 119–139.

James, H. 1959. Flicker: An unconditioned stimulus for imprinting. *Canadian Journal of Psychology*, *13*, 56–67.

James, H., and Binks, C. 1963. Escape and avoidance learning in newly hatched domestic chicks. *Science*, *139*, 1293–1294.

Kilham, P., Klopfer, P. H., and Oelke, H. 1968. Species identification and colour preferences in chicks. *Animal Behaviour*, *16*, 238–244.

King, J. A. 1958. Parameters relevant to determining the effects of early experience upon the adult behavior of animals. *Psychological Bulletin*, *55*, 46–58.

King, J. A. 1968. Species specificity and early experience, In: *Early Experience and Behavior*. G. Newton and S. Levine (Eds.). C. C. Thomas, Springfield, Ill., pp. 42–64.

Klopfer, P. 1967. Stimulus preferences and imprinting. *Science*, *156*, 1394–1396.

Klopfer, P. H., and Hailman, P. J. 1964. Basic parameters of following and imprinting in precocial birds. *Zeitschrift fuer Tierpsychologie*, *21*, 755–762.

Kovach, J. K. 1971. Effectiveness of different colors in the elicitation and development of approach behavior in chicks. *Behaviour*, *38*, 154–168.

Kovach, J. K., and Hichox, J. 1971. Color preferences and early perceptual discrimination learning in domestic chicks. *Developmental Psychobiology*, *4*, 255–267.

Kovach, J. K., Fabricius, E. and Fält, L. 1966. Relationships between imprinting and perceptual learning. *Journal of Comparative and Physiological Psychology*, *61*, 449–454.

Kuo, Z. Y. 1924. A psychology without heredity. *Psychological Review*, *31*, 427–451.

Lehrman, D. S. 1953. A critique of Konrad Lorenz's theory of instinctive behavior. *Quarterly Review of Biology*, *28*, 337–363.

Lehrman, D. S. 1970. Semantic and conceptual issues in the nature-nurture problem. In: *Development and Evolution of Behavior*. L. R. Aronson, E. Tobach, D. S. Lehrman, and J. S. Rosenblatt (Eds.). Freeman, San Francisco, pp. 17–52.

Lorenz, K. Z. 1937. The companion in the bird's world. *Auk*, *54*, 245–273.

Lorenz, K. Z. 1950. The comparative method in studying innate behaviour patterns *Symposium of the Society for Experimental Biology*, *4*, 221–268.

Lorenz, K. Z. 1966. *On Aggression*. Methuen, London.

MacDonald, G. 1968. Imprinting: Drug-produced isolation and the sensitive period. *Nature* (*London*), 1158–1159.

Marley, E., and Morse, W. H. 1966. Operant conditioning in the newly hatched chicken. *Journal of Experimental Analysis of Behavior*, *9*, 95–103.

McDougall, W. 1921. *An Introduction to Social Psychology* (14th ed.). J. W. Luce, Boston.

Meyer, M. E., and Frank, L. H. 1970. Food imprinting in the domestic chick: A reconsideration. *Psychonomic Science*, *19*, 43–45.
Moltz, H. 1963. Imprinting: An epigenetic approach. *Psychological Review*, *70*, 123–138.
Montagu, M. F. A. (Ed.) 1968. *Man and Aggression*. Oxford University Press, New York.
Polt, J. M. 1969. Effect of imprinting experience on discrimination learning in chicks. *Journal of Comparative and Physiological Psychology*, *69*, 514–518.
Polt, J. M., and Hess, E. H. 1966. Effects of social experience on the following response in chicks. *Journal of Comparative and Physiological Psychology*, *61*, 268–270.
Quine, D. A., and Cullen, J. M. 1964. The pecking response of young arctic terns (*Sterna macrura*) and the adaptiveness of the "releasing mechanism." *Ibis*, *106*, 145–173.
Quinta, T. 1966. Use of an electrified center board in the study of chicks on the visual cliff. *Perceptual and Motor Skills*, *22*, 169–170.
Ratner, A. M., and Hoffman, H. S. 1974. Evidence for a critical period for imprinting in Khaki Campbell ducklings (*Anas platyrhynchos domesticus*). *Animal Behaviour*, *22*, 249–255.
Sackett, G. P. 1963. A neural mechanism underlying unlearned, critical period, and developmental aspects of visually controlled behavior. *Psychological Review*, *70*, 40–50.
Salzen, E. A. 1970. Imprinting and environmental learning. In: *Development and Evolution of Behavior*. L. R. Aronson, E. T. Tobach, D. S. Lehrman, and J. S. Rosenblatt (Eds.). Freeman, San Francisco, pp. 158–178.
Schleidt, W. 1962. Die historische Entwicklung der Begriffe "Angeborenes auslösendes Schema" and "Angeborener Auslösemechanismus" in der Ethologie. *Zeitschrift für Tierpsychologie*, *19*, 697–732.
Schneirla, T. C. 1966. Behavioral development and comparative psychology. *Quarterly Review of Biology*, *41*, 283–303.
Sluckin, W. 1973. *Imprinting and Early Learning* (2nd ed.). Aldine, Chicago.
Smith, F. V. 1960. Towards definition of the stimulus situation for the approach response in the domestic chick. *Animal Behaviour*, *8*, 197–200.
Smith, F. V., and Hoyes, P. A. 1961. Properties of the visual stimuli for the approach response in the domestic chick. *Animal Behaviour*, *9*, 159–166.
Storr, A. 1968. *Human Aggression*. Atheneum, New York.
Taylor, A., Sluckin, W., and Hewitt, R. 1969. Changing colour preferences of chicks. *Animal Behaviour*, *17*, 3–8.
Thorpe, W. H. 1963. Ethology and the coding problem in germ cell and brain. *Zeitschrift fuer Tierpsychologie*, *20*, 529–551.
Tinbergen, N. 1951. *The Study of Instinct*. Oxford University Press, London.
Whalen, R. E. 1971. The concept of instinct. In: *Psychobiology: Behavior from a Biological Perspective*. J. L. McGaugh (Ed.). Academic Press, New York, pp. 53–72.
Zolman, J. F. 1968. Discrimination learning in young chicks with heat reinforcement. *Psychological Record*, *18*, 303–309.
Zolman, J. F. 1969. Stimulus preferences and form discrimination learning in young chicks. *Psychological Record*, *19*, 407–416.
Zolman, J. F., and Lattin, W. J. 1972. Development of brightness preference in young chicks: Effects on brightness discrimination learning. *Journal of Comparative and Physiological Psychology*, *79*, 271–283.
Zolman, J. F., Chandler, S. D., and Black, D. 1972. Visual discrimination learning of the young chick: Key-peck conditioning with heat reinforcement. *Developmental Psychobiology*, *5*, 181–187.
Zolman, J. F., Pursley, D. G., Hall, J. A., and Sahley, C. L. 1975. Form preferences in successive discrimination learning of young chicks. *Journal of Comparative and Physiological Psychology*, *89*, 1180–1191.

PHYSIOLOGICAL MEDIATION

5

James L. McGaugh

COGNITION AND CONSOLIDATION

The history of science is replete with instances where experiments have yielded compelling data against all logic and wisdom.

—David Krech (1972)

There are certain facts concerning the nature of learning in laboratory animals as well as ordinary human beings that make it difficult (and perhaps even impossible) for us to discover the neural processes and processing which enable us to learn and remember. Some of the most important and perplexing of these facts were revealed by the research of Edward Chace Tolman and his students in the Department of Psychology at Berkeley. It is through the Berkeley influence that we learned that we must distinguish learning from performance. Performance is observed. Making inferences about learning on the basis of changes in performance is a complex matter, since performance is also influenced by many factors other than learning. The well-known "latent learning" experiments demonstrated the importance of the learning-performance distinction (Tolman and Honzik, 1930; Tolman, 1932, 1951). From Tolman and his students we also learned that learning does not consist simply of acquiring the ability to make specific responses in the presence of particular stimulation. Learning consists of acquiring information about "what-leads-to-what." That is, learning is cognitive. This conclusion is supported by extensive evidence from studies of latent learning, problem solving, and place vs. response learning (Tolman, 1948). Additional facts revealed by

---

James L. McGaugh • Department of Psychobiology, School of Biological Sciences, University of California, Irvine, California.

Karl Lashley provided still further evidence against a simple S-R associationistic view of learning (Lashley, 1950). Rats as well as human beings readily use information acquired under one set of conditions in order to behave appropriately under changed conditions. While this cognitive view of learning was vigorously challenged (Hull, 1951; Hilgard, 1956; Miller, 1959), it is well supported by evidence and is widely accepted.

The task of understanding the neural basis of learning would no doubt be a much easier one if learning *did* consist of the acquisition of specific responses in the presence of specific stimulation. If that were the case, it might be possible to discover the neural circuitry underlying the learned response as well as the changes in circuitry which enable learning to occur (Lashley, 1933). But the facts that changes in stimulus conditions do not necessarily alter the performance of learned responses and that the performance of learned responses can and does vary in the presence of relatively constant external stimulus conditions argue against theories which propose that learning involves the development of precise neural circuitry which connects receptors with muscles and glands (Tolman and Brunswik, 1935; Lashley, 1949).

Thus the findings of Tolman and Lashley make it difficult indeed to develop either a simple or a sensible view of the neural basis of learning. David Krech had the good fortune of learning these lessons directly from Tolman, with whom he studied as a graduate student, and from Lashley, with whom he studied as a postdoctoral fellow. Lewis Petrinovich and I had the good fortune of learning these lessons directly from David Krech when we were graduate students in the "enriched environment" provided by the Berkeley psychology department in the mid-1950s. The faculty at Berkeley at that time, in addition to Krech, included Tolman, Robert Tryon, Egon Brunswik, Benbow Ritchie, Al Riley, Leo Postman, and Mark Rosenzweig. Most of these faculty regularly participated in Tolman's seminar on animal learning. We were all permanently influenced by the heated discussions of cognitive theory which took place at Tolman's seminars. Another major influence at Berkeley was the seminar on brain biochemistry and behavior offered by Krech, Rosenzweig, and Edward Bennett. Through these influences, and in particular those of David Krech, we learned that (1) the processes of learning and memory are enormously complex; (2) learning must be studied with a healthy respect for individual differences—in particular, those differences which are of genetic origin; (3) efforts to understand learning and memory—including individual differences—might profitably be pursued through studies of brain biochemistry and behavior; (4) the proper study of man's memory (or human memory if you prefer) is best accomplished by experiments investigating rats' retention. Krech now feels, as I will point out later in this chapter, that some of us learned the last of these lessons much too well (Krech, 1972).

Making Memory

As I noted, the facts provided by behavioral studies of learning make it difficult to develop a neurobiological theory of learning. Those who have not been discouraged by these facts have responded in one of several ways. Some investigators have continued to assume that learning must consist of the formation of specific neuronal circuits and that the facts of learning will eventually be explained by such circuitry (Kandel and Spencer, 1968). Others have attempted to develop complex neurobiological theories of learning which do not assume that specific neuronal circuits are required for learning (John, 1972). A third approach makes no assumption about neuronal circuitry but focuses, rather, on an attempt to understand the neurobiological conditions which either favor or impair animals' ability to acquire and retain information. The guiding assumption of this approach is that an understanding of brain states which influence learning and memory will provide important clues to the neuronal processes which underlie learning and memory (McGaugh and Herz, 1972; McGaugh and Gold, 1974; Gold and McGaugh, 1975*a*). Obviously, the use of this approach allows one to investigate the neurobiology of learning and memory without having to confront directly the uncomfortable facts provided by Tolman and Lashley and their students. This approach also readily accommodates research concerning individual differences in learning as well as studies of brain chemistry and learning. And, finally, the approach is well suited for those of us who were "reared" at Berkeley and influenced by Krech (Jarvik, 1972; McGaugh, 1966; Petrinovich, 1967).

In this chapter, I will summarize some of the findings from my laboratory concerning the modulating influences on learning and memory of drugs, hormones, and electrical stimulation of the brain. Our findings clearly indicate that such treatments can enhance and impair the storage of newly acquired information. And we believe that these findings may well help us understand the nature of brain states which favor memory storage. Before reviewing this evidence, I would like to provide a bit of historical context. This research grew out of several lines of evidence and theory which converged in the late 1940s. It is of particular interest to note, and will be emphasized later in the chapter, that this research problem stemmed from clinical findings and experimental research based on human subjects.

Retrograde Amnesia and Memory Consolidation

In 1900 Mueller and Pilzecker suggested that the neural processes underlying memory perseverate for some time after a learning experience and that such perseveration results in the fixation or consolidation of the newly acquired memory trace. The "perseveration-consolidation" hypothesis was proposed as a means of explaining retroactive interference as observed in laboratory studies of human verbal learning and retention. McDougall (1901) pointed out that the hypothesis provided an explanation of the retrograde amnesia observed following head injury. Head injury might produce amnesia by impairing the consolidation of memory of recent experiences. Clinical evidence summarized by Russell and Nathan in 1946 strongly supports this interpretation; patients with head injuries typically have a permanent loss of memory for events which occurred within minutes, hours, or sometimes days prior to the injury. Generally, the degree of retrograde amnesia depends on the severity of the head injury. In the mid-1940s, there was growing evidence that the newly developed electroconvulsive therapy (ECT; or electroconvulsive shock, ECS) treatments also produced retrograde amnesia (Mayer-Gross, 1943) in patients. Subsequently Duncan (1949) and Gerard (1949) demonstrated that ECS treatments produced retrograde amnesia in laboratory animals. It was also in 1949 that Hebb (1949) and Gerard (1949) proposed the dual-trace hypothesis of memory storage. According to this hypothesis, the neural perseveration following a training experience is based on reverberating neural circuits. The reverberation provides a basis for recent memory and leads to the consolidation of the stable long-term memory trace. According to this view, head injury and ECT (or ECS) treatments produce retrograde amnesia because they interfere with the reverberating neuronal activity initiated by recent experiences. This hypothesis is quite similar to that proposed earlier by Mueller and Pilzecker.

In the early 1950s, these "new" findings and hypotheses had many implications for research on the neurobiology of learning and memory. If memory consolidation occurs over time following learning, it should be possible to investigate the neurobiological processes involved in the consolidation of the permanent memory trace. Perhaps individual differences in learning and retention are based in part on individual differences in memory consolidation efficiency. Further, if consolidation processes are subject to disruptive influences, then perhaps they are also susceptible to influences which might enhance consolidation. My first research on this problem was stimulated by this last implication.

Drug Facilitation of Learning and Memory

When we were graduate students in the seminar on brain chemistry and behavior, in the mid-1950s, Petrinovich and I became interested in the effects of drugs on learning. Our initial undertaking was a comprehensive review of all published research concerned with this problem. Our seminar report was the first draft of our review, which subsequently underwent countless revisions until we decided (arbitrarily but mercifully) to publish it 10 years later (McGaugh and Petrinovich, 1965).

It was during the course of preparing the original review that we discovered Lashley's findings (1917) that maze learning is enhanced by low doses of strychnine sulfate. Lashley's study provided the most convincing evidence available at that time that learning could be enhanced by a drug. Further, this finding seemed to fit well with the consolidation hypothesis and the dual trace hypothesis. Thus Petrinovich and I decided to see whether we could confirm and extend Lashley's findings. Our initial experiment clearly confirmed Lashley: rats given low doses of strychnine sulfate each day before they were trained on an alley maze (Lashley III) made fewer errors than controls in learning the maze (McGaugh and Petrinovich, 1959).

While these results confirmed those of Lashley, they did not provide any clarification of how the drug influenced learning. The enhanced performance produced by the drug might be due either to an action on neurobiological processes underlying learning or to effects on sensory and motivational processes affecting the performance of learned responses. With the procedures used, it was possible only to conclude that acquisition performance was improved. Our hope was, of course, that the facilitating effect of strychnine was due its influences on learning (i.e., cognitive) processes and not to other influences on performance. In the first series of experiments designed to provide clarification of these questions (McGaugh, 1961; McGaugh and Thomson, 1962; Petrinovich, 1963), we found that strychnine facilitated learning in a variety of learning tasks which used different motivation and response requirements. Further, similar effects were obtained with other stimulant drugs including a synthetic strychninelike compound, diazadamantanol (McGaugh *et al.*, 1961), pentylenetetrazol (Hunt and Krivanek, 1966), and nicotine (cf. Bovet *et al.*, 1966; Oliverio, 1968).

With all of the drugs studied, but most particularly with strychnine, the dose used is critical. Petrinovich (1967) found that strychnine can either facilitate or impair learning—depending on the particular dose used as well as the strain of animals used as subjects. Thus the evidence gathered since 1959 clearly indicates that the effects originally reported by Lashley can be obtained with a wide variety of experimental conditions. Such findings make it less likely that the effects are due to influences on sensory or motivational processes since the requirements of the tasks used in the different experiments vary considerably.

It seems reasonable to conclude that CNS stimulants enhance the acquisition and retention of learned responses by modulating memory storage processes, i.e., by stimulating the consolidation of cognitive processes. However, the evidence that strychnine and other drugs can directly affect performance of learned responses cannot be disregarded (cf. Zalmanson, 1929; Benevento and Kandel, 1967). Obviously, the questions about the learning vs. performance effects of a drug cannot be answered in any simple clear-cut manner by experiments in which the animals are drugged while acquiring and performing learned responses. There are many ways in which drugs can alter behavior and there is no direct way of distinguishing between influences on learning processes and other influences on behavior.

A different way of approaching this problem was suggested by the experimental studies of retrograde amnesia. As I noted above, such studies suggested that the processes underlying memory storage remain susceptible to experimental influences for a fairly long period of time following training. On the basis of this evidence, we reasoned that it might be possible to facilitate memory storage by administering drugs *after* training. With this procedure of posttraining administration, the animals can be trained and subsequently tested under normal nondrugged conditions. The drug can be administered shortly after training and retention trials can be given after the drug is metabolized or excreted.

A number of experiments conducted in my laboratory, and subsequently in other laboratories, examined the effects of posttraining drug administration on learning and retention. In these studies, animals, usually rats, were given daily training trials and injected with a CNS stimulant shortly after the last trial. Using this general experimental procedure, learning facilitation was found with a variety of tasks and with several drugs including strychnine, picrotoxin, caffeine, pentylenetetrazol, amphetamine, nicotine, physostigmine, and diazadamantanol. In studies using discrimination tasks, oddity discrimination, delayed response performance, and avoidance responding, as well as mazes, animals given posttrial injections of CNS stimulants learned with fewer errors and/or trials than animals injected with control solutions (cf. McGaugh, 1959; Breen and McGaugh, 1961; Paré, 1961; Hudspeth, 1964; Oliverio, 1968; Franchina and Moore, 1968; Doty and Doty, 1966; McGaugh, 1973). While most of these experiments used rats and mice as subjects, comparable findings have been obtained in studies using monkeys (Bowman and Harlow, personal conversation). The magnitude of the facilitating effect obtained with posttrial administration depends on many factors including the drug, the dose, the species and strain, and the task.

As I noted, we have assumed that by using the posttrial administration procedure, the animals are not under the drug's influence either during training or during the subsequent testing.Most of the drugs used are fairly rapidly metabolized or excreted, so it is likely that with posttrial injections the drugs are almost completely eliminated within 24 hr—the typical interval between training trials. Clearest evidence for this has been provided by studies in which the time of injection is varied in different groups of animals. In a series of studies (McGaugh *et al.*, 1962; McGaugh and Krivanek, 1970; Krivanek and McGaugh, 1968, 1969), we found that learning was enhanced by posttrial drug injections only if the injections occurred within an hour following training.

While the early posttrial studies were in progress, it occurred to us that the posttrial injections might be rewarding to the animals. It was well known at that time that posttrial electrical stimulation could serve as a reward. This hypothesis could not explain the facilitating effects of pretrial injections but could well explain the retrograde facilitating effects found with posttrial injections. Evidence against this hypothesis was obtained in two studies.

The first study (Westbrook and McGaugh, 1964) investigated the effects of posttrial drug administration on latent learning using the experimental procedures developed by Tolman and his students (Tolman and Honzik, 1930). Hungry and thirsty rats were given a series of unrewarded trials in a maze. After each trial, they received either a drug injection (diazadamantanol) or an injection of a control solution. Neither group showed improved performance over the series of unrewarded trials. Thus there was no evidence that the drug injections were rewarding. Subsequently, the drug injections were discontinued and a highly palatable food reward was given at the end of each trial. Under these conditions, both groups learned, but the degree of learning was significantly greater in the rats that had previously received the posttrial drug injections. These results indicate that the injections facilitated the learning that was not evidenced in performance (i.e., latent learning) during the initial series of unrewarded trials.

The second study (Petrinovich *et al.*, 1965) investigated the effect of posttrial injections of strychnine on memory in a delayed alternation task using the experimental procedures developed by Petrinovich and Bolles (1957). Rats were first trained to alternate their choice of goal boxes in a T-maze. Water was available on each trial in the goal box which was *not* entered on the preceding trial. When the response was well learned, the interval between trials was lengthened. At the shorter intervals the animals performed well, but at intervals of several hours the rats' performance reverted to a chance level. The animals were apparently unable to remember their last response when the intertrial interval was long. However, with long intertrial intervals their performance of the delayed alternating response was significantly improved by injection with strychnine immediately after the trial preceding the delayed test. In other words, with this procedure posttrial injections *decreased* the probability that the animals would repeat the response made prior to the injection. Such effects would not be expected were the injections acting simply as a reward. The drug appeared to improve performance by enhancing the rats' memory of the previous response.

I have summarized only a restricted selection of studies that have been conducted to investigate the effect of CNS stimulants on learning. A number of more extensive reviews of the problem have been published (McGaugh, 1968, 1973; Dawson and McGaugh, 1973; McGaugh and Herz, 1972). Overall, the findings of these studies have provided strong evidence that memory storage processes can be enhanced by administration of drugs after training. The effect is readily obtained with a variety of drugs, strains and species of subjects, and types of learning tasks. The phenomenon of drug enhancement of memory seems well established. However, these experiments shed very little light on the neurobiological basis or bases of the effects. I will return to this problem in a subsequent section.

Modulating Effects of Electrical Stimulation of the Brain

Most experimental studies of memory consolidation have used treatments which interfere with memory. In a series of studies conducted in my laboratory, we have confirmed and extended the earlier findings that retrograde amnesia is produced by ECS (McGaugh, 1966; McGaugh and Dawson, 1971). We, as well as other investigators, have also shown that retrograde amnesia can be produced by direct electrical stimulation of a number of brain regions (McGaugh and Gold, 1976; Kesner and Wilburn, 1974). Further, we have shown that memory can be impaired by low-intensity electrical stimulation which produces neither convulsions nor brain seizure after discharges (McGaugh, 1974; Gold *et al.*, 1974). The gradient of retrograde amnesia obtained in these studies depends on many conditions, including the strain of animals, the training task, the intensity and duration of the current, and the specific brain region stimulated (McGaugh and Gold, 1976). It is clear from these findings that memory storage processes remain susceptible to brain stimulation for minutes or even hours following training. It is also clear that retrograde amnesia gradients do not provide direct measures of the time course of memory consolidation: they are products of the experimental conditions under which they are obtained (McGaugh and Dawson, 1971; Gold *et al.*, 1973*a*, *b*).

There is also extensive evidence that memory can be enhanced by posttraining electrical stimulation of the brain. For example, in an elegant series of experiments, Bloch and his colleagues (Bloch, 1970) gave rats electrical stimulation of the mesencephalic reticular formation immediately after training sessions. Rate of learning was enhanced by the stimulation. Further, they found that the amnesia produced by postsession administration of the depressant drug fluothane could be prevented if the electrical stimulation of the reticular formation were given in the interval between the termination of the training and the administration of the fluothane.

In a series of experiments in my laboratory, we have confirmed Bloch's finding that learning is enhanced by postsession electrical brain stimulation. In one study (Denti *et al.*, 1970), we gave rats reticular stimulation immediately after each training trial on a one-way active avoidance task. The learning of the group given postsession stimulation was superior to that of animals which had electrodes implanted but which did not receive stimulation. But the learning of the stimulated animals was inferior to that of control rats which did not have electrodes implanted. Thus the posttrial stimulation appeared to partially compensate for a lesion-produced impairment of learning. However, Bloch's findings indicate that facilitation of learning by posttrial electrical stimulation of the reticular formation can also be obtained in studies in which the lesion produced by the implantation of the electrode does not impair learning (Bloch, 1970).

In other experiments, we found that learning is facilitated by posttraining electrical stimulation of the ventral hippocampus (Landfield *et al.*, 1973). Rats were given one trial for several days on a simple active avoidance task using shock motivation. The performance of the controls bearing implanted electrodes was inferior to that of the unimplanted controls. Two groups of animals received electrical stimulation either 5 sec or 5 min after each training trial. The performance of animals given the stimulation 5 sec after each trial almost equaled that of the unoperated controls, while the performance of animals given the stimulation 5 min after the trial was as poor as that of the nonstimulated controls. The lack of effectiveness of the delayed stimulation suggests that the effect of the stimulation given immediately after training is not due to a general or nonspecific effect of daily brain stimulation treatments.

In an extensive series of studies conducted in my laboratory, Paul Gold has demonstrated that memory can be impaired or enhanced by posttrial electrical stimulation of the amygdala (Gold *et al.*, 1973*b*, 1975*a*, *b*; Handwerker *et al.*, 1974). In these experiments, rats were trained on a simple task and then given low-intensity stimulation of the amygdala. The stimulation produced retrograde amnesia in experiments using a variety of tasks including inhibitory avoidance, active avoidance, and discrimination learning. The effect is readily produced by unilateral as well as bilateral stimulation. Further, Gold has found that the same type of stimulation can produce either impairment of memory or facilitation of memory, depending on the experimental conditions. As is shown in Figure 1, animals given posttraining amygdala stimulation show poor retention following training on an inhibitory avoidance task in comparison with either unimplanted controls or controls bearing amygdala electrodes if a relatively high level of footshock is used during training (left side of figure). However, if a low-level footshock is used during training, the implanted animals have poor retention. Further, with low-level footshock, posttrial stimulation of the amygdala facilitates retention (right side of figure). These findings indicate that brain stimulation does not simply disrupt or

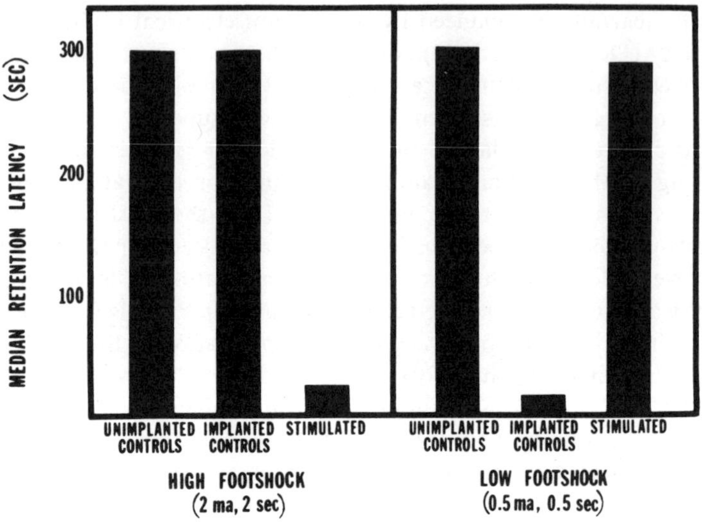

Figure 1. Effect of posttrial amygdala stimulation on retention of inhibitory avoidance training. Rats ($N = 8$ per group) received bilateral stimulation (10 sec 25–30 μA, 0.1 msec 100 Hz monophasic, bipolar electrodes) 30 sec after a training trial. Retention was measured 24 hr later. From Gold *et al.* (1975*b*).

enhance memory. Rather, the stimulation modulates memory storage processes: the effect of the stimulation appears to depend on the animal's internal state at the time of the stimulation.

Alterations in memory storage have been produced by stimulation of many other brain regions, including the cortex, hippocampus, caudate nucleus, substantia nigra, and mesencephalic reticular formation (Zornetzer, 1974; Sideroff *et al.*, 1974; Wyers *et al.*, 1968; Haycock *et al.*, 1973; Routtenberg and Holzman, 1973; Bloch, 1970). One possible interpretation of such findings is that these are brain regions in which memory systems are located (Kesner and Wilburn, 1974). As Gold and I have argued, however, it can be concluded only that these are regions in which stimulation is effective in modulating memory storage (Gold and McGaugh, 1975*a*). Further studies are needed to determine the causes of the modulation. Stimulation of any brain region might well produce widespread changes in brain states because of alterations such as release of hormones and associated changes in states of arousal.

Endogenous Memory Modulators

Most of the research from my laboratory has involved treatments such as electrical brain stimulation and administration of stimulant drugs whose actions on the central nervous system are poorly understood. Thus these studies have provided few clues to the basis of the modulating influences of these treatments on memory. One possibility is that these treatments act directly on cellular storage processes. Another possibility is that the treatments affect processes which are normally involved in modulating memory storage. Gold and I have suggested (Gold and McGaugh, 1975*a*) that an experience affects memory in two ways. First, the experience initiates processes leading to the storage of information. Second, the experience produces more general effects including changes in state of arousal and associated release of hormones. We have suggested that these "nonspecific" consequences of stimulation might well play an important role in serving to modulate the degree of storage of the information provided by the experience. Treatments which affect memory might do so by affecting either the storage system or the "nonspecific" modulation systems. Further, this hypothesis suggests that different training conditions might produce different degrees of retention simply because of different "nonspecific" consequences of the training. The impairing and enhancing effects of experimental treatments such as brain stimulation might be due to alterations in normal modulating influences such that memories which would otherwise be strong are weakened (amnesia) and memories which would otherwise be weak are strengthened (facilitation).

In recent years, several endogenous substances have been suggested as possibly playing a modulating role in memory storage. Kety (1972) has suggested that catecholamines, particularly norepinephrine, released in affective states might have the effect of promoting memory storage. De Wied and his associates (de Wied, 1974) have shown that ACTH and peptide fragments of ACTH alter retention. It is probably the case that all of the treatments which affect memory storage have profound influences on catecholamine systems as well as pituitary and adrenal activity. Further, recent studies have shown that administration of pituitary and adrenal hormones as well as treatments which alter catecholamine metabolism can produce both retrograde amnesia and facilitation of memory storage. Gold and van Buskirk (1975, 1976*a*, 1977) have examined the effects of posttrial simultaneous administration of several hormones including epinephrine, norepinephrine, and ACTH on the retention by rats of an inhibitory avoidance response. Moderate doses of these hormones were found to enhance retention if the hormone was administered within a few minutes after training. A high dose of ACTH impaired retention. Hormones administered 2 hr after training did not affect subsequent retention. These findings provide clear evidence that memory storage processes are influenced by hormones administered after training and thus provide support for the view that hormones may be directly involved in the modulation of memory storage. It is not clear, however, how peripherally administered hormones modulate central neural processes since there is much evidence suggesting that these hormones do not pass the blood-brain barrier. It is possible that small amounts might pass the barrier—particularly in the region of the hypothalamus. It is also possible that the peripheral injections may cause the release of ACTH or directly influence the CNS by altering circulatory activity. There is evidence that peripherally administered hormones affect levels of brain as well as peripheral catecholamines (Gold and van Buskirk, in preparation). Thus while it is not clear exactly how peripherally administered hormones affect brain activity it is clear that they do produce alterations in brain functioning. It remains to be determined whether all of these hormones have central effects or whether they have peripheral effects which have a common action centrally.

There is much recent evidence suggesting that retention is influenced by posttraining alteration in brain catecholamines. For example, amphetamine enhances retention when administered shortly after training (Krivanek and McGaugh, 1969; McGaugh, 1973). However, it has not yet been shown that this effect is due to an action on central catecholamines. Somewhat more direct evidence has been provided by studies using drugs which block catecholamine biosynthesis. Several experiments have shown that retention is impaired by drugs which inhibit the synthesis of norepinephrine. Diethyldithiocarbamate (DDC) and fusaric acid block norepinephrine synthesis by inhibiting the enzyme dopamine-β-hydroxylase. Several studies have shown that retention is impaired by either pretrial or posttrial administration of DDC (Randt *et al.*, 1971; Osborne and Kerkut, 1972). In a series of recent experiments, we have examined the effects of posttrial alterations in catecholamine levels on retention. Our findings are based on studies of the effects of DDC on retention of an inhibitory avoidance response in mice and are shown in Figure 2. The mice in this experiment were injected with DDC at one of several times ranging from 24 hr before training to 3 hr after training. Improvement of retention was found only if the drug was administered within 3 hr before training or 1 hr after training (McGaugh *et al.*, 1975). At the dose of DDC used, the levels of norepinephrine are significantly lowered for several hours following administration. We have also obtained comparable results in studies using rats and other types of training tasks (van Buskirk *et al.*, 1976). These results are consistent with the interpretation that the retention deficit produced by DDC is due to the decrease in norepinephrine produced by inhibition of dopamine-β-hydroxylase. However, these findings must be interpreted cautiously, for DDC chelates heavy metals and undoubtedly influences other brain systems which involve metal-requiring enzymes. DDC also produces brain seizures. However, we have found no relationship between the occurrence of brain seizures and amnesia in animals treated with DDC.

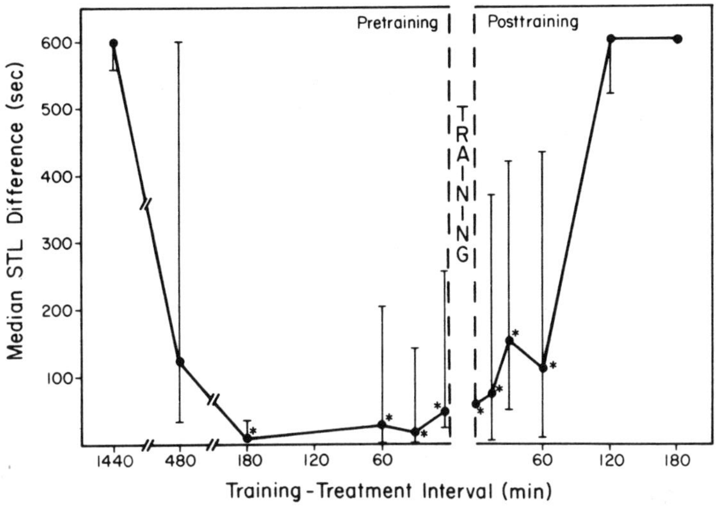

Figure 2. Effects of training-treatment interval on diethyldithiocarbamate (DDC) induced retention deficits for inhibitory avoidance learning in mice. Different groups of mice received DDC, 900 mg/kg intraperitoneally, at various times before or after training on a one-trial, step-through, inhibitory avoidance task. Seven days after training, test step-through latencies were assessed. Each point represents the median step-through latency (STL) difference for 16 animals. Error bars indicate the interquartile ranges. Animals receiving saline had a value of 600 (271.8–600) sec. From McGaugh *et al.* (1975).

Another approach to the problem is that of administering catecholamines directly to the brain to see whether such treatment will affect retention. We have found some evidence that, in mice, memory can be facilitated by posttrial intraventricular administration of catecholamines (Haycock *et al.*, 1976; McGaugh *et al.*, 1975). Somewhat clearer evidence of a role for catecholamines in memory has been provided by recent studies in which animals were given DDC before training and intraventricular injections of norepinephrine after training. In the first study using these procedures, Stein *et al.* (1975) found that the memory deficit produced by DDC was significantly attenuated by norepinephrine (10 mg) if the intraventricular injection was given immediately after training. Administration of norepinephrine 2 hr or more after the training did not affect retention. Subsequent studies in my laboratory have confirmed these findings (Meligeni *et al.*, 1975). In these experiments, rats were injected with DDC (680 mg/kg) 30 min before receiving a training trial on an inhibitory avoidance task. Immediately after the training trial, norepinephrine was injected into the lateral ventricle by means of an implanted cannula. As Figure 3 shows, learning was impaired in the DDC-treated animals. However, a dose of 1.0 mg of norepinephrine attenuated the retention deficit produced by the DDC. These findings provide additional support for the view (Kety, 1970, 1972) that central norepinephrine plays a role in memory storage. Obviously, additional studies are needed to determine whether substances other than norepinephrine might also attenuate DDC-induced retention deficits.

Figure 4 is an illustration of the results of another recent experiment in my laboratory, in which we found that DDC-induced retention deficits can also be attenuated by peripheral subcutaneous injections of norepinephrine (Meligeni *et al.*, 1975). This effect, like that found by Gold and van Buskirk, which indicated that retention is enhanced by posttrial subcutaneous injections of norepinephrine, is difficult to interpret in terms of a direct action of norepinephrine on the brain. The peripheral effects might act indirectly, for example, through influences on the pituitary gland or on the circulatory system.

Other recent attempts to investigate the role of catecholamines in memory have involved the use of brain lesions. Most of the norepinephrine-containing terminals in the cerebral cortex appear to arise from cell bodies of the locus coeruleus, which is located in the midbrain. Lesions of this structure produce a decrease in cortical norepinephrine. There is some evidence to suggest that locus coeruleus lesions produce deficits in learning (Anlezark *et al.*, 1973).

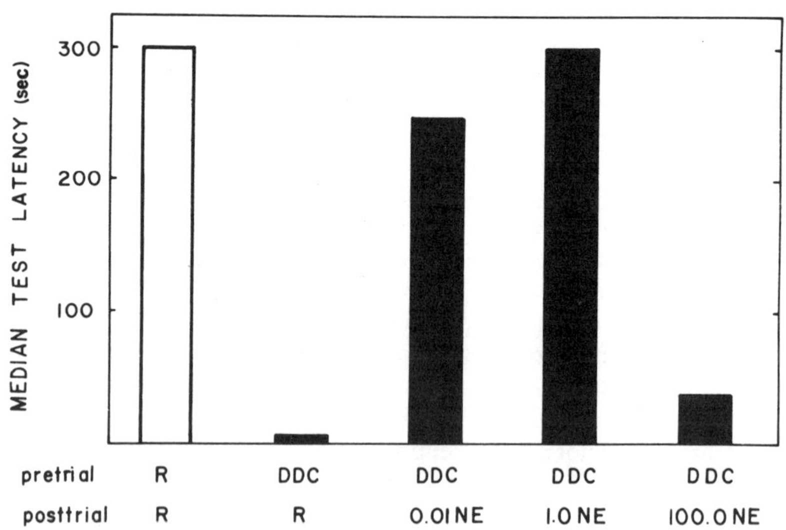

Figure 3. Effect of pretraining administration of diethyldithiocarbamate followed by posttrial intraventicular norepinephrine on retention of a one-trial inhibitory avoidance response in rats. From Meligeni *et al.* (1975) (DDC: 680 mg/kg[i.p.]; NE: μg/μl[i.v.]; FS: 2ma–2 sec).

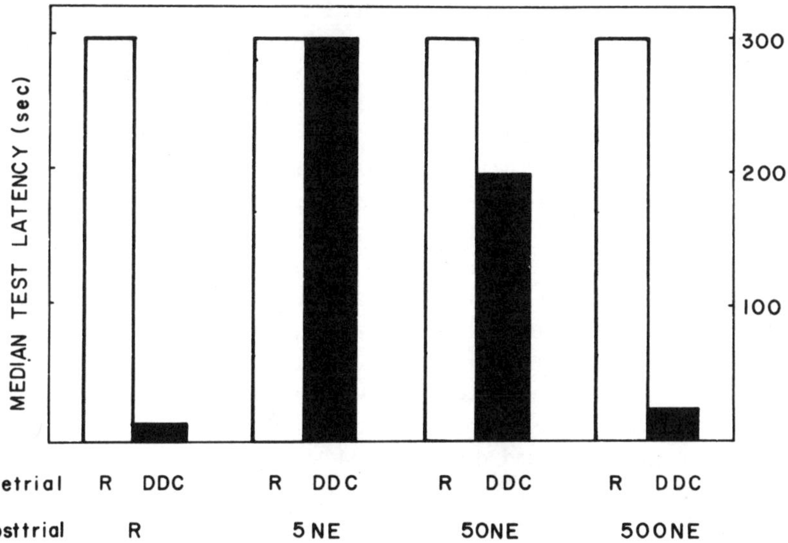

Figure 4. Effect of pretraining administration of diethyldithiocarbamate followed by posttrial subcutaneous norepinephrine on retention of a one-trial inhibitory avoidance response in rats. From Meligeni *et al.* (1975) (DDC: 680 mg/kg[i.p.]; NE: μg/kg[s.c.]; FS: 2 ma, 2 sec).

However, this effect has not been confirmed (Amaral and Foss, 1975). Recently, Zornetzer and Gold (1975) reported that animals with a unilateral locus coeruleus lesion have an increased susceptibility to ECS-induced amnesia. In normal (i.e., unlesioned) mice, ECS produced amnesia for inhibitory avoidance training only if the treatment was administered shortly after the training. However, in mice with locus coeruleus lesions, an ECS treatment produced a retention deficit even if the treatment was administered several days after the training. The lesion (which was made immediately after training) did not, by itself, affect retention.

Sleep and Memory Modulation

The effects of locus coeruleus lesions reported by Zornetzer and Gold (1975) are strikingly similar to the effects of REM sleep deprivation reported several years ago by Fishbein *et al.* (1971). In the latter study, mice were trained on an inhibitory avoidance task and then deprived of REM sleep for 2 days. An ECS given immediately after termination of the REM deprivation produced a retention deficit, while an ECS given 6 hr later had no effect. In normal mice, ECS produced amnesia only when given shortly after the training. In view of the evidence (Jouvet, 1967) that the locus coeruleus plays some role in REM sleep, it might be that the loss of REM sleep and associated hormonal and neuronal activity is the basis for the effects found by Zornetzer and Gold as well as for those found by Fishbein and colleagues.

Evidence from studies by Bloch and his colleagues has provided additional support for the view that REM sleep may influence memory storage processes (Leconte *et al.*, 1973; Leconte and Hennevin, 1973). In these studies, rats were trained daily on an active avoidance task. During the early stages of training, REM sleep increased after each training session. The amount of REM sleep occurring after training decreased after the animals had learned the task but increased again if they were then taught a new task. Further, learning was retarded by depriving animals of REM sleep for several hours immediately after each training session. Similar findings have been reported by Pearlman and Becker (1973). It is not yet clear just what aspects of REM deprivation are responsible for the influence on retention. It might be that hormones released during REM sleep normally serve as memory storage modulators. There is some evidence that the learning deficit produced by REM sleep deprivation is related to a decrease in catecholamines. Hartmann and Stern (1972) reported that L-dopa (a precursor of dopamine and norepinephrine) attenuates the impairing effects of REM deprivation on retention.

Brain States and Individual Differences

Experimental studies of learning and memory generally focus on group differences—particularly those differences that can be attributed to differences in experimental treatments. A constant source of annoyance to the experimenters is the fact that individuals differ in their ability to learn and retain information. Animals of different ages and different strains and species differ in their behavior. Further, different animals are differentially affected by different experimental treatments. While it is clear why differences are sources of annoyance for those of us who are looking for general laws, it should also be clear that careful attention to individual differences might help us to understand the bases of our experimental treatments.

There is some evidence to suggest that individual differences in learning and retention are based on differences in brain functioning. Several studies have shown that, for example, learning ability declines with age (Gold *et al.*, 1975*c*; Gold and McGaugh, 1975*b*; Freund and Walker, 1971; Ray and Barrett, 1973). Older rats and mice seem to benefit selectively from spacing of training trials when many trials are given on a learning task (McGaugh and Cole, 1965; Oliverio and Bovet, 1966). Further, old rats are particularly susceptible to the facilitating and impairing effects, on retention, of posttraining drug administration (Doty and Doty, 1964, 1966). All of these findings suggest that there are age-related changes in the efficiency of memory storage processes—as well as an increased susceptibility to modulating influences. In some ways, old animals appear to be like animals with locus coeruleus lesions.

Current research in my laboratory has provided additional evidence that memory processes change with age (Gold and McGaugh, 1975*b*). In these studies, rats of 60 days, 1 year, and 2 years of age were trained on simple tasks (inhibitory avoidance and visual discrimination) and then given retention tests hours, days, or weeks later. Figure 5 shows the results of our studies of retention of an inhibitory avoidance response. Sixty-day-old animals show retention over a period of 6 weeks. One-year-old animals forget within 3 weeks and 2-year-old animals forget within a 1-week period. Figure 6 shows the results of our studies of retention of a visual discrimination response. As can be seen, the findings are similar to those obtained with the inhibitory task. Rate of forgetting appears to increase with age.

We do not know what processes are responsible for these age-related changes in forgetting. These changes might be due to numerous conditions associated with aging, including vascular changes and metabolic changes. However, it might be that the decline in retention is caused by a loss of specific endogenous processes, such as hormones and transmitters, which are involved in the modulation of memory storage. If the decline in memory is due to a loss

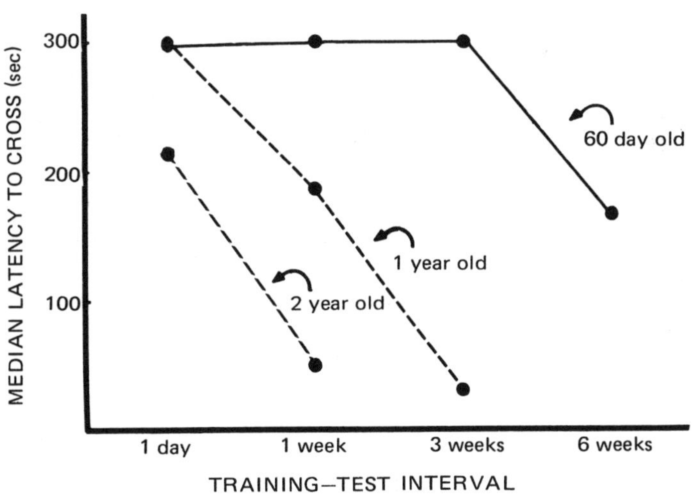

Figure 5. Retention performance of rats of three ages trained in an inhibitory avoidance task and retested 1 day, 1 week, 3 weeks, or 6 weeks later. Rate of forgetting varies directly with the age of the animals. From Gold and McGaugh (1975*b*).

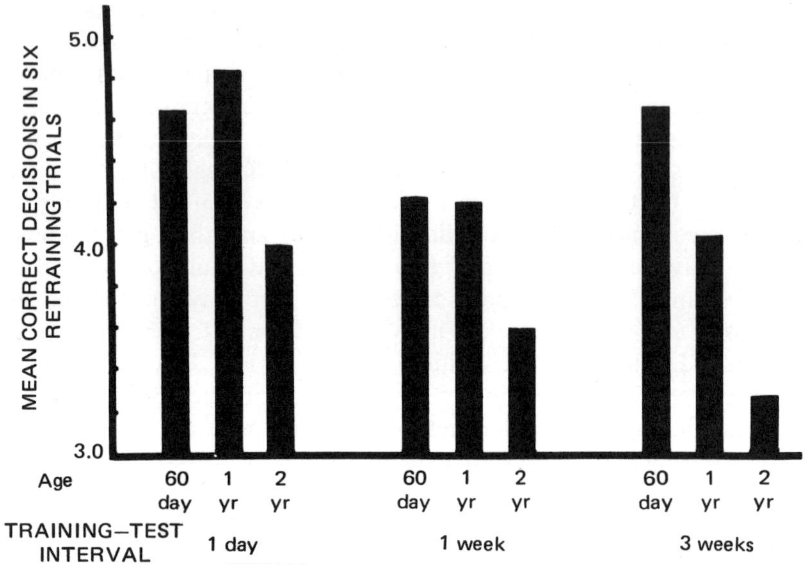

Figure 6. Retention performance of animals trained in a discriminated avoidance Y-maze and tested for retention 1 day, 1 week, or 3 weeks later. The retention measure was the number of correct choices on six test trials. The retention performance measured 3 weeks after training suggests that in this task, as in the inhibitory avoidance task, the rate of forgetting is directly related to the age of the animals. From Gold and McGaugh (1975*b*).

of specific substances, when it might be possible to attenuate the memory decline by resupplying the critical substances. To date, this possibility has not been extensively investigated. It is well worth considering whether other individual differences in learning and retention including strain differences as well as differences produced by brain damage and disease are due at least in part to differences in physiological processes which are involved in modulating memory storage.

Of Rats and People

All of the experiments I have reviewed in this chapter are based on studies using laboratory animals—mainly rats and mice. As I noted earlier in the chapter, however, most of the ideas or hypotheses or theories that led to this research originally came from observations of memory dysfunction in human patients. Our studies of rats' retention are generally consistent with the clinical observations of man's memory.

As yet, however, there have been very few studies of the effects of drugs, hormones, and brain stimulation on human memory. It seems reasonable to assume that findings based on studies using rats, mice, and monkeys should apply as well to people. Certainly it would be of considerable interest to know whether memory in humans—particularly those with disorders of memory—might be enhanced by drugs and hormones.

Recently Krech has argued that it is essential that we consider explicitly the implications of findings based on studies using laboratory animals for our understanding of human memory:

> Most of us . . . started our brain chemistry and behavior research with some people-based observation or intuition or hunch. We then, being experimental scientists, went on to our rats and pigeons and mice and goldfish. We did the best we knew how. Good. But this is my plea, let us venture forth again, let us be quicker than we have been to check out our rat-pigeon-goldfish-mouse findings on people. Let us not, in remaining away from man whence all our first hunches flow, suffocate in our animal laboratories. (Krech, 1972).

It may well be the proper time to take Krech's advice. Certainly there are many findings of recent studies of the kind I have summarized in this chapter which have clear implications for studies of human memory.

Cognition, Consolidation, and Complexity

It has been said (and emphasized by Krech) that there is no phenomenon, however complex, which when examined carefully will not turn out to be even more complex. This conclusion is certainly valid for the phenomenon (or phenomena) of memory. We think we are beginning to understand some of the processes which are involved in modulating the processes involved in storing new information—in consolidating cognition. As yet, however, we remain ignorant of almost all of the important issues concerning the neurobiology of memory (McGaugh, 1976). We do not know how information is selected for storage (why do we remember only some of our experiences?) We do not know where memories are stored in the nervous system and we do not know how the storage is accomplished. We do not know how memories are recalled. And we have developed no coherent explanation of the embarrassing facts of behavior revealed by Tolman and Lashley and their students.

Findings of studies of memory storage modulation may lead to an understanding of brain states which are favorable for information storage. The findings might also lead to the understanding of as well as the development of treatments for disorders of human memory. If so, our research with rats and mice will have served good purpose.

ACKNOWLEDGMENTS

I wish to thank my professor, David Krech, my colleague, Lew Petrinovich, and my many students for their contribution to the ideas and the research findings discussed in this chapter.

References

Amaral, D. G., and Foss, J. A. 1975. Locus coeruleus lesions and learning. *Science, 188,* 377.

Anlezark, G. M., Crow, T. J., and Greenway, A. P. 1973. Impaired learning and decreased cortical norepinephrine after bilateral locus coeruleus lesions. *Science, 181,* 682.

Benevento, L. A., and Kandel, G. L. 1967. Influence of strychnine on classically conditioned defensive reflexes in the cat. *Journal of Comparative and Physiological Psychology, 63,* 117–120.

Block, V. 1970. Facts and hypotheses concerning memory consolidation. *Brain Research, 24,* 561–575

Bovet, D., McCaugh, J. L., and Oliverio, A. 1966. Effects of post trial administration of drugs on avoidance learning of mice. *Life Sciences, 5,* 1309–1315.

Breen, R. A., and McGaugh, J. L. 1961. Facilitation of maze learning with posttrial injections of picrotoxin. *Journal of Comparatives and Physiological Psychology, 54,* 498–501.

Dawson, R. G., and McGaugh, J. L. 1973. Drug facilitation of learning and memory. In: *The Physiological Basis of Memory.* J. A. Deutsch. Academic Press, New York, pp. 77–111.

Denti, A., McGaugh, J. L., Landfield, P., and Shinkman, P. 1970. Facilitation of learning with posttrial stimulation of the reticular formation. *Physiology and Behavior, 5,* 659–662.

de Wied, D. 1974. Pituitary-adrenal system hormones and behavior. In: *The Neurosciences.* F. O. Schmitt and F. G. Worden (eds.). M.I.T. Press, Cambridge, Mass., pp. 653–666.

Doty, B. A., and Doty, L. A. 1964. Effect of age and chlorpromazine on memory consolidation. *Journal of Comparative and Physiological Psychology, 57,* 331–334.

Doty, B. A., and Doty, L. A. 1966. Facilitative effects of amphetamine on avoidance conditioning in relation to age and problem difficulty. *Psychopharmacologia, 9,* 234–241.

Duncan, C. P. 1949. The retroactive effect of electroshock on learning. *Journal of Comparative and Physiological Psychology, 42,* 32–44.

Fishbein, W., McGaugh, J. L., and Swarz, J. R. 1971. Retrograde amnesia: Electroconvulsive shock effects after termination of rapid eye movement sleep deprivation. *Science, 182,* 80–82.

Franchina, J. J., and Moore, M. H. 1968. Strychnine and the inhibition of previous performances. *Science, 160,* 903–904.

Freund, G., and Walker, D. W. 1971. The effect of aging on acquistion and retention of shuttle box avoidance in mice. *Life Sciences, 10,* 1343–1349.

Gerard, R. W. 1949. Physiology and psychiatry. *American Journal of Psychiatry, 106,* 161–173.

Gold, P. E. and McGaugh, J. L. 1975*a*. A single-trace, two-process view of memory storage processes. In: *Short-Term Memory*. D. Deutsch and J. A. Deutsch (eds.). Academic Press, New York, pp. 355–378.

Gold, P. E., and McGaugh, J. L. 1975*b*. Changes in learning and memory during aging. In: *Neurobiology of Aging*. J. M. Ordy and K. R. Brizzee (eds.). Plenum Press, New York, pp. 145–158.

Gold, P. E., and van Buskirk, R. B. 1975. Facilitation of time-dependent memory processes with posttrial epinephrine injections. *Behavioral Biology*, *13*, 145–153.

Gold, P. E., and van Buskirk, R. B. 1976*a*. Enhancement and impairment of memory processes with posttrial injections of adrenocorticotropic hormone. *Behavioral Biology*, *16*, 387–400.

Gold, P. E., and van Buskirk, R. 1976*b*. Hormonally mediated noradrenergic modulation of memory processes. In preparation.

Gold, P. E., and van Buskirk, R. B. 1977. Effects of posttrial hormone injections on memory processes. *Hormones and Behavior*, in press.

Gold, P. E., Macri, J., and McGaugh, J. L. 1973*a*. Retrograde amnesia gradients: Effects of direct cortical stimulation. *Science*, *179*, 1343–1345.

Gold, P. E., Macri, J., and McGaugh, J. L. 1973*b*. Retrograde amnesia produced by subseizure amygdala stimulation. *Behavioral Biology*, *9*, 671–680.

Gold, P. E., Zornetzer, S. F., and McGaugh, J. L. 1974. Electrical stimulation of the brain Effects on memory storage. In: *Advances in Psychobiology*, Vol. 2. G. Newton and A. Riesen (eds.). Wiley Interscience, New York, pp. 64–75.

Gold, P. E., Edwards, R. M., and McGaugh, J. L. 1975*a*. Amnesia produced by unilateral, subseizure, electrical stimulation of the amygdala in rats. *Behavioral Biology*, *15*, 95–105.

Gold, P. E., Hankins, L., Edwards, R. M., Chester, J., and McGaugh, J. L. 1975*b*. Memory interference and facilitation with posttrial amygdala stimulation: Effect on memory varies with footshock level. *Brain Research*, *86*, 509–513.

Gold, P. E., van Buskirk, R., and McGaugh, J. L. 1975*c*. Age-related changes in learning and memory. In: *Survey Report on the Aging Nervous System*. G. J. Maletta (Ed.). U.S. Government Printing Office, Washington, D.C., pp. 169–178.

Handwerker, M. J., Gold, P. E., and McGaugh, J. L. 1974. Impairment of active avoidance learning with posttraining amygdala stimulation. *Brain Research*, *75*, 324–327.

Hartmann, E., and Stern, W. C. 1972. Desynchronized sleep deprivation: Learning deficit and its reversal by increased catecholamines. *Physiology and Behavior*, *8*, 585–587.

Haycock, J. W., Deadwyler, S. A., Sideroff, S. I., and McGaugh, J. L. 1973. Retrograde amnesia and cholinergic systems in the caudate-putamen complex and dorsal hippocampus of the rat. *Experimental Neurology*, *41*, 201–213.

Haycock, J. W., van Buskirk, R. B., and McGaugh, J. L. 1976. Facilitation of retention with posttrial intraventricular administration of catecholamines. In preparation.

Hebb, D. O. 1949. *The Organization of Behavior*, Wiley, New York.

Hilgard, E. R. 1956. *Theories of Learning*, Appleton-Century-Crofts, New York.

Hudspeth, W. J. 1964. Strychnine: Its facilitating effect on the solution of a simple oddity problem by the rat. *Science*, *145*, 1331–1333.

Hull, C. L. 1951. *Essentials of Behavior*. Yale University Press, New Haven.

Hunt, E., and Krivanek, J. 1966. The effects of pentylenetetrazol and methylphenoxypropane on discrimination learning. *Psychopharmacologia*, *9*, 1–16.

Jarvik, M. E. 1972. Effects of chemical and physical treatments on learning and memory. *Annual Review of Psychology*, *23*, 457–486.

John, E. R. 1972. Statistical versus switchboard theories of memory. *Science*, *177*, 850–864.

Jouvet, M. 1967. Neurophysiology of the states of sleep. *Physiological Review, 47*, 117–177.

Kandel, E. R., and Spencer, W. A. 1968. Cellular neurophysiological approaches in the study of learning. *Physiological Review, 48*, 65–134.

Kesner, R. P., and Wilburn, M. W. 1974. A review of electrical stimulation of the brain in the context of learning and retention. *Behaviorial Biology, 10*, 259–293.

Kety, S. S. 1970. The biogenic amines in the central nervous system: Their possible roles in arousal, emotion, and learning. In: *The Neurosciences.* F. O. Schmitt (Ed.). Rockefeller University Press, New York, pp. 324–336.

Kety, S. S. 1972. Brain catecholamines, affective states and memory. In: *The Chemistry of Mood, Motivation, and Memory*, Vol. 4 of *Advances in Behavioral Biology.* J. L. McGaugh (Ed.). Plenum Press, New York, pp. 65–80.

Krech, D. 1972. Discussion. In: *The Chemistry of Mood, Motivation, and Memory*, Vol. 4 of *Advances in Behavioral Biology.* J. L. McGaugh (Ed.). Plenum Press, New York, pp. 217–223.

Krivanek, J., and McGaugh, J. L. 1968. Effects of pentylenetetrazol on memory storage in mice. *Psychopharmacologia, 12*, 303–321.

Krivanek, J. A., and McGaugh, J. L. 1969. Facilitating effects of pre- and posttrial amphetamine administration on discrimination learning in mice. *Agents and Actions, 1*, 36–42.

Landfield, P. W., Tusa, R., and McGaugh, J. L. 1973. Effects of posttrial hippocampal stimulation on memory storage and EEG activity. *Behavioral Biology, 8*, 485–505.

Lashley, K. S. 1917. The effects of strychnine and caffeine upon the rate of learning. *Psychobiology, 1*, 141–170.

Lashley, K. S. 1933. Integrative functions of the cerebral cortex. *Physiological Review, 13*, 1–42.

Lashley, K. S. 1949. Persistent problems in the evolution of mind. *Quarterly Review of Biology, 24*, 28–42.

Lashley, K. S. 1950. In search of the engram. In: *Symposium of the Society for Experimental Biology*, No. 4. Cambridge University Press, Cambridge, pp. 454–482.

Leconte, P., and Hennevin, E. 1973. Characteristiques temporelles de l'augmentation de sommeil paradoxal consecutif a l'apprentissage chez le rat. *Physiology and Behavior, 11*, 677–686.

Leconte, P., Hennevin, E., and Bloch, V. 1973. Analyse des effets d'un apprentissage et de son niveau d'acquisition sur le sommeil paradoxal consécutif. *Brain Research, 49*, 367–379.

Mayer-Gross, W. 1943. Retrograde amnesia. *Lancet, 2*, 603–605.

McDougall, W. 1901. Facilitative and disruptive effects of strychnine sulphate on maze learning. *Psychological Reports, 8*, 99–104.

McGaugh, J. L. 1959. Some neurochemical factors in learning. Ph.D. thesis. University of California, Berkeley.

McGaugh, J. L. 1961. Facilitative and disruptive effects of strychnine on maze learning. *Psychological Reports, 8*, 99–104.

McGaugh, J. L. 1966. Time-dependent processes in memory storage. *Science, 153*, 1351–1358.

McGaugh, J. L. 1968. Drug facilitation of memory and learning. In: *Psychopharmacology: A Review of Progress.* D. H. Efron *et al.* (Eds.). U.S. Government Printing Office, Washington, D.C., PHS Publ. No. 1836, pp. 891–904.

McGaugh, J. L. 1973. Drug facilitation of learning and memory. *Annual Review of Pharmacology, 13*, 229–241.
McGaugh, J. L. 1974. Electroconvulsive shock: Effects on learning and memory in animals. In: *Psychobiology of Convulsive Therapy*. M. Fink, S. S. Kety, J. L. McGaugh, and T. A. Williams (Eds.). V. H. Winston, Washington, D.C., pp. 85–97.
McGaugh, J. L. 1976. Neurobiological aspects of memory. In: *Biological Foundations of Psychiatry*. R. G. Grenell and S. Gabay (Eds.). Raven Press, New York, pp. 499–525.
McGaugh, J. L., and Cole, J. M. 1965. Age and strain differences in the effect of distribution of practice on maze learning. *Psychonomic Science, 2*, 253–254.
McGaugh, J. L., and Dawson, R. G. 1971. Modification of memory storage processes. In: *Animal Memory*. W. K. Honing and P. H. R. James (Eds.). Academic Press, New York, pp. 215–242.
McGaugh, J. L., and Gold, P. E. 1974. Conceptual and neurobiological issues in studies of treatments affecting memory storage. In: *The Psychology of Learning and Motivation*, Vol. 8. G. H. Bower (Ed.). Academic Press, New York, pp. 233–262.
McGaugh, J. L., and Gold, P. E. 1976. Modulation of memory processes with electrical stimulation of the brain. In: *Neural Mechanisms of Learning and Memory*. M. Rosenzweig and E. Bennett (Eds.). MIT Press, Cambridge, Mass., pp. 549–560.
McGaugh, J. L., and Herz, M. J. 1972. *Memory Consolidation*, Albion, San Francisco.
McGaugh, J. L., and Krivanek, J. 1970. Strychnine effects on discrimination learning in mice: Effects of dose and time of administration. *Physiology and Behavior, 5*, 1437–1442.
McGaugh, J. L., and Petrinovich, L. 1959. The effect of strychnine sulphate on maze-learning. *American Journal of Psychology 72*, 99–102.
McGaugh, J. L., and Petrinovich, L. F. 1965. Effects of drugs on learning and memory. *International Review of Neurobiology, 8*, 139–196.
McGaugh, J. L., and Thomson, C. W. 1962. Facilitation of simultaneous discrimination learning with strychnine sulphate. *Psychopharmacologia, 3*, 166–172.
McGaugh, J. L., Westbrook, W. H., and Thomson, C. W. 1961. Strain differences in the facilitative effects of 5-5-diphenyl-1-3-diazadamantan-6-ol (1757 I.S.) on maze learning. *Journal of Comparative and Physiological Psychology, 54*, 502–505.
McGaugh, J. L., Thomson, C. W., Westbrook, W. H., and Hudspeth, W. J., 1962. A further study of learning facilitation with strychnine sulphate. *Psychopharmacologia, 3*, 352–360.
McGaugh, J. L., Gold, P. E., van Buskirk, R. B., and Haycock, J. W. 1975. Modulating influences of hormones and catecholamines on memory storage processes. In: *Hormones, Homeostasis and the Brain*, Vol. 42 of *Progress in Brain Research*. W. H. Gispen, van Wimersma, T. B. Greidanus, B. Bohus, and D. de Wied (Eds.). Elsevier, Amsterdam, pp. 151–162.
Meligeni, J. A., Ledergerber, S. A., and McGaugh, J. L. 1975. Reversal of diethyldithiocarbamate induced amnesia by norepinephrine. In: *Neuroscience Abstracts*. Society for Neuroscience, Bethesda, Md., p. 514.
Miller, N. E. 1959. Liberalization of basic S-R concepts: Extension to conflict behavior, motivation, and social learning. In: *Psychology: A Study of a Science*, Vol. 2. S. Koch (Ed.). McGraw-Hill, New York, pp. 196–292.
Mueller, G. E., and Pilzecker, A. 1900. Experimentelle Beitrage zur Lehre vom Gedachtniss. *Zeitschrift fuer Psychologie, 1*, 1–288.
Oliverio, A. 1968. Effects of nicotine and strychnine on transfer of avoidance learning in the mouse. *Life Sciences, 7*, 1163–1167.

Oliverio, A., and Bovet, D. 1966. Effects of age on maze learning and avoidance conditioning of mice. *Life Sciences*, *5*, 1317–1324.

Osborne, R. H., and Kerkut, G. A. 1972. Inhibition of noradrenalin biosynthesis and its effects on learning in rats. *Comparative and General Pharmacology*, *3*, 359–362.

Paré, W. 1961. The effect of caffeine and seconal on a visual discrimination task. *Journal of Comparative and Physiological Psychology*, *54*, 506–509.

Pearlman, C., and Becker, M. 1973. Brief posttrial REM sleep deprivation impairs discrimination learning in rats. *Physiological Psychology*, *1*, 373–376.

Petrinovich, L. F. 1963. Facilitation of successive discrimination learning by strychnine sulphate. *Psychopharmacologia*, *4*, 103–113.

Petrinovich, L. F. 1967. Drug facilitation of learning: Strain differences. *Psychopharmacologia*, *10*, 375–378.

Petrinovich, L., and Bolles, R. 1957. Delayed alternation: Evidence for symbolic processes in the rat. *Journal of Comparative and Physiological Psychology*, *50*, 363–365.

Petrinovich, L., Bradford, D., and McGaugh, J. L. 1965. Drug facilitation of memory in rats. *Psychonomic Science*, *2*, 191–192.

Randt, C. T., Quartermain, D., Goldstein, M., and Anagnoste, B. 1971. Norepinephrine biosynthesis inhibition: Effects on memory in mice. *Science*, *172*, 498–499.

Ray, O. S., and Barrett, R. J. 1973. Interaction of learning and memory with age in the rat. In: *Psychopharmacology and Aging*. C. Eisdorfer and W. E. Fann (Eds.). Plenum Press, New York, pp. 17–39.

Routtenberg, A., and Holzman, N. 1973. Memory disruption by electrical stimulation of substantia nigra, pars compacta. *Science*, *181*, 83–86.

Russell, W. R. and Nathan, P. W. 1946. Traumatic amnesia. *Brain*, *69*, 280–300.

Sideroff, S., Bueno, O., Hirsch, A., Weyand, T., and McGaugh, J. L. 1974. Retrograde amnesia initiated by low-level stimulation of hippocampal cytoarchitectonic areas. *Experimental Neurology*, *43*, 285–297.

Stein, L., Belluzzi, J. D., and Wise, C. D. 1975. Memory enhancement by central administration of norepinephrine. *Brain Research*, *84*, 329–335.

Tolman, E. C. 1932. *Purposive Behavior in Animals and Men*. Century, New York.

Tolman, E. C. 1948. Cognitive maps in rats and men. *Psychological Review*, *55*, 189–208.

Tolman, E. C. 1951. *Collected Papers in Psychology*. University of California Press, Berkeley, 289 pages.

Tolman, E. C., and Brunswik, E. 1935. The organism and the causal texture of the environment. *Psychological Review*, *42*, 43–77.

Tolman, E. C., and Honzik, C. H. 1930. Introduction and removal of reward, and maze performance in rats. *University of California Publications in Psychology*, *4*, 338–342.

van Buskirk, R. B., Haycock, J. W., Gold, P. E., and McGaugh, J. L. 1976. Modification of memory processes in rats by diethyldithiocarbamate and fusaric acid. In preparation.

Westbrook, W. H., and McGaugh, J. L. 1964. Drug facilitation of latent learning, *Psychopharmacologia*, *5*, 440–446.

Wyers, E. J., Peeke, H. V. S., Williston, J. S., and Herz, M. J. 1968. Retroactive impairment of passive avoidance learning by stimulation of the caudate nucleus. *Experimental Neurology*, *22*, 350–366.

Zalmanson, A. N. 1929. Conditioned defense reflexes after local poisoning of the cortical motor centers with strychnine and cocaine. *Vysshaya Nervnaya Deyatel'nost*, Moscow, GIZ, 39–48 (*Psychological Abstracts*, *8*, 1943, 21).

Zornetzer, S. F. 1974. Retrograde amnesia and brain seizures in rodents: Electrophysiological and neuroanatomical analyses. In: *The Psychobiology of Convulsive Therapy*.

M. Fink, S. S. Kety, J. L. McGaugh, and T. A. Williams (Eds.). V. H. Winston, Washington, D.C.

Zornetzer, S. F., and Gold, M. S. 1975. Effects of locus coeruleus lesions on the susceptibility of labile memory to disruption. In: *Neuroscience Abstracts.* Society for Neuroscience, Bethesda, Md., p. 821.

6

Thomas H. Roderick, Richard E. Wimer, and Cynthia C. Wimer

GENETIC MANIPULATION OF NEUROANATOMICAL TRAITS

I detect no beginnings of a unified theory of learning, and general laws thereof. If and when we do arrive at a reasonably respectable theory and reasonably general laws, they will encompass both behavioral and physiological variables, with different weights for each variable and for each species and perhaps for each individual.

—David Krech

It was probably in 1954 at the Berkeley Faculty Club, around the large table in the middle of the dining room, where there gathered regularly for lunch an exciting conglomeration of individuals representing a variety of academic disciplines, mutually attracted to each other for who knows what reasons, that David Krech held forth on his new research forays into the field of brain chemistry and behavior. Imagine his enthusiasm! . . . the vast horizons opening up with elucidation of the biochemical basis of behavioral patterns; imagine the responses! . . . some looking up, others with eyes steadfast on their soup bowls. Probably Everett Dempster from the Department of Genetics at least raised his eyebrows, for his interests were vast and specifically encompassed the question of the extent of genetic variation in the causes of behavioral variation. Krech, persisting, undoubtedly continued telling of Melvin Calvin's interest in the problem and the already significant scientific role Edward Bennett was taking in the biochemistry of the visual and somesthetic areas of the rat brain.

Thomas H. Roderick • The Jackson Laboratory, Bar Harbor, Maine. *Richard E. Wimer and Cynthia C. Wimer* • Division of Neurosciences, City of Hope National Medical Center, Duarte, California.

Krech probably said directly to Dempster that he also ought to take an active part in the behavioral or biochemical studies of this new team, because, after all, look at the tremendous insight psychologist Robert Tryon gave behaviorists through his genetic manipulation of maze performance.

Dempster had a new student (T.H.R.) who at the time was playing somewhat aimlessly with Drosophila. This student's main interests were evolution and mammalian genetics, ideal interests for the Krech team. In any case, it was within 2 weeks that the student set out from Hilgard Hall to the Life Science Building to meet this man Krech and to experience more of the excitement that Dempster had imparted. All meetings with Krech left this student about one-third cowed, one-third encouraged, and one-third inspired. The mix was probably appropriate and, in any case, the first meeting was successful. It began an adventure into interdisciplinary research on an exciting frontier with professors and graduate students who in some cases remain collaborators over 20 years later.

The influence of Robert Tryon's previous work on both geneticists and psychologists made a selection program a certainty sooner or later. So it began: two-way selection for acetylcholinesterase activity in the visual and somesthetic areas of the rat brain. It was surprisingly successful and it provided the extreme biochemical phenotypes which were ultimately tested for their visual and spatial preferences in the Krech hypothesis box. Concomitant with the selection study was a study of the F_2 *between two inbred strains, high and low in cholinesterase activity, respectively. The* F_2 *showed the phenotypic variation expected for cholinesterase activity but surprisingly, in the light of the hypothesis, showed no correlation between enzyme activity and spatial preference in Krech's hypothesis box. But by that time the first generation had already responded dramatically to selection, and the genetics of brain chemistry was exciting in itself. Further along the way other behaviors, such as spontaneous activity, were studied, but none clearly showed an association with cholinesterase activity.*

The student geneticist left Berkeley with his Ph.D. and his wife, a top technician and sometime coauthor in Bennett's lab. His research experience had been exceptional because of both the personal and the scientific association with Krech and others of the team. It had also left him with a surprising finding of a tremendous phenotypic variation in brain chemistry, and particularly that 70% of it was due to additive genetic variation. This was about as high a heritability as has ever been reported. Why was there such high genetic control over the variation in acetylcholinesterase activity in the brain? What were the functional, behavioral, and evolutionary implications of such a fact? Was this also true for other traits of the brain, anatomical as well as chemical? If no unequivocal behavioral effects could be found from altering fundamental neurochemical traits in the brain, could they be found from altering anatomical traits within the brain? Would characteristics of brain anatomy also respond easily to selection pressure?

The collaborative association of two psychologists (R. E. W. and C. C. W.) with the geneticist began at The Jackson Laboratory, Bar Harbor, Maine. The ease and the enthusiasm with which the association developed were based in part on one of the psychologists (R. E. W.) having spent a graduate year at Berkeley, where he met and heard both David Krech and Robert Tryon, and also based on both psychologists' common graduate training at McGill University, where Donald Hebb's zeal permeated the department—making all research an adventure. To the collaboration T. H. R. brought his experience in genetic techniques and his Krech-inspired interest in relationships between brain and behavior; R. E. W. brought a commitment to the study of biological variables underlying individual differences in behavior and a desire to exploit genetic materials in the study of these differences; and C. C. W. brought an interest in applying the concepts and techniques of psychometrics to the study of individual differences.

This chapter is both a summary and an appraisal of the results of 10 years of collaborative research effort between a geneticist interested in behavior and two pyschologists interested in genetics. The research in which we collaborated entailed the study of neuroanatomical traits in the house mouse, and the determination of associated differences in behavior.

There are many important questions concerning genetics and behavior. One that is fundamental to our understanding of evolution concerns the extent to which behaviorally variable traits, particularly those within the so-called normal range of variability, are due to genetic variability among individuals. Further, there is the question of the nature of behavioral traits which have a high genetic component. Because they are relevant to the understanding of behavior, the above questions can be asked of neurochemical and neuroanatomical traits as well. Further, there is the question of whether genetic manipulation can be employed to bring about alterations in neurobiological traits which exhibit high genetic variability such that their causation and function might be clarified by examination of correlated responses in other traits. We were attempting to use genetic manipulation, particularly selective breeding, to produce controlled variability in brain morphology in order that this last question might be examined.

The actual initiating stimulus was provided by Storer, whose interests in longevity had led him to collect data on the brain weights of house mice from 18 inbred strains. He found highly significant and substantial strain differences (Storer, 1967). This provided evidence at the outset that there should be appreciable genetic variability for at least some gross neuroanatomical traits. Storer's work was also directive, for it suggested a "twenty-questions" research strategy beginning with what could be established with respect to gross morphological characteristics of the central nervous system and proceeding sequentially to successively finer aspects on the basis of the answer to the previous "question."

The idealized program to manipulate neuroanatomical traits would have three major characteristics. First, the population of animals would possess abundant genetic and phenotypic variability. From our point of view, it did not matter too much whether the genetic variability was based on a few or many genes so long as a sizable phenotypic alteration could be achieved in a relatively short time, i.e., so long as much of the phenotypic variation was genetic in origin and additive in nature. The means of Storer's strains appeared to distribute across a broad range, and this, with the relatively small within-strain variability, was evidence for both a substantial genetic contribution and the involvement of many genes. All that was necessary was that a good part of this genetic variation be additive rather than epistatic (i.e., not dependent on an interaction involving very specific combinations of genes present at different loci). Second, the genes acting in concert would specify precise interpretable variations in specific nervous system morphology. Finally, all associated behavioral differences would be dramatic, easily measured and defined, and informative. The degree of departure from these most desirable characteristics could not, unfortunately, be determined in advance.

The first two "questions" were defined in terms of these desirable characteristics. The first question was whether there is a substantial amount of usable genetic variation associated with size of the brain and with size of the specific portions of the central nervous system. The second question was whether there are any detectable associated differences in behavior. The answers were, as we shall next show, generally encouraging.

The First Question: Is There a Substantial Amount of Usable Genetic Variation Associated with Size of the Brain and Some of Its Divisions and What Is the Nature of the Variation?

A foundation population from which one begins a selective breeding program should have substantial genetic variability. One way to achieve this is to use an outbreeding feral population as a foundation stock. Another way is to form a foundation stock from crosses of a sufficient number of inbred strains which are as genetically independent as possible. The argument here is that genetically independent strains are themselves random samples of a hypothetical genetically heterogeneous population. Eight strains which were both reasonably accessible to other investigators and as genetically independent as possible were chosen. Lack of appreciable common ancestry among the strains was determined from articles concerning their early origins (Staats, 1966). Figure 1a shows the strains and the manner in which they were crossed to produce the first foundation stock.

Mechanics of the Selection Process

In the foundation population, two litters (first litters from two mating pairs) were selected at random and crossed such that the males of one were mated to the females of the other and *vice versa.* When most of the matings had produced two litters, the parents were killed with carbon dioxide and their brains were removed and weighed immediately. Details of the dissection are given in an earlier paper (Roderick *et al.*, 1973). At this time, the animals were usually between 100 and 150 days of age—a time of relative stability in brain weight. The criterion for selection was the rank of the midparent value for brain weight, i.e., the mean of the brain weights of each mating pair. Offspring of the two highest mating pairs were saved for mating for the next generation and constituted the first generation of the high line. Similarly, the offspring of the two lowest pairs were saved for mating and constituted the first generation of the low line. We decided not to choose parents for the control line from the remaining matings because that would essentially be selecting the intermediate values in the initial generation. Instead, matings were made up from the second litters of the two original mating pairs, and

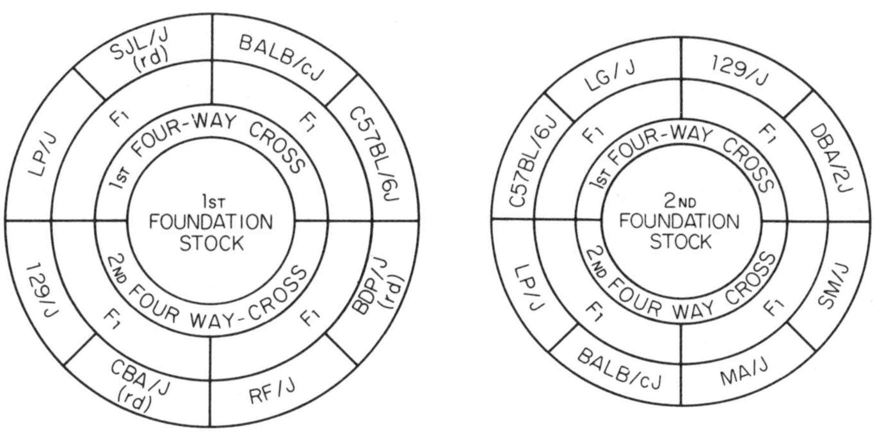

Figure 1. Two foundation populations formed by crossing separate strains in a specific manner. Three of the strains which made up the first foundation stock were homozygous for retinal degeneration (*rd*). All strains making up the second foundation population had normal retinas.

two mating pairs for the control line were chosen randomly from them. This trio of lines constituted a high, a control, and a low line, respectively, and was called Selection 6 (Sel-6) because it was the sixth selection program in our laboratory. A concurrent replication was run. In order to accomplish this, another trio of lines was set up from two other mating pairs in the foundation stock and was called Selection 7 (Sel-7). Two mating pairs were usually chosen within each selected line, and therefore a double first cousin breeding scheme was generally used in each generation (Roderick, 1960). In later generations, there were not always enough offspring from only two selected matings and sometimes the offspring of a third, fourth, or more mating pairs were used as well. In such cases, a round-robin mating scheme was used to minimize inbreeding. That is, females of family 1 were mated to males of family 2, females of family 2 were mated to males of family 3, and so forth until the circle was completed. When these deviations were necessary, the pair with the next midparent rank was chosen, and thus there were occasions for some between-litter selection. The means for each generation were calculated from the means of the midparent values of all sacrificed pairs in that line and generation. The selection differentials were calculated from the unweighted means of all selected pairs whether they contributed offspring to the next generation or not.

Responses to Selection for Brain Weight

Figures 2 and 3 show the results of selection for brain weight. The point for each generation usually represented means of at least eight mating pairs (16 individuals) except for later generations in the selected line, when some means were based on as many as 25 midparents because of so much sterility. Selection response in both experiments was immediate and extensive. The ranges of individual brain weights of the high lines were virtually apart from the ranges of the low lines by the third selected generation. The ranges of the selected lines were distinct from those of the controls at about generation 12 in Sel-6 and a little later in Sel-7. Realized heritabilities for the separation of the lines in five generations were 0.53 in Sel-6 and 0.74 in Sel-7. These values are close to those for genetic determination (0.62–0.67) found in our study of variation between and within inbred strains (Roderick *et al.*, 1973) and suggest that the great portion of the variation there must also have been additive.

Except for the high line in Sel-6, one can see evidence for a plateauing of response in later generations. The response in Sel-6 was greater in both directions than that in Sel-7, and responses in both experiments were approximately symmetrical. The brains of animals of the high lines were ultimately 50% heavier than those of the lows. That difference amounted to about 0.2 g. Brain weights of extreme individuals of the high lines were well over twice the weights of extremes in the low lines.

All these descriptions reveal the rather dramatic response to selection despite the fact that the need to mate animals prior to measurement reduced the potential selection differential considerably. A part of the answer to the first question, then, is that a great deal of genetic variability was available in the foundation population and that much of it for brain weight was additive and therefore usable in selective breeding.

There was evidence for other sources of variation as well. Quite obvious in several places, particularly in Sel-6, is the simultaneous upward or downward shift of all the lines in consecutive generations, even as the lines continued to separate from each other. At this time, we can only speculate about

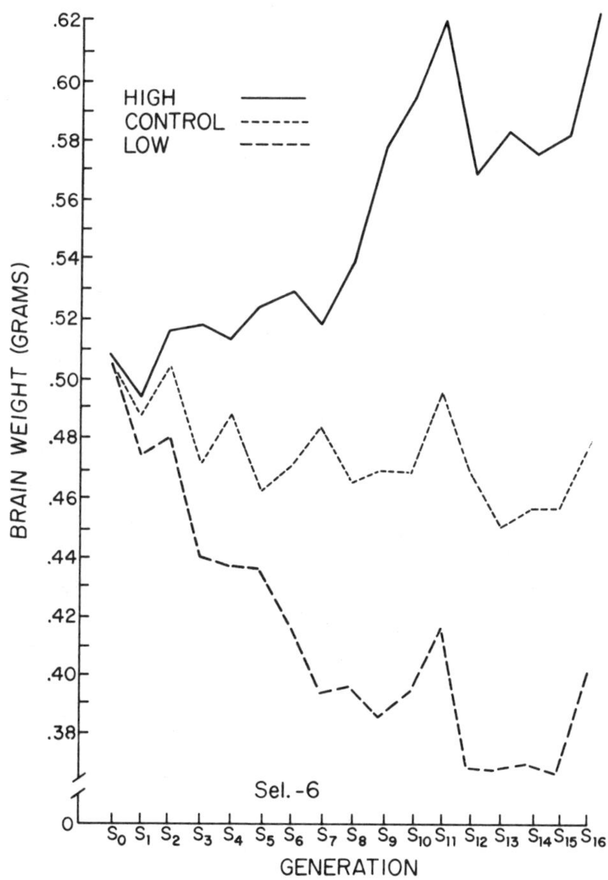

Figure 2. Selection 6: Selection for brain weight from the first foundation population.

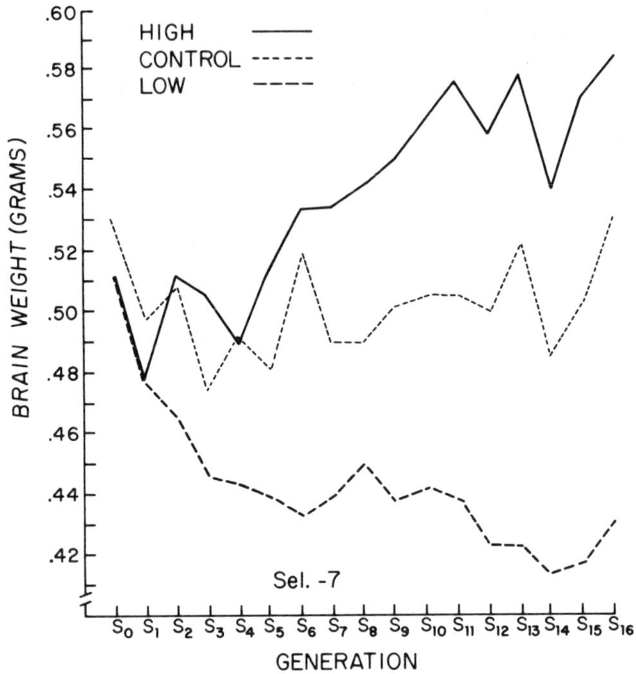

Figure 3. Selection 7: An independent replication of selection for brain weight also from the first foundation population. This experiment was run concurrently with Selection 6.

the environmental factors that cause these shifts. Some of it could be attributable to slight differences in ages of animals between generations. Possibly some of it is ascribable to changes in technical assistance from time to time, although we were careful to attempt to maintain a consistency in our techniques. Other parts of it may be due to rather important seasonal or daily weather conditions which are unknown at present. We could not ascribe any of it to necessary but slight improvements in laboratory conditions over the course of this program. The slight gradual decline in the means of both control lines, particularly in the early generations of Sel-7 and throughout the experiment in Sel-6, suggests an effect of inbreeding depression. The increase in the inbreeding coefficient, however, was only about 6% per generation.

There was a significant decline in fertility in both low lines around the seventh generation of selection and in the high line of Sel-6 around generation 10. The problem was so severe that there was danger of losing the lines even with relaxation of selection pressure.

Because of the fertility problem and because of our desire to see if we could exceed the incipient plateaus, we crossed the lines of the two experiments in generation 11: high by high, control by control, and low by low, respectively, with no lapse in the selection pressure. The breeding and selection procedures were continued in the same manner in these hybrid populations, which were now called Sel-16.

Figure 4 shows the results of further selective breeding from these crosses. Included in the figure are the values of the parental lines for one generation prior to and after the cross. Although there was immediate recovery of fertility, a further substantial change in brain weight beyond that already achieved did not occur. These results indicate that many of the same genes had been selected in both original experiments and that most of the additive genetic variation had been exhausted by generation 11.

During the course of these experiments, it was discovered that some

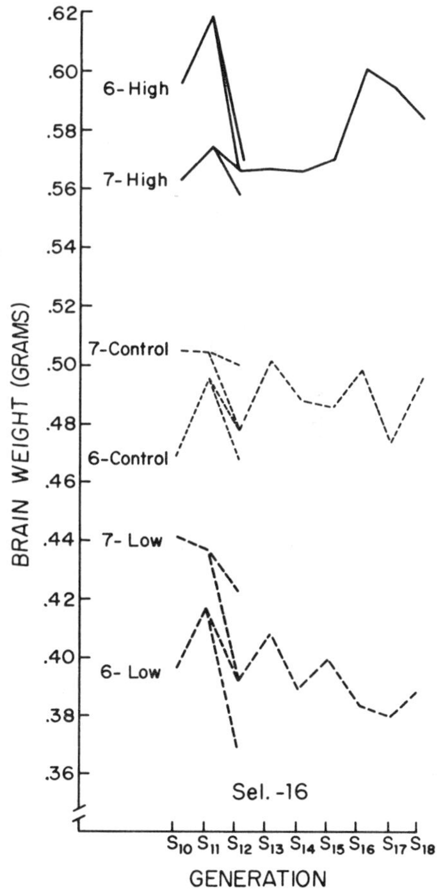

Figure 4. Continued selection for brain weight after crossing the lines of Sel-6 and Sel-7, respectively. This experiment was called Sel-16.

animals from the selected lines behaved as if they were incapable of learning in a visual performance test. Subsequent histological study revealed that they had imperfect retinas, caused by a recessive condition known as retinal degeneration (*rd/rd*; Sidman and Green, 1965). We found three of the lines making up the first foundation stock to have the condition. By the time we recognized this problem, some of the selected lines were already fixed for this condition or nearly so. Thus selection against it was of no avail. At this time, we formed the second foundation stock (Figure 1*b*) from eight genetically independent strains, all of which were known to be free of the *rd* condition. From this stock, we began another selection program for brain weight (Sel-17) and others to be described later. It is sufficient for the purposes of this chapter to say that the response to selection in Sel-17 was very similar to that in Sel-6 and Sel-7.

Correlated Responses to Selection for Brain Weight

Traits other than the trait selected which respond either positively or negatively during the course of selection are said to have shown a correlated response. The trait is then known as a correlated character. In a selection experiment, it is necessary to distinguish true correlated characters from those which change during the course of selection for reasons other than a genetic correlation with the selected trait. Genetic drift in a small population, for example, could account for a spurious change in another trait (Falconer, 1960). If a trait always changes with the selected trait in repeated selection experiments, there is fairly good evidence for a true correlated response. Further corroboration of a genetic association can be obtained by examining the correlation of the traits among single individuals in a genetically heterogeneous population.

Correlated responses are important to ascertain, for they can provide clues about other traits which are in the same causative pathway (developmental or physiological) as the selected trait. On the other hand, characters might be outside a narrowly defined causative pathway but be correlated because both are influenced independently by some of the same initial gene effects. At best, we hoped for no correlated characters except those concerned with brain weight and its developmental or physiological consequences. The extent to which that was not the case and to which unknown characters outside this pathway influenced behavior were the extent of the weakness in this experimental approach. A similar remark can be made concerning *any* genetic approach. We were particularly concerned, therefore, with discovering possible correlated traits which were not in the causative pathway from genes to brain weight to behavior, but which themselves might have affected the behaviors which we studied.

Body weight was a positively correlated character both in Sel-6 and, to a lesser degree, in Sel-7. In Sel-6, the high, control, and low selected lines showed the same rank order in body weight from generation 3 onward. By generation 16, the mean body weights of those lines were 54.4, 43.2, and 31.8 g, respectively. The response was similar but occurred later in Sel-7. The selected high and low lines showed a similar rank order in body weight from generation 5 onward, but the control line was above the high line in body weight until generation 7, after which it generally fell between the selected lines but still very close to the high line. By generation 16, the mean body weights of those lines were 40.6, 37.6, and 26.2 g, respectively.

Spinal cords were dissected out, weighed, and measured (Roderick *et al.*, 1973) to determine whether other parts of the central nervous system were responding to selection for brain weight. For Sel-6, the mean weights of spinal cords for generation 15 of the high, control, and low lines were 0.1677, 0.1359, and 0.1152 g, respectively. Mean lengths of spinal cords were 4.50, 4.23, and 3.74 mm, respectively. There was almost no overlap between the lines in midparent values of spinal cord weights and lengths. The similar values for Sel-7 were 0.1606, 0.1474, and 0.0984 g and 4.42, 4.27, and 3.80 mm, respectively. The same generalization can be made about the nature of distributions in Sel-7 except for the spinal cord lengths of the high and control lines, which overlapped considerably.

Hagerich (1968) studied animals in the twelfth generation of Sel-6 and Sel-7 in order to determine whether weight differences were associated with changes in volume or in density. She removed the brains, embedded them in paraffin, cut them into frontal sections 15 μm thick, and mounted them on glass slides. The sections were stained with cresyl violet and luxol fast blue. Coded slides were examined and the density of cells in the neocortex was determined by means of projections of photographs on a grid at specified magnifications. Using other animals, she dropped fresh brains into distilled water in 10-ml graduated cylinders and employed a graduated syringe to measure the volume of water that the brains displaced. She found the brains of mice of the high lines to have greater volume than those of mice of the low lines. Because she found no differences in the density of cells in the neocortex between the selected lines, she concluded that cell number and not cell size was the determining factor. Preliminary studies of the relation between whole brain DNA and brain weight by Dravid *et al.* (1972) also suggested that the variations in brain weight originated largely in cell number. Gould (1966) studied brains from the selected lines to see if there were changes in the proportions of certain component structures of the brain. He removed the brains, stained them, and sectioned them coronally. Enlarged tracings of the sections were made with the aid of a projecting microscope. Areas of different brain regions were then measured with a polar planimeter. He examined 30 sections per brain. Although he found significant differences between the lines for all areas measured, he found no difference in the ratio of any of the component structures to the total brain.

We consider the above findings to be preliminary and plan to do further work on correlated responses. Our tentative conclusion is that selection for brain weight has also altered body weight and spinal cord weight and length. Selection for brain weight has altered the volume of the brain as well. The changes in brain weight have apparently been brought about mostly by changes in cell number and not in cell size. Although brains of inbred strains differ dramatically in the relative proportions of components of the brain (R. Wimer *et al.*, 1969), the proportionality within the brains of animals of the selected lines appears to have remained about the same.

Selection for Ratio Phenotypes

Whether the brain could be altered in weight and size was a very general question, but the first one which we wished to ask. General, though somewhat more precise, questions concerning specific portions of the central nervous system remained. Could portions be exaggerated or diminished by selective breeding? Our study of brain weight suggested that selection for absolute weight or volume of any component or portion of the brain would result in simultaneous proportional alteration of all components of the brain. Therefore, it seemed reasonable to breed for relative proportions of certain components, although we suspected in advance that this might be a more difficult adjustment for the brain to accommodate and that there might be far less additive genetic variance for such proportions.

Two structures, the neocortex and the hippocampus, were chosen for study because of their great interest with respect to brain function and behavior and because of the relative ease of defining their boundaries in sectional material. The methods for preparing and measuring these structures were similar to those of Gould (1966) mentioned earlier and are given in detail in a previous report (R. Wimer *et al.*, 1969). Briefly, the brains were cut into 10-μm sections and the sampling points were the three sections corresponding to 25, 50. and 75% of the total longitudinal length of the structure as estimated by the number of sections. The areas of the brain structures were measured with a planimeter and the volume of each structure was estimated. The ratio score for each animal was the estimated volume of the structure divided by the estimated volume of the total "brain" (see below). The study of nine inbred strains revealed a genetic determination of 0.39 for the proportion of neocortex to total "brain" and 0.25 for the proportion of hippocampus to total "brain." The genetic determination, estimated this way, is comprised of dominance and epistatic genetic variance as well as the usable additive genetic variance. These estimates were sufficiently high, however, to make us believe there was some additive genetic variance which could be utilized in a selective breeding program. Two more foundation populations were derived from the second foundation stock (Figure 1), and the two independent selection programs were begun. We used the same breeding scheme as that employed in the experiments involving brain weight. A statistically significant divergence of the high and low lines was achieved in both selection programs in the first generation. However, these separations disappeared in subsequent generations, and significant separation of the lines was never achieved thereafter. This was a particular disappointment because the structures are of considerable interest to us and because measuring the criterion for each animal was expensive and tedious. The experiments were terminated and the lines were discarded.

We wished to pursue the selection for proportionality a bit further. So we considered again another question about total brain weight. It had been suggested by Krompecher and Lipak (1966) that the ratio of brain weight to spinal cord weight might be a more sensitive predictor of behavorial capacity than absolute brain weight. It seemed possible that selection for such a ratio might not produce a correlated response for body weight. We estimated the genetic correlation between brain and spinal cord weight to be +0.60 (Roderick *et al.*, 1973), which meant that there was a substantial part of their genetic variance that these two major divisions of the central nervous system did not share. We had found that the coefficient of genetic determination of their ratio was about 0.30–0.35, which also left room for the possibility of usable additive genetic variance. We therefore established Sel-18, a selection program for ratio of brain weight to spinal cord weight, from the second foundation population. The same procedures were used as in previous selection experiments. The midparent values were calculated as the means of the individual ratios of the pair. Figure 5 shows the results of selection. A rather consistent difference developed between the high and low lines, although the two control lines equaled or exceeded both selected lines in several instances. We also examined the possibility of correlated responses in body weight, brain weight, and spinal cord weight. The two control lines and selected lines did not behave in any consistent or orderly pattern which would have indicated that a correlated response had occurred for these traits.

Comment

Studies of brain weight provide an ample basis for optimism with regard to our future ability to manipulate at least some of the component traits

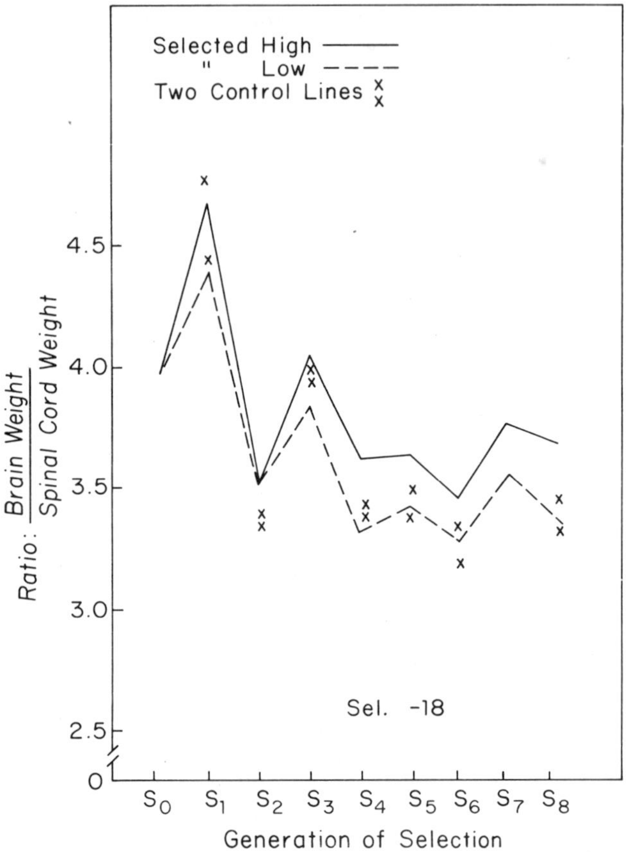

Figure 5. Selection for the ratio of brain weight to spinal cord weight.

which underlie it. Heritability is high and many loci appear to be involved. Results for ratio phenotypes, however, need not necessarily be viewed as a comparable occasion for pessimism. On the basis of studies of inbred strains (Roderick *et al.*, 1973; R. Wimer *et al.*, 1969), we *know* that identifiable genetic control exists for the sizes of some specific portions of the central nervous system. Further, selective breeding for the ratio of brain weight to weight of the spinal cord was moderately successful and might have achieved a much greater separation with continued selection. More sophisticated techniques for determining the selection criterion, techniques based on the genetic variances and covariances of the component phenotypes, might have been employed. The question of the manipulability of ratio traits, then, has not been completely answered.

The Second Question: Are There Detectable Associated Differences in Behavior?

The value of selective breeding is that it has the potential to exaggerate a phenotypic mean well beyond the normal range found in genetically heterogeneous natural populations. Therefore, any subtle correlated responses, particularly in behavior, might be exaggerated as well and thus be made more discernible. Further, a larger amount of measurement error is tolerable in the comparison of phenotypic extremes than is in the assessment of individuals within the normal range of variability.

But selective breeding as an approach to understanding mechanisms has two intrinsic difficulties which detract from simple interpretations of relationships of traits. The first is the problem of associated responses in nongenetically related traits. Changes in such adventitiously associated traits can come about by genetic drift, particularly when there is a limited number of pairs of parental mice (in our case usually two or three pairs) selected to produce all the progeny for the ensuing generation in each line. Thus there is a good possibility for random fixation or loss of alleles associated with various biochemical, morphological, or physiological traits which go unnoticed but which have significant consequences for behavior. In comparing our selected lines, we might then observe a spurious association between our selected trait and a behavioral trait. One way around this problem is to conduct several simultaneous replications of the selection experiment, because a true genetically correlated trait should respond consistently in all replications. Selection experiments are expensive, so this is an impractical solution. A better way to verify that these associations are truly genetic is to examine both traits in a genetically heterogeneous population, where the phenotypic association should persist, although possibly not so obviously because the selected trait is not exaggerated there. To employ this strategy of confirmation requires a higher level of behavioral reliability, which might not be attainable.

The second difficulty with this approach, and with a genetic approach in general, is that a genetically correlated character outside a causative pathway of specific interest might itself influence behavior. We call these characters "indirectly conjoined traits." For example, in our brain weight studies one must consider the possibility that body weight, the indirectly conjoined trait, has an influence on behaviors that we studied. A study of a genetically heterogeneous population will not help clarify the matter, as it would simply confirm the presence of a genetic association between the traits. One is left with looking for the most likely indirectly conjoined traits and, at best, proving they did not change and therefore could have had no effect in any observed behavioral changes. What would be most desirable for clear interpretation and insight into mechanisms would be to find only "directly conjoined traits," i.e., those correlated characters which fall directly in the causative pathway from genes to brain to behavior.

The Brain Weight Trait

The first behavioral studies of mice in the selection experiment for brain weight utilized mice of the third generation of selection (C. Wimer and Prater, 1966). Brains were removed and weighed upon completion of behavioral testing. The numbers of mice employed and the mean weights of brains of mice of the various groups with standard deviations are shown in Table 1. The difference in brain weight between the high and low lines was already highly significant ($F = 98.76$, df $= 1/51$, $P < 0.01$). The major behavioral results of interest were those obtained from an open-field activity test and from brightness discrimination learning performance in the water maze (R. Wimer and Weller, 1965; Waller *et al.*, 1960). In keeping with the overall strategy to be employed, analyses of variance were first performed to determine the presence of reliable behavioral differences between the high and low selected lines. Behavioral results obtained from these two tests are summarized in Table 2. The results clearly indicated statistically significant differences between highs and lows both in the number of squares entered in the open field and in the number of days of training required to attain the

Table 1. Sample Sizes (n), Mean Brain Weights in Grams (M), and Standard Deviations (SD) for Mice at the Third, Fourth, Seventh, and Tenth Generations of Selection for Absolute Brain Weight[a]

Generation	Lines[b]	*n*	*M*	SD
Three	H6 + H7	28	0.4910	0.0212
	C6 + C7	24	0.4739	0.0270
	L6 + L7	28	0.4462	0.0153
Four	H6 + H7	28	0.4990	0.0313
	C6 + C7	31	0.4770	0.0258
	L6 + L7	27	0.4519	0.0221
Seven	H6 + H7	18	0.5118	0.0300
	C6 + C7	17	0.4802	0.0320
	L6 + L7	18	0.4319	0.0301
Ten	H7	20	0.5483	0.0319
	C6	17	0.4570	0.0211
	C7	18	0.4722	0.0158

[a] The information pertains to mice employed in the behavioral studies.
[b] The letters indicate the nature of the line: H and L are lines for which selection was exercised in, respectively, the high and low brain weight direction; C indicates unselected controls. The numbers 6 and 7 refer to the two selection replications, for which averages were used in generations 3, 4, and 7.

Table 2. Selected Behavioral Comparisons of Both High and Both Low Lines Selected for Absolute Brain Weight at the Third Generation of Selection [a]

	Means comparisons					Individual comparisons: unselected controls		
	Means							
	Highs	Lows	*F*	df	*P*	*r*	df	*P*
Open field, squares entered	117.64	93.21	4.03	1/55	<0.05	+0.370	22	N.S.
Water maze, days to criterion	4.72	5.96	5.65	1/52	<0.05	−0.305	17	N.S.

[a] Pearson product-moment correlations (*r*'s) for mice of the unselected controls are included as well.

acquisition criterion in the water maze. There therefore existed potential positive causative associations of brain weight with open-field activity and with speed of learning in the water maze. Pearson product-moment correlations were next computed between brain weight and these behavioral traits using values obtained for individual mice of the unselected control populations. The correlations obtained, also included in Table 2, provided independent substantiation for the presence of the associations suggested from comparisons of the highs and lows. These results provided both evidence for a satisfactory level of reliability for some behavioral tests and support for the contention of previous investigators (Hamilton, 1935; Lashley, 1949; Rensch, 1956, 1964) that brain size and behavioral capacity, particularly learning performance, are positively related.

Mice of some of the selected lines for brain weight and their controls were studied at the fourth (Terris, 1964) and the seventh (Ackerman, 1965) generations of selection. Terris measured activity in the open field and performance in learning a brightness discrimination in the water maze. Ackerman studied spatial discrimination learning in a water maze. The brain weight values obtained are summarized in Table 1. The behavioral results are summarized in Table 3. Noteworthy was the failure of both experimenters to agree with behavioral differences between lines observed by C. Wimer and Prater (1966) at the third generation. These behavioral discrepancies might have resulted from a change in the composition of this complex morphological trait as selection progressed, i.e., a change in the nature of the brain-behavior association for the intermediate or later-diverging subtraits. Alternatively, changes in the nature of the brain-behavior association might have developed at more extreme ranges of all or some of the specific morphological subtraits. Also noteworthy was that, in every instance, the signs of correlations involving mice of the unselected controls were in agreement with those obtained by C. Wimer and Prater.

Table 3. Summary of Behavioral Results Obtained for Mice of the Selection Experiment for Absolute Brain Weight for the Fourth and Seventh Generations of Selection and/or for Their Corresponding Unselected Controls

	Means comparisons						Individual comparisons: unselected controls		
	Means			F	df	P			
	Highs	Lows	Controls				r	df	P
Fourth generation									
Open-field test, squares entered	144	144	N/A	0.00	1/44	N.S.	+0.10	23	N.S.
Water maze, brightness discrimination, trials to criterion	6.31	6.12	N/A	0.04	1/44	N.S.	−0.03	23	N.S.
Seventh generation									
Water maze, spatial discrimination, trials to criterion	6.09	N/A	6.86	0.16	1/33	N.S.	−0.12	21	N.S.

Note that mice of the low line are omitted from the presentation of Ackerman's behavioral results. The cause for this was retinal degeneration. Once this difficulty became apparent, the eyes of all mice employed in behavioral testing were subsequently examined histologically for the presence of this retinal condition. Behavioral results for mice exhibiting retinal degeneration were then excluded from all final statistical analyses. Nearly all of Ackerman's results for mice of the low lines had to be excluded on this basis, so that analysis had to be restricted to results from some mice of the unselected controls and the highs.

By the tenth generation of selection, retinal degeneration was, for all practical purposes, fixed in both of the low lines and in one of the highs. Behavioral testing of mice of the tenth generation was therefore carried out using mice from one replication of the high line and from both replications of the control line (C. Wimer *et al.*, 1969). Individual mice subsequently determined to possess retinal degeneration were excluded from all statistical analyses of behavior which are to be reported. Brain weights of mice for which behavioral results are given are presented in Table 1. The behavioral tests included the open field, brightness discrimination learning in the water maze, and original learning and reversal learning of activity or passivity. (With respect to the active-passive task, activity-matched groups of highs and activity-matched groups of controls were originally trained to be active *or* passive for 3 days and then reversed to training for the opposite condition.

Electrical shock was used to punish undesired responses. Activity was defined as any locomotor movement of the feet, including rearing. All other behavior, such as freezing, grooming, and sniffing, was called passive. Total amount of activity per session was recorded and analyzed.) Results of the various behavioral tests are summarized in Table 4. Since the active-passive task was employed for the first time with mice of this tenth generation, no comparisons with previous results are possible. Results for the open-field test (administered for 2 days at the third generation and for 1 day at the fourth) and the water maze, however, can be compared. When means comparisons are made (compare Tables 2, 3, and 4), results for both the open-field test and the water maze appear once more to be consistent with the associations

Table 4. Summary of Behavioral Results Obtained for Mice of One Line (H7) [a] *Selected for High Absolute Brain Weight and of Two Lines (C6 and C7) of Unselected Controls* [b]

Task and measure	Means comparisons						Individual comparisons: unselected controls		
	Means			F	df	P			
	H7	C6 + C7	C6				r	df	P
Open-field test, squares entered									
Day 1	221	128	N/A	27.27	1/56	<0.01	+0.17	33	N.S.
Day 2	173	100	N/A	16.85	1/56	<0.01	−0.15	33	N.S.
Day 3	154	84	N/A	15.39	1/56	<0.01	−0.15	33	N.S.
Water maze, brightness discrimination, trials to criterion	4.16	7.25	N/A	6.10	1/44	<0.01	+0.06	25	N.S.
Active-passive learning task, minutes of shock									
Original learning, active	0.50	N/A	0.85	12.12	1/17	<0.01	−0.28	6	N.S.
Original learning, passive	0.42	N/A	0.26	2.51	1/17	N.S.	−0.08	7	N.S.
Reversal learning, active	0.75	N/A	1.03	7.30	1/17	<0.05	−0.48	7	N.S.
Reversal learning, passive	0.36	N/A	0.12	5.30	1/17	<0.05	+0.45	6	N.S.

[a] The letter indicates the nature of the line: H stands for a line for which selection is exercised in the high brain weight direction, while C indicates an unselected control. The numbers 6 and 7 are used to designate the two selection replications.
[b] Data were obtained at the tenth generation of selection.

with brain weight observed in mice of the third generation. That is, higher brain weight once again appears to be positively related to activity in the open field and speed of learning in the water maze. Pearson product-moment correlations obtained for mice of the unselected controls were consistent with those obtained by C. Wimer and Prater (1966) and by Terris (1964) for early activity levels in the open field, but also suggested a change in the direction of the association with brain weight over ensuing days. The correlational result for trials to criterion in the water maze obtained for mice of the controls was not consistent with respect to sign with the results obtained by C. Wimer and Prater, by Terris, or by Ackerman (1965), but did not differ appreciably from zero. Results from the active-passive task are of great interest. While no differences were observed between the high line (H7) and the control line (C6) with respect to first-day activity (no shock administered), the highs consistently performed better in learning active avoidance and the controls performed better in learning passive avoidance. There were no differences between highs and controls with respect to reversal learning *per se*, for highs were superior on the reversal from passive to active, while the controls were superior on the reversal from active to passive. Pearson product-moment correlations for original learning and reversal learning obtained from individual mice of the unselected control line provided support for the conclusion, tentatively reached by means comparison, that brain weight is positively related to active avoidance conditioning and negatively related to passive conditioning. The superiority of high-brain-weight mice with respect to learning performance may have to be qualified with respect to activity components involved in what is to be learned. Indeed, activity characteristics may be the more common source of genetically associated differences in learning performance, and not learning ability *per se*.

Others have performed behavioral studies of mice of these lines as well. Elias (1969) studied spatial discrimination reversal learning at the fourteenth generation of selection. He utilized lines in which a high proportion of mice did not exhibit retinal degeneration (H7, C6, and C7). Behavioral results for individual mice found to possess retinal degeneration were excluded from statistical analyses. Utilizing means comparisons, Elias observed no difference between highs and controls for original learning, but found highs to exhibit superior reversal learning performance. Correlational studies among individual mice were not reported. Collins (1970) studied high, low, and unselected control mice of Sel-16 (see above) at the fifteenth generation of selection. Mice were reared either individually (isolated) or in groups of ten with toys, etc. (enriched). Means comparisons obtained for a spatial (go left or right) reversal-learning task in the water maze produced striking behavioral contrasts with results obtained in previous studies: the control-line mice, intermediate with respect to the brain weight trait (but probably not with respect to retinal degeneration), performed worse than did either lows or highs on both original and reversal problems! The source of the markedly inferior performance of the controls is presently unclear. Neither of Collins' rearing conditions was equivalent to those used previously, so genotype-environment interactions may have been involved (cf. Cooper and Zubek, 1958; Fuller and Wimer, 1973; Erlenmeyer-Kimling, 1972). On the other hand, no attempt was made to discriminate mice possessing retinal degeneration, and the behavioral consequence of this condition (which should have been less prevalent in the controls) may have enhanced performance for both lows and highs. A more recent study by Fuller *et al.* (1973) favors the involvement of a difference in the Sel-16 lines, or of a gene-environment interaction. The issue is clearly not settled. Consistent with a previous finding (Elias, 1969), Sel-16 highs were found to be superior to lows on spatial discrimination reversal performance in the water maze (see also Fuller *et al.*, 1973). For additional information on studies of our stocks by others, see Fuller and Geils (1972, 1973) and Gonsiorek *et al.* (1974).

A great deal was learned from all of these studies. Evidence was obtained for at least a moderate association between brain weight and reversal learning in the water maze (Elias, 1969; Fuller *et al.*, 1973). Furthermore, there was some evidence (C. Wimer and Prater, 1966; C. Wimer *et al.*, 1969) that original learning performance in the water maze might be positively related as well, particularly if one granted that brightness discriminations are more difficult than spatial ones and hence likely to be more discriminating (Ackerman, 1965; Elias, 1969). When obtained, results of Pearson product-moment correlations among unselected controls were generally supportive (Ackerman, 1965; Terris, 1964; C. Wimer and Prater, 1966), although not always (C. Wimer *et al.*, 1969). All studies provided some evidence to support a positive association between brain weight and activity in the open field (Terris, 1964; C. Wimer and Prater, 1966; C. Wimer *et al.*, 1969). Further, the active-passive task provided a clue that activity level may have been one component source for some of the observed differences in learning performance.

It is one thing to realize intellectually and remotely that genetic drift may produce adventitious changes in gene frequencies for unselected relevant traits during the course of selection. It is another to agonizingly observe a gene (*rd*) with potentially enormous ramifications and consequences for behavior increase in frequency and become fixed before one's eyes (but see Fuller *et al.*, 1973). And it occurred despite the precaution of conducting a replicated selection experiment! Adventitious or not, how many genes of major consequence were increasing or decreasing in frequency? The results of means comparisons obtained at early generations of selection when adventitious traits should not have diverged so markedly were clearly the most worthy of trust.

Ratio Traits

Since none of the ratio selection experiments (relative volumes of neocortex or hippocampus, weight of brain to weight of spinal cord) achieved marked morphological separation, no behavioral studies of these lines were performed. However, group comparisons need not be restricted to selected lines: *any* genetically heterogeneous randomly mated population of mice which possesses adequate phenotypic range may be tested behaviorally and then divided subsequently into groups on the basis of extremeness with respect to morphological trait. Or it can be subjected to correlational analysis of individuals when behavioral reliability makes this approach feasible. The examination of multiple morphological traits in this way offers possibilities of (1) a variety of animal sortings for the study of different brain-behavior associations when morphological traits are independent and (2) analyses of covariance (for means comparisons) and partial correlations (for individual comparisons) when they are not (e.g., C. Wimer *et al.*, 1971). Studies of parent-offspring correlations in two generations would offer the capacity to determine the additive component of genotypic variance for both morphological and behavioral traits, and their genetic correlation as well (Falconer, 1960). The first study of brain-behavior associations using some of this strategy confirmed its potential value.

The morphological traits examined were (1) total volume of that portion of the brain which is overlaid with neocortex ("brain" volume), (2) absolute volume of hippocampus, (3) absolute volume of neocortex, (4) the ratio of hippocampal volume to "brain" volume (hippocampal ratio), and (5) the ratio of neocortical volume to "brain" volume (neocortical ratio) (C. Wimer *et al.*, 1971). All volumes were estimates obtained from determination of the rostrocaudal length of the region and from planimetric measures of enlarged photographs of three brain sections corresponding to 25%, 50%, and 75% of that length. Nearly all the morphological traits had previously been shown to possess a substantial amount of genotypic variability (R. Wimer *et al.*, 1969). The mice studied were randomly bred from the second foundation stock, which did *not* include retinal degeneration. Behavioral tests included open-field activity, active shock-escape *or* passive shock-avoidance learning in a jump box (R. Wimer *et al.*, 1968), and brightness *or* spatial discrimination learning followed by reversal learning in a modified water maze (C. Wimer *et al.*, 1971). Learning tasks were given under temporally massed *or* distributed conditions of practice. The mice were subsequently killed and morphological traits were determined for all brains.

Table 5. Pearson Product-Moment Correlations between Five Morphological Traits for a Genetically Heterogeneous Population of House Mice (df = 52)

	Hippocampal volume		Neocortical volume	
	Absolute	Ratio	Absolute	Ratio
Volume of "brain"	+0.65 [a]	−0.32 [b]	+0.87 [a]	−0.04
Hippocampal volume				
Absolute	—	+0.50 [a]	+0.49 [a]	−0.18
Ratio		—	−0.37 [a]	−0.16
Neocortical volume				
Absolute			—	+0.45 [a]
Ratio				—

[a] $P < 0.01$.
[b] $P < 0.05$.

The correlations between morphological traits obtained for individuals are presented in Table 5. Morphologically distinct groups were created by independent sortings of mice into high, intermediate, and low thirds for each morphological trait. The morphological trait separations obtained are summarized in Table 6. Behavioral results for the hippocampal ratio and neocortical ratio groups are presented in Figure 6. Figure 6a shows the day-to-day decrement in open-field activity for mice in the three hippocampal ratio groups. For the hippocampal ratio groups, it is apparent that the lows were more active and the highs less active on all 5 days, but that there was no difference between groups in the rate of decline in activity across days. For the neocortical ratio groups (Figure 6b), there was no difference between groups on day 1, but highs remained more active than lows on later days. A contingency table was constructed to verify that hippocampal and neocortical ratio classifications were independent (see Table 7). χ^2 test carried out on this table resulted in $\chi^2 = 1$, df $= 4$, $P > 0.90$, indicating independent assignment to neocortical and hippocampal ratio groups. Neocortical and hippocampal ratios, then, appear to have had independent and different effects on open-field activity.

Hippocampal ratio sorting of mice into three morphological trait groups for the passive shock-avoidance task with two temporal conditions of practice would have resulted in too few mice per cell. (Half the mice had been trained on the active shock-escape task instead.) Mice receiving the passive shock-avoidance task were accordingly divided at the median into two groups, one having a higher hippocampal ratio and the other having a lower hippocampal ratio. Results for these two morphological trait groups for massed and distributed temporal practice conditions are presented in Figure 7a. The superiority of the higher hippocampal ratio group for the massed-practice condition is readily apparent, with superiority in performance increasing over trials. The small difference between morphological trait groups under the

Table 6. Means (M) and Standard Deviations (SD) of Volume[a] and Ratio Estimates for Mice of a Genetically Heterogeneous Population Independently Divided into Thirds (Highs, Intermediates, and Lows) for Each of Five Morphological Traits

	Total volume of "brain"		Hippocampal volume				Neocortical volume			
			Absolute		Ratio		Absolute		Ratio	
Morphological groups	*M*	SD	*M*	SD	*M*	SD	*M*	SD	*M*	SD
Highs ($n = 18$)	0.1848	0.0099	0.0139	0.0008	0.0828	0.0046	0.0476	0.0039	0.2717	0.0103
Intermediates ($n = 18$)	0.1634	0.0044	0.0120	0.0004	0.0745	0.0016	0.0414	0.0010	0.2538	0.0056
Lows ($n = 18$)	0.1434	0.0084	0.0106	0.0007	0.0664	0.0035	0.0362	0.0020	0.2386	0.0064

[a] Measurement units are cubic centimeters.

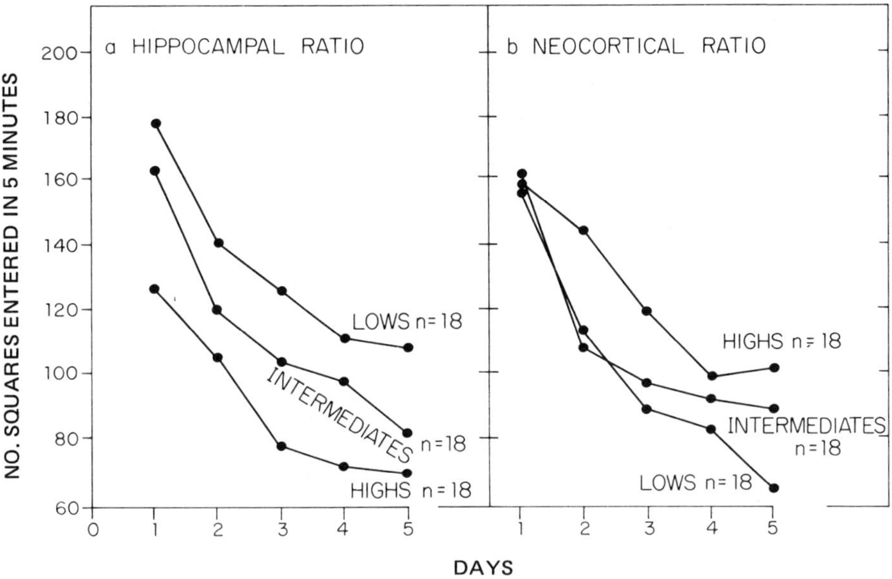

Figure 6. Mean open-field activity levels for a genetically heterogeneous population of house mice divided into three groupings on the basis of their individual hippocampal ratios (a) or their neocortical ratios (b).

Table 7. A Contingency Table to Show the Number of Mice Assigned to Each of Three Groups for Hippocampal Ratio and for Neocortical Ratio

Hippocampal ratio	Neocortical ratio		
	High	Intermediate	Low
High	6	5	7
Intermediate	5	7	6
Low	7	6	5

distributed-practice condition was in the same direction, although not statistically significant. Figure 7(b), shows results for high, intermediate, and low hippocampal ratio groupings with practice conditions combined. The superiority of high-ratio mice over both intermediates and lows is highly apparent. The intermediate-ratio mice do not appear to have performed much better than did the lows. Neocortical ratio groups did not differ in passive shock avoidance.

Neither the active shock-escape task nor the discrimination learning tasks discriminated among groups sorted for either hippocampal or neocortical ratio.

Selected correlations between behavioral and morphological traits are summarized in Table 8. All of the correlations of absolute hippocampal volume and ratio with open-field activity were significantly negative, indicating that the mouse with the larger hippocampus tends to be less active. Some of the correlations of open-field activity with neocortical ratio were significantly positive, indicating that the mouse with the larger neocortical ratio tends to be more active in some fashion. A significant positive correlation for the massed condition of practice was obtained between high performance on the passive avoidance task and high hippocampal ratio. Consistent with the results obtained from means comparisons, no significant correlations were observed between any morphological traits and behavioral measures for either the active shock-escape task or for discrimination learning performance in the water maze.

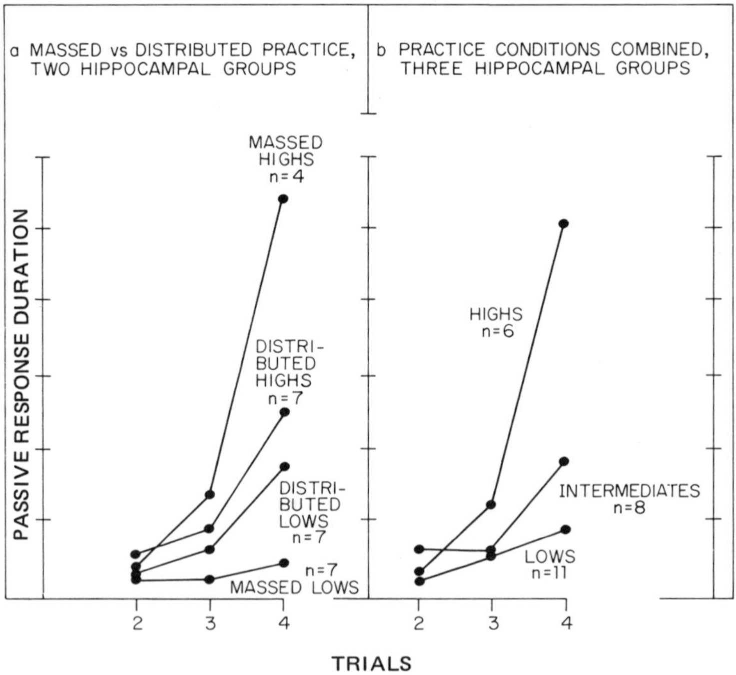

Figure 7. Mean durations of a passive response for a genetically heterogeneous population of house mice administered passive shock-avoidance training. (a) Performance levels for higher and lower hippocampal ratio groupings for two temporal conditions of practice. (b) Performance levels when results for the two practice conditions are combined and high, intermediate, and low hippocampal ratio groupings are formed.

Table 8. Selected Pearson Product-Moment Correlations Obtained from Individual Comparisons for the Determination of Possible Associations between Behavioral and Morphological Traits

Behavioral test/measure	n	Total forebrain volume	Hippocampal volume: Absolute	Hippocampal volume: Ratio	Neocortical volume: Absolute	Neocortical volume: Ratio
Open field/squares entered						
Day 1	54	−0.19	−0.55 [a]	−0.48 [a]	+0.04	+0.16
Day 2	54	−0.21	−0.44 [a]	−0.33 [b]	−0.06	+0.28 [b]
Day 3	54	−0.24	−0.51 [a]	−0.39 [a]	−0.08	+0.28 [b]
Day 4	54	−0.23	−0.45 [a]	−0.33 [b]	−0.13	+0.18
Day 5	54	−0.05	−0.43 [a]	−0.32 [b]	−0.06	+0.29 [b]
Total	54	−0.23	−0.54 [a]	−0.42 [a]	−0.07	+0.27 [b]
Passive task/latency						
Trial 1	25	−0.05	−0.06	+0.13	+0.10	+0.27
Trials 2–4 (massed)	11	−0.09	+0.41	+0.67 [b]	−0.25	−0.42
Trials 2–4 (distributed)	14	−0.09	−0.02	+0.09	+0.12	+0.38

[a] $P < 0.01$.
[b] $P < 0.05$.

Neocortical ratio was related to rate of decline in activity over days in the open field, and to nothing else measured. Hippocampal ratio was negatively related to overall level of activity, and to the ease with which activity level could be decreased by punishment. Substantial, and not infrequently significant, correlations between morphological and behavioral traits were obtained. Much of the variation in the morphogical traits may have been associated with differences in genotype (R. Wimer *et al.*, 1969), although this could not be established on the basis of examination of mice of this single generation.

Comment

These results provide strong support for the potential value of behavioral studies such as ours. It *is* possible to identify some substantial behavioral differences when house mice differ with respect to brain weight, or with respect to the size of some specific portions of their brains. It therefore appears possible that a substantial part of the genetically associated variability in behavior which occurs in house mice will eventually be found to be due to differences in brain morphology. It seems reasonable to anticipate that studies employing more specific and precisely defined morphological traits will succeed in establishing stronger and more reliable associations with behavior than those which we have as yet been able to achieve.

Appraisal

Our initial research program was directed toward providing answers to two questions. The first was concerned in part with whether there is a substantial amount of additive genetic variance associated with brain weight, and with the nature of that variation. The response to selection was dramatic and continued over many generations, so the answer was that there is a great deal of additive variance and the trait is multifactorial. The first question was also concerned with whether there is substantial usable genetic variability for size or weight of specific portions of the central nervous system. Studies of strain differences in relative volumes of neocortex and of hippocampus with respect to total volume of "brain" (R. Wimer *et al.*, 1969) and of weights of brain and spinal cord (Roderick *et al.*, 1973) all agreed in indicating the presence of (1) genetic variability affecting size of all portions of the central nervous system and (2) genetic systems of lesser, but nevertheless appreciable, consequence associated with the size of some of its specific divisions. However, selection experiments for relative volumes of neocortex and hippocampus were failures, and selection for relative weight of spinal cord showed only a limited response.

The second question was whether there are any detectable associated differences in behavior. The answer to this question was affirmative. Behavioral studies of animals selected for brain weight revealed differences between highs and lows in open-field activity and in maze-learning performance at early generations when moderate response to selection had occurred (C. Wimer and Prater, 1966). Behavioral studies of genetically heterogeneous mice which were subsequently sacrificed for determination of their relative volumes of neocortex and hippocampus revealed marked differences in pattern of decline in open-field activity across days with neocortical ratio and in overall level of activity with hippocampal ratio. Further, learning performance of a passive avoidance task was found to be related to hippocampal ratio.

Implications of Our Findings

The implications of these answers would seem to be as follows: There is substantial genetically associated variation in the size and weight of the central nervous system of the house mouse which commonly involves all divisions which have been examined. Weights and volumes are complex morphological traits in that they represent the net unanalyzed effect of a potentially large variety of component traits. However, both the response to selection for brain weight and the speed with which it occurred indicate that the genetic systems associated with the principal more specific traits have substantial additive genotypic variance. Preliminary evidence indicates that cell number is one component trait involved (Dravid *et al.*, 1972; Hagerich, 1968). There is reason to believe that, once identified, the principal underlying traits can be manipulated genetically.

There is less marked, but nevertheless appreciable, independent genetically associated variability in the weights and volumes of the specific divisions of the mouse central nervous system which have been examined. Substantial progress with respect to such ratio phenotypes may require the employment of a mathematically more sophicated selection criterion and the identification and utilization of more specific component morphological traits (e.g., Barber *et al.*, 1974).

It would appear that genetically associated variability in morphological traits is associated with some of the genetically associated variability in behavior which has been observed in house mice. Further, the degree of association between morphological trait and behavioral trait may in some instances be very substantial, for relatively strong associations have been identified in a genetically heterogeneous population of mice. Inconsistencies and equivocal results concerning the nature of these associations may be anticipated, however, until both morphological and behavioral traits are defined more precisely and analyzed in greater detail (cf. contrasting behavioral associations of brain weight and "brain" volume, and Fuller *et al.*, 1973).

Other Genetic Approaches

Much has been learned not only with respect to the specific questions asked but also with respect to the most efficient and informative manner in which these questions could have been asked. As we have seen, answers could have been obtained much more efficiently had the basic strategy of employing selection *not* been chosen. In addition to the difficulties mentioned above, there are other problems with selective breeding experiments: inefficiency, unreproducibility, and difficulties in maintenance of lines. The problem of inefficiency is simply the time required to produce differences, sometimes several years. The problem of unreproducibility stems from our inability to reconstitute precisely any heterogeneous population and to control probabilistic events involving allelic loss or fixation over several generations of selection. Differences brought about by genetic drift can seriously affect one's ability to generalize from only one or two replications (Falconer, 1973). We have already discussed the limitation that this places on our experimental approach. The other major disadvantage is maintaining the lines. Inbred strains are the survivors among a larger group of lines which failed to withstand inbreeding. From our experience, this is true not only for lines derived from feral populations but also for lines derived from crosses between independent successfully inbred laboratory strains. So, not only is there a problem in counteracting the lack of fitness usually associated with selected variables, but there is also the problem of inbreeding depression as the lines are continued.

There are more efficient research strategies available. One strategy is to cross mice from two inbred strains which are at the opposite phenotypic extremes for the trait in order to produce an F_1 hybrid. Mice of the F_1 hybrid are then backcrossed with mice of the parental strains to produce sets of segregating first backcross progeny (Green, 1974). This mating scheme can produce information within a single year. Further, errors such as inclusion of stocks with retinal degeneration (see our experiments described above) can be remedied quickly. The only step involving probabilistic events is the backcross progeny, but each genotype in that generation has a single and replicable probability of occurrence. An additional advantage is that the backcross progeny generally exhibit lower mortality and higher reproductive performance than do mice of inbred strains. One major disadvantage of this strategy employing only two inbred strains is the difficulty of generalizing to a population on the basis of a limited sample of genotypes and phenotypes. Another source of difficulty is linkage disequilibrium when major genes are involved. Relatively closely linked genes, as they existed in the parental strains, would tend to act as a unit until a sufficient number of generations had provided an opportunity for them to recombine and to reach equilibrium, and thereafter to occur independently. One may misinterpret the effects of major genes until linkage equilibrium is reached. This further limits our ability to generalize about genetic effects or causative interactions because many genes of interest are potentially closely linked to genes with major biochemical or morphological effects which may have consequences, although spurious, for behavior (cf. R. Wimer, 1973). Thus examination of parental strains, F_1 hybrids, and first backcross progeny can only result (as in the case of examination of a limited number of selected lines) in the identification of *potential* causative associations. Corresponding genetically heterogeneous populations for the verification of causative behavioral associations are the F_3 and subsequent generations of mice initiated by intercrossing F_1 mice and generated through random mating of the resulting progeny of the F_2 generation. We have successfully employed a genetically heterogeneous population for the study of brain-behavior associations (studies of neocortical and hippocampal ratios presented above). Precise information concerning the additive component of the genotypic variance for the morphological trait can be obtained through the determination of phenotypic correlations between parents and offspring as this mating strategy is executed.

There are other new approaches to the study of behavioral genetics. One exciting approach employs recombinant inbred lines (Bailey, 1971), independent lines inbred from the F_2 of a cross between two genetically independent inbred strains. Because rapid inbreeding "freezes" close linkages before they recombine, these lines are most useful in assessing linkage relationships of major gene differences existing between the two original strains. For studies of the genetic component of variation in brain or behavior, these lines can provide evidence for the number of loci contributing to the phenotypic variation, the degree of dominance of major genes involved, and the linkage of some otherwise intractable "behavioral" genes to loci exhibiting common genetic polymorphisms. The technique has already been used in a genetic analysis of fighting behavior in mice (Eleftheriou *et al.*, 1974).

Other potentially useful tools for studying the genetics of brain and behavior are the recently developed chromosomal inversion systems in the mouse (Roderick and Hawes, 1974). Even a rather large chromosomal inversion, i.e., about 40 centiMorgans, which is about 3% of the genome of the mouse and two-thirds of the genetic length of the "average" chromosome, will completely "inhibit" recombination in the inverted region. Thus whole segments of chromosome from one inbred strain can be placed on the genetic background of another strain with the end result being a strain identical to the original except for new specific and well-located pieces of chromosome. One of the advantages is the possible location of areas of the genome with special influence on behavioral or quantitative traits. A similar, more rapid, but less powerful experiment is to study the behavior or phenotype of interest in an F_2 from a cross of two strains, one with the inversion, as long as the inverted segment can be identified by genetic markers.

In both of these new approaches, one can break apart for study segments of the genome which control a quantitative trait. These chromosome segments are large enough so that they may reveal specific smaller segments of importance underlying such traits. Furthermore, the possible components of complex mechanisms underlying a quantitative trait may be parceled out if different segments contain different correlated characters.

Some Assumptions Which Were Implicit in Our Work

No matter what genetic research strategies are employed, the experimenter must be aware constantly of the special limitation, as well as the advantage, of the genetic approach to brain-behavior associations. The general advantage is relatively straightforward, for our ultimate goal is to account for uniformity and variability of behavior in populations of *intact* organisms. It is when genes are viewed as precise tools for the study of specific brain-behavior associations that the limitation exists—the possible existence of indirectly conjoined traits, one type of pleiotropism.

Concern for normal variability and minimization of severe pleiotropism causing indirectly conjoined traits have been continuing implicit themes throughout both this presentation and the entire research program. The inbred strains studied to establish the presence of genotypic variability or crossed to create foundation populations for genetic selection experiments were thought to be free of gross behavioral abnormalities or externally detectable neurological anomalies. The anticipation was that such "normal" inbred strains would eventually be found to contain mutant genes or more complex genetic systems with relatively subtle morphological effects having high potential biological significance for the species. The hope was also present that the relatively subtle would also prove eventually to be the morphologically more specific and precise. There are many known neurological mutants of the house mouse which have been identified on the basis of animal caretaker's observations of behavioral abnormality or of externally detectable morphological traits. Thus most behaviorally detected neurological mutants run in circles, shake, convulse, or exhibit gross motor incoordination (Sidman *et al.*, 1965). Some indication of the types of mice identified on the basis of externally observable morphological anomalies is provided by mutant names such as "brain hernia," "hydrocephalus-1," and "cerebral degeneration." While a gross behavioral anomaly need not necessarily be indicative of gross and diffuse alterations within the nervous system, it certainly cannot be thought to favor their absence. Although such gross anomalies may not be thought to represent meaningful biological experiments for those who are behaviorally oriented, they may serve admirably for the needs of the experimenter in another discipline (Caviness *et al.*, 1972; Rakic and Sidman, 1973; Sidman, 1968).

Also implicit throughout this presentation and the entire program has been the strategic decision to begin with brain and to proceed to behavior. The wisdom of such an approach depends on one's beliefs concerning the nature and complexity of the behaviors one intends to study and on one's present conceptions of the functional organization of the central nervous system. It was our intention that the behaviors be among the traditional ones of interest for the psychologist, e.g., open-field activity, maze learning, and active and passive avoidance learning. Differences in such behaviors were believed *not* to predominantly involve relatively precise species-specific behavioral components, but rather to involve psychologically complex processes of inhibition, learning, and motivation. Such behaviors appeared more likely to involve interactions between general biological computer functions of the central nervous system (e.g., Miller *et al.*, 1960; Powers, 1973) than highly behavior-specific neuronal circuits (e.g., Mayr, 1974). Since genetically associated variation in our behaviors might originate in biochemical or morphological traits potentially involving interactions between many regions of the brain, the probability of successfully establishing an associated morphological trait appeared to be low. Therefore, it was thought prudent first to establish morphological variation and then to proceed to associated behavioral variation. The more "ethological" the behavior, the greater the potential power of genetic dissection of the behavioral phenotype itself would appear to be (e.g., Buckley, 1969; Dilger, 1962; Rothenbuhler, 1964). The most efficient way, and perhaps the only way, into the nervous system for some ethological traits might entail the study of underlying associated neurophysiological traits (cf. Bentley and Hoy, 1974).

Concerns about the selective advantages of behavioral traits and their distributions in populations are clearly central with respect to our understanding of the probable evolution and maintenance of specific behaviors, and of the greater capacity for certain behaviors than for others (Bolles, 1970; Dobzhansky, 1972; Hinde and Stevenson-Hinde, 1973; Russell, 1958; Sheldon, 1968; Seligman, 1970). Knowledge of how nervous systems function, and of the biochemical, morphological, and physiological traits which lie in the causative pathways between primary gene action and behavior (Fuller, 1957), is also clearly central with respect to our understanding of how behavioral evolution may have occurred, how behavioral variability is presently maintained, and how behavior and the capacities for behaviors might be altered (Diamond and Hall, 1969; Hodos and Campbell, 1969; Hirsch, 1967). We have clearly only just begun.

Acknowledgments

Besides our indebtedness to Professor David Krech, we wish to acknowledge the valuable collaboration and discussions with Dr. John B. Storer and Dr. John L. Fuller. We also are grateful for the assistance of several students and technicians, particularly Georgia Hall, William Mace, Florence Leland, Jane Harris, Virginia Hoagland, Patricia McFarland, and Carol Wildman. We would also like to thank Drs. R. L. Collins, R. L. Sprott, and J. E. Vaughn for critical readings of our manuscript. This work was supported by NIH Research Grants HD 02491 from the National Institute of Child Health and Human Development and NS 10284 from the National

Institute of Neurological Diseases and Stroke. The Jackson Laboratory is fully accredited by the American Association for Accreditation of Laboratory Animal Care.

References

Ackerman, D. F. 1965. Escape learning in mice selected for brain weight. Unpublished student paper, Jackson Laboratory, Bar Harbor, Me.

Bailey, D. W. 1971. Recombinant-inbred strains: An aid to finding identity, linkage, and function of histocompatibility and other genes. *Transplantation, 11*, 325–327.

Barber, R. P., Vaughn, J. E., Wimer, R. E., and Wimer, C. C. 1974. Genetically-associated variations in the distribution of dentate granule cell synapses upon the pyramidal cell dendrites in mouse hippocampus. *Journal of Comparative Neurology, 156*, 417–434.

Bentley, D., and Hoy, R. R. 1974. The neurobiology of cricket song. *Scientific American, 231*, 34–44.

Bolles, R. G. 1970. Species-specific defense reactions and avoidance learning. *Psychological Review, 77*, 32–48.

Buckley, P. A. 1969. Disruption of species-typical behaviour patterns in F_1 hybrid *Agapornis* parrots. *Zeitschrift fuer Tierpsychologie, 26*, 737–743.

Caviness, V. S., Jr., So, D. K., and Sidman, R. L. 1972. The hybrid reeler mouse. *Journal of Heredity, 63*, 241–246.

Collins, R.-A. 1970. Experimental modification of brain weight and behavior in mice: An enrichment study. *Developmental Psychobioloy, 3*, 145–155.

Cooper, R. M., and Zubek, J. P. 1958. Effects of enriched and restricted early environments on the learning ability of bright and dull rats. *Canadian Journal of Psychology, 12*, 159–164.

Diamond, I. T., and Hall, C. W. 1969. Evolution of neocortex *Science, 164*, 251–262.

Dilger, W. C. 1962. The behavior of lovebirds. *Scientific American, 206*, 88–98.

Dobzhansky, Th. 1972. Genetics and the diversity of behavior. *American Psychologist, 27*, 523–530.

Dravid, A. R., Wimer, R. E., and Herschman, H. R. 1972. Biochemical bases for genetically determined brain weight phenotypes. *Transactions of the American Society of Neurochemistry, 3*, 1972 (abstract).

Eleftheriou, B. E., Bailey, D. W., and Denenberg, V. H. 1974. Genetic analysis of fighting behavior in mice. *Physiology and Behavior, 13*, 773–777.

Elias, M. F. 1969. Differences in spatial discrimination reversal learning for mice genetically selected for high brain weight and unselected controls. *Perceptual and Motor Skills, 28*, 707–712.

Erlenmeyer-Kimling, L. 1972. Gene–environment interaction and the variability of behavior. In: *Genetics, Environment and Behavior.* L. Ehrman, G. S. Omenn, and E. Caspari (Eds.). Academic Press, New York, pp. 181–208.

Falconer, D. S. 1960. *Quantitative Genetics.* Ronald Press, New York.

Falconer, D. S. 1973. Replicated selection for body weight in mice. *Genetical Research, 22*, 291–321.

Fuller, J. L. 1957. The genetic base: Pathways between genes and behavioral characteristics. In: The Nature and Transmission of the Genetic and Cultural Characteristics of Human Populations, Proceedings of the 1956 Annual Conference, Milbank Memorial Fund, 40 Wall St., New York.

Fuller, J. L., and Geils, H. D. 1972. Brain growth in mice selected for high and low brain weight. *Developmental Psychobiology, 5* 307–318.

Fuller, J. L. and Geils, H. D. 1973. Behavioral development in mice selected for differences in brain weight. *Developmental Psychobiology, 6*, 469–474.

Fuller, J. L., and Wimer, R. E. 1973. Behavior genetics. In: *Comparative Psychology: A Modern Survey*. D. A. Dewsbury and D. A. Rethlingshafer (Eds.). McGraw-Hill, New York, pp. 197–237.

Fuller, J. L., Brady-Wood, S., and Elias, M. F. 1973. Effects of retinal degeneration and brain size upon spatial reversal learning in mice. *Perceptual and Motor Skills, 36*, 947–950.

Gonsiorek, J. C., Donovick, P. J., Burright, R. G., and Fuller, J. L. 1974. Aggression in low and high brainweight mice following septal lesions. *Physiology and Behavior, 12*, 813–818.

Gould, J. 1966. Effects of changes in total brain size on specific brain structures in mice. Unpublished student paper, Jackson Laboratory, Bar Harbor, Me.

Green, E. L. 1974. Some systems of mating useful in mouse genetics. *Experimentation Animale, 7*, 1–14.

Green, M. C. 1966. Mutant genes and linkages. In: *Biology of the Laboratory Mouse* (2nd ed.). E. L. Green (Ed.). McGraw-Hill, New York, pp. 87–150.

Hagerich, J. A. 1968. Investigation of the causes of brain weight variation in mice. Unpublished student paper, Jackson Laboratory, Bar Harbor, Me.

Hamilton, J. A. 1935. The association between brain size and maze ability in white rats. Unpublished Ph.D. dissertation, University of California, Berkeley.

Hinde, R. A., and Stevenson-Hinde, J. (Eds.) 1973. *Constraints on Learning: Limitations and Predispositions*. Academic Press, New York.

Hirsch, J. (Ed.) 1967. *Behavior-Genetic Analysis*. McGraw-Hill, New York.

Hodos, W., and Campbell, C. B. G. 1969. *Scala naturae:* Why there is no theory in comparative psychology. *Psychological Review, 76*, 337–350.

Krompecher, St., and Lipak, J. 1966. A simple method for determining cerebralization: Brain weight and intelligence. *Journal of Comparative Neurology, 127*, 113–120.

Lashley, K. S. 1949. Persistent problems in the evolution of mind. *Quarterly Review of Biology, 24*, 28–42.

Mayr, E. 1974. Behavior programs and evolutionary strategies. *American Scientist, 62*, 650–659.

Miller, G. A., Galanter, E., and Pribram, K. H. 1960. *Plans and the Structure of Behavior* Holt, Rinehart and Winston, New York.

Powers, W. T. 1973. *Behavior: The Control of Perception*. Aldine, Chicago.

Rakic, P., and Sidman, R. L. 1973. Weaver mutant mouse cerebellum: Defective neuronal migration secondary to abnormality of Bergmann glia. *Proceedings of the National Academy of Sciences of the United States of America, 70*, 240–244.

Rensch, B. 1956. Increase of learning capability with increase of brain-size. *American Naturalist, 90*, 81–95.

Rensch, B. 1964. Memory and concepts of higher animals. *Proceedings of the Zoological Society (Calcutta), 17*, 207–221.

Roderick, T. H. 1960. Selection for cholinesterase activity in the cerebral cortex of the rat. *Genetics, 45*, 1123–1140.

Roderick, T. H., and Hawes, N. L. 1974. Nineteen paracentric chromosomal inversions in mice. *Genetics, 76*, 109–117.

Roderick, T. H., Wimer, R. E., Wimer, C. C., and Schwartzkroin, P. A. 1973. Genetic and phenotypic variation in weight of brain and spinal cord between inbred strains of mice. *Brain Research*, *64*, 345–353.

Rothenbuhler, W. C. 1964. Behavior genetics of nest cleaning in honey bees. IV. Responses of F_1 and backcross generations to disease-killed brood. *American Zoologist*, *4*, 111–123.

Russell, W. M. S. 1958. Evolutionary concepts in behavioral science. I. Cybernetics, Darwinian theory and behavioral science. *General Systems*, *3*, 18–28.

Seligman, M. E. P. 1970. On the generality of the laws of learning. *Psychological Review*, *77*, 406–418.

Sheldon, M. H. 1968. Learning. In: *Analysis of Behavioral Change*. L. Weiskrantz (Ed.). Harper and Row, New York, pp. 127–157.

Sidman, R. L. 1968. Development of interneuronal connections in brains of mutant mice. In: *Physiological and Biochemical Aspects of Nervous Integration*. F. D. Carlson (Ed.). Prentice-Hall, New York, pp. 163–194.

Sidman, R. L., and Green, M. C. 1965. Retinal degeneration in the mouse; location of the *rd* locus in linkage group XVII. *Journal of Heredity*, *56*, 23–29.

Sidman, R. L., Green, M. C., and Appel, S. H. 1965. *Catalog of the Neurological Mutants of the Mouse*. Harvard University Press, Cambridge, Mass.

Staats, J. 1966. The laboratory mouse. In: *Biology of the Laboratory Mouse* (2nd ed.). E. L. Green (Ed.). McGraw-Hill, New York, pp. 1–9.

Storer, J. B. 1967. Relation of lifespan to brain weight, body weight and metabolic rate among inbred mouse strains. *Experimental Gerontology*, *2*, 173–182.

Terris, A. D. 1964. Behavior differences in mice selected for brain size. Unpublished student report, Jackson Laboratory, Bar Harbor, Me.

Waller, M. P., Waller, P. F., and Brewster, L. A. 1960. A water maze for use in studies of drive and learning. *Psychological Reports*, *7*, 99–102.

Wimer, C., and Prater, L. 1966. Some behavioral differences in mice genetically selected for high and low brain weight. *Psychological Reports*, *19*, 675–681.

Wimer, C., Roderick, T. H., and Wimer, R. E. 1969. Supplementary report: Behavioral differences in mice genetically selected for brain weight. *Psychological Reports*, *25*, 363–368.

Wimer, C., Wimer, R. E., and Roderick, T. H. 1971. Some behavioral differences associated with relative size of hippocampus in the mouse. *Journal of Comparative and Physiological Psychology*, *76*, 57–65.

Wimer, R. E. 1973. Dissociation of a phenotypic correlation: Response to posttrial etherization and to temporal distribution of practice trials. *Behavior Genetics*, *3*, 379–386.

Wimer, R. E., and Weller, S. 1965. Evaluation of a visual discrimination task for the analysis of the genetics of a mouse behavior. *Perceptual and Motor Skills*, *20*, 203–208.

Wimer, R. E., Symington, L., Farmer, H., and Schwartzkroin, P. 1968. Differences in memory processes between inbred mouse strains C57BL/6J and DBA/2J. *Journal of Comparative and Physiological Psychology*, *65*, 126–131.

Wimer, R. E., Wimer, C. C., and Roderick, T. H. 1969. Genetic variability in forebrain structures between inbred strains of mice. *Brain Research*, *16*, 257–264.

7

Mark R. Rosenzweig and Edward L. Bennett

ENRICHED ENVIRONMENTS: FACTS, FACTORS, AND FANTASIES

As we prepared to write this chapter and reviewed the varied and sometimes contradictory reactions of some investigators to our reports on effects of environment on brain and behavior, an old story came to mind: A villager was accused of returning a borrowed teapot in poor condition. Vehemently he replied, "In the first place, I never borrowed it; in the second place, I returned it in perfect condition; in the third place, the teapot was already dented when I got it!" Thus the initial criticism of our work was that our results were unlikely or probably unreproducible; that is, the effects didn't exist in the first place. This charge, we believe, has been abundantly answered by replications of the findings, in other laboratories as well as our own. Cragg (1972) has stated: "Initial incredulity that such differences in social and psychological conditions could give rise to significant differences in brain weight, cortical thickness, and glial cell numbers seems to have been overcome by the continued series of papers from Berkeley reporting consistent results. Some independent confirmation by workers elsewhere has also been obtained" (p. 42). A second criticism was the opposite of the first—that the brain is known to be so plastic that almost any experience

---

Mark R. Rosenzweig • Department of Psychology, University of California, Berkeley, California. *Edward L. Bennett* • Lawrence Berkeley Laboratory, University of California, Berkeley, California.

can produce measurable effects in it. And a third criticism has been that although the effects exist they should not properly be attributed to experience—that is, to learning and memory—but are really due to other factors such as stress or accelerated maturation. It is these latter two criticisms that we plan to take up in this chapter. A brief review of the cerebral effects caused by differential environments and of the history of their discovery will help to set the stage for the rest of this report.

As pointed out in our first discussion of this question at the 1959 Pittsburgh symposium (Rosenzweig *et al.*, 1961), we began research with the enriched and impoverished conditions after obtaining unexpected results indicating that formal training produced changes in brain chemistry. To enhance the opportunities for differential learning and thus "to maximize the possibility of obtaining relatively sizable effects," we then designed a program involving varied informal experience. Specifically, we set up three experimental conditions: (1) The baseline condition was originally called Social Control and was later called Standard Colony (abbreviated SC in either case). In this condition, three rats of the same sex were assigned to a usual colony cage (32 by 20 by 20 cm) with no special stimulation. (2) The enriched environmental condition was first called Play and Training, then Environmental Complexity and Training (ECT), and eventually Enriched Condition (EC). In this condition, 10–12 rats of the same sex were assigned to a large cage (70 by 70 by 46 cm) equipped with varied stimulus objects (ladders, blocks of wood, etc.). In our first experiments (Krech *et al.*, 1960), the ECT cage contained a small wooden maze and two wooden objects selected each day from a set of seven. Later we increased the variety by placing about six objects in the cage each day from a set of about 25 objects of varied forms and materials (chains, plastic tubes, light bulbs, etc., as described and illustrated in Rosenzweig and Bennett, 1969). The rats were also placed for 30 min daily in a 75- by 75-cm open field with patterns of barriers that were changed daily. Until 1966, the rats were also given a few trials a day of maze training, but this formal training was later dropped from the schedule, so ECT became EC. (3) The Isolated or Improverished Condition (IC) has single rats living in cages about the size of colony cages. Originally these cages were kept in dimly lighted sound-deadened rooms, and the cages had solid side walls to prevent the rats from seeing each other. Later, as will be described, we found that it was the lack of cagemates that seemed to be the essential feature of the IC treatment; animals housed alone in colony cages in a brightly lit and active laboratory room developed brain measures indistinguishable from those of rats in the original IC condition.

These environmental conditions were originally found to produce differences in cholinesterases, AChE-ChE (Krech *et al.*, 1960), then in weights of brain sections (Rosenzweig *et al.*, 1962), then in thickness of cerebral cortex (Diamond *et al.*, 1964), and eventually in a large variety of brain measures (Rosenzweig *et al.*, 1972*a*). For readers who wish additional information about the variety of brain changes induced by differential experience, the following are references to some other articles and reviews: Bennett (1976), Geller (1971), Greenough (1976), Rosenzweig *et al.* (1972*a,c*).

In the 1959 report we wrote of focusing down on the crucial aspects of the environmental situation, and we attempted experimentally to rule out several tied variables—differential activity, differential handling, and diet. In collaboration with David Krech during the period 1958–1966 and with Marian C. Diamond during 1960–1974, we pushed a two-pronged attack on the problem, on the one hand studying effects of formal training on brain measures and on the other hand examining the roles of various factors in the informal environmental situations. This chapter will be restricted to the latter aspect, and among the factors to be considered are the following: locomotion, handling, stress, endocrine mediation of the effects, fluid content of brain, differential rates of maturation, social grouping, and active vs. passive experience. Other evidence will also be considered concerning the hypothesis that differential memory formation plays a role in producing the cerebral effects. This account will extend from our initial research on these questions up to the present (1974)* and will draw upon the work of other laboratories as well as our own.

Are the EC-IC Brain Differences Due to Variables Other Than Differential Opportunity to Learn?

Effects of Handling and of Locomotion

Two of the most obvious ways in which the ECT and IC conditions differed from each other were that rats in ECT were handled more often and they showed more locomotor activity than their littermates in IC. Furthermore, many studies have shown effects of at least early handling on behavior and on physiology of rodents. Of course, the amount of handling received by ECT rats was not great—simply being picked up to be placed in the open field and removed from it, and brief handling when stimulus objects were changed or when the rats were moved from one cage to another. The IC rats were picked up every week or two for weighing. Even though differences in handling did not seem to be marked, we nevertheless wanted to control for this factor.

* A few further references have been added since this chapter was submitted.

In our intial publications on the ECT-IC effects, we therefore reported further experiments run to determine whether differential handling and locomotion might account for the effects (Krech *et al.*, 1960; Rosenzweig *et al.*, 1961). In the two experiments on handling, some rats were handled 2 min each day, for either 30 or 60 days, while littermates were never handled. In the experiment on possible effects of greater locomotor activity, the active group had access to individual running wheels at all times. We concluded "that handling alone probably contributes very little to the observed ECT effect, and that sheer locomotor activity plays no role at all" (Krech *et al.*, 1960, p. 518). More work on this was considered necessary, however, since neither of the experiments on handling lasted as long as the ECT-IC experiments, and the experiment on differential activity included only eight pairs of rats. Futhermore, ECT had both more handling and greater locomotion, and the combination of these factors might be important. We therefore subsequently performed an experiment to test the effects of combined activity plus handling (A+H). The A+H group was handled daily and could locomote in individual running wheels, while littermate groups were in ECT or IC; the experiment extended for the standard length, from 25 to 105 days of age. The results (Rosenzweig *et al.*, 1968) showed no effects of handling plus locomotion except perhaps in the somesthetic region of cortex. It was clearly established that the EC-IC effects could not be attributed either to the greater amount of handling or to the greater amount of locomotion or to the combination of these two factors in the enriched compared to the improverished condition.

Subsequent experiments have offered further corroboration for this conclusion. In experiments on effects of formal maze training, rats in a runway control group have run back and forth in a 2.1-m-long straight alley 50 times or more per day over a 30-day period, and this has not produced differences in cerebral measures (brain weights, AChE and ChE, and RNA and DNA) from those of rats not having this locomotor experience.

Concerning handling, two further kinds of experiments show that this treatment can be omitted from programs that, nevertheless, produce unusually large effects of environmental complexity. We will later report pronounced cerebral effects produced by placing rats in an outdoor field for 30 days; during this time they were not touched by the experimenters, but their brains showed enhanced EC effects at the end of the experimental period (Rosenzweig and Bennett, manuscript). Kuenzle and Knüsel (1974) set up a "superenriched environment" in which rats traversed a bridge between two complex environment cages, shuttling back and forth to get to food and water. Conditions were changed over the month-long experimental period so that the rats had to traverse a maze and open appropriate gates in the apparatus, but the rats were not handled. The superenriched environment, despite the lack of handling, was reported to produce greater brain effects than the usual Berkeley EC environment which includes handling.

A study on behavioral effects of handling in the context of EC and IC experience was reported by Greenough *et al.* (1972). One group of rats was placed in EC, one in IC with no handling, and one in IC with daily handling. When they were tested subsequently for maze learning, the performance of EC rats was superior to that of the two IC groups, which did not differ from each other.

Experiments to be reported below on stress also introduced the variable of handling. Some IC rats received the usual infrequent handling, while others were removed from their cages daily and carried to another room for a stress treatment. Handling plus stress did not cause these IC groups to differ from each other in our usual brain measures.

We conclude that neither postweaning handling, nor differential locomotion, nor the combination of the two can give rise to the EC-IC effects.

Can Stress Account for the EC-IC Effects?

Stress has probably been the most frequently suggested alternative explanation for the EC-IC effects. As in the teapot story, some have seen stress as affecting the IC rats (e.g., Geller, 1971), while others, on the contrary, have suggested that the stimulation of the EC rats might be stressful (e.g., Welch *et al.*, 1974). Daly (1973) has provided useful comparative perspective by relating laboratory environments to the natural microhabitats of burrowing rodents. He concludes that laboratory procedures, such as handling, are overstimulative for the preweanling pup that is "normally confined to the postnatal womb of a hole or burrow," but that the standard laboratory condition "becomes an impoverished environment at that stage [weaning] when the young animal would become active over a wider range" (p. 438). It should be noted that almost all of the studies reviewed in this chapter concern postweaning treatments, and it is during this period that Daly points out that stimulation beyond standard colony conditions is required in order to approach the normal situation for the rat.

In our *Science* paper of 1964 (Bennett *et al.*, 1964), we asked whether isolation stress of the IC rats could be the cause of the differences between them and their enriched-experience littermates. This seemed a hypothesis worth considering because isolation had been reported to be stressful for rats. According to a group of Canadian investigators (Balász *et al.*, 1962; Hatch *et al.*, 1963), isolated rats of the Wistar strain became so aggressive that they could not be handled with bare hands and they developed caudal dermatitis. A current review of the isolation syndrome will be found in Greenough (1976), and a comprehensive review of this syndrome with particular reference to mice has been prepared by Valzelli (1973).

The following two lines of evidence from our experiments made us doubt that isolation stress accounted in any large measure for the ECT-IC differences: (1) Rats of the strains we studied did not show any obvious symptoms of stress in the isolated condition. They did not become aggressive, they did not develop caudal dermatitis, and their adrenal glands did not become enlarged. (2) Use of the standard colony condition showed that ECT rats differed significantly from SC littermates, and "the bulk of the effects on cerebral weight and on acetylcholinesterase activity is due to enriching rather than restricting the experience [in relation to that] of our colony animals" (Bennett *et al.*, 1964, p. 615). (While later research has confirmed the existence of significant EC-SC differences, these may be either larger or smaller than SC-IC differences, depending on the brain measure considered and, for certain measures, on the age of the rats at exposure to the environmental conditions. For example, in regard to depth of occipital cortex, the SC-IC difference exceeds the EC-SC when rats are in the conditions from 25 to 55 days of age, whereas the opposite is true when the experimental period runs from 60 to 90 days of age; see Figures 7A and 7B in Rosenzweig *et al.*, 1972*c*.)

Even if IC could be shown to be stressful, this would not prove that it caused the EC-IC effects. In fact, we had evidence to demonstrate that stress due to unavoidable electrical shock does not produce cerebral effects similar to those of our differential environments. The results of five experiments, conducted in 1959–1960, were reported at the International Congress of Psychology in 1966 and published later (Rosenzweig, 1968). In these experiments, each shock subject received intermittent unavoidable electrical shock for 12 min daily. At the same time, the littermate control was placed in a similar experimental enclosure but with no shock and in a different room. The first two experiments lasted 2 weeks and the other three each lasted 4 weeks. Two weeks or less of EC-IC suffices to produce clear brain weight effects (Rosenzweig, 1969; Ferchmin *et al.*, 1970; Bennett, 1976).

In all five experiments, employing a total of 42 littermate pairs of five different strains, the terminal body weight was lower in the shocked than in the control rats; overall the difference amounted to 6% ($P < 0.01$). Adrenal weights were taken in the first four of these experiments and were 6% greater in the shocked rats ($P < 0.10$); the ratio of adrenal to body weight was 14% greater in the shocked rats ($P < 0.001$). Although the stress of shock affected body weight and the ratio of adrenal weight to body weight, it had little effect on brain measures. None of the four cortical regions yielded a significant difference, the occipital and somesthetic areas showing somewhat greater weights in the shocked rats and the remaining dorsal cortex and ventral cortex weighing somewhat less in the shocked rats than in the controls. Total cortex weighed 2.3% less in the shocked rats ($P < 0.05$). When allowance was made, through analysis of covariance, for reduction of body weight by shock, the difference in cortical weight shrank and became nonsignificant. Even if the absolute weights are considered, the pattern of differences over cortical areas does not parallel that of EC-IC differences. AChE activity was analyzed in only one of these experiments. It showed no significant differences between shocked and control rats for any brain region.

Subsequently, Geller and Yuwiler (1968) and Geller (1971) reported on effects of 30 days of EC or IC following weaning. Under their conditions, IC, compared to EC, showed increase in norepinephrine in the caudate nucleus. There were also signs that the IC rats had been under stress early in the experiment, since IC showed increased values of transaminases and a 4% increase in adrenal weight ($P < 0.05$). Neither the serum nor the adrenal corticosteroids were elevated at sacrifice, so Geller concluded "that some time during the 30 days of the experiment the ICs had adapted to the condition and were no longer responding with adrenal activation . . . . However, the adrenal weight change was not reversible and the transaminase activity remained at a higher basal level" (Geller, 1971, pp. 284–285). In a subsequent experiment, groups were kept in the differential conditions for 2½, 6, 11, or 16 days. Geller reports that "Adrenal corticoids were higher in the ICs during the first part of the exposure but by 11 days no difference could be seen" (1971, p. 286). The data show that the difference was never greater than 4% and never reached significance (Figure 4, p. 287), so any effect on adrenal corticoids remains doubtful.

In considering these results of Geller, one aspect of the experiments requires mention—the usually early age of weaning. The rats were weaned at approximately 19 days of age, some as young as 16 days and the oldest at 21 days. Sixteen days is only 2 days after the rat pup's eyes and ears open, and temperature regulation is still incomplete in such young rats. Most laboratories wean rats at about 25 days of age. It seems quite possible that isolation may be stressful for 19-day-old rats but not for rats weaned at a more normal age. Thus it is not clear whether the findings of Geller on prematurely weaned rat pups are relevant to other studies in which rats were weaned at a normal age.

The possible role of stress on EC-SC-IC effects was studied experimentally in our laboratories by Riege and Morimoto (1970). They asked not only "Does IC or, for that matter, EC entail stress?" but also "Even if overt stress is used, can this produce brain differences found in the EC-IC experiments?" In three experiments, environmental complexity and stress yielded a clear double differentiation in effects on brain weights and adrenal weights (Riege and Morimoto, 1970, Table 5). That is, EC vs. IC caused the usually significant differences in brain weight measures but no significant effects in adrenal weights. Stress (being tumbled each day in a rotating drum) did not cause any significant differences in brain weights, but it produced significant increases in adrenal weights. In regard to total AChE activity, stress produced increases among both EC and IC rats, but these were only half the size of the EC-IC effects. In total ChE activity, stress also produced some effects but again they were generally smaller than the EC-IC effects. Concentrations of some biogenic amines (norepinephrine, dopamine, and serotonin) were also measured. Here both stress and environment produced effects, but the two patterns of effects were quite different. Thus there was no indication that IC was stressful in these experiments (since there was no EC-IC difference in adrenal weight), and even when overt stress was employed it did not produce any brain weight effects or a pattern of chemical effects that resembled those of EC vs. IC.

Up to now we have considered stress only as possibly occurring in the isolation condition. Elsewhere we have noted that the enriched condition might cause the stress of "information overload" (Rosenzweig *et al.*, 1972*c*, p. 258). The possibility also exists that living in a grouped condition may be a cause of stress. An indication of this sort comes from the work of Welch and Welch (in preparation). They housed rats either singly or in groups for a 1-year period following weaning. At the end of the year, the grouped rats "had elevated blood pressure, kidney pathology and endocrine change suggestive of greater stress." This result is opposite to that reported by Geller, but these results of the Welches may be restricted to prolonged periods of group living, or, as we have pointed out earlier, Geller's results may be restricted to rats that are placed in the differential environments at a premature weaning age. Whether, in fact, the enriched condition, the condition of group living, or the impoverished condition represents a stress for the rat in certain experiments should not contradict the reasoning reported here. That is, neither our enriched nor our impoverished condition has produced symptoms of stress in comparison with the standard colony condition, and, furthermore, when overt stress of electrical shock or tumbling has been employed, it has not produced the patterns of alteration of cerebral measures seen with the enriched or impoverished conditions.

The weight of the evidence seems to us clearly to refute the hypothesis that EC-IC cerebral effects can be attributed to stress. We are not, of course, challenging the findings that stress can effect brain and behavior in many ways, but we wish to emphasize that stress vs. nonstress conditions do not yield effects like those produced by EC vs. IC.

Hormonal Mediation of Environmental Effects?

Although the experiments of the preceding section seem clearly to rule out stress as the cause of the cerebral EC-SC-IC effects, it might still be possible that hormonal functions mediated these effects of differential experience. That is, the differential experience might lead to alteration in hormonal activity which could, in turn, affect the nervous system. We therefore tested the hypothesis that the pituitary gland is essential to occurrence of the EC-IC effects (Rosenzweig *et al.*, 1972*b*). The pituitary gland was chosen not only to eliminate its secretions but also to diminish and cut off from environmental influence the secretions of the glands controlled by the pituitary—the thyroid, the adrenal cortex, and the gonads.

Three experiments were run, two with male Fischer rats and one with male Long-Evans rats. In each case, some animals were hypophysectomized shortly after weaning. Then, 5–10 days later, the animals were placed in one of four experimental conditions (to which they had been preassigned) and were kept there for 30 days. The four conditions were these: EC-hypophysectomized, EC-control, IC-hypophysectomized, and IC-control. Results for hypophysectomized animals were used only in the cases that showed verified complete hypophysectomy at sacrifice. The results of these experiments demonstrated that, although hypophysectomy stunts bodily growth and checks brain growth somewhat, significant EC-IC brain differences nevertheless occurred in both the brain weights and brain chemical measures of the operated animals. If the operation had prevented the occurrence of EC-IC effects, then it would have been necessary to determine which gland or glands are essential, to verify this by the procedures of replacement therapy, and so on. Since our results did not, however, implicate hormonal mediation of the experiential effects, we have not pursued work in the endocrine direction further; this may be someone else's cup of tea.

The one indication of possible hormonal effects on these brain measures comes from work of Diamond *et al.* (1971) on EC-IC effects in female rats. They reported that whereas EC-IC differences in thickness of cortex occur in females, these effects can be obscured in the case of pregnant rats. Greenough (1976) has also commented on the possibility of hormonal mediation of EC-IC effects, pointing out that endocrine effects might be expected to occur rather generally throughout the cortex, whereas the EC-IC effects are seen to be strongly differentiated regionally.

Maturational Effects?

Brains from EC rats show, when compared to those of their IC littermates, greater cortical weight, a greater glial/neural ratio, and fewer neurons

Table 1. EC-IC Percentage Differences in Brain Weights and Body Weights in Experiments with Different Starting Ages and Durations of 30 Days or More (1960–1974)

Age at start (days)		Duration (days)							
		30 (267)[a]	37 (24)	45 (23)	60	80 (206)	100 (46)	130 (58)	160 (22)
25	Occipital cortex	9.6[b]	6.1[b]	8.0[b]	—	7.3[b]	9.8[b]	8.5[b]	11.4[b]
	Total cortex	5.2[b]	4.6[b]	6.4[b]		4.2[b]	6.6[b]	6.8[b]	2.5[c]
	Rest of brain	0.1	0.9	2.6[c]		−0.8[d]	0.7	1.6[d]	−3.3[c]
	Total brain	2.3[b]	2.4[d]	4.2[b]		1.2[b]	3.2[b]	3.7[b]	−0.9
	Cortex/rest	5.0[b]	3.6[b]	3.6[b]		5.1[b]	5.8[b]	5.2[b]	6.1[b]
	Body weight	−8.9[b]	−4.7[d]	1.1		−7.7[b]	−4.8[c]	−7.5[b]	−6.8[d]
		(133)[a]							
60	Occipital cortex	7.2[b]	—	—	—	—	—	—	—
	Total cortex	5.5[b]							
	Rest of brain	1.9[b]							
	Total brain	3.4[b]							
	Cortex/rest	3.6[b]							
	Body weight	−0.8							
						(45)[a]			
105	Occipital cortex	—	—	—	—	10.9[b]	—	—	—
	Total cortex					5.4[b]			
	Rest of brain					1.7[d]			
	Total brain					3.2[b]			
	Cortex/rest					3.7[b]			
	Body weight					−0.1			

[a] Number of pairs is given in parenthesis.
[b] $P < 0.001$.
[c] $P < 0.01$.
[d] $P < 0.05$.

per unit of cortical volume. Similar changes are found when adult rats are compared to young. Very young (preweanling rats) raised in a complex environment open their eyes earlier than animals raised in a less complex environment (Malkasian and Diamond, 1971). It has been suggested (e.g., Sperry, 1968) that rats raised in EC would mature more rapidly than rats raised in IC, and it is therefore appropriate to inquire to what extent EC-IC brain differences merely reflect differences in rate of maturation.

In a recent review (Rosenzweig *et al.*, 1972*c*), we summarized several lines of evidence which we believed made untenable the concept of more rapid maturation as a major factor contributing to the effects of differential environments. We have reported that there is no critical period for producing EC-IC effects in brain weight. During the last several years, additional data regarding this point have been accumulated, and a summary for several brain areas is given in Table 1. Rather similar effects are produced in brain weights with experiments extending over a variety of age ranges and durations, and there does not appear to be a critical age prior to which differential environments must be initiated. Cummins *et al.* (1973) have also reported brain weight differences among rats assigned to differential environments at weaning and kept in EC or IC for about 500 days. Maturational effects would be expected to become insignificant during such a lengthy period, but the obtained effects were as large as those found with the usual shorter periods. EC rats have also been shown to have thicker cortices in experiments run over a variety of age ranges and durations (Diamond, this volume).

The fact that many of the EC-IC differences are opposite in direction to changes produced by maturation is even more compelling evidence. Cortical thickness is greater in the EC rat than in the improverished. However, while all regions of the cerebral cortex—dorsal, lateral, anterior, and posterior—increase rapidly in depth between 6 and 10 days postnatally, and more slowly to 26 days, after this age a gradual decrease in depth occurs (Diamond *et al.*, 1975). That is, after 26 days of age, maturation leads to reduced cortical thickness, whereas EC increases it. The ratio of cortical to subcortical weight has been a very reliable measure that distinguishes EC from IC animals; the EC rats have a greater cortex/subcortex weight ratio than do the IC littermates. However, maturation has been shown to lead to a marked decrease in this ratio (Bennett and Rosenzweig, 1971; Riege, 1971).

Several biochemical measures that distinguish EC rats from IC rats also show opposed EC-IC and maturational effects. The enzyme acetylcholinesterase shows a marked increase in activity per milligram from 25 to 105 days of age (Bennett *et al.*, 1961, and unpublished), yet animals maintained in EC over this time period have lower levels of cortical AChE activity than do their IC littermates (Rosenzweig *et al.*, 1972*c*). The nucleic acid concentration in occipital cortex is another measure that is responsive to differential environments as well as to maturation, as can be seen in Table 2.

Table 2. Influence of Age and Environmental Conditions on RNA/DNA Ratio: Occipital Cortex

Age (days) of rats		Duration of EC-IC period	RNA/DNA		Percent difference between EC and IC	Number of pairs EC>IC [a]	*P*
Start	Sacrifice		EC	IC			
26	30	4	2.224	2.060	8.0	13/14	0.001
28	59	31	1.974	1.784	10.6	12/12	0.001
25	150	125	1.730	1.633	6.0	10/12	0.01
97	264	167	1.660	1.552	7.0	7/9	0.01
330	360	30	1.638	1.559	5.0	9/11	0.01

[a] Number of littermate pairs in which EC value was greater than IC value.

The ratio of RNA to DNA is significantly higher in occipital cortex of EC rats compared to the impoverished. The higher ratio for the EC rats is obtained in both young and old rats and in experiments of several durations. The EC-IC difference in this ratio is caused primarily by a decrease in the DNA/mg of the EC rat, and partially by a very small but nonsignificant increase in RNA/mg. Although the RNA/DNA ratio increases with EC, it can be seen in the table to decrease with maturation. From 30 to 360 days, both EC and IC rats show decreases in RNA to DNA ratio of over 30% ($P < 0.001$). The decrease with age occurs primarily because of a relatively large decrease in RNA/mg. There is little or no change in DNA/mg with age after 40 days.

Thus it is clear that a number of anatomical and biological measures are differentially modified by maturation and by enriched environments, so we conclude that EC-IC differences cannot be attributed to maturational effects.

Can Differences in Water Content of Brain Account for EC-IC Effects?

Another tempest in the teapot concerns, appropriately enough, water. It is frequently suggested that cortical weight and depth changes are due to an increase in water content or edema rather than an actual increase in tissue. Most recently this suggestion was made by Welch *et al.* (1974). Again, several different measures, some indirect and some direct, lead us to reject this suggestion.

The first indirect evidence is provided by our findings concerning AChE and ChE activities. Activity per unit of tissue weight typically goes down for AChE with enriched experience, whereas it goes up for ChE. Mere increases in water content of tissue would lead to similar decreases in both measures. Total cortical AChE activity is greater in the EC rat than in the IC rat. An even greater difference in favor of the EC rat is found when total ChE is determined (Rosenzweig *et al.*, 1972*c*). No changes in total activity would be anticipated if the major cerebral change were in the water content. The protein content, as a percentage of wet weight, is another indirect measure that argues against a mere increase in water content as a major factor producing the EC-IC weight differences. In 1962, in three experiments, protein content was determined in rats raised in differential environments. It was found to vary directly with tissue weight (Bennett *et al.* 1964). Occurrence of edema would be expected to reduce protein per unit of tissue weight, but this was not found.

A third indirect argument is provided by the RNA and DNA measures that we have recently obtained. Here again, if changes in water content were the primary cause of weight differences, both RNA and DNA would be expected to decrease, and by similar relative amounts, in the cortex of EC rats. Instead, we have found a differential effect; DNA has shown large and significant decreases per unit weight, whereas RNA has remained constant or even increased slightly. Thus the RNA/DNA ratio is increased in the EC rats when compared to the IC rats. This change, in the case of the occipital cortex, has averaged about 7.5%, and has shown an increase in about 85% of the over 500 EC-IC pairs analyzed to date.

It should also be noted that biochemical and anatomical differences between EC and IC animals exhibit marked regional differences. For example, the effects found in the occipital cortex are generally large, while those in the somesthetic cortex are typically much smaller. Therefore, if edema is occurring, it must be highly localized.

Direct measures of EC-IC effects on wet weight and dry weight of brain were made in 1969. Both wet and dry weights were compared for 11 pairs of rats individually (Bennett *et al.*, 1969). More recently, wet and dry weights were determined for pooled tissue samples from 23 pairs of rats. Typical EC-IC differences were obtained using these dry weights. The data from both experiments have been summarized in Rosenzweig *et al.* (1972*c*).

Hoover and Diamond (1976) have recently shown that the occipital cortex of female rats maintained in differential environments from 60 to 90 days of age did not differ in water content as a percent of wet weight ($N = 11$ pairs). Geller (1971) has also reported that male rats raised in differential environments for 30 days beginning at weaning did not differ in water content ($N = 8$ pairs).

The only direct evidence that water content of brain may differ because of differential environments has come from a comparison made by de Feudis (1974) of mice living in grouped conditions with mice living in isolated conditions. In this case, aggregated mice were reported to have a 7.5% lower ratio of dry weight to wet weight than isolated mice for the cortex, and a 4.8% lower ratio for the hemispheres (percentages were recalculated to correct errors in the original). (It should be noted that data from only 13 mice—7 aggregated and 6 isolated—were used for these determinations.)

While further investigation of the effect of aggregation on water content of mice may be justified, we do not believe that water content is a major factor in producing brain weight difference as a result of EC and IC environments that we have used for rats, mice, gerbils, or peromyscus.

Does Altered Sensory Input Produce the EC-IC Effects?

Sensory stimulation is an obvious aspect of differential environments, and it is readily controlled, so it is not surprising that some research has been done to evaluate the role of stimulation in producing cerebral EC-IC effects. In many discussions, however, it seems to be taken for granted that the sensory factor is of major importance; we believe that it will be worthwhile to examine the role of this factor explicitly. Two separate questions will be considered: (1) Is the environment outside the cage important; that is, what is the role of ambient stimulation? (2) Should the effects of complex vs. impoverished environments be attributed to effects of restricted or distorted sensory input?

Is Extracage Stimulation Effective?

In our initial design of experiments on the effects of differential environments on rat brain and behavior, we chose convenient, but not extreme, conditions which we believe would maximize the observed cerebral differences. We supposed that the varied activity of experimenters in the busy EC room would contribute to enrichment and that the lack of general stimulation in the separate isolation room would heighten the IC effect. Other investigators have also presented both intracage and extracage stimuli in their enriched conditions and have assumed that the results they obtained were due to both sources; this is true of the behavioral study of Gardner *et al.* (1974), to be discussed later, and also of the paper of Mailloux *et al.* (1974) reporting effects of enriched visual experience on cortical evoked potentials in the rat. The latter group (Edwards *et al.*, 1969) had already obtained significant effects with an EC condition similar to ours and apparently added extracage stimuli in the replication in an attempt to enhance the results.

The presumed effectiveness of extracage stimuli in the EC-IC experiments had to be subjected to experimental tests. (We had also supposed initially that the small amount of training in ECT contributed to the cerebral effects, but we later found that the role of this factor was negligible.) We had operational concerns with the necessity of using the isolation room—frequently it is convenient to house IC rats within the main colony rooms, e.g., when some animals are being given daily injections of drugs, or in case of limitation of space. A further reason for investigation was several reports, albeit somewhat contradictory, which suggested that extracage environment was an important factor in determining subsequent maze performance (Forgays and Forgays, 1952; Hymovitch, 1952).

Further experiments (1965–1966) showed that the usual extracage environment did not modify the results obtained with either EC or IC animals. That is, IC animals kept in the EC room had brain weights virtually identical to those of the IC animals run at the same time in the IC room, and *vice versa*. Additionally, clear EC-IC differences developed in an experiment in which the IC rats were kept in colony wire cages on the same racks on which 2-hr EC groups spent 22 hr per day.

Although rats raised in IC conditions in the main laboratory or in the isolation room did not differ in cerebral measures, rats isolated in an extremely impoverished environment (IEI) did have cerebral values that differed even more from those of the EC group than did the values of the usual IC group (Krech *et al.*, 1966). To obtain this extreme condition, cages were suspended individually in fiberglass boxes, and these boxes were placed in an audiometric test chamber.

Continuing concern with the possible influence of extracage perception on rats has been the subject of several recent articles. Some of the reports have been contradictory. For example, Lavallee (1969, 1970) reported that rats given daily slide shows from weaning to 80 days of age were superior in problem solving to the control rats which saw only a blank screen. Attempts in our laboratory to replicate these findings (Ricard, unpublished) were unsuccessful. In two experiments, using Fischer rats, Ricard found that the animals given the daily slide show were inferior to the controls on the Hebb-Williams maze. In addition, in a parallel experiment, no differences in cerebral weight or enzymatic measures were found between the visually deprived and stimulated rats.

Singh *et al.* (1967, 1970) reported that rats that could observe vertical stripes from their cage developed both behavioral and cerebral differences from rats whose cages faced a blank wall. Particularly large differences were reported in AChE activity; the group which had visualized the stripes had twice the AChE activity in posterior cerebral cortex as did the controls (1967). An attempt to replicate this experiment in our laboratory by Maki (1971) showed no cerebral differences as a consequence of the extracage stimuli.

Two experiments run during 1973 gave even clearer evidence that direct interaction of the rats with the stimulus objects is necessary to obtain the usual EC-IC cerebral effects (Ferchmin *et al.*, 1975). These experiments, termed the "observer" experiments, included three groups of animals—the usual EC rats, the IC rats, and the Observer Condition (OC) rats. The OC rats were placed in small wire-mesh cages inside the EC cage (Figure 1). Thus they were exposed to all of the general noises, sights, and smells of the laboratory. In addition, the OC group had a small amount of contact with the EC rats through the wire mesh of the OC cages. In designing this experiment, it was thought, based on the literature of "observational learning," that the mere act of watching the EC animals at close hand might make the OC group more like EC rats than like IC rats in both brain weight and behavior. The results were clearly just the opposite. The brain weights of the OC rats

Figure 1. Rats in the Observer Condition within an enriched environment cage.

were essentially identical to those of the IC rats. Behaviorally, when tested for exploratory behavior in a Greek cross apparatus, these observer rats, like the IC rats, showed a significantly lower level of exploration than the EC rats. For some measures, the scores were even more extreme than those of the ICs.

We see no evidence to date that extracage stimuli, either visual or other, above the levels available in IC contribute independently to the EC-IC differences in behavior or especially in brain development. Any investigator who believes the extracage stimuli to be effective in determination of EC-IC differences is encouraged to present evidence that this is more than fantasy.

Differentiation between Effects of Complex Environment and Effects of Restricting or Distorting Sensory Input

Our doubt that extracage stimuli are effective in the EC situation should not be taken to mean that we ignore reports that under certain circumstances certain types of animals can be affected strongly by visual stimuli without the necessity for direct contact with the stimulus objects. But a brief review of these experiments will, we believe, reveal that the effects of restricted or distorted sensory input cannot serve as a basis for explaining the EC-IC effects.

A number of papers have reported that modified early experience in kittens or monkeys alters the receptive fields of cells in the visual cortex (Hirsch and Spinelli, 1960; Blakemore and Cooper, 1970; Pettigrew, 1974). It is not yet clear to what extent these phenomena will be found in other species. Rabbits did not show modification of cortical receptive fields when raised with exposure to only horizontal or vertical stripes (Mize and Murphy, 1973), although this is the situation that produced clear modification in the kittens of Blakemore and Cooper (1970). Earlier work with rats seem to show little effect of visual deprivation on perceptual capacity, as measured on tests of pattern discrimination or on the visual cliff. Recent experimenters have, however, found some perceptual changes in rats as a function of early experience. Thus Walk and Walters (1973) found that rats kept in the dark for 30 days after birth could not discriminate a 4-inch depth but could discriminate a 6-inch depth; controls reared in a normal light-dark cycle discriminated well on both the 4-inch and 6-inch tests. The rats reared in the dark for 30 days recovered the ability to discriminate the 4-inch depth after 48 hr of light, but rats kept in the dark for 60 days had not recovered after 12 days of light. Tees (1974) has found that differential ability to perceive depth did not depend on experience in light at 20 days of age, but thereafter dark-reared rats did not improve at the same rate or acquire the same degree of discriminative ability as did their light-experienced counterparts. It appears therefore that a complex story about effects of light experience on ability in the rodent is developing. It must be recalled, however, that rats in both the usual EC and IC situations have light experience; the differences are only in the complexity of their visual and other surroundings.

Especially now that Hubel and Wiesel have reported anatomical evidence of altered cortical connections resulting from abnormal early stimulation (see their papers, Society for Neurosciences meeting, 1974), it seems appropriate to ask whether such sensory effects could be the basis for the cerebral effects of differential experience. Indeed, Blakemore and Mitchell entitled their 1973 paper "Environmental Modification of the Visual Cortex and the Neural Basis of Learning and Memory." But it seems to us that the effects of altered early sensory exposure are not likely to provide a general model for neural events in learning or for effects of differential experience. Let us compare certain aspects of the sensory effects and of the experiential effects with the aid of Table 3.

Role of Age. First consider the role of age of subjects in production of the effects. The effects of sensory exposure are limited to early life. Hubel and Wiesel (1962) reported that binocular organization of receptive fields in kittens has a sensitive period that extends from about the fourth to the eighth week after birth; later than this, little effect can be produced. Blakemore and Mitchell (1973) reported that for orientation of lines effects can be obtained from the third to the fourteenth week, with particular sensitivity

Table 3. Differences between Effects of Altered Sensory Exposure and Effects of Enriched Experience

	Effects of restricted or distorted sensory exposure	Effects of enriched experience (interaction with a complex environment)
Effects are produced readily in adults	No	Yes
Effects are produced by simple exposure to stimuli	Yes	No

during the fourth and fifth weeks. The restriction of these effects to a narrow age range clearly limits the generality of these findings to learning, since cats can learn throughout their life span. In contrast to the narrow age range during which effects of sensory exposure can be induced, effects of enriched experience have been found in rats at each age at which they have been tested. Thus Malkasian and Diamond (1971) found that preweaning experience had significant effects on size of neuronal perikarya. We have found typical effects on brain weights whether we put rats into the differential environments at 25, 60, 100, or 180 days of age. Riege (1971) in our laboratory obtained EC-SC-IC differences in rats assigned to differential environments at 285 days of age. Cummins *et al.* (1973) kept rats in differential environments until 500 days of age; subsequent training and maze testing then induced further brain changes in the previously isolated rats.

Effects of Simple Exposure to Stimuli. The changes in cortical receptive fields have been induced by simply restricting stimulation or by distorting it; at least, no requirement for active participation by the animal has been stated. In fact, it has been reported that receptive fields can be altered by presenting restricted stimuli to animals that have been immobilized by pharmacological agents. On the contrary, we have found that cerebral effects of enriched experience do not occur without the active participation of the subjects. We have just seen that rats placed in small OC cages within the large EC cage do not develop the brain values of EC rats—even though they share the sights, sounds, and smells of the EC cage (Ferchmin *et al.*, 1975). We have also reported that even rats placed singly in EC cages, and lacking all social stimulation, do develop EC brain values *if* they are primed to interact with the varied stimulus objects (Rosenzweig and Bennett, 1972).

It appears that living under standard colony conditions is perfectly adequate to bring about normal development of sensory-perceptual systems, but it is not sufficient to produce full development of brain and of problem-solving ability.

We recognize that species differences may play a role in these comparisons, since most research on sensory restriction has been done with cats or monkeys, whereas most work with enriched experience has been done with rodents. More direct species comparisons are needed with these research designs, and our group hopes to be able to pursue research on enriched experience with carnivores.

On the basis of currently available observations, we believe that the cerebral and behavioral effects of enriched experience should not be attributed to the effects of sensory exposure.

Relative Effectiveness of Inanimate and Social Stimulation

Having just eliminated extracage stimulation as playing any important role in determining the EC-IC cerebral differences—and having previously eliminated such factors as handling, locomotion, and stress—we now come to the factors of social stimulation and stimulation from the varied objects in the EC situation. We have considered the possible importance of social stimulation in previous papers (Rosenzweig, 1970; Rosenzweig *et al.*, 1972*c*), but further findings and discussion suggest that this factor now requires more searching evaluation. Thus Welch *et al.* (1974) have reported "that mere group living sufficed to increase brain weight without a complex physical environment being involved . . . . Our results suggest that the stimuli required for cerebral cortical enlargement are not as specific as the experience of learning to cope with structural complexity as Rosenzweig *et al.* suggest" (pp. 79–80). Welch *et al.* showed that rats living in a group of 12 for 1 year developed differences in brain weights and in brain RNA and DNA, compared to rats housed singly; environmental enrichment was not investigated. In a behavioral study, Morgan (1973) compared isolated rats to rats raised with both cagemates and varied objects; the isolates were inferior in problems involving acquisition and reversal of complex motor skills. No difference in performance was found, however, between rats raised in social groups that were distinguished by the presence or absence of varied stimulus objects. The behavioral differences were therefore attributed entirely to the social factor (isolation vs. grouping).

We recognize that there are many studies on a variety of effects of aggregation vs. isolation, especially in mice. It would be beyond the scope of this chapter to review such studies which do not compare effects of social stimulation with those of inanimate stimulation. For the interested reader, information about aggregation studies is found in de Feudis (1972, 1974) and Valzelli (1973).

Enrichment or Impoverishment from the Standard Colony Baseline

We had considered some effects of social grouping in our 1964 *Science* paper (Bennett *et al.*, 1964). In three experiments with S_1 rats, we had included groups housed in colony conditions, three to a cage (SC). We had found that in weight of cortex and in total AChE "the ECT group differed significantly from the SC group and differed further from them than did the IC group. Thus the bulk of the effects on cerebral weight and acetylcholinesterase activity is due to enriching rather than to restricting the experience of our colony animals." This was true both for animals assigned to the differential conditions at weaning (25 days of age) and for animals assigned at 105 days of age.

The relative contributions of enrichment and improverishment to brain measures were discussed extensively in Rosenzweig *et al.* (1972*c*) by comparing EC to SC and IC to SC. Let us summarize briefly some of the principal results for experiments of 80-day duration begun at weaning (in conditions from 25 to 105 days of age) and at 105 days (105–185), noting that the relative importance of enrichment and improverishment differs both with age and with the brain measures considered. Since the overall EC-IC differences are small but significant, it should be apparent that results of partialing these differences between the two factors should be taken as indicative only. For the five experiments run from 25 to 105 days, the cortical brain weight differences were chiefly due to enrichment (EC-SC, 2.8%, $P < 0.001$; IC-SC, −0.9%, N.S.), the subcortical weight differences were chiefly the result of impoverishment (EC-SC, 0.5%, N.S.; IC-SC, 2.1%, $P < 0.01$), and the cortical/subcortical ratio showed roughly equal results of both factors (EC-SC, 2.3%, $P < 0.001$; IC-SC, −3.0%, $P < 0.001$). Obviously the overall EC-IC differences are the sums of the two effects—for the cortical/subcortical ratio, 5.3%, $P < 0.001$. When experiments are started at weaning, the IC rats come to develop greater body weights than either EC or SC. When the percentage differences of brain weights are adjusted for covariance on body weight, the IC-SC differences then become somewhat greater than EC-SC in cortex as well as in subcortex. In several enzymatic measures—AChE per unit of weight, ChE/weight, and ChE/AChE—the effects were almost entirely due to impoverishment in the day 25–105 experiments. In contrast, for the three experiments run from 105 to 185 days, enrichment was clearly more effective than impoverishment in both cortical weight (EC-SC, 4.3%, $P < 0.001$; IC-SC, 1.6% $P < 0.05$) and the cortical/subcortical weight ratio (EC-SC, 3.2%, $P < 0.001$; IC-SC, −0.6% N.S.). For chemistry, only AChE/weight was determined for the older animals; the effects were small and were chiefly attributable to enrichment rather than to impoverishment.

Effects of EC, SC, and IC for still older rats were reported by Riege (1971). The brain weight measures were responsive both to enrichment above the SC baseline and to impoverishment. The cortical/subcortical ratio showed chiefly enrichment effects.

We have recently measured RNA and DNA in occipital cortex of rats assigned to EC, SC, and IC at weaning. For RNA/DNA, both EC and IC differed significantly from SC and in opposite directions. The effects of enrichment and of impoverishment were roughly similar in magnitude for these young rats. In experiments in which 100-day-old or 200-day-old rats were assigned to the three conditions for 30 days, the RNA/DNA ratios were similar in the SC and IC groups but were significantly greater in the EC group.

Anatomical effects in EC, SC, and IC—cortical depths, cell size, and synaptic lengths—are discussed by Diamond in her chapter in this volume. As for the weight and chemical measures, the relative effectiveness of enrichment and impoverishment depends on both the starting age and the measure considered. For still another anatomical measure, branching of cortical dendrites, Greenough and Volkmar (1973) have attributed the effects almost entirely to enrichment.

Concerning behavior, which is not our main focus in this chapter, we have found both EC-SC and IC-SC differences, and these varied with both the age of exposure to the differential environments and the test employed. Both of these factors have also come out in studies by other workers (see review in Rosenzweig, 1971).

The foregoing studies show clearly that there are effects of both enrichment and impoverishment on a number of brain measures. One obvious way in which the EC, SC, and IC situations differ is in the size of the social groups. Since the EC animals lived in groups of 12, whereas SC lived in groups of 3, the possibility remained that the EC-SC brain differences reflected mainly the sizes of the social groups rather than the differences in the inanimate environments. Two recent papers from other laboratories will be noted in which the most enriched situation has the largest group size, and so the two factors are confounded. Let us consider these studies briefly.

Kuenzle and Knüsel (1974) in Switzerland designed a "superenriched" environment. A group of 70 rats were housed in two large interconnected cages and had to shuttle back and forth across a bridge with changing gates and signals in order to find food and water. Over the 29-day experimental period, the rats found successively more complicated problems and also had to perform athletic feats in order to survive. In two replications, groups were run simultaneously in the superenriched environment and in a reproduction of the Berkeley EC situation. The super EC rats were found to surpass the regular EC rats in weight of occipital cortex, in length of the cerebral hemispheres, in ChE/AChE in occipital cortex, but not in RNA/DNA in occipital cortex. While these results are encouraging in showing even greater brain plasticity than found heretofore, it is clear that this experiment confounds the factors of social and inanimate enrichment, since the super EC was greater along both dimensions. Also, the stress on agility in the super EC renders questionable the assertion of Kuenzle and Knüsel that the super-enriched condition "is superior to the original [EC] in that it confronts the animal with true learning situations," whereas "the original setup mostly improves the animals' motor performance but does not provide for genuine learning situations."

Gardner *et al.* (1974) have measured separate effects of environmental and social enrichment on several behavioral tests. They kept male Long-Evans rats in one of four conditions, starting at 21 days and lasting for 60–70 days: (1) Perceptually enriched–socially enriched (PE-SE), in groups of 22 or 23 in large cages filled with varied objects that were moved or changed every 3 days; there were also extracage visual and auditory stimuli (flashing Christmas-tree lights and intermittent radio music). (2) Perceptually enriched–socially isolated (PE-SI), in small individual cages with a single object that was changed every 3 days; extracage visual and auditory stimuli as for PE-SE. It is clear that the perceptual enrichment as well as group size differed between PE-SE and PE-SI. (3) Perceptually impoverished–socially enriched (PI-SE), in groups of 22 or 23 in large cages of the same size as for PE-SE, but without stimulus objects. The room was dark and the cages were surrounded by sound-attenuating material, and white masking noise was delivered constantly. (4) Perceptually impoverished–socially impoverished (PI-SI), in individual cages kept, like PI-SE, in the dark and with sound attenuation and masking noise. PI-SI is similar to our condition of Isolation in Extreme Impoverishment (Krech *et al.*, 1966) and is thus more extreme than our usual IC condition.

On a one-trial passive avoidance step-down test, rats from all four conditions showed similar pretraining latencies, but there were significant differences in retention latencies. Both SE groups showed long latencies (excellent retention), and PE-SI showed good retention, but PI-SI gave little evidence of learning. Other animals from the same conditions were used to study memory consolidation by administration of electroconvulsive shock at varying intervals following a step-down trial. The investigators concluded that the socially impoverished rats suffered from a slowing of the consolidation process. All the rats were then tested for exploration in a Hebb-William maze used as an open field. The perceptually enriched groups explored more than the PI groups ($P < 0.01$), whereas the social variable had no effect. (It should be noted that this experiment did not distinguish between effects of intra- and extracage environmental stimulation.) On almost every measure Gardner *et al.* (1974) found significant interaction between the perceptual and social factors. This may well be true, but it could be in part an artifact that occurred because the perceptual enrichment was distinctly unequal for the PE-SE and the PE-SI groups.

Inanimate and Social Stimulation

Our first experiments comparing IC with groups of 12 in either EC or in a large cage without varied stimulus objects were done with male inbred Fischer rats as subjects (Rosenzweig, 1971). In two experiments, animals were placed in the differential conditions at 60 days of age and remained there for 30 days until sacrifice at 90 days of age. In all, seven experimental conditions were used; this was a reason for employing Fischer rats as subjects, since they are inbred and a littermate design did not have to be used; it would not have been possible to obtain sufficient litters with seven S_1 rats, and the Fischer animals had shown generally similar effects to our S_1 and S_3 strains in previous experiments. The seven conditions were as follows: Rats of one group in each experiment remained isolated in individual colony cages (IC) for 24 hr per day. One group of 12 lived for 24 hr per day in the usual EC conditions, while another group of 12 lived in an empty EC cage; this was called the Large Cage (LC), and we have more recently referred to it as the Group Condition (GC). Further groups were also placed in LC or EC for only 2 hr per day, since we had found that 2 hr of enriched experience suffices to bring about many of the same brain effects as does 24 hr per day (Rosenzweig *et al.*, 1968).

Brain weight measures at sacrifice showed that the animals placed in EC for either 24 or 2 hr per day differed significantly from the IC rats; on the other hand, the animals placed in groups of 12 in LC for either 24 or 2 hr per day did *not* differ significantly from the IC animals. The animals placed singly in EC or LC did not differ from the IC animals. Since the animals placed in groups of 12 in LC did not come to show significant differences from the IC animals, we concluded that social stimulation was not sufficient to bring about major differences from IC. In retrospect, it seems that we should have been concerned about not finding any differences between LC and IC, since we had previously reported significant differences between SC and IC. It may be that the Fischer strain of rats is not as much affected by social stimulation as is the Berkeley S_1 strain.

In conjunction with recent experiments in which groups of animals are given access to a maze 24 hr a day and required to run through it as they shuttled back and forth between food and water, we have included a control group placed in a large EC cage which is not furnished with the usual stimulus objects. Results of these experiments suggest that the subjects of the S_1 strain showed greater cerebral effects of grouping than did the Fischer subjects in the previous experiments reported above. Table 4 presents some of the results of EC, GC, and IC on brain weights and RNA/DNA ratio from these recent experiments. It will be seen that GC vs. IC shows about half as large an effect as EC vs. IC in weight of occipital cortex and weight of total cortex and about two-thirds the effect in the cortical/subcortical ratio. The comparison of EC with GC shows that the regular EC produces significantly larger brain weight effects in all areas—occipital cortex, total cortex, and the cortical/subcortical ratio. RNA and DNA were analyzed in only two cortical sections—occipital and the combination of somesthetic and remaining dorsal cortex. The RNA/DNA ratio of both cortical areas analyzed is significantly larger for animals raised in EC than for those raised in GC, and, in turn, the ratio for GC animals is significantly larger than for IC rats. Again the GC values are about half way between the EC and the IC values. Thus we can be sure that experience in the enriched condition produces significantly larger brain effects than does simple social living in a group of 12, but social living itself produces significant effects as compared with isolation.

The effects of living in the laboratory-enriched environment themselves are smaller than the effects of living in a seminatural environment, and this further shows that the stimulus situation is important as well as the size of the social group. The outdoor Seminatural Environment (SNE) was described briefly in Rosenzweig *et al.* (1972*a*). This condition has now been employed in a number of experiments where littermate S_1 male animals could be compared after either 30 days in SNE or 30 days in EC. The results show

Table 4. Percentage Differences between Brain Values of Rats in Enriched Condition (EC), Group Condition (GC), and Impoverished Condition (IC) [a]

	Occipital cortex	Somesthetic plus remaining dorsal cortex	Total cortex	Rest of brain	Cortex/Rest
A. Brain weights					
EC vs. IC	6.1 [b]	4.6 [b]	5.5 [b]	0.9	4.5 [b]
GC vs. IC	2.8 [d]	1.3	2.7 [c]	−0.4	3.1 [b]
EC vs. GC	3.2 [d]	3.3 [b]	2.7 [c]	1.3	1.4 [d]
B. RNA/DNA					
EC vs. IC	9.8 [b]	4.4 [b]	—	—	—
GC vs. IC	5.8 [b]	1.8 [c]	—	—	—
EC vs. GC	3.8 [b]	2.5 [b]	—	—	—

[b] $P < 0.001$.
[c] $P < 0.01$.
[d] $P < 0.05$.

that to a high level of significance 12 animals in the outdoor environment develop larger cortical weights and cortical/subcortical weight ratios than do their littermates in the EC condition.

(In discussion of work with the seminatural environment, we have found that some investigators presume that rats placed in a relatively large area will scatter and avoid social contacts or conflicts. It may therefore be worth putting on the record that laboratory rats of the two strains that we have studied in this situation [Fischer and S_1] prefer to stay together. We find them resting together under boards, or staying together in tunnels that they burrow.)

Another way to show the importance of inanimate stimulation comes from experiments in which the social factor was excluded but in which the cerebral enrichment effects were obtained. In a series of experiments begun in 1967, we found that rats receiving a daily injection of methamphetamine, before being put in the enriched condition for 2 hr a day, developed larger than usual brain weight effects. In her doctoral thesis, Su-Yu Chang (1969) reported that the animals given methamphetamine showed *less* social interaction than animals given saline injections, whereas the methamphetamine animals showed a greater than usual amount of interaction with the stimulus objects. In further research along this line (Rosenzweig and Bennett, 1972), we found that placing rats singly in EC (SEC) for 2 hr per day resulted in signficant differences from IC if the animals were given small injections of methamphetamine before the daily period in the enriched environment but not if they were given injections of saline. We therefore concluded that anatomical and chemical changes characteristic of EC will develop in the rat brain whenever the animal interacts with a relatively complex environment for at least a minimum daily period over at least a minimum duration of days. "Social stimulation, which heretofore has always been included in the enriched condition, is now found not to be necessary" (p. 304). Finding that social stimulation is not required to produce the EC-IC effects of course does not reveal whether or not social stimulation will contribute to the EC effect if the social condition is present.

We conclude that social living, while it has clear effects on brain measures, cannot account entirely for effects of our laboratory-enriched condition. Furthermore, additional environmental enrichment, while the size of the group is held constant, can bring about even larger cerebral effects. It is clear that the social condition itself warrants further study; perhaps the social condition is important in part because it provides opportunities for certain types of learning. And certainly the social condition is required as a control for other conditions in which animals are grouped together while effects of their factors are being studied.

Discussion

Major Factors in Environmental Enrichment

From the research reviewed above, it appears that some factors can now be set aside as having little or no importance in producing EC-IC cerebral effects. These factors than can now be safely disregarded include differential handling, differential locomotion, stress, and differential rates of maturation. Extracage stimulation seems to be of little importance, provided that some light and sound are present as in IC; removal of all visual and auditory stimulation, as in IEI, did produce effects of sensory deprivation. On the other hand, it appears that both the stimulation of contact with varied stimulus objects and social stimulation contribute independently to the enrichment. The experiments reviewed above show that a number of investigators have manipulated either or both of these factors, as Figure 2 illustrates. Considerable progress has already been made in mapping these two dimensions. Let us consider some of the results in terms of this figure.

The social dimension in Figure 2 is presented simply in terms of the number of animals living together, from one up. The enrichment of environment in terms of complexity of inanimate stimulus objects is more difficult to scale, and the ordinal scale presented here is purely intuitive. For example, how can one rank the relative enrichment of the large outdoor field (SNE), that of the Ferchmin procedure (FEC) with its variety of cages (Ferchmin *et al.*, 1970) and that of the complex "superenriched" environment in the Swiss laboratory (SE)? They differ from each other in several dimensions, but, since we could not readily decide which was more complex, we have given them the same rating; later research may settle such a question.

Some investigators have attempted to disentangle the effects of these two factors by varying one and hold the other constant. For example, we have done this by exposing single rats to a number of different experimental environments, as shown in the left-hand column of Figure 2. For single animals exposed under normal conditions of motivation, the inanimate environment apparently has relatively little effect; only extreme impoverishment (IEI) produced significantly different brain values from the IC condition. Even putting single rats in the enriched condition (SEC) did not bring about much difference, unless the single animals were exposed to it after having been administered an excitant drug which increased their interaction with the varied stimulus objects, and in that case they did differ from IC littermates in the EC direction. In the case of animals living in a group of 12, it has been easier to show the effect of environmental enrichment on cerebral measures. Here we have found that rats in SNE exceed rats in EC in several cerebral measures, and the EC rats in turn surpass rats

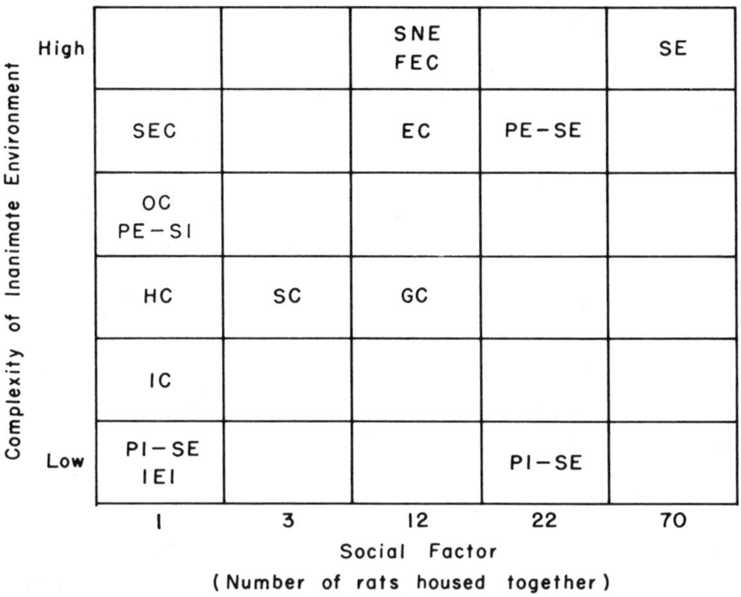

Figure 2. Representation of differential environments in terms of two main variables—inanimate stimulation and social grouping. The conditions have been described in the text, and the abbreviated designations are as follows. Rosenzweig *et al.*: EC (Environmental Complexity), FEC (Ferchmin EC), GC (Group Condition), HC (Home Cage), IC (Impoverished Condition), IEI (Isolated in Extreme Impoverishment), OC (Observer Condition), SC (Standard Colony), SEC (Single-Animal EC), SNE (Seminatural Environment). Gardner *et al.*: PE-SE (Perceptually Enriched–Socially Enriched), PE-SI (Perceptually Enriched–Socially Isolated), PI-SE (Perceptually Isolated–Socially Enriched), PI-SI (Perceptually Isolated–Socially Isolated). Kuenzle and Knüsel: SE (Superenriched Environment) and EC.

in GC in several measures. Thus there seems to be an interaction between environment and group size, the effects of environment showing up clearly with groups of 12 but being definitely smaller in the case of individual animals. We have discussed this previously (Rosenzweig and Bennett, 1972), pointing out that animals in a group tend to keep each other active, and this brings them into frequent contact with the inanimate stimulus objects as well as with each other; thus social grouping heightens the effects of inanimate enrichment.

This rather simple two-dimensional display could be complicated considerably by taking into account other variables and thus making a multidimensional display. Let us note some of these other variables. Age at which animals are exposed to the differential environments might well be taken into account. Even though we have found no critical period for these effects, it nevertheless seems to be true that somewhat larger effects are obtained when animals are placed in the differential environments at an early age than when they are already fully adult. The duration of exposure, both hours of exposure per day and number of days in the experimental period, also merits study. This will have to be investigated separately for different cerebral measures, since it appears that only a few days bring about clear effects in cerebral weights and nucleic acid concentrations whereas many weeks are required for clear effects in cholinesterase activity. The types of stimuli used could also be a subject of investigation. To date, we have used a variety of readily obtainable objects and gadgets without particular reference to the preferences of the animal subjects. One could well investigate the effectiveness of species-specific stimuli, such as odors produced by animals or animal products. One of the most important directions in which research should be extended, it seems to us, is to investigate the effects with other species of experimental animals. To date, we have found rather similar effects in four species of rodents—laboratory rats, laboratory mice, gerbils, and feral *Peromyscus*. It seems important to extend this research to other orders of mammals. Many theorists already have seized upon the results obtained with rodents and have extrapolated them freely to other orders, including man. Clearly it is important to know whether the results obtained to date, or similar effects, will be found in other mammalian orders. We believe that an important next step will be to run similar experiments with cats. With this species, we can use the same multiple litter designs that have been successful with rodents, and research with cats is both feasible and relatively economical. In the long run, of course, it would be important to extend this research further to primates.

The Role of Learning in Producing Effects of Environmental Enrichment

A much debated question has been whether differential opportunity for learning is one of the major causes of cerebral differences resulting from experience in differential environments. As we noted near the start of this chapter, we embarked upon the research with the differential environment because of our unexpected early findings that training in different formal programs led to changes in brain chemistry. We set up the differential environments in order to increase the differential opportunity to learn with the hope that this would enhance the brain differences, and in fact such increased differences were obtained. It is of course not certain that these larger cerebral effects could be attributed to learning and memory as such.

Others who have done research in this area have maintained that learning must be involved in producing these cerebral differences. Thus Greenough

(1976) states that "it would be much more difficult to argue that EC rats do *not* learn more than their cage housed counterparts than it is to argue that they do." He presents several specific reasons to support the conclusion that differential memory formation is at least one component in producing these cerebral effects: First, both the behavioral and the cerebral effects of environmental complexity appear to be potentiated by drugs that affect memory formation. In this regard, he cites our reports (Bennett *et al.*, 1973; Rosenzweig and Bennett, 1972) that daily administration of excitant drugs potentiates the effects of environmental complexity upon brain measures. He also notes reports that effects of complex environment upon maze learning are enhanced by daily administration of strychnine (LeBoeuf and Peeke, 1969; Peeke *et al.*, 1971). Second, Greenough notes that our group and others have found effects of environmental complexity on brain weights and nucleic acids after only a few days in the differential environments, and thus the time scale is compatible with that of experiments on learning and memory (Ferchmin *et al.*, 1970). Furthermore, brain weight differences occur even when exposure to environmental complexity is restricted to as little as 2 hr per day for 30 days, again a daily period comparable to that of many learning experiments (Rosenzweig *et al.*, 1968). Third, Greenough points out that behavioral effects of enriched experience seem to be greatest on tasks which are rather similar to the complex environment, especially mazes.

Gardner *et al.* (1974) consider a number of types of learning that probably take place in the enriched situation. They note that rats living in a social group sometimes display aggressive behavior and this provides opportunities for passive avoidance learning that may then transfer to other situations. Perceptually enriched rats may learn to explore objects and spatial arrangements, and this may generalize positively to the open field and to maze situations. They also suggest that there may be specific alterations in brain mechanisms subserving learning and memory.

Seligman (1975) suggests that another type of learning occurs—learning to control situations or, on the contrary, to be helpless:

> In any deprivation or enrichment study, it is easy to overlook the deprivation and enrichment of control. When an experimenter adds toy blocks and mazes to the laboratory environment of a rat, he not only adds more things, but he adds more *control* over things. The environment is enriched not only because the block is there, but because the animal interacts with it; he sniffs it, overturns it, chews it. I doubt very much that adding objects, without allowing concomitant control, would yield any effects of enrichment (p. 146).

The experiment of Ferchmin *et al.* (1975) has, in fact, provided evidence that stimuli that do not provide an opportunity for control do not yield either cerebral or behavioral effects of enrichment.

We can adduce further evidence that demonstrates that learning takes place in the enriched situation. Thus McCall *et al.* (1969) have tested the responses of rats to objects that have previously been placed in their cages and novel objects. There are clear differences in the reactions to these classes of objects, thus showing that the animals have learned to distinguish them. Further evidence of learning in the EC situation comes from a recent study by Parsons and Spear (1972). In three experiments, two with weanlings and one with adult rats, the animals first learned in an active avoidance situation. Animals were kept in either an enriched or a standard laboratory environment for 60 days before being given a retention test. Environmental enrichment in the interim period resulted in greater forgetting of the active avoidance response than did the standard laboratory environment. The experimenters concluded that learning in the complex situation resulted in extraexperimental interference with retention of the avoidance response.

The evidence and the reasoning summarized in this section of the discussions offer strong support for the conclusion that learning and memory formation are taking place at a greater rate in the EC than in the SC or IC situations. It remains to be shown how the learning and memory formation are tied to the observable changes in cerebral measures, and this will undoubtedly provide a fertile field for further research. In our own laboratory, we are pursuing investigations of formal training in situations which we hope will produce cerebral effects in ways that can more readily be related to learning than has been true in the past.

L'Envoi

The experimentation and conceptualization reviewed in this chapter span many years, and, as we have noted, arose out of the still earlier concerns that David Krech and we shared concerning the role of neurochemical variables in individual differences in problem solving. We look back with pleasure to 1954, when we began a dozen years of interdisciplinary collaboration with David Krech, who was responsible for many of the ideas and research techniques discussed here. While we remain cautious about the relations between learning and cerebral effects in our rats, we are certain of the stimulation and learning that we gained from our collaboration with David Krech, and we think back to many lively discussions, over many cups of tea.

Acknowledgments

Our research described in this chapter has extended over many years, and numerous individuals have made important contributions to it. Particular acknowledgment and appreciation are due Mrs. Marie Hebert, who has made the thousands of brain dissections needed to obtain all of the data summarized in this report. Hiromi Morimoto, assisted by Mrs. Hebert, has done all of the analyses for acetylcholinesterase and cholinesterase, RNA and DNA, water, and other constituents. Over the past few years, Donald Dryden has been responsible for much of the animal care, maintenance, and behavioral testing. Arun Prakash has ably compiled the data and performed the statistical analysis. Finally, Mrs. Jessie Langford has skillfully kept the records of the project and has patiently and accurately typed and retyped the manuscripts. In addition to these staff members, several students—both undergraduate and graduate—have been active in various aspects of this research; two postdoctoral fellows deserve special mention—Walter H. Riege and Pedro A. Ferchmin.

Along with the dedication of those who have helped us, another factor, money, has also been necessary. Over the years, several grants have provided this essential support. These have included NSF Grants GB-8011, GB-11840, and GB-30368, a grant from NIMH (MH-07903), and a grant from the Office of Education (OEG-0-9-140398). The U.S. Atomic Energy Commission, through the Lawrence Berkeley Laboratory, provided support for this project from its inception.

References

Balázs, T., Murphy, J. B., and Grice, H. C. 1962. The influence of environmental changes on the cardiotoxicity of isoprenaline in rats. *Journal of Pharmacy and Pharmacology*, *14*, 750–755.

Bennett, E. L. 1976. Brain effects of differential experience and training. In: *Neural Mechanisms of Learning and Memory*. M. R. Rosenzweig and E. L. Bennett (Eds.). M.I.T. Press, Cambridge, Mass., pp. 279–287.

Bennett, E. L., and Rosenzweig, M. R. 1971. Potentials of an intellectually enriched environment. In: *Progress in Human Nutrition*. S. Margen (Ed.). Avi Publishing Co., Westport, Conn., pp. 210–224.

Bennett, E. L., Rosenzweig, M. R., Krech, D., Ohlander, A., and Morimoto, H. 1961. Cholinesterase activity and protein content of rat brain. *Journal of Neurochemistry*, *6*, 210–218.

Bennett, E. L., Diamond, M. C., Krech, D., and Rosenzweig, M. R. 1964. Chemical and anatomical plasticity of brain. *Science*, *146*, 610–619.

Bennett, E. L., Rosenzweig, M. R., and Diamond, M. C. 1969. Rat brain: Effects of environmental enrichment on wet and dry weights. *Science*, *163*, 825–826.

Bennett, E. L., Rosenzweig, M. R., and Wu, S.-Y. C. 1973. Excitant and depressant drugs modulate effects of environment on brain weight and cholinesterases. *Psychopharmacologia*, *33*, 309–328.

Bennett, E. L., Rosenzweig, M. R., and Diamond, M. C. 1974. Effects of successive environments on brain measures. *Physiology and Behavior*, *12*, 621–631.

Blakemore, C., and Cooper, G. F. 1970. Development of the brain depends on the visual environment. *Nature* (*London*), *228*, 467–468.

Blakemore, C., and Mitchell, D. E. 1973. Environmental modification of the visual cortex and the neural basis of learning and memory. *Nature* (*London*), *241*, 467–468.

Chang, S.-Y. 1969. Changes produced in rat brain by environmental complexity and drug injection. Doctoral dissertation, University of California, Berkeley.

Cragg, B. G. 1972. Plasticity of synapses. In: *The Structure and Function of Nervous Tissue*, Vol. IV. G. H. Bourne (Ed.). Academic Press, New York, pp. 2–60.

Cummins, R. A., Walsh, R. N., Budtz-Olsen, O. E., Konstantinos, T., and Horsfall, C. R. 1973. Environmentally-induced changes in the brain of elderly rats. *Nature* (*London*), *243*, 516–518.

Daly, M. 1973. Early stimulation of rodents: A critical review of present interpretations. *British Journal of Psychology*, *64*, 435–460.

de Feudis, F. V. 1972. Effects of isolation and aggregation on the water content of mouse brain. *Biological Psychiatry*, *5*, 207–211.

de Feudis, F. V. 1974. Differences in brain and body weights of mice caused by differential housing. *Experientia*, *30*, 207–210.

Diamond, M. C., Krech, D., and Rosenzweig, M. R. 1964. The effects of an enriched environment on the histology of the rat cerebral cortex. *Journal of Comparative Neurology*, *123*, 111–119.

Diamond, M. C., Johnson, R., and Ingham, C. A. 1971. Brain plasticity induced by environment and pregnancy. *International Journal of Neuroscience*, *2*, 171–178.

Diamond, M. C., Johnson, R. E., and Ingham, C. A. 1975. Morphological changes in the young, adult and aging rat cerebral cortex, hippocampus, and diencephalon. *Behavioral Biology*, *14*, 163–174.

Edwards, H. P., Barry, W. F., and Wyspianski, J. O. 1969. Effect of differential rearing on photic evoked potentials and brightness discrimination in the albino rat. *Developmental Psychobiology*, *2*, 133–138.

Ferchmin, P. A., Eterovic, V. A., and Caputto, R. 1970. Studies of brain weight and RNA content after short periods of exposure to environmental complexity. *Brain Research*, *20*, 49–57.

Ferchmin, P. A., Bennett, E. L., and Rosenzweig, M. R. 1975. Direct contact with enriched environment is required to alter cerebral weights in rats. *Journal of Comparative and Physiological Psychology*, *88*, 360–367.

Forgays, D. G., and Forgays, J. W. 1952. The nature of the effect of free-environmental experience on the rat. *Journal of Comparative and Physiological Psychology*, *45*, 322–328.

Gardner, E. B., Boitano, J. J., Mancino, N. S., D'Amico, D. P., and Gardner, E. L. 1974. Environmental enrichment and deprivation: Effects on learning, memory and exploration. *Physiology and Behavior*, *14*, 321–327.

Geller, E. 1971. Some observations on the effects of environmental complexity and isolation on biochemical ontogeny. In: *Brain Development and Behavior*. M. B. Sterman, D. J. McGinty, and A. M. Adlinolfi (Eds.). Academic Press, New York, pp. 277–296.

Geller, E., and Yuwiler, A. 1968. In: *Ontogenesis of the Brain*. L. Jilek and S. Trojan (Eds.). Charles University, Prague, p. 277.

Greenough, W. T. 1976. Enduring brain effects of differential experience and training. In: *Neural Mechanisms of Learning and Memory*. M. R. Rosenzweig and E. L. Bennett (Eds.). M.I.T. Press, Cambridge, Mass., p. 255–278.

Greenough, W. T., and Volkmar, F. R. 1973. Pattern of dendritic branching in occipital cortex of rats reared in complex environments. *Experimental Neurology*, *40*, 491–504.

Greenough, W. T., Madden, T. C., and Fleischmann, T. B. 1972. Effects of isolation, daily handling, and enriched rearing on maze learning. *Psychonomic Science*, *27*, 279–280.

Hatch, A., Wiberg, G. S., Balázs, T., and Grice, H. C. 1963. Long-term isolation stress in rats. *Science, 142*, 507.

Hirsch, H. V. B., and Spinelli, D. N. 1970. Visual experience modifies distribution of horizontally and vertically oriented receptive fields in cats. *Science, 168*, 869–871.

Hoover, D. M., and Diamond, M. C. 1976. Effects of norethynodrel administration on the rat visual cortex exposed to differential environment: A preliminary study of electrolytes and water. *Brain Research*, in press.

Hubel, D. H., and Wiesel, T. N. 1962. Receptive fields, binocular interaction and functional architecture in the cat's visual cortex. *Journal of Physiology, 160*, 106–154.

Hymovitch, B. 1952. The effects of experimental variations on problem-solving in the rat. *Journal of Comparative and Physiological Psychology, 45*, 313–321.

Krech, D., Rosenzweig, M. R., and Bennett, E. L. 1960. Effects of environmental complexity and training on brain chemistry. *Journal of Comparative and Physiological Psychology, 53*, 509–519.

Krech, D., Rosenzweig, M. R., and Bennett, E. L. 1966. Environmental impoverishment, social isolation and changes in brain chemistry and anatomy. *Physiology and Behavior, 1*, 99–104.

Kuenzle, C. C., and Knüsel, A. 1974. Mass training of rats in a superenriched environment. *Physiology and Behavior, 13*, 205–210.

Lavallee, R. J. 1969. The effects of early visual and motor experience on adult problem solving in hooded and albino rats. *Psychonomic Science, 17*, 21–22.

Lavallee, R. J. 1970. Effects of visual form and distance experience before maturity on adult problem-solving ability in the rat. *Developmental Psychology, 2*, 257–263.

LeBoeuf, B. J., and Peeke, H. V. S. 1969. The effect of strychnine administration during development on adult maze learning in the rat. *Psychopharmacologia, 16*, 49–53.

Mailloux, J. G., Edwards, H. P., Barry, W. F., Rowsell, H. C., and Achorn, E. G. 1974. Effects of differential rearing on cortical evoked potentials of the albino rat. *Journal of Comparative and Physiological Psychology, 87*, 475–480.

Maki, W. S., Jr. 1971. Failure to replicate effect of visual pattern restriction on brain and behaviour. *Nature (London) New Biology, 233*, 63–64.

Malkasian, D. R., and Diamond, M. C. 1971. The effects of environmental manipulation on the morphology of the neonate rat brain. *International Journal of Neuroscience, 2*, 161–170.

McCall, R. B., Lester, M. L., and Dolan, C. G. 1969. Differential rearing and the exploration of stimuli in the open field. *Developmental Psychology, 1*, 750–762.

Mize, R. R., and Murphy, E. H. 1973. Selective visual experience fails to modify receptive field properties of rabbit striate cortex neurons. *Science, 180*, 320–323.

Morgan, M. J. 1973. Effects of post-weaning environment on learning in the rat. *Animal Behaviour, 21*, 429–442.

Parsons, P. J., and Spear, N. E. 1972. Long-term retention of avoidance learning by immature and adult rats as a function of environmental enrichment. *Journal of Comparative and Physiological Psychology, 80*, 297–303.

Peeke, H. V. S., LeBoeuf, B. J., and Herz, M. J. 1971. The effect of strychnine administration during development on adult maze learning in the rat. II. Drug administration from day 51 to 70. *Psychopharmacologia, 19*, 262–265.

Pettigrew, J. D. 1974. The effect of selective visual experience on stimulus trigger features of kitten cortical neurons. *Annals of the New York Academy of Sciences, 228*, 393–405.

Riege, W. H. 1971. Environmental influences on brain and behavior of old rats. *Developmental Psychobiology, 4*, 157–167.

Riege, W. H., and Morimoto, H. 1970. Effects of chronic stress and differential environments upon brain weights and biogenic amine levels in rats. *Journal of Comparative and Physiological Psychology*, *71*, 396–404.

Rosenzweig, M. R. 1968. Effects of experience on brain chemistry and brain anatomy. *Atti della Accademia Nazionale dei Lincei*, *109*, 43–63.

Rosenzweig, M. R. 1970. Evidence for anatomical and chemical changes in the brain during primary learning. In: *Biology of Memory*. K. Pribram and D. Broadbent (Eds.). Academic Press, New York, p. 69–85.

Rosenzweig, M. R. 1971. Role of experience in development of neurophysiological regulatory mechanisms and in organization of the brain. In: *Early Childhood: The Development of Self-regulatory Mechanisms*. D. C. Walcher and D. L. Peters (Eds.). Academic Press, New York, p. 15–33.

Rosenzweig, M. R., and Bennett, E. L. 1969. Effects of differential environments on brain weights and enzyme activities in gerbils, rats, and mice. *Developmental Psychobiology*, *2*, 87–95.

Rosenzweig, M. R., and Bennett, E. L. 1972. Cerebral changes in rats exposed individually to an enriched environment. *Journal of Comparative and Physiological Psychology*, *80*, 304–313.

Rosenzweig, M. R., Krech, D., and Bennett, E. L. 1961. Heredity, environment, brain biochemistry, and learning. In: *Current Trends in Psychological Theory*. University of Pittsburgh Press, Pittsburgh, pp. 87–110.

Rosenzweig, M. R., Krech, D., Bennett, E. L., and Diamond, M. C. 1962. Effects of environmental complexity and training on brain chemistry and anatomy: A replication and extension. *Journal of Comparative and Physiological Psychology*, *55*, 429–437.

Rosenzweig, M. R., Krech, D., Bennett, E. L., and Diamond, M. C. 1968. Modifying brain chemistry and anatomy by enrichment or impoverishment of experience. In: *Early Experience and Behavior*. G. Newton and S. Levine (Eds.). Charles C Thomas, Springfield, Ill., pp. 258–298.

Rosenzweig, M. R., Love, W., and Bennett, E. L. 1968. Effects of a few hours a day of enriched experience on brain chemistry and brain weights. *Physiology and Behavior*, *3*, 819–825.

Rosenzweig, M. R., Bennett, E. L., and Diamond, M. C. 1972*a*. Cerebral changes in response to experience. *Scientific American*, *226*(*2*), 22–29.

Rosenzweig, M. R., Bennett, E. L., and Diamond, M. C. 1972*b*. Cerebral effects of differential environments occur in hypophysectomized rats. *Journal of Comparative and Physiological Psychology*, *79*, 56–66.

Rosenzweig, M. R., Bennett, E. L., and Diamond, M. C. 1972*c*. Chemical and anatomical plasticity of brain: Replications and extensions, 1970. In: *Macromolecules and Behavior* (2nd ed.). Appleton-Century-Crofts, New York, pp. 205–277.

Seligman, M. E. P. 1975. *Helplessness: On Depression, Development, and Death*. Freeman, San Francisco.

Singh, D., Johnston, R. J., and Klosterman, H. J. 1967. Effect on brain enzyme and behavior in the rat of visual pattern restriction in early life. *Nature* (*London*), *216*, 1337–1338.

Singh, D., Maki, W. S., Jr., Johnston, R. J., and Klosterman, H. J. 1970. Effect of visual pattern restriction in early life on brain enzyme, body weight and learning in the rat. *Nature* (*London*), *228*, 471–472.

Sperry, R. W. 1968. Plasticity of neural maturation. 27th Symposium of Social and Developmental Biology, *Developmental Biology*, *Supplement 2*, 306–327.

Tees, R. C. 1974. Effect of visual deprivation on development of depth perception in the rat. *Journal of Comparative and Physiological Psychology*, *86*, 300–308.
Valzelli, L. 1973. The "isolation syndrome" in mice. *Psychopharmacologia*, *31*, 305–320.
Walk, R. D., and Walters, C. P. 1973. Effect of visual deprivation on depth discrimination of hooded rats. *Journal of Comparative and Physiological Psychology*, *85*, 559–563.
Welch, B. L., Brown, D. G., Welch, A. S., and Lin, D. C. 1974. Isolation, restrictive confinement or crowding of rats for one year. I. Weight, nucleic acids and protein of brain regions. *Brain Research*, *75*, 71–84.

8

Marian Cleeves Diamond

ANATOMICAL BRAIN CHANGES INDUCED BY ENVIRONMENT

Twenty-six years ago I began to study the structure and function of the brain, because I believed that the greatest plague inflicting mankind was initiated by the brain. Ecclesiastes tells us that vanity and vexation of spirit are the characteristics of man, whether he be rich or poor. And only a creature with a brain would invent and suffer from such cognitive ills. If the biological basis of behavior were found, perhaps man's existence could be a better lot. By understanding the structural and functional mechanisms of behavior, man might even solve his ancient emotional problems. Just how far have we come? Only after joining the team of Krech, Rosenzweig, and Bennett did I think I was taking steps in the right direction toward correlating learning behavior with brain anatomy. The purpose of this chapter is to present a collection of information which attempts to understand how the microscopic structure of the forebrain changes during the lifetime of one mammal, the rat, whether it be during normal development and aging or during life in artificially provided environments. Both external and internal environmental manipulations affect brain morphology. The experiments to be reported here involve primarily external factors which were manipulated by exposing animals to various degrees of environmental complexity. Since neurons are extraordinarily difficult to study *in vivo* without interfering with the subject, most information is accumulated from preserved material, and, for the same reason, neurons are studied from lower animals and not from human beings.

Marian Cleeves Diamond • Department of Physiology-Anatomy, University of California, Berkeley, California.

The Young, Adult, and Aging Forebrain

The normal development and aging pattern is presented first to serve as a standard for comparison with brain changes induced by environment. A literature search for information on quantitative changes in the anatomy of the forebrain during development and aging indicates a sparsity of complete data. In 1917, Sugita measured the thickness of the rat cortex during aging, but his samples were small for each age group, and the sections measured did not correspond to those commonly used today. A recent study in our laboratory (Diamond *et al.*, 1975*a*) showed the changes in depth during development and aging, using at least 15 rats per age group from 6 to 650 days, of not only the cortex but the hippocampus and diencephalon as well (Figure 1). (Figure 2 designates the positions of the areas measured.) Figure 1 shows that all parts of the cortex, anterior, posterior, medial, and lateral, increase in depth rapidly until 26 days of age, and then there is a 9% decrease in cortical depth between 26 and 650 days of age. A search for hemispheric dominance in the rat showed the right hemisphere to be thicker than the left in all age groups with but a few small reversals. The right medial (B) and the lateral (D) segments (Figure 2) are on the average between 2 and 3% greater than the comparable left hemisphere segments, whereas the dorsal (C) segment is between 5 and 7% greater in the right than in the left hemisphere. These quantitative hemispheric differences are apparent throughout the lifetime of the rat.

In contrast to the cortex, the hippocampal depth continues to increase until 650 days of age (Figure 1, middle section). The initial rise in depth from 6 to 10 days is very similar to the pattern of cortical growth, but instead of reaching a maximum at 26 days a slow 9% increase is seen by 650 days.

As in the cortex and the hippocampus, the greatest increases in diencephalon dimensions occur between 6 and 10 days of age, and then, like the hippocampus, the diencephalon continues to increase until 650 days. Apparently both the hippocampus and diencephalon are increasing in dimensions (by about 9–10%) with aging, while the cortex is decreasing by 9% or possibly stretching over the increasing subcortical mass (Figure 1).

In an attempt to understand the changes occurring in the constituents of the cortex with development and aging, different measurements have been taken on cell number and size. At birth, the rat has 94–97% of the adult number of neurons (Schade and Ford, 1965). In 1968, Brizzee and colleagues found an absence of any significant decrease in neuron density between 109–113 days and 763–972 days of age, but an increase in number of glial cells was noted. There was no difference in the distribution of neurons through cortical layers as a function of aging. The glial population was greater in the aged brain at all levels of the cortex except between the two

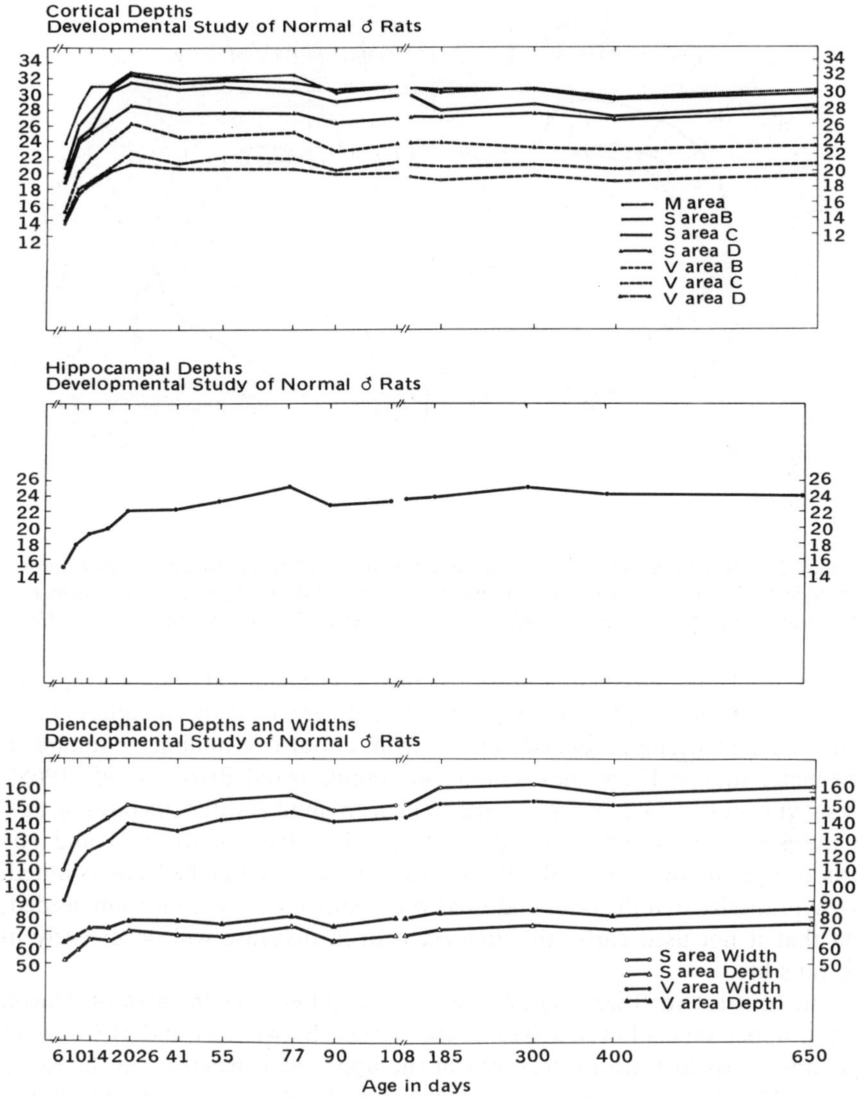

Figure 1. Developing and aging curves of the Long-Evans rat, cortical depth, hippocampal depth, and diencephalon width and depth from 6 to 650 days of age. The ordinate shows the measurements in millimeters at 22.5× magnification. The M area represents a tissue sample taken immediately before the anterior crossing of the corpus callosum. The S area is at the level of the crossing of the anterior commissure and the V at the level of the posterior commissure. The hippocampal depths were taken at the V level. From Diamond *et al.* (1975*a*).

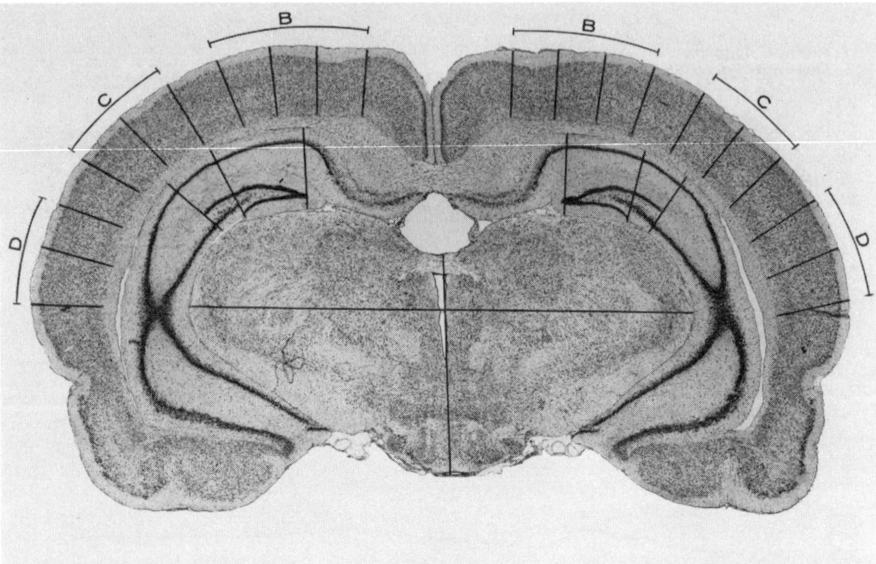

Figure 2. A transverse section of the rat brain at the level of the posterior commissure to indicate the position of the measurements for cortical depth, B, C, and D segments; hippocampal depth; and diencephalon width and depth. From Diamond *et al.* (1975*a*).

deepest levels measured. In a more recent study (Diamond *et al.*, 1976*a*), we counted neurons on photomicrographs of segment B of the occipital cortex (Figure 2), enlarging an area of cortex from about one millimeter square to one meter square. From these counts we found, as did Brizzee *et al.* (1968), no significant loss (4% N.S.) in cortical neuron number after 108 days of age, in the period from 108 to 650 days of age. However, between 41 and 108 days of age an 18% ($p < 0.001$) decrease in neuron number was counted. We hypothesize that the rat is endowed with many more neurons than needed, and that if not used early, the greatest neuron decrease will occur early in the rat's life.

In contrast to Brizzee *et al.*, we did find differences in rates of neuron loss in upper versus lower halves of the cortex. Between 41 and 108 days of age, a 9% loss in neurons occurred in the upper half; whereas, in the lower half, a 24% loss took place. Between 108 and 650 days of age, the upper layers lost 7%, and the lower layers, only 1%. Thus, the association layers apparently lose cells continuously with aging; whereas, cells in the projection layers are lost only in the early years.

At birth, the nuclei and perikarya are less than half the adult size (Schade and Baxter, 1960). By 6 days of age, the mean perikaryon volume has increased by 60% compared to that of the 1-day-old animal (Brizzee and

Jacobs, 1959). Measurements of neuronal nuclear volume in the visual cortex show a sharp decrease, about 30%, between 26 and 41 days of age, and thereafter a 13% decrease until 650 days (Diamond *et al.*, 1976*a*).

With regard to glial number and aging, Brizzee *et al.* (1968) found a moderate increase in packing density of the glial cells in the cerebral cortex throughout the life-span of the animal from 109–113 to 763–972 days. Glial counts were completed more recently on the photographs used for neuron determinations (Diamond *et al.*, 1976*a*). By counting about 450 glial cells/animal in 13 animals/age group, we found a decrease of 34% ($p < 0.001$) between 41 and 108 days of age, but only a 4% (N.S.) decrease between 108 and 650 days of age. The neuron and glial aging pattern was identical in this latter period. Using a DNA analysis, Enesco (1967) and Mandel and Bieth (1952) suggest the possibility that no change in total cell numbers occurs in the rat brain after the fourteenth postnatal day. These data show that the analyses of DNA content in whole brains are not really a very meaningful approach to following patterns of glial and neuron populations.

Brizzee *et al.* (1968) found the total rat brain weight and the weight of the major subdivisions greater in aged than in young adult rat brains. The ratio of forebrain weight to total brain weight increased significantly from young adult to old rats. Thus brain weight measures, including all parts of the forebrain, do not necessarily agree with measures on histological preparations (Diamond *et al.* 1975*a*). Loss of water during the histological preparations of the tissues may be one significant factor.

In summary, from examination of the data on the developing and aging forebrain it appears that the rat cerebral cortex increases in depth until 26 days of age and then slowly decreases until at least 650 days, whereas the hippocampus and diencephalon both continue to increase in dimensions until 650 days of age. The right cerebral hemisphere is thicker than the left in every cortical region measured between the ages of 6 and 650 days. The rat has about 95% of its neurons at birth and appears to lose or redistribute them most rapidly in the first 100 days. Both the volume of cortical neurons and the cortical depth show a considerable decrease during this time period. Between 100 and 650 days of age, there is very little difference in neuronal and glial number per unit area of rat cortex.

Effects of Environment on the Preweaned Rat Cortex

Having examined some data available on the growth and development of the postnatal forebrain of the rat, it is of interest to learn how some extrinsic factors from the environment influence these brain dimensions. During the first 26 days of the rat's life, the cortex is growing most rapidly, and it was during this preweaning period that we (Malkasian and Diamond, 1971) placed rats in modified enriched and impoverished environments. Before the pups were 6 days of age, we found that the mothers disturbed the nest too violently to allow several mothers and their pups to live together in a single cage. So at 6 days of age three groups of animals were formed: (1) one mother with her three male pups remained in a standard colony cage (Unifamily Environment, UFE); (2) three mothers with three male pups each were placed together in a single large cage (Multifamily Environment, MFE); (3) three mothers with three male pups each were placed together in a single large cage with various metal objects (Enriched Condition–Multifamily Environment, EC-MFE). The UFE vs. EC-MFE cohort was divided into three age groups to be sacrificed at 14, 19, and 28 days of age. The results showed no cortical depth differences between 28-day-old UFE and MFE rats in either the somatosensory or occipital cortices, but the EC-MFE had significantly greater cortical depth than the UFE at all age groups (Figure 3 shows such changes in the occipital cortex). At 14 days of age, there were cortical depth differences as large as 16% in the EC-MFE animals compared to the UFE animals, and as large as 12% at 28 days. These findings suggest that some regions of a neonate cortex may be morphologically more responsive to the external environment than is the adult brain, which has been reported to demonstrate changes in the range of 5–10%. In addition, the neuronal nuclear and perikaryon areas in the somatosensory cortex were significantly greater in the EC-MFE animals than in those from the UFE in the 28 day old group.

Not only did the cortical differences between the UFE and the EC-MFE rats show marked differences at 14 days of age, the earliest period measured, but also, in the EC-MFE animals, the eyes opened 1 day earlier, giving an additional measure indicating that maturation of the nervous system was enhanced by the enriched environment. Increased neurogenesis may have resulted in increased rate of innervation of the orbital structures facilitating earlier eye opening (Eayrs, 1951).

Thus these results, when compared with the rapid growth curve of the cortex from the preweaned rat, indicate that maturation can be enhanced during the preweaning period.

Effects of Environment on Postweaned Male Rat Cortical Depth

In order to study the effects of environment on the rat brain, three types of environmental conditions are commonly used in our laboratory: Enriched (EC), Impoverished (IC), and Standard Colony (SC). EC animals were housed in a large cage (70 by 70 by 46 cm) and had access to stimulus objects (toys) which were changed daily. The EC animals were placed for 30 min in

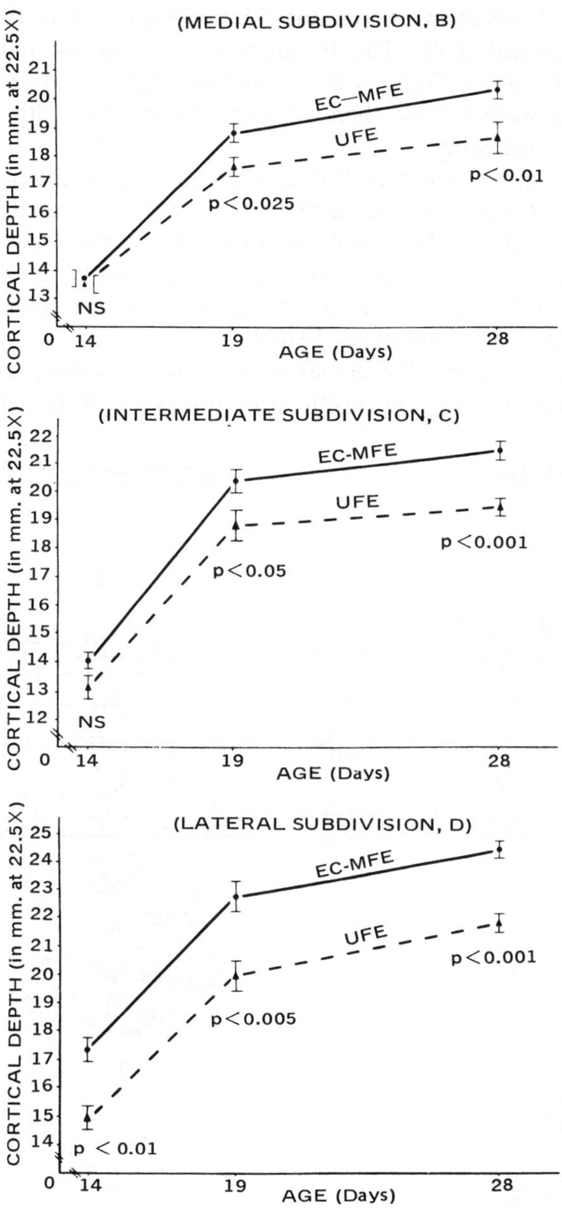

Figure 3. Depth of the occipital cortex in the preweaned Long-Evans rat as a function of age, comparing the Unifamily Environment with the Enriched Condition–Multifamily Environment rats. See Figure 2 for the approximate position of the B, C, and D segments in this experiment. From Malkasian and Diamond (1971).

the field of a Hebb-Williams apparatus (75 by 75 cm) where the pattern of barriers was changed daily. The IC animals were housed individually in small cages (32 by 20 by 20 cm) with no stimulus objects or maze experience. The SC animals were housed three to a small cage also with no stimulus objects or maze experience.

In the original experiments dealing with anatomical measures and enriched and impoverished environments, 80 days was considered as a reasonable time to bring about changes in brain structure. Since those first experiments, the duration has been decreased gradually from 80 days to 30 to 15 to 7 to 4 days and to 1 day, even though no changes were found during the 1-day experiments (Diamond *et al.*, 1976*b*).

Figures 4 and 5 show the dorsal view of the rat brain, with the lines 1 through 10 representing the positions of transverse histological sections

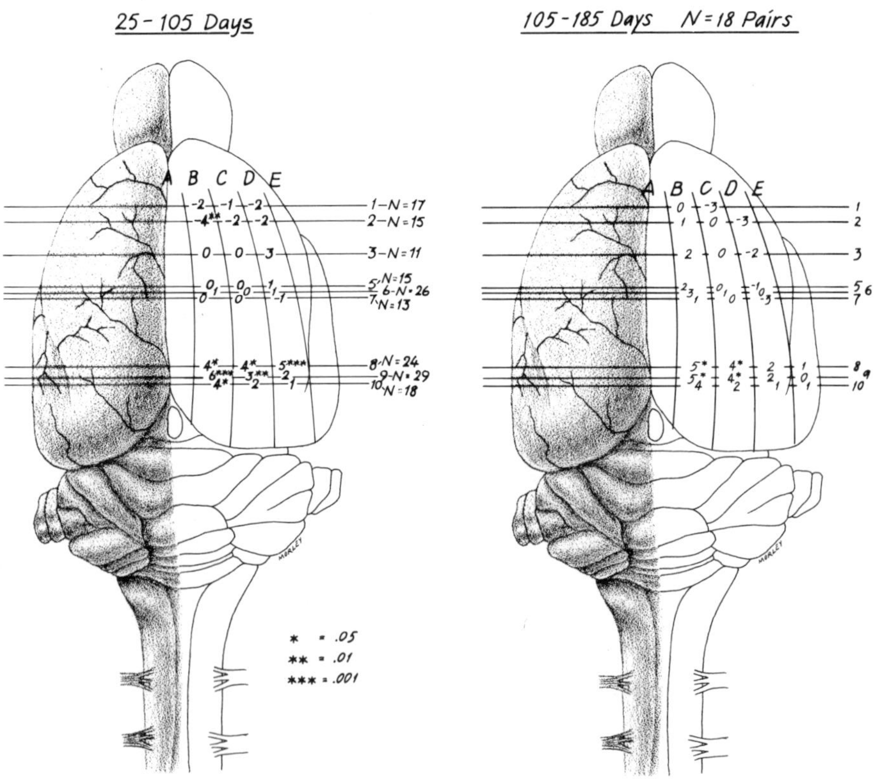

Figure 4. Left: Percent differences in cortical depth measures between rats in enriched or impoverished environment from 25 to 105 days of age. Right: Percent differences for rats in the same conditions also for 80 days, but from 105 to 185 days of age. From Diamond *et al.* (1972).

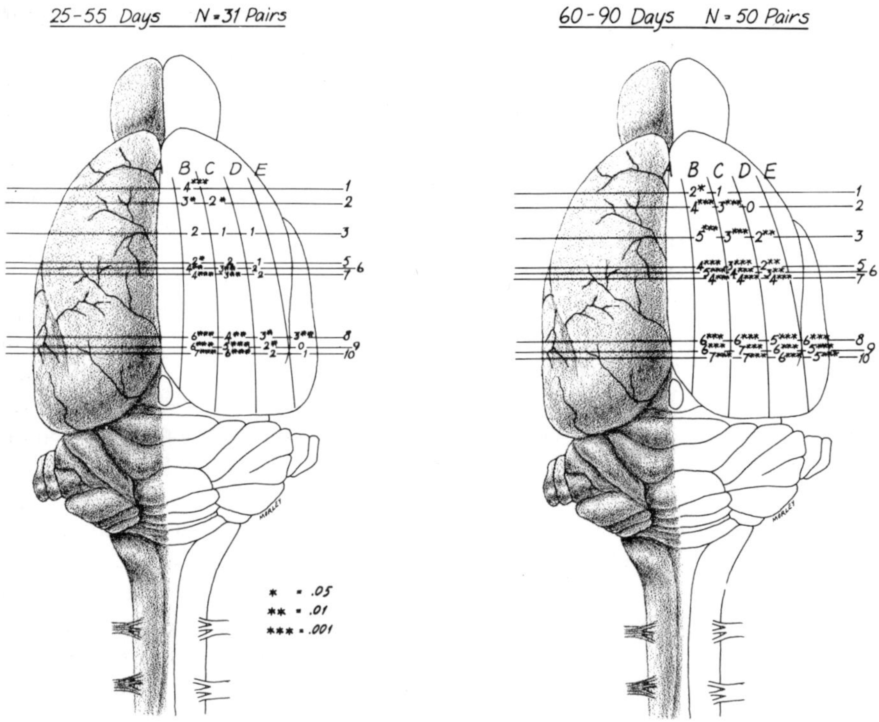

Figure 5. Left: Percent differences in cortical depth measures between rats in enriched or impoverished environment from 25 to 55 days of age. Right: Percent differences for rats in the same conditions also for 30 days, but from 60 to 90 days of age. From Diamond *et al.* (1972).

measured for cortical depth changes. The numbers on the brain represent the percent differences in cortical depth changes between enriched and impoverished environments. Figure 4 represents the cortical depth changes after two different 80-day periods, from 25 to 105 days and from 105 to 185 days. In both of these periods, the greatest cortical depth differences are seen in the occipital cortex, but in none of the sections compared was the cortical depth significantly different between the two 80-day groups. Figure 5 shows the depth changes for two different 30-day periods, from 25 to 55 days and from 60 to 90 days. Even though it appears that the cortical depth changes are greater in the 60–90 day group, the results of the two 30-day groups do not differ significantly from one another except in the lateral occipital cortex (lines 8, 9, and 10, segments D and E). The young 30-day group (25–55) does not differ markedly from the two 80-day groups. However, the older 30-day group (60–90) is significantly greater than both the 80-day groups in most of the segments compared.

Figures 6, 7, and 8 compare the enriched and impoverished conditions with a third condition, the standard colony. In Figure 6, the two 30-day groups are presented, showing that impoverishment is manifest by a thinner cortex than that of the standard colony animal in most sections measured, whereas the effects of enrichment are most pronounced in the occipital cortex, sections 8, 9, and 10. The effects of enrichment appear to be greater, but are not significantly so, in the 60–90 day group than in the 25–55 day group. Figure 7 shows that, with 15 days' duration, effects of both enriched and impoverished environments are seen, but primarily effects due to impoverishment. With 4 days of experience, environmental effects are evident but for different reasons dependent on the age of the group. For example, the top part of Figure 8 shows that if animals are placed in their respective conditions at 26 days of age, primarily the effect of impoverishment is manifest; however, if adult animals enter their conditions at 60 days, the results, as seen in Figure 8 (bottom), indicate primarily an effect due to the enriched condition.

These data indicate the importance of several factors to be taken into consideration in correlating anatomy and behavior. The effects of age and duration of exposure to various environments have been known previously to bring about different patterns of behavior, but that brain structure is altered in different areas depending on age and duration is something new. Animals isolated immediately at weaning demonstrate abnormal behavior

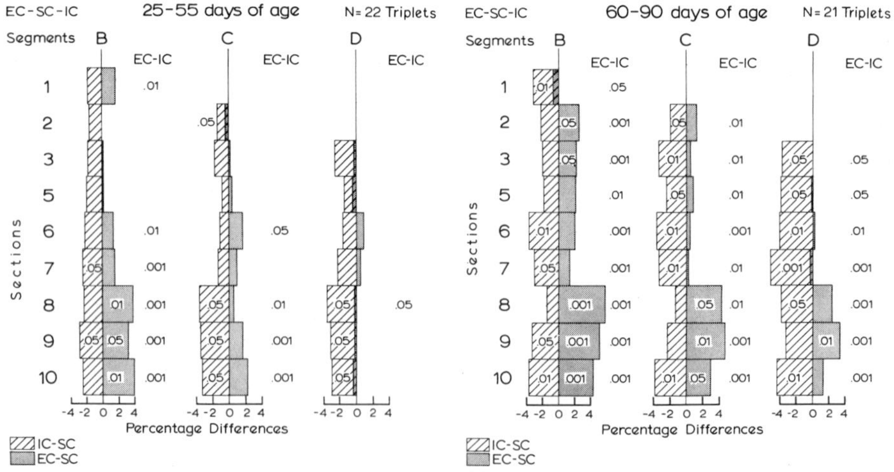

Figure 6. Left: Comparisons are made between the percent cortical depth differences from enriched, standard colony, and impoverished rats in their conditions from 25 to 55 days of age. The sections 1–10 are shown in Figures 4 and 5. The diagonally striped bars represent the effects of impoverishment compared to the standard colony rat and the stippled areas the effects of enrichment. Right: Percent cortical depth differences for another age group, from 60 to 90 days of age. From Diamond *et al.* (1972).

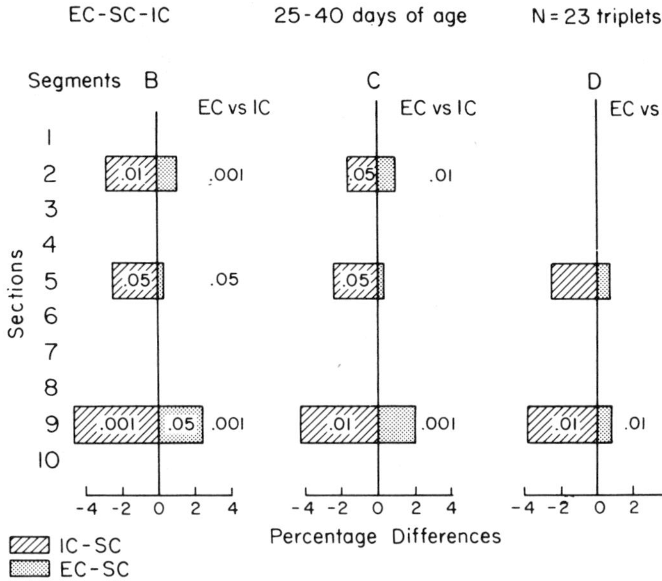

Figure 7. Percent cortical depth differences for three sections, 2, 5, and 9, from enriched, standard colony, and improverished rats in their environments from 25 to 40 days of age. From Diamond *et al.* (1975*b*).

during adulthood. The present results with rats have shown that isolation for 4 days after weaning reduces cerebral cortical structure, but if the rats are continued in the enriched or the impoverished environment for 30 days the effects of isolation remain and the effect of enrichment eventually develops. Similarly, if rats enter the enriched or the impoverished condition at 60 days of age, only the effects of enrichment are measurable after 4 days, but after 30 days effects of isolation also appear.

Effects of Environment on the Cortical Depth of Castrated Male Rats

Since it had been shown in the Long-Evans strain of rats that the occipital cortical depth differences induced by enriched or impoverished environment in the male rat are greater than those in the female rat (Diamond *et al.*, 1971), we (McDonald and Diamond, unpublished data) were interested in learning if hormones secreted by the testis were responsible for this cortical depth difference. Two groups of animals were studied, those castrated at birth before the brain was essentially male, and those castrated at 30 days of age. Both groups were placed in an enriched or impoverished environment

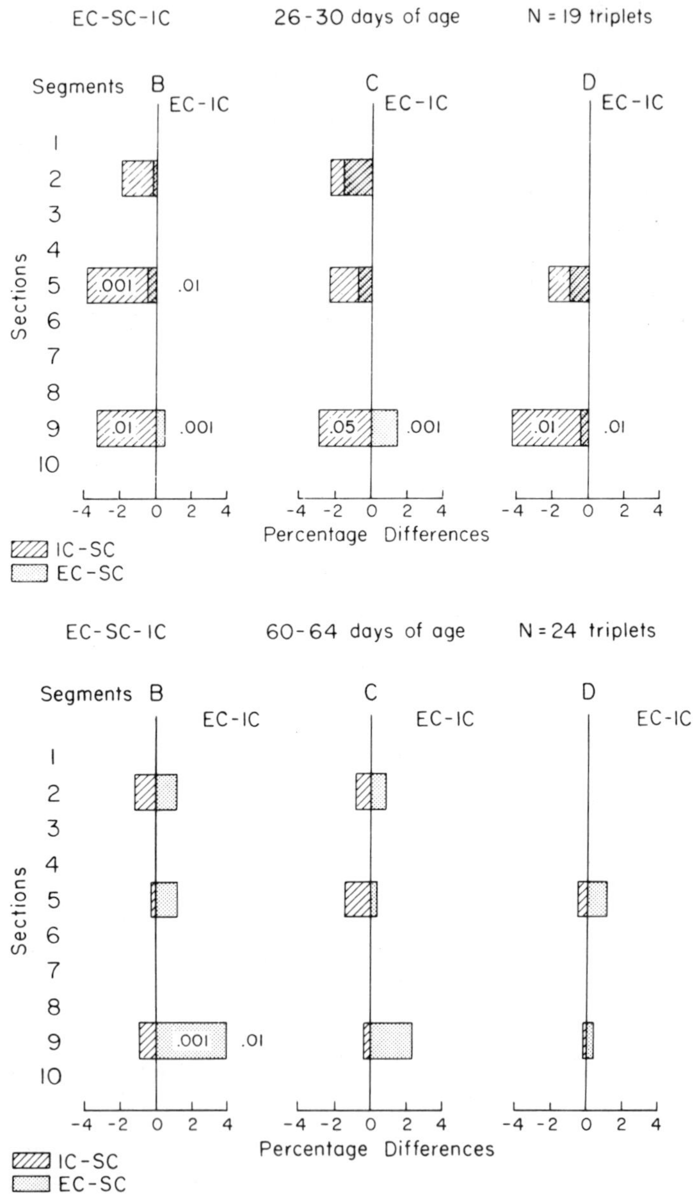

Figure 8. Top: Percent cortical depth differences for three sections, 2, 5, 9, from enriched, standard colony, and impoverished rats in their environments from 26 to 30 days of age. Bottom: Same comparisons made for animals in their environments also for 4 days, but from 60 to 64 days of age. From Diamond *et al.* (1975*b*).

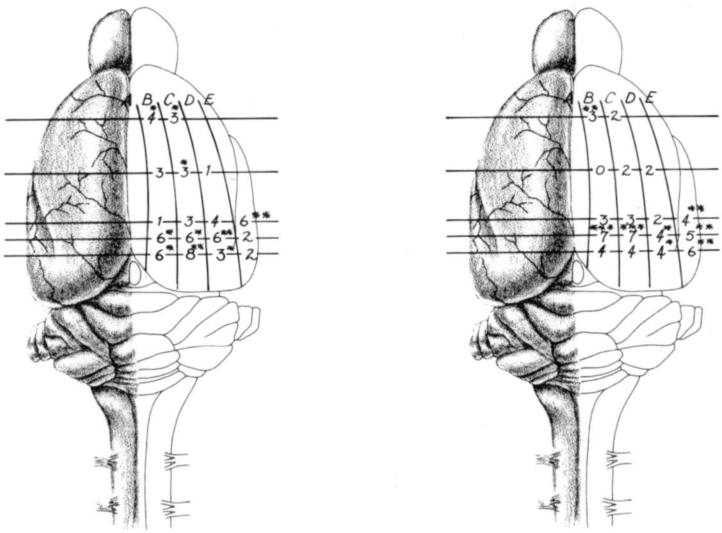

Figure 9. Left: Percent cortical depth differences between enriched and impoverished animals castrated at birth ($N = 11$ pairs). Right: Percent cortical depth differences between enriched and impoverished animals castrated at 30 days of age ($N = 12$ pairs). From McDonald and Diamond (1974).

from 60 to 90 days of age, and both groups clearly displayed the environmental effects seen with the intact male animal (Figure 9), indicating that something other than the male hormones was responsible for the male and female cortical depth differences. Experiments are now in progress to determine the brain changes in ovariectomized enriched and impoverished rats.

Effects of Environment on the Cortical Depth of Female Rats

That sex hormones may change the brain is not a new notion. Some 90 years ago, Gowers (1885) suggested that sex hormones affect brain function, when he noted that epileptic seizures varied with the phase of the menstrual cycle. In our research dealing with environment and brain changes, we did not anticipate sex hormones to play an important part, for in 1971 Rosenzweig, Bennett, and Diamond showed that enriched and impoverished conditions can cause brain changes in the absence of the pituitary gland in male rats when the hormones stimulating the gonads are reduced. That sex hormones may play a role in our environmental changes was discovered quite by accident. The experiment shedding light on this subject derived from a study designed to examine the brains of offspring from parents experiencing varied environmental conditions. Before examining the brains of the off-

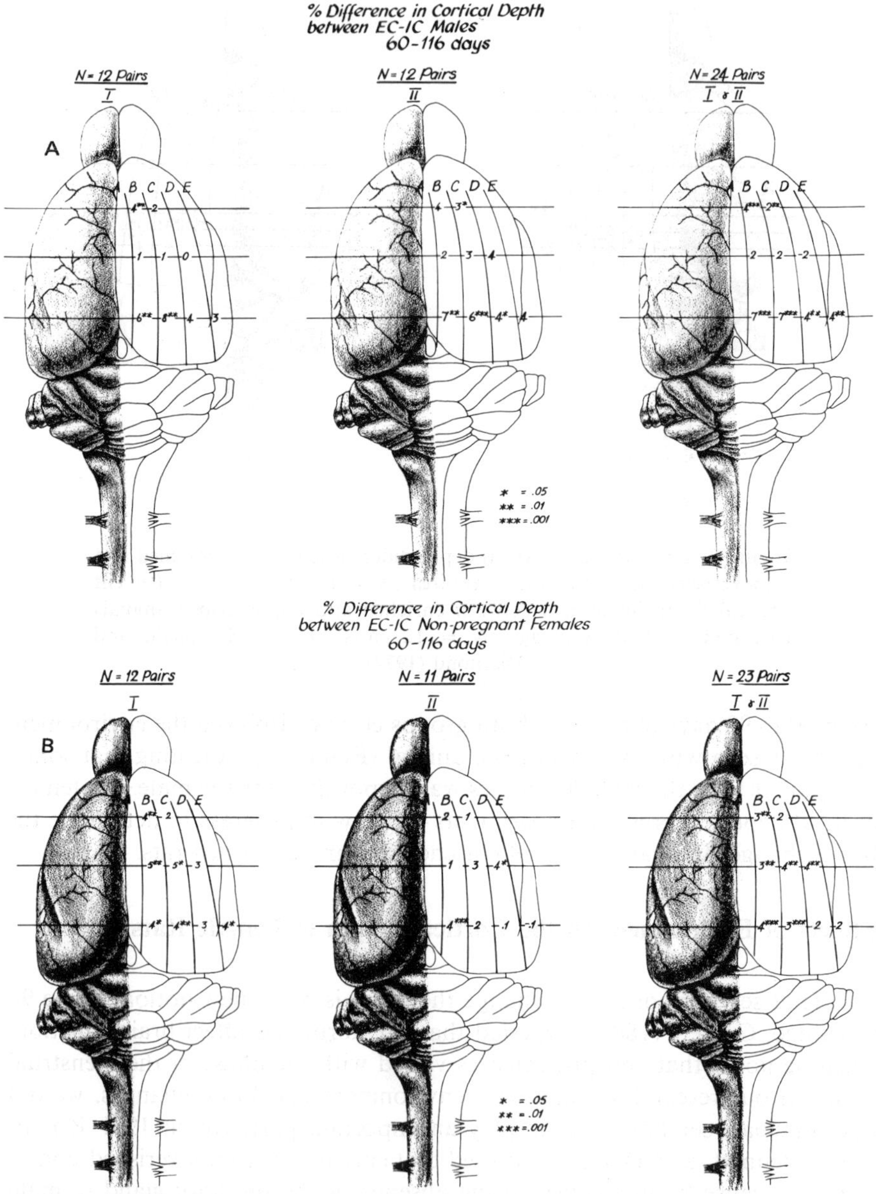

Figure 10. This figure is divided into three sections, A, B, and C. A: Percent cortical depth differences between enriched and impoverished Long-Evans male rats in their conditions from 60 to 116 days of age. I represents results from the initial experiment, II results from the replication experiment, and III the combination of results from I and II. B: Percent cortical depth differences for nonpregnant Long-Evans female rats. C: Percent cortical depth differences for the postpartum females. From Diamond *et al.* (1971).

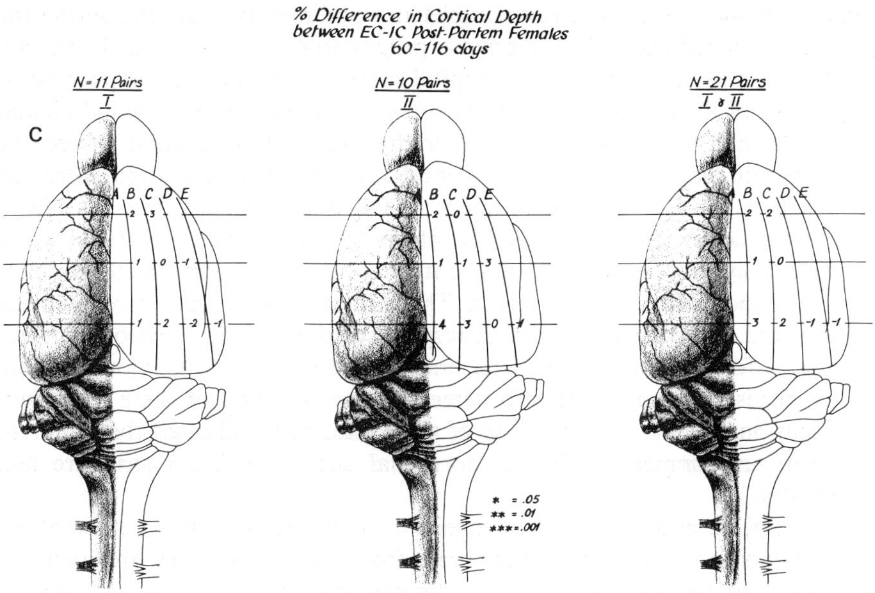

Figure 10 (continued).

spring, it was necessary to confirm morphological changes in the brains of both sets of parents. The changes in the male brains were confirmed, but an unexpected result concerning the postpartum female brain altered the direction of the experimental approach. A lack of experimental difference between the enriched and impoverished postpartum females was observed (Diamond *et al.*, 1971) (Figure 10). In the nonpregnant female, significant depth differences were found in the medial area of the frontal, somesthetic, and occipital cortex. The differences found in the occipital cortex in the non-pregnant female were significantly smaller than those found in the Long-Evans male of the same age. However, in the nonpregnant female significant differences were seen in the somesthetic area that were not present in the male of the Long-Evans strain (Figure 10). Why the male occipital cortex responds more than does the female occipital cortex while the female somesthetic cortex responds more than the male somesthetic cortex is not clear. Of course, these results offer opportunity for speculation about differences between male and female brains, with one being more responsive to visual sensations and the other to peripheral sensations, but at present no valid scientific measures support these speculations.

To return to the lack of cortical depth differences between enriched and impoverished postpartum rats, more information is now available than at the time of the original publication in 1971. In an attempt to understand the reasons for the changes in the impoverished pregnant rat's brain, we (Hoover and Diamond, 1976) have just completed a preliminary study measuring the effects of norethynodrel, a synthetic progesterone-like compound, on Na, water, Cl, and K content in the occipital cortex of enriched and impoverished rats. Half of the animals in each environment were given norethynodrel, and the other half served as controls. Norethynodrel administration altered the response of the cortex to environmental enrichment. Norethynodrel-treated animals in the enriched environment had a thinner cortex and less Na in the visual cortex than did the EC controls. No differences in cortical water and electrolytes were seen between control and norethynodrel-treated animals in the impoverished environment. These data suggest that norethynodrel altered the ability of the cortex to respond to the enriched environment but had no effect on the cortex of the impoverished animals. Obviously, more work needs to be done here to determine the meaning of these important implications. In the meantime, all of these data have indicated that different external environments influence hormonal action on brain structure and chemistry.

From the original report on effects of pregnancy on rats in different environments, it was evident that the brain from the impoverished pregnant rats had reached the depth of not only the enriched female cortex but also the impoverished male cortex. That the impoverished pregnant female cortex reached the depth of the male cortex but did not surpass it causes one to question whether there is a "ceiling effect" in cortical depth. At no time have the environmental conditions stimulated the cortical depth of the postweaned rat to go beyond 10%. As mentioned previously, a 16% difference in cortical depth was encountered between the enriched and the impoverished preweaned rat, at the time when normal maturation was apparently being accelerated. In the future, postweaned rats could possibly be exposed to more rigorous environmental conditions to determine if larger depth differences can be induced. (I have always said that one of my dreams was to cause the rat cortex to form its first convolution!)

Effects of Environment on the Hippocampus of Male Rats

The hippocampus is known to be associated with learning and memory. For example, hippocampal damage has been found to retard performance on complex mazes, discrimination reversal, and alternation (Thomas *et al.*, 1968; Kimble, 1968; Isaacson and Kimble, 1972). Thus it appeared a natural area of the brain to examine in relation to enriched and impoverished environments. Walsh *et al.* (1969) found a 6% ($p < 0.05$) difference in hippocampal depth between eight pairs of enriched and impoverished rats. More recently, we have completed an extensive study with 224 pairs of postweaned rats comparing the hippocampal depth between enriched and impoverished animals for many age groups and varied durations. At no time were significant changes in hippocampal depth encountered (Diamond *et al.*, 1975*b*) (Table 1). It is not clear why Walsh *et al.* (1969) were able to show hippocampal differences; whereas, no significant differences were found in our laboratory. Perhaps the entorhinal cortex and not the hippocampus should be measured in enriched and impoverished animals, for McLardy (1970) reported that only when the entorhinal cortex was removed was a deficit seen in recent memory; no deficit occurred with bilateral removal of the hippocampus or fascia dentata. Recent evidence does show the entorhinal cortex responds to an enriched environment (Diamond *et al.*, 1976*b*).

Effects of Environment on Cortical Cell Number

The changes occurring in the cerebral cortical depth measurements as a consequence of environment having been observed, a logical next step is examination of the constituents within the cortex which could be responsible for such depth changes. Determining the number of cells in an area of the cortex is one consideration. We hope that mechanized techniques will soon be used accurately to differentiate cell types in the brain. At the present, nothing is more effective than the human eye to detect the subtle differences in size and density of the cell bodies in the cerebral cortex. The classification of all the glia in between the morphologically clearly distinguished glia creates a major problem. The differentiation between endothelial cells and certain glia

Table 1. Percent Differences in Hippocampal Depth between Environmentally Enriched and Impoverished Rats

Duration in days	Ages	Percent difference	Number of EC>IC (pairs)	*P*
1	60–61	1.1	13/24	N.S.
4	60–64	0.6	11.5/24	N.S.
4	26–30	0	12/20	N.S.
7	25–32	−1.2	10/22	N.S.
15	25–40	−0.5	9/23	N.S.
30	25–55	1.0	10/20	N.S.
30	60–90	2.0	11.5/20	N.S.
80	25–105 [a]	1.9	17/31	N.S.
80	105–185	−1.3	10/18	N.S.
160	25–185	−0.6	11/22	N.S.
		Total	115/224	

[a] Age group most comparable to that of Walsh *et al.* (1969).

is another hindrance to precise, automated brain cell counts. In the meantime, three methods of cell counts have been employed on brains from animals in their environments from 25 to 105 days of age: (1) The number of neurons and glia were counted in each microscopic field, proceeding from the pia surface to the corpus callosum (Diamond *et al.*, 1964). (2) An autoradiographic examination was made of the rate of glia multiplication due to an enriched environment (Altman and Das, 1964). (3) Overlapping photomicrographs were combined into one composite picture of an area of the occipital cortex 1.00 by 0.75 mm. Differential cell counts of neurons and glia were made from each animal (Diamond *et al.*, 1966). Although neurons were counted in both the microscopic and the composite picture methods, no significant differences in the number of neurons were detected between the two experimental groups of animals. By the initial method of counting cells in each microscopic field, a higher glia/neuron ratio in the enriched brain was seen, for the decrease in glia per microscopic field was significantly less than the decrease in neurons. By the autoradiographic technique, the investigators reported an increase in labeled cells in the cortical radiation and in the corpus callosum of the enriched animals but did not attempt to differentiate types of cells. By the examination of the cells in the enlarged, composite picture, an absolute increase in glial cells in the enriched brain was found, compared to the impoverished brain, giving a higher glia/neuron ratio of 16% ($p < 0.02$). Essentially all three methods have led to the same conclusion that there is a difference in glia count between the brains of enriched and impoverished animals. It is yet to be determined whether enrichment or impoverishment is responsible for this difference by comparing the counts with those from a standard colony littermate. For the 25–105 day age group, the differences in depth measures are due more to the enriched condition than to the impoverished condition, so one might predict the glia differences also will follow this direction. The difference in glia counts may be attributed to any one of a number of functions mentioned previously (Diamond *et al.*, 1966): to supply additional neuronal nutritional needs, to support newly formed fibers, to regulate ionic movement in the brain, to give additional specificity to synaptic membranes, to respond to axoplasmic movement, to regulate vascular flow, or to encode experience.

Effects of Environment on Neuronal Nuclear and Perikarya Areas

In one initial experiment (Diamond *et al.*, 1966), we expressed concern over the lack of increase in perikarya area in the enriched rats, for we had hypothesized that the cortical depth increases might be due in part to dendritic branching, which presumably would demand greater perikarya dimensions. But from camera lucida drawings we could find no significant differences between the enriched and impoverished groups. However, with the projection of the cells using a microfilm reader, with the larger image to measure, significant differences in both perikarya area and in the nuclei of the perikarya were found, 17% ($p < 0.001$) and 20% ($p < 0.01$), respectively (Diamond, 1967). These large cellular changes were found in brains from animals in enriched and impoverished conditions from 25 to 105 days of age. In 1971, Malkasian and Diamond reported perikarya and nuclear changes of 16% and 19%, respectively, in the somatosensory cortex of preweaned rats living in enriched and impoverished environments from 6 to 26 days of age. In more recent experiments (Diamond *et al.*, 1975*b*), perikarya and nuclear dimensions have been measured in rats living in the environmental conditions for 30 days, from 25 to 55 and from 60 to 90 days of age, and in an older 80-day group, from 105 to 185 days of age. However, in none of these groups were significant differences between enriched and impoverished animals found in the nuclear area. Only nuclear area was measured because of the high positive correlation found between it and perikarya area in the 25–105 day group. In only two durations measured, from 25 to 105 and from 60 to 90 days, do the perikarya and nuclei show changes in response to external environment; in the former age group both nuclei and perikarya show changes, and in the latter only the perikarya.

Effects of Environment on Dendritic Branching

In 1966, Holloway investigated whether the dendritic branches of stellate neurons in the occipital cortex were responding to environmental manipulation from 25 to 105 days of age. He found that they were. In a later experiment in small, medium, and large pyramidal neurons and in stellate neurons, enriched rats consistently had more higher-order dendritic branches than their impoverished littermates (Greenough and Volkmar, 1973). The standard colony rats were closer to the impoverished animals in higher-order branching. In the pyramidal neurons, the branching differences occurred primarily in the basal dendrites. No consistent differences in the length of branches were found by either Holloway or Greenough and Volkmar. In examining areas other than the occipital cortex, Greenough *et al.* (1973) could not detect any dendritic differences in the frontolateral cortex, but in the temporal cortex smaller but reliable differences were seen in layer 5 pyramidal cell basal dendritic branching. We are presently collaborating with Smit and Uylings, Brain Research Institute, the Netherlands, to determine if dendritic branching occurs in older rats as a consequence of the enriched and impoverished environments (from 112 to 142 days of age). In this experiment, the enriched rats have been exposed to the seminatural enriched condition at the University of California Field Station for Research in Animal Behavior rather than the usual laboratory enrichment cages, in an attempt to produce significantly greater anatomical changes than those formed in the laboratory. The seminatural condition consists of outdoor enclosures having a dirt-covered concrete base 30 by 30 ft and a screen over the top. Significant increases in dendritic branching have been found in older enriched animals (Uylings *et al.*, 1976).

Effects of Environment on Dendritic Spines and Synapses

Speculations have been made for a long time pointing to the synapse as a primary site concerned with memory mechanisms. Many of the synapses in the cerebral cortex are found on dendritic spines. In an attempt to understand the role of the dendritic spine in the brain's response to enriched and impoverished environments, Globus *et al* (1973) counted spines on basal, apical, and oblique dendrites from the occipital cortical pyramidal neurons. Only the basal dendrites from the enriched animals had a greater number of spines when compared with basal dendrites from impoverished animals, implying an increased number of intracortical connections. The logical next step was to measure the environmentally induced morphological change at the region of functional interaction between two nerve fibers, namely at the synapse. The first experiments of Mollgaard *et al.* (1971) examined synapses at the electron microscopic level and provided evidence that the structure of the synapse can be altered by environment. The length of the postsynaptic thickening in asymmetrical synapses in layer III of the occipital cortex was shown to be considerably longer in the enriched animal than in the impoverished. Not only were the synapses longer but also they were fewer per unit area in the enriched animals compared to the impoverished animals exposed to their environments from 25 to 55 days. These results, showing the plasticity of the synapse, were encouraging, but they did not indicate clearly whether the enriched or the impoverished condition was responsible for the synaptic changes, so it was necessary to repeat the experiment comparing both conditions with a third, the standard colony condition.

Recent (Diamond *et al.*, 1975*b*, 1976*b*) initial and replication experiments studied synapses in enriched, impoverished, and standard colony animals from 25 to 55 days of age. Although the large differences shown by Mollgaard and colleagues were not repeated, an 8% ($p < 0.01$) difference in postsynaptic thickening length in layer IV between 675 synapses from enriched rats and 680 synapses from impoverished rats was found. This synaptic difference was due primarily to the impoverished condition, as shown by comparison with standard colony littermates (Table 2). A smaller sample from layer III

Table 2. Percent Difference in Postsynaptic Length for EC-SC-IC Using All Animals Studied

	Number of animals	Number of synapses	Length of synapse (mm)	Condition compared	Percent difference	P
Expt. I						
EC	7	306	11.4	EC-SC	0.1	N.S.
SC	7	306	11.3	SC-IC	6.7	<0.10
IC	8	359	10.6	EC-IC	6.8	<0.05
Expt. II						
EC	10	369	12.2	EC-SC	1.5	N.S.
SC	9	312	12.0	SC-IC	5.4	N.S.
IC	8	321	11.4	EC-IC	6.9	<0.10
Expts. I + II						
EC	17	675	11.8	EC-SC	1.1	N.S.
SC	16	618	11.7	SC-IC	6.3	<0.05
IC	16	680	11.0	EC-IC	7.5	<0.01

showed changes of the same order of magnitude as those in layer IV. The number of synapses per unit area of neuropil was 15% ($p < 0.01$) more in the impoverished than in the enriched animals, and this difference was primarily due to impoverishment. Thus, environmental experience does significantly affect synaptic length and number. That synapses can be modified by environment has also been supported by West and Greenough (1972), who measured not only the postsynaptic thickening length but also the bouton diameter and the length of the region of tight aposition of the pre- and postsynaptic processes in type 1 synapses in layers I, II, and VI of the occipital cortex. In these studies, the only measure showing significant differences was the length of the postsynaptic thickening, with the enriched rats having the greater length by 14%.

The results of Mollgaard *et al.* (1971), West and Greenough (1972), and Diamond *et al.* (1975*b*) all indicate that synapses respond to environmental changes by either increasing or decreasing their dimensions. In 1971, Soleto and Palay also concluded that synaptic rearrangements are continuously taking place in the brain even under so-called normal conditions. Raisman (1969) demonstrated that the central nervous system is capable of synaptic rearrangements after a destructive lesion has been placed in the brain. Along similar lines, Lynch *et al.* (1973) have provided data indicating different forms of postlesion growth in the hippocampus of the rat. All of these combined sources support the idea that the synapse is constantly subject to change in response to the external environment.

Duration of Anatomical Effects

By examining one region of the cortex, the medial occipital area, from animals exposed to the different environments at different ages and for varying periods of time, the periods of maximum response to the environments become evident (see Table 3). Animals in the environments for 4 and 7 days develop 3–4% enriched vs. impoverished differences, but by 15 days a 7% difference is seen which is as large a difference as that found with the longer durations, 30 or 80 days. However, if animals are kept in their conditions for 160 days, differences greater than 7% do not develop, but actually are less, becoming more similar to the values seen with the short durations, 4–7 days. From these data, it is apparent that the occipital cortical depth difference between enriched and impoverished rats becomes diminished after 80 days.

If one examines the data from the somesthetic cortex in contrast to the occipital cortex, for the various age groups and for the different durations, only two groups, from 25 to 55 days and from 60 to 90 days, show significant depth differences between enriched and impoverished environments. No distinct increase in cortical depth is seen in the somesthetic area as the duration of the experiment increases, for at 4 days a 3% significant difference is seen and at 30 days a 3–4% significant difference is present, with no further increase for a longer duration. Evidently, one cannot speak of general overall cortical changes due to environmental stimulation for different periods, for some cortical regions indicate greater differences with longer durations, and some do not.

Table 3. Percent Differences in Medial Occipital Cortical Depths between Environmentally Enriched and Impoverished Rats

Duration in days	Ages	Percent differences	Number of EC>IC (pairs)	*P*
1	60–61	0.7	10/24	N.S.
4	60–64	2.9	17/24	0.01
4	26–30	3.7	15/20	0.001
7	25–32	3.8	19.5/22	0.001
15	25–40	7.1	22/23	0.001
30	25–55	6.6	25/30	0.001
30	60–90	6.7	45.5/50	0.001
80	25–105	7.9	22/22	0.001
80	105–185	5.0	13/18	0.05
160	25–185	3.0	16/22	0.05
		Total	205/255	
		Total minus the 1-day group	195/231	

Summary

What do all of these anatomical changes mean with regard to brain function? Knowledge of an increase or a decrease in the size of a structure is not necessarily of great value unless a functional correlation can be made. However, size changes by themselves within specific areas of the brain are useful as regional indicators of continued functional interaction. With the somesthetic cortex responding differently to an enriched environment than the occipital cortex, and the medial area differently from the lateral, there is little wonder that it is difficult to design a behavioral test to determine the functional significance of the effect of a multiple environment. In attempts to correlate behavioral performance with increased cortical structure, the most frequently cited finding indicates that the enriched rat makes fewer errors in less time in a reversal discrimination test than does the impoverished rat (Krech *et al.*, 1962). However, LeBoeuf and Peeke (1969) and Peeke *et al.* (1971) found no effect on Lashley III maze learning between animals from enriched and impoverished environments.

In a recent attempt to refine the experimental approach and to correlate anatomical changes with learning, rats were given a series of maze patterns in increasing complexity, and the cortical depth of a trained rat was compared with that of an untrained but maze-familiar littermate. Preliminary results indicate cortical depth differences between trained and untrained littermates (Diamond, Malkasian, and Johnson, 1974, unpublished). In one sense, the training in this experiment could be referred to as learning, and yet, on the other hand, it could be called enrichment of environment. How does one really establish an endpoint which is clearly defined as learning? With all of the effort that has gone into brain research correlated with learning, few sharply defined end points are available. It is, perhaps, at this time that one turns to simple animals, with a less complicated appearing system of nerve cells, but even here, with fewer cells, the limited number of cells must tackle some tasks carried on by many cells in the more complex animals. So which is actually the simpler system? At present, no one approach with invertebrates or vertebrates will clarify "how the brain learns." Investigators will continue to add peripheral and central knowledge to the pile and eventually the pieces will fit together, possibly to show a very simple mechanism.

In conclusion, the work concerned with enriched and impoverished environments and brain structure has shown that the brain grows with use (see Table 4). Since the brain consists partly of nerve cells, studies on the neurons have demonstrated that every part of the cell measured to date, from the nucleus to the synapse, can increase or decrease depending on whether the environment is stimulating or not. We have learned that certain parts of the cortex respond by changing size when the duration of exposure to

Table 4. Summary of Anatomical Changes Measured in the Medial Occipital Cortex

Measurement and condition	N (pairs)	Experimental duration in days	Percent difference	P
I. Cortical depth differences between enriched and impoverished rats				
A. Preweaned Long-Evans males	7	6–14	2	N.S.
	7	6–19	7	0.01
	19	6–26	9	0.01
B. Postweaned S_1 males	24	60–61	0.7	N.S.
	20	26–30	4	0.001
	24	60–64	3	0.01
	22	25–32	4	0.001
	23	25–40	7	0.001
	30	25–55	7	0.001
	50	60–90	7	0.001
	22	25–105	8	0.001
	18	105–185	5	0.05
	22	25–185	3	0.05
C. Castrated Long-Evans males, neonates	11	60–90	6	0.05
D. Castrated Long-Evans males, at 30 days of age	12	60–90	7	0.001
E. Nonpregnant Long-Evans females	23	60–116	4	0.001
F. Postpartum Long-Evans females	21	60–116	3	N.S.
G. Newborns from Long-Evans enriched and impoverished parents	30	95–116	0	N.S.
II. Cortical depth differences between enriched and standard colony postweaned S_1 males	20	26–30	0.5	N.S.
	24	60–64	4	0.001
	23	25–40	3	0.05
	22	25–55	3	0.05
	21	60–90	5	0.001
III. Cortical depth differences between standard colony and impoverished S_1 males	20	26–30	3	0.01
	24	60–64	1	N.S.
	23	25–40	5	0.001
	22	25–55	2	0.05
	21	60–90	4	0.05
IV. Difference in glial number between enriched and impoverished S_1 males	17	25–105	14	0.01
V. Difference in neuronal area between enriched and impoverished S_1 males	12	60–90	4	0.05
	20	25–105	12	0.001

Table 4. (Continued)

Measurement and condition	N (pairs)	Experimental duration in days	Percent difference	P
VI. Difference in neuronal nuclear area between enriched and impoverished S_1 males	20	25–55	2	N.S.
	19	60–90	2	N.S.
	20	25–105	12	0.001
	18	105–185	−1	N.S.
VII. Difference in postsynaptic length between				
Enriched and standard colony S_1 males	13	25–55	1	N.S.
Standard colony and impoverished S_1 males	13	25–55	6	0.05
Enriched and impoverished S_1 males	13	25–55	8	0.01

the environmental condition is long, and others when the duration is short. Essentially, the brain increases in size with exercise as does skeletal muscle, but size alone does not tell how the muscle functions. The mechanism by which actin and myosin interact explains how the muscle contracts. Is there any reason to believe that a nerve cell which has increased in size with use is a center for memory storage? Perhaps the increase in size in the nerve cell means that all existing components of the cell have increased in activity to form new connections which are possibly the site of memory. By constant use of a newly formed or enlarged, existing synapse, memory is retained, and with disuse it is lost. The memory mechanism cannot be as simple as this, for on this basis how does one explain the retrieval of long-term memory, memory not used for decades? Not only by the presence or absence of a synapse, for the synapse structure can be modified within days. Perhaps a synapse does not completely disappear with disuse. Is there a minimum size a synapse can reach and still serve as a memory site? An investigation on the persistence of synaptic changes might prove useful in helping to understand further the structural changes related to memory functions. We have only just begun, with the real questions and answers still ahead.

References

Altman, J., and Das, G. D. 1964. Autoradiographic examination of the effects of enriched environment on the rate of glial multiplication in the adult rat brain. *Nature* (*London*), *204*, 1161–1163.

Brizzee, K. R., and Jacobs, L. A. 1959. Early postnatal changes in neuron packing density and volumetric relationships in the cerebral cortex of the white rat. *Growth*, *23*, 337–347.

Brizzee, K. R., Sherwood, N., and Timiras, P. 1968. A comparison of cell populations at various depth levels in cerebral cortex of young adult and aged Long-Evans rat. *Journal of Gerontology*, *23*(*3*), 289–297.

Diamond, M. C. 1967. Extensive cortical depth measurements and neuronal size increases in the cortex of environmentally enriched rats. *Journal of Comparative Neurology*, *131*, 357–364.

Diamond, M. C., Krech, D., and Rosenzweig, M. R. 1964. The effects of an enriched environment on the histology of the rat cerebral cortex. *Journal of Comparative Neurology*, *123*, 111–119.

Diamond, M. C., Law, F., Rhodes, H., Lindner, B., Rosenzweig, M. R., Krech, D., and Bennett, E. L. 1966. Increases in cortical depth and glia number in rats subjected to enriched environment. *Journal of Comparative Neurology*, *128*, 117–125.

Diamond, M. C., Johnson, R. E., and Ingham, C. A. 1971. Brain plasticity induced by environment and pregnancy. *International Journal of Neuroscience*, *2*, 171–178.

Diamond, M. C., Rosenzweig, M. R., Bennett, E. L., Lindner, B., and Lyon, L. 1972. Effects of environmental enrichment and impoverishment on rat cerebral cortex. *Journal of Neurobiology*, *3*(*1*), 47–64.

Diamond, M. C., Johnson, R. E., and Ingham, C. A. 1975*a*. Morphological changes in the young, adult and aging rat cerebral cortex, hippocampus, and diencephalon. *Behavioral Biology*, *14*, 163–174.

Diamond, M. C., Lindner, B., Johnson, R. E., Bennett, E. L., and Rosenzweig, M. R. 1975*b*. Differences in occipital cortical synapses from environmentally enriched, impoverished and standard colony rats. *Journal of Neuroscience Research*, *1*(*2*), 109–119.

Diamond, M. C., Johnson, R., Ingham, C., Rosenzweig, M., and Bennett, E. L. 1975*c*. Effects of differential experience on neuronal nuclear and perikarya dimensions in the rat cerebral cortex. *Behavioral Biology*, *15*, 107–111.

Diamond, M. C., Johnson, R. E., and Gold, M. 1976*a*. Differential cell counts in young adult and aging rat cerebral cortex. Unpublished.

Diamond, M. C., Ingham, C. A., Johnson, R. E., Bennett, E. L., and Rosenzweig, M. R. 1976*b*. Effects of environment on morphology of rat cerebral cortex and hippocampus. *Journal of Neurobiology*, *7*(*1*), 75–86.

Eayrs, J. T. 1951. The factors governing the opening of the eyes in the albino rat. *Journal of Anatomy*, *85*, 330–337.

Enesco, H. 1967. A cytophotometric analysis of DNA content of rat nuclei in aging. *Journal of Gerontology*, *22*, 445–448.

Globus, A., Rosenzweig, M. R., Bennett, E. L., and Diamond, M. C. 1973. Effects of differential experience on dendritic spine counts in rat cerebral cortex. *Journal of Comparative and Physiological Psychology*, *82*, 175–181.

Gowers, W. R. 1885. *Epilepsy and Other Chronic Convulsive Diseases*. William Wood & Co., New York.

Greenough, W. T., and Volkmar, F. R. 1973. Pattern of dendritic branching in occipital cortex of rats reared in complex environments. *Experimental Neurology*, *40*, 491–504.

Greenough, W. T., Volkmar, F. R., and Juraska, J. M. 1973. Effects of rearing complexity on dendritic branching in frontolateral and temporal cortex of the rat. *Experimental Neurology*, *41*, 371–378.

Holloway, R. L., Jr. 1966. Dendritic branching: Some preliminary results of training and complexity in rat visual cortex. *Brain Research*, *2*, 393–396.

Hoover, D., and Diamond, M. C. 1976. The effects of norethynodrel administration on the rat visual cortex exposed to differential environment: A preliminary study of electrolytes and water. *Brain Research*, *103*, 139–142.

Isaacson, R. L., and Kimble, D. P. 1972. Lesions of the limbic system: Their effects upon hypotheses and frustration. *Behavioral Biology*, *7*, 767–793.

Kimble, D. P. 1968. Hippocampus and internal inhibition. *Psychological Bulletin*, *70*, 285–295.

Krech, D., Rosenzweig, M. R., and Bennett, E. L. 1962. Relations between brain chemistry and problem solving among rats raised in enriched and impoverished environments. *Journal of Comparative Physiological Psychology*, *55*, 801–807.

LeBoeuf, B. J., and Peeke, H. V. S. 1969. The effect of strychnine administration during development on adult maze learning in the rat. *Psychopharmacologia* (*Berlin*), *16*, 49–53.

Malkasian, D. R., and Diamond, M. C. 1971. The effects of environmental manipulation on the morphology of the neonate rat brain. *International Journal of Neuroscience*, *2*, 161–170.

Mandel, P., and Bieth, R. 1952. Étude comparée du développement biochimique des cerveaux chez quelques de mammiferes. *Comptes Rendus Hebdomadaires des Séances de l'Académie des Sciences*, *235*, 485–487.

McDonald, M., and Diamond, M. C. 1974. Unpublished data.

McLardy, T. 1970. Memory function in hippocampal gyri but not in hippocampi. *International Journal of Neuroscience*, *1*(*2*), 113–118.

Mollgaard, K., Diamond, M. C., Bennett, E. L., Rosenzweig, M. R., and Lindner, B. 1971. Quantitative synaptic changes with differential experience in rat brain. *International Journal of Neuroscience*, *2*, 113–128.

Peeke, H. V. S., Le Boeuf, B. J., and Herz, M. J. 1971. The effect of strychnine administration during development on adult maze learning in the rat. II. Drug administration from day 51 to day 70. *Psychopharmacologia* (*Berlin*), *19*, 262–265.

Raisman, G. 1969. Neuronal plasticity in the septal nuclei of the adult rat. *Brain Research*, *14*, 25–48.

Rosenzweig, M. R., Bennett, E. L., and Diamond, M. C. 1971. Chemical and anatomical plasticity of brain: Replications and extensions. 1970. In: *Macromolecules and Behavior* (2nd ed.). J. Gaito (Ed.). Appleton-Century-Crofts, New York.

Schade, J. P., and Baxter, C. F. 1960. Changes during growth in the volume and surface area of cortical neurons in the rabbit. *Experimental Neurology*, *2*, 158–178.

Schade, J. P., and Ford, D. H. 1965. *Basic Neurology*. Elsevier, New York, p. 134.

Soleto, C., and Palay, S. L. 1971. Altered axons and axon terminals in the lateral vestibular nucleus of the rat. *Laboratory Investigation*, *25*, 653–671.

Sugita, N. 1917. Comparative studies on the growth of the cerebral cortex. *Journal of Comparative Neurology*, *28*, 495–591.

Thomas, G. J., Hostetler, G., and Barker, D. J. 1968. Behavioral functions of the limbic system. In: *Progress in Physiological Psychology*, Vol. 2. E. Stellar and J. M. Sprague (Eds.). Academic Press, New York.

Uylings, H. B. M., Diamond, M. C., and Veltman, W. A. M. 1976. Dendritic outgrowth in the visual cortex of adult rats under different environmental conditions. Submitted for publication.

Walsh, R. N., Budtz-Olsen, O. E., Penny, J. E., and Cummins, R. A. 1969. The effects of environmental complexity on the histology of the rat hippocampus. *Journal of Comparative Neurology*, *137*, 361–366.

West, R. W., and Greenough, W. T. 1972. Effect of environmental complexity on cortical synapses of rats: Preliminary results. *Behavioral Biology*, *7*, 270–284.

SOCIAL AND COGNITIVE ISSUES

9

Kenneth R. Hammond

THE SOCIAL IMPLEMENTATION OF COGNITIVE THEORY

Krech, Tolman, and Brunswik form the core of what future historians of psychology will call "the Berkeley Group." These psychologists will be praised, as they have been praised, not only for their academic contributions but also for their efforts to relate their scientific work to the world outside the laboratory. All three tried to *implement* their ideas, although each sought implementation in a different way.

Krech sought to implement cognitive theory through political action, through his leadership in the establishment of the Society for the Study of Social Issues, and by writing books that were focused on the psychology of human behavior in its social context. *Theory and Problems of Social Psychology* (Krech and Crutchfield, 1948) not only explained social psychology to undergraduates but also provided them with a coherent theoretical system they could *use*—an achievement yet to be matched in social psychology.

Tolman sought implementation by a conscious, obvious anthropomorphism; he endowed his research animals with cognitive abilities that other psychologists shrank from attributing even to human beings. It was clear that he meant to theorize about man while studying the behavior of rats. "Cognitive Maps in Rats and Men" (1948), an article which has had, and will have, a long life, made it clear that he was concerned with implementing cognitive theory for the society of his life and times.

Brunswik, whose prose is as obtuse as Krech's is clear, sought imple-

---

Kenneth R. Hammond • Institute of Behavioral Science, University of Colorado, Boulder, Colorado.

mentation by insisting that psychologists study behavior in the social circumstances in which it is found. Implementation and research went hand in hand; it was the business of psychologists to study human beings (as well as animals) in the ecology in which they function, that is, in circumstances representative of their natural habitat, rather than in laboratories where oversimplified circumstances prevent generalization to the complexities of real life. Cognitive theory, studied in society, would be applicable to behavior in society; thus cognitive theory could be implemented directly (Brunswik, 1952, 1956).

The present chapter is intended to continue this tradition of the Berkeley Group. It focuses on the implementation of cognitive theory in the Krech-Tolman-Brunswik tradition. It directs itself to the *cognitive* (Tolman) aspects of *social problems* (Krech), and to the cognitive *representation of the circumstances* (Brunswik) which give rise to these problems.

We proceed by first considering a key idea that each man contributed to cognitive theory and research. Since each of them made a large number of theoretical contributions, the choice of *one* concept is necessarily a highly personal matter. I have chosen to call attention to three concepts that have had a large influence on those of us who have developed what is now called "social judgment theory" (Hammond *et al.*, 1975).

Three Concepts

Krech

The central idea acquired from Krech's theorizing about cognition is that knowledge is organized. This idea began with Krech's observations of rats running a nonsolvable maze, and led to his conclusion that rats had "hypotheses" about the cues which led to food, because they were observed to choose alleys *systematically*. That is, they based their choice of an alley at one time on visual cues, at another time on response (right and/or left turn) patterns, and so on. Moreover, the change from the use of one set of cues to another was abrupt, rather than gradual. That observation gave rise to the idea of a *noncontinuous* change from one set of hypotheses to another, from one organized "cognitive structure" to another (see Krechevsky, 1932).

The theory that a series of organized cognitive structures (or systems) replaced one another found its culmination in *Theory and Problems of Social Psychology*, where it provided meaning for those social psychologists who needed a richer theory of human behavior in its social context than that provided by the major alternative—a cold, clear-eyed, thin, stimulus-response behaviorism. Moreover, the general theory *still* provides a meaningful conceptual framework for social psychologists.

There are difficulties, however. The theory of organized cognitive structures was a theory ahead of its time; it was a theory ahead of the research technology available to it. As a result, it never developed an empirical base.

However, the concept of organized cognition was not only important to Krech, it was important to Tolman as well. He emphasized the organizing function of cognition by making use of an analogy, the "cognitive map."

Tolman

The choice of the map analogy was a good one, for every map represents a series of relations. As Webster defines it, a map indicates the "relative position and size" of a variety of things, including people and even ideas. The most common maps represent the relative physical position and size of cities and towns, but of course any set of relations, physical or otherwise, can be mapped into another set.

Tolman thought of and applied the concept of a "map" because he was running rats in mazes and he believed the rats were indeed learning the physical location of the food in relation to other objects; moreover, he believed these objects could be used as cues to the location of food. Tolman used the map analogy to emphasize his belief that the animal acquired a representation of the physical relations between objects and that the representation of these relations constituted *knowledge* which could be applied when it was appropriate to apply it: when the animal was hungry, for example.

The point to be observed here is that it was the research technology of the 1930s and 1940s which gave rise to Tolman's concept of the cognitive map. Had he been using a problem box instead of a maze, the map analogy might well not have occurred to him. And although the analogy had power (it readily conveyed the idea of relations as a fundamental cognitive unit), the limitations of his technology (the rat maze) also limited Tolman's ability (and the ability of his students) to pursue the complex theoretical implications of the concept he invented. Introduced almost 30 years ago, the idea remained largely unexplored, mainly because the research technology for exploring it was not available. Technology adequate for that purpose is available now, however, and later in this essay I will indicate how Tolman's concept of a cognitive map can now be used in the study of human judgment. Before doing so, however, we turn to the last of the three, Brunswik, and to a consideration of his admonition that unless the research environment is representative of the usual habitat of the animal being studied, the results cannot be generalized, and, therefore, are of little use.

Brunswik

If Krech *shocked* the psychologists who thought that they had purged such "mentalistic" concepts as "hypotheses" from scientific psychology, and if Tolman *annoyed* the stimulus-response psychologists by introducing the "map" analogy (and contrasting it with the "telephone switchboard" theory of the stimulus-response psychologists), Brunswik can be said to have *baffled everyone* (including Krech and Tolman) by rejecting the idea of the systematic design of experiments, and by arguing that experiments should, instead, be representative. And although Krech's "hypotheses" are now part of the common vocabulary of psychologists, and although the representational implication of Tolman's "cognitive maps" is implicit in one form or another in virtually all current cognitive theorizing, it must be said that Brunswik's principal ideas remain—30 years later—beyond the pale (and ken) of virtually all of psychology. Yet it is Brunswik's contribution (1952, 1956) that leads directly to the social implementation of the cognitive theory of the Berkeley Group. Since it can be confidently anticipated that the reader will be either wholly innocent of or seriously misinformed about Brunswik's main ideas, a brief explanation is required.

The central idea is straightforward; generalization requires representation. As everyone knows, if research findings from the *organisms* studied in the laboratory or survey are to be generalized (i.e., applied) to the organisms not studied, the organisms studied must be representative of those not studied. Brunswik's point is that the same logic must be applied to the *circumstances* in which the organism is studied. In short, the design of the experiment or study must be *fully* representative; it should not be representative with regard to the selection of subjects on the one hand and nonrepresentative with regard to the selection of circumstances on the other.

This suggestion seems reasonable enough: who would want to quarrel with what appears to be no more than a straightforward argument for the consistent application of the standard rule for inductive inference? The implications of this apparently innocent plea for methodological consistency, however, are quite another matter, for it means that variables suspected of having important effects on behavior must not be separated from one another in order to determine their separate effects. And as Brunswik persistently emphasized, social behavior takes place in a context which involves confused and confusing sets of entangled variables. In order to understand the behavior that emerges in that context, psychologists must study behavior in that context. Only if they do will the results of that research be directly generalizable (and that means applicable) to the social context in which the behavior is found. Direct applicability makes implementation possible, if not likely. Therefore, the shift in research design urged by Brunswik seems essential if the basic theoretical ideas of Krech and Tolman are to be implemented. (The details of Brunswik's argument are summarized in *The Psychology of Egon Brunswik*, edited by Hammond, 1966. The most comprehensive original sources are Brunswik, 1952, 1956.)

Brunswik's suggestion regarding the representative rather than the systematic design of experiments has seldom been acknowledged, let alone put into practice; it has been more or less politely ignored. The reasons are threefold: First, Brunswik presented his ideas in such fine detail and difficult prose that few people ever bothered to read, much less understand, his argument. Second, representative design raises serious difficulties in the interpretation of research results. Third, it is extremely difficult to carry out his suggestions in most instances.

Was the Berkeley Group really ahead of its time? The evidence is everywhere, but one seldom finds it in such pristine form as in the 1973 address of the President of the Division of Experimental Psychology (Jenkins, 1974). Reporting on a lifelong series of experiments on memory, he reveals that he has now discovered that associationism is wrong and must be rejected in favor of "contextualism," which he says, "demand[s] an understanding of all 'the higher mental processes' at once" (p. 794). No one worked this idea out more systematically and responsibly than Krech and Crutchfield in *Theory and Problems of Social Psychology* (1948), and Tolman's writings are full of it. But there was no reference to Krech or Tolman in Jenkins' presidential address. Jenkins also discovered that "a whole theory of an experiment can be elaborated without contributing in an important way to the science because the situation is *artificial and nonrepresentative* . . ." [italics mine]. And, finally, 40 years after the Berkeley Group had made this point he observes that "contextualism stresses relating one's laboratory problems to the *ecologically valid* [Brunswik's term!] problems of everyday life" (p. 794). No reference to Brunswik. Evidently the ideas of the Berkeley Group were so far ahead of their time that they are going to be *re*discovered.

A Fork in the Road

Innovative, provocative, and right (!) as the Berkeley Group may have been, they did not succeed in establishing a strong empirical base for their ideas. As in so many other cases, final, clear-cut answers were not achieved. Some questions were reformulated, and some were set aside to wait until new research technology appeared which would permit new approaches. And, in fact, two types of technology did appear in the 1950s and 1960s; (1) new techniques for invading the organism (e.g., implants) and (2) new techniques for mathematical analysis (electronic computers). As a result, some of

Krech's students were able to pursue the physiological, biochemical aspects of the Berkeley Group's cognitive theory in the hope, as Krech put it, "that the smallest unit of analysis will provide the greatest level of generality." Some of that work is described in the other chapters in this volume.

But the author of this chapter chose to pursue a more abstract approach. The possible use of new computer technology, combined with mathematical-statistical techniques, was explored in an effort to study human judgment in the context of social psychology. This approach resulted in a series of studies carried out within the framework of what is now called social judgment theory (Hammond *et al.*, 1975). It was learned that computer technology would make it possible for the investigator (and the subject) to *see* cognitive maps displayed on the screen of a computer graphics terminal. And not only it is possible to see cognitive maps immediately after they have been formed, they can also be *manipulated*, i.e., changed by the experimenter and/or the subject. Making cognitive maps visible raises new and interesting problems of course, and all of them would have intrigued the Berkeley Group.

Observing Cognitive Maps

Tolman based his hopes on learning about the properties of a rat's cognitive map by conducting experiments. Experiments, he hoped, would show that the rat *knew* where the food was, and would thereby show that the rat was not merely making a series of specific responses to a series of specific stimuli. Social judgment theorists have taken a different approach. Instead of conducting experiments to prove the existence of cognitive maps, social judgment theorists take the utility of the concept for granted. They proceed by asking their subjects to exercise their judgment with regard to a series of cases representative of a given problem. (Usually the data are presented to subjects in profile form, as in Figure 1, on the screen of an interactive computer graphics terminal.) Once the individual has made a series of judgments with regard to a series of profiles, the subject or experimenter may immediately request a computer-generated display of the mathematical-statistical properties of the cognitive map the subject used in making his judgments with regard to the task in question. For example, one may request a display which will show the *weight* that was attached to each dimension of the judgment task (see Figure 2). One may also request a display which will show the shape of the function forms that were used in relating each dimension (or "cue") to the judgments (see Figure 3).

The three illustrations were taken from a study of labor-management negotiations. Figure 1 presents one of a series of labor contracts which the negotiators rated in terms of acceptability. The contract shown in Figure 1

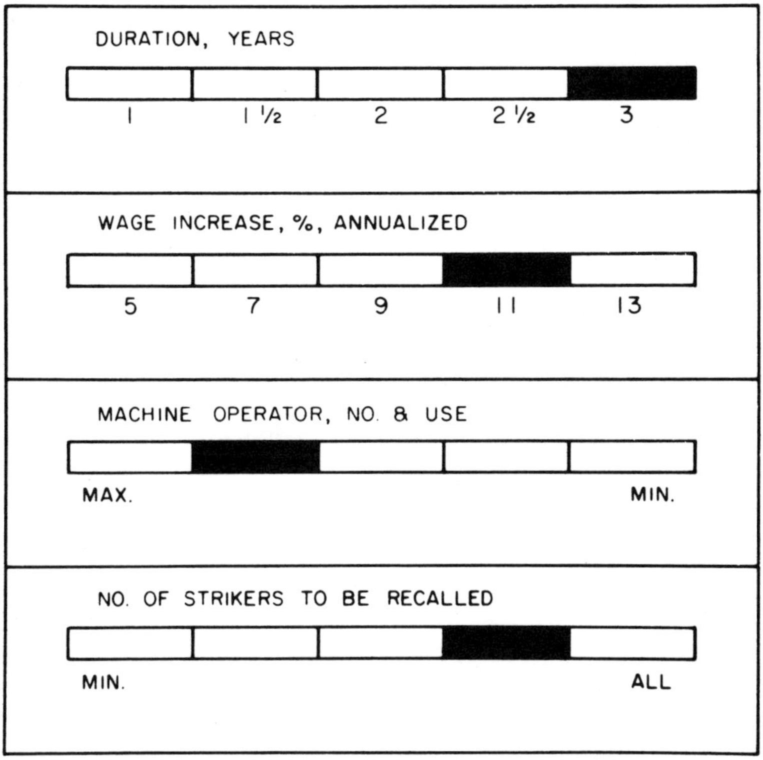

Figure 1. An example of a profile displayed on a computer graphics device.

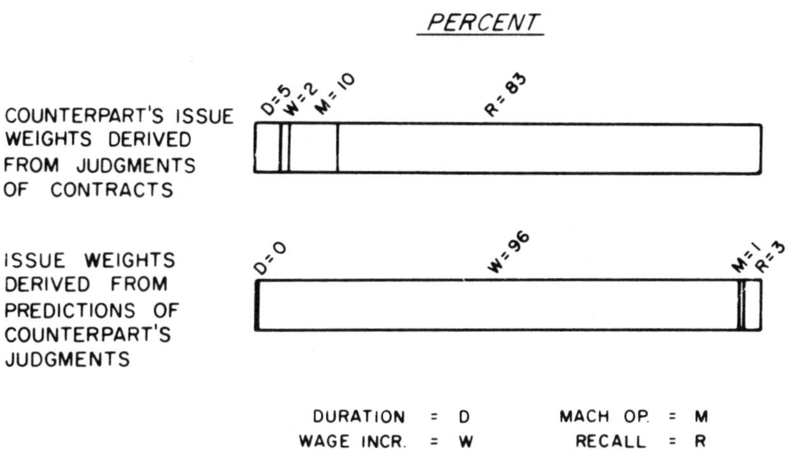

Figure 2. An example of a computer graphics display of weights.

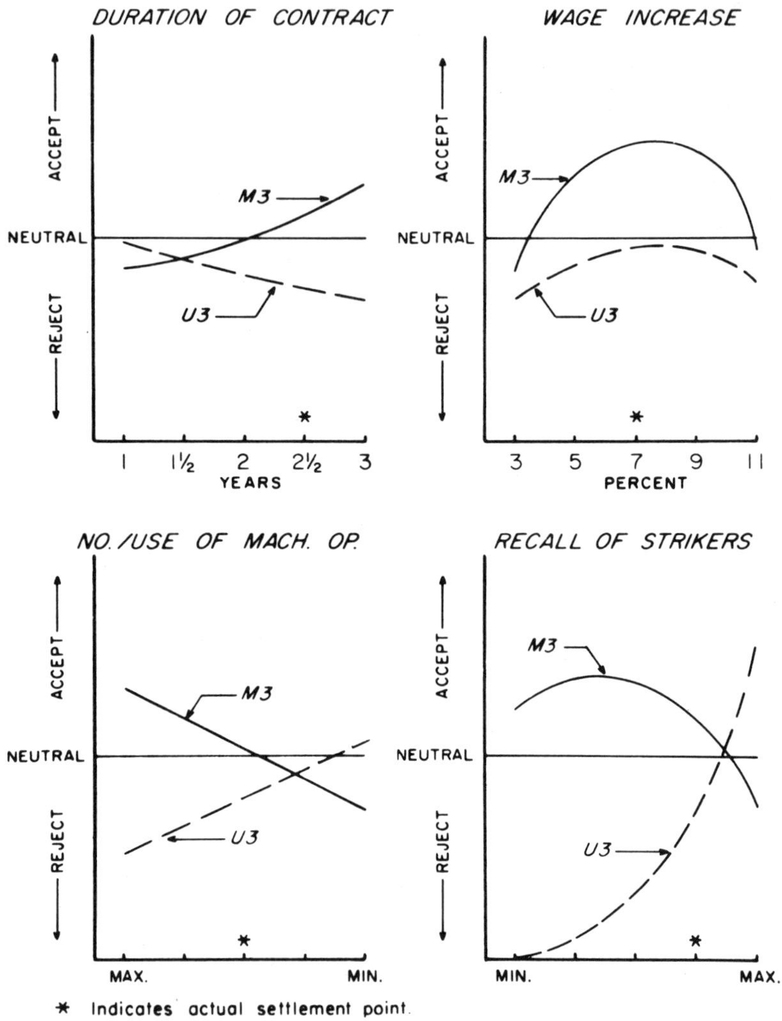

Figure 3. An example of a computer graphics display of function forms.

indicates that the contract would be of 3 years' duration, that the wage increase would be 11%, that almost the maximum number of "machine operators" would be rehired, and that nearly all the strikers would be recalled. Application of appropriate statistical analysis (see Hammond *et al.*, 1975) permits the extraction of the relative weights each negotiator placed on each of the four contract issues. Figure 2 presents a computer-generated display of the different weights one union negotiator (top line) placed on each of the four issues (length of bar segment indicates amount of weight). The union negotiator placed a weight of 83% on the "recall of strikers" issue and a weight of only 2% on the "wages" issue. When called upon to predict the acceptability of each contract for this union negotiator, his counterpart from management predicted that this union negotiator would place a weight of 96% on the "wages" issue and only 3% on "recall of strikers." This large misunderstanding is provocative, and becomes particularly so when one learns that the prediction took place after nearly 7 months of intense (and bitter) across-the-table bargaining between these two people. Similar results were obtained from two other pairs of union-management negotiators.

Figure 3 illustrates a display of function forms for a union and management pair. The results show that the union negotiator had a slight preference for a shorter contract and the management negotiator a slight preference of a longer contract. Both had *nonlinear* function forms with regard to wage increases. Their policies differed quite markedly with regard to the "machine operator" issue and the "recall of strikers" issue. Note the location of the actual settlement points. Displays of this sort, as well as others, may be presented immediately after the person rates a series of profiles. (See Balke *et al.*, 1973, for details concerning this study.)

These are the concepts Brunswik used in his description of the organism's use of information in representatively designed experiments. Because persons must cope with cognitive tasks (e.g., making a judgment about the acceptability of a labor contract) in which the network of relations is uncertain and interdependent, people can do little more than apply differential weights and function forms to various dimensions of the task. And because of the confusing entanglement of uncertain data, people have great difficulty in reporting accurately on what weights and function forms were used. Computer graphics technology, however, makes it possible to see this aspect of one's cognitive map immediately.

Display of weights and function forms for the various cues or dimensions of the task that the person includes in his judgment is also relevant to Tolman's consideration of the "width" of cognitive maps. For example:

> What are the conditions which favor narrow strip-maps and what are those that favor broad comprehensive maps not only in rats but also in men? (Tolman, 1948, p. 205)

The "width" of cognitive maps can be readily ascertained in the mathematical-statistical representations of cognitive maps provided by computer technology by displaying the number of variables (as well as their dependence) considered by the person exercising his judgment.

In addition, the extent to which *control* was exercised over the execution of the judgment policy can be displayed. That procedure was introduced because of the distinction Tolman drew between learning and performance. Hammond and Summers (1972) put the matter only slightly differently by drawing a distinction between *knowledge* and *cognitive control* over the execution of that knowledge. Just as Tolman pointed out that knowledge was not isomorphic with performance, Hammond and Summers pointed out that a person's knowledge of the properties of a judgment task was not isomorphic with the manner in which he executed his judgments. The accuracy of a person's judgments will diminish to the extent that a person lacks perfect cognitive control over his judgments, even though he may have perfect knowledge of the task properties. And just as one person cannot see the weights and function forms that another person uses in making these judgments, neither can one person see the degree of cognitive control exercised by another person. This quantity is, therefore, displayed for persons to see so that lack of control can be separated from incorrect knowledge.

A further advantage of the display of cognitive maps is that the persons making the judgments can evaluate the judgments that he in fact made—and *change* the judgment policy that produced those judgments, if he wishes, with complete control. That can be done by simple operations (pointing with a light pen, pressing a key on the keyboard), thus changing *weights* and *function forms* in a controlled way.

Moreover, if the properties of the task are known, the judge may *compare* the properties of his cognitive map with those of the judgment task. That is, the subject may see his cognitive representation of the weights and function forms of the task and compare this representation with those of the task. One may then change his judgment policy so as to maximize judgmental accuracy (as part of one's training, for example).

This procedure has resulted in the introduction of a new concept—*cognitive feedback*—the effectiveness of which confirms the emphasis of the Berkeley Group on the representational aspects of the cognition. Until this procedure was introduced, virtually all learning theory (aside from that proposed by the Berkeley Group) assumed that learning was contingent upon *outcome feedback*. Thus subjects were exposed to a variety of stimulus presentations, made a response, and were then exposed to the correct answer. How could learning occur without giving the learner the correct answer? Because no procedures were available for displaying information relevant to *cognition*, researchers were forced into accepting and using the research paradigm that implicitly assumed outcomes (often interpreted as "reinforcements") to be essential to learning. As matters stand now, however, feedback that is oriented to cognition is available, and its use places the concept of cognitive feedback in clear opposition to that of traditional, stimulus-response based outcome feedback.

Research results make it clear that outcome feedback is less effective than cognitive feedback (see Deane *et al.*, 1972; Hammond, 1971; Hammond *et al.*, 1973; Lindell, 1973; Slovic *et al.*, 1972; Summers *et al.*, 1970; Todd and

Hammond, 1965). Moreover, outcome feedback *impedes* learning when presented in conjunction with cognitive feedback (Hammond *et al.*, 1973) and complex tasks may not be learned at all if subjects are given outcome feedback only (Goldberg, 1971; Hammond, 1971; Deane *et al.*, 1972).

Cognitively oriented feedback concerning weights and functional relations can now be presented in pictorial form. But what about those organizing principles that were central to Krech's theory of cognition? Some progress has been made toward making these visible. Consider Proposition IV from *Theory and Problems of Social Psychology* which asserts that "The ease and rapidity of the cognitive reorganization process are a function of the differentiation, isolation, and rigidity of the original cognitive structure" (p. 135). These aspects of cognitive structure can now be displayed readily enough in the present state of the art. "Differentiation" may be displayed in terms of the *number* of variables taken into account by the person making the judgment. "Isolation" can be displayed in terms of the *interdependencies* among these variables. And "rigidity" may be displayed in terms of the *persistence* of a given judgment policy (or "cognitive structure") over various conditions. All well and good. What cannot be done at present, however, is precisely what Krech would insist upon: the display of various *organizing principles*. That problem warrants discussion, for it brings us to an interesting paradox.

Prior to the initiation of research on social judgment, psychologists had expected to find that human beings organize knowledge in rather complex ways, and, therefore, that rather complex principles would have to be invoked in order to describe the process. More than a decade of research into human judgment, however, has shown clearly that *simple* principles of organization (such as adding or averaging) are remarkably good predictors of people's judgments in a wide variety of situations, despite the fact that common experience and nearly all psychological theory tell us otherwise. Worse still, it can also be shown that a *variety* of simple principles are successful predictors (Goldberg, 1971) of judgments. In short, whereas most psychological theories (or models) of cognitive activity are long on sophistication and short on predictive utility, simple models are not only embarrassingly simple but also embarrassingly high on predictive utility.

Whether these findings speak more to the weakness of our research procedures or to the general validity of simple descriptions of human cognitive activity is uncertain. What is certain, however, is that social judgment theorists, spurred by the disbelief of laymen and colleagues (among whom Krech is sure to be included), will continue to pursue the problem: Is it true that more complex principles of organization need to be employed in order to describe cognitive maps accurately? If so, and it probably is so, how can those principles be described and displayed in pictorial fashion so that people can see, and thus understand, what they are doing? Even more important, how can pictures of complex organizing principles be displayed so that people can see that *their* way of organizing knowledge is different from *yours*?

This matter is of critical importance, for, as things stand now, it is virtually impossible for human beings to explain to one another how they organize data into a judgment. Until we overcome the challenge that Krech put before us, the paradox will remain, and social judgment theorists will continue to use simple descriptive organizing principles that work, fully cognizant that they may very well work for the wrong reason. Technology has not *entirely* caught up with Krech.

Cognitive Maps and Conflict

Perhaps the most important result of displaying the mathematical–statistical properties of cognitive maps is that it allows *two* persons to compare their judgment policies and thus to see directly those aspects of their judgment policies that lead to different judgments. In short, two (or more) persons can see the cognitive bases of a dispute arising from differing judgments. That is a significant innovation, of course, for without such computer-generated displays of cognitive maps each person must rely on reports offered by the other about the characteristics of his judgmental policy. And if there is any firm generalization that can be made about persons who are quarreling over the correctness of their judgments, it is that everyone treats such reports with considerable skepticism—*as they should.* The skepticism is misplaced, however. It is usually caused by suspicion of the *motives* of the other, rather than his inability to report accurately on the cognitive activity which produced the judgment. It is appropriate to be skeptical of the completeness and accuracy of an introspective report of the cognitive activity that led to a given judgment, not because every report is necessarily motivated by evil intent to deceive, but because human beings cannot report adequately regarding their cognitive maps. (A decade of judgment research shows clearly that human beings describe their own cognitive activity incompletely and inaccurately, even with regard to rather simple judgment tasks.) Because people do not have a useful framework by which to describe the cognitive aspects of the judgment process, and because they have learned from experience that reports of the process that are offered are seldom helpful, people have little recourse but to explain the cognitive activity of the other person in *noncognitive* terms. Thus the judgments of the *other* person are explained by referring to his motives ("he made that judgment because he wants to *get*") or to his emotions ("she made that judgment because she was *angry*"). Since both parties to the dispute turn to noncognitive explanations for the cognitive behavior of the other, the course of disputes is predictable, and predictably dismal. Since motives can always be found (*post hoc*) for any behavior, the circular explanation is self-confirming. Supported by the security of circular reasoning, by the comfort of folklore as old as humanity, and by psychoanalysis (now part of folklore), the overemphasis on motives will die hard.

It is, therefore, not strange that the cognitive bases for quarrels were never systematically investigated until recently (see Hammond, 1965). Ten years and roughly 30 investigations later (Hammond and Brehmer, 1973; Hammond *et al.*, 1975), it is clear that it is unnecessary to appeal to motives (or emotions) to explain interpersonal conflict arising from different judgments. Such quarrels can have, and do have, a purely cognitive basis.

An assertion that interpersonal conflict may rest primarily, if not wholly, on cognitive differences, and that cognitive processes may themselves account for difficulties in conflict resolution, challenges credulity. Indeed, the idea is so foreign to accepted doctrine that no amount of laboratory research will dispel that incredulity. Cognitive theory must meet the test of implementation in the real world outside the laboratory.

Implementation

Application of theory and research to the world outside the laboratory is interesting and valuable only when both are counterintuitive, or at least strange enough to make the layman dubious. Otherwise, success or failure would not convey information. Social judgment theory meets this general criterion, particularly with regard to its insistence on the importance of cognitive processes in interpersonal conflict. Parallel with the informative aspects of testing new approaches, however, is the resistance encountered by new ideas arriving from a behavioral scientist's laboratory. And, of course, in the late 1960s and early 1970s, any social psychologist armed with a computer terminal, prepared to argue that interpersonal conflict is largely a cognitive matter, and eager to help settle disputes was likely to be viewed with considerable suspicion. As Leon Rappoport put it: "The people we were most interested in studying were not likely to let us into their offices, let alone into their heads!" (personal communication).

Given these circumstances, it is surprising that implementation of social judgment theory has moved as far as it has in the past 5 years. Examples of the application include citizen participation in planning (Stewart and Gelberd, 1972), determination of policies about community goals (Steinmann and Stewart, 1973), and modeling of physicians' judgments (Stewart *et al.*, 1975*b*). Stewart *et al.* (1975*a*) describe the usefulness of social judgment theory for technology assessment, Flack and Summers (1971) illustrate its application to water resource planning, and Brady and Rappoport (1973) detail its relevance to policy about nuclear safeguards. In addition, Balke *et al.* (1973) show that cognitive factors can play a far larger role in labor-management negotiations than had been suspected. Adelman *et al.* (1975) also show the utility of cognitive theory in a dispute involving corporate policy, and Steinmann *et al.* (1975) describe the use of cognitive theory in the problems of public land acquisition for "open space" or urban "green belts." Miller (1973) indicates the usefulness of cognitive theory in reducing conflict in families with problem children, as well as in managing conflict between police and minority youth. Perhaps the most interesting implementation of cognitive theory has occurred in psychiatric hospitals, where it has been found that chronic schizophrenic patients can make use of computer-generated cognitive maps to improve their judgmental ability. Results indicate that such displays may be more efficacious in this regard than currently used psychoactive drugs (Hammond and Joyce, 1975).

Conclusion

Mathematical treatment of the Krech-Tolman-Brunswik theory, together with modern computer technology, has achieved what could not be achieved with the rat maze—direct visual display of a cognitive map. And although that step has not taken us nearly as far as we need to go, it has permitted the successful implementation of the cognitive theory of the Berkeley Group. More accurately, that step has permitted successful implementation of *part* of their cognitive theory, for only three of the ideas they produced have been mentioned here. Further implementation will surely be forthcoming as new research technology permits the exploration of the rich assortment of ideas offered to us by the Berkeley Group.

Finally, a personal note, I have described an intellectual adventure undertaken by me for which the port of embarkation was the Department of Psychology at the University of California at Berkeley, time of preparation being the late 1930s and the late 1940s. Although this expedition is not yet complete, it is nearing its end. I hope I will be forgiven, therefore, if I make my gratitude explicit now to David Krech, Edward Tolman, and Egon Brunswik—and I must also mention Robert Tryon and Alfred Kroeber—for inspiring the effort and charting the course. They were truly great intellectuals of their time, who never forgot, or wearied of, their obligations to humanity.

References

Adelman, L., Stewart, T. R., and Hammond, K. R. 1975. A case history of the application of social judgment theory to policy formulation. *Policy Sciences*, *6*, 137–159.

Balke, W. M., Hammond, K. R., and Meyer, G. D. 1973. An alternative approach to labor-management negotiations. *Administrative Science Quarterly*, *18*, 311–327.

Brady, D., and Rappoport, L. 1973. Policy-capturing in the field: The nuclear safeguards problem. *Organizational Behavior and Human Performance*, *5*, 330–347.

Brunswik, E. 1952. The conceptual framework of psychology. In: *International Encyclopedia of Unified Science*, Vol. 1, No. 10. University of Chicago Press, Chicago.

Brunswik, E. 1956. *Perception and the Representative Design of Psychological Experiments* (2nd ed.). University of California Press, Berkeley.

Deane, D. H., Hammond, K. R., and Summers, D. A. 1972. Acquisition and application of knowledge in complex inference tasks. *Journal of Experimental Psychology*, *92*, 20–26.

Flack, J. E., and Summers, D. A. 1971. Computer aided conflict resolution in water resource planning: An illustration. *Water Resources Research*, *7*, 1410–1414.

Goldberg, L. R. 1971. Five models of clinical judgment: An empirical comparison between linear and nonlinear representations of the human inference process. *Organizational Behavior and Human Performance*, *6*, 458–479.

Hammond, K. R. 1965. New directions in research on conflict resolution. *Journal of Social Issues*, *21*, 44–66.

Hammond, K. R. (Ed.) 1966. *The Psychology of Egon Brunswik*. Holt, Rinehart and Winston, New York.

Hammond, K. R. 1971. Computer graphics as an aid to learning. *Science*, *172*, 903–908.

Hammond, K. R., and Brehmer, B. 1973. Quasi-rationality and distrust: Implications for international conflict. In: *Human Judgment and Social Interaction*. L. Rappoport and D. A. Summers (Eds.). Holt, Rinehart and Winston, New York, pp. 338–391.

Hammond, K. R., and Joyce, C. R. B. (Eds.) 1975. *Psychoactive Drugs and Social Judgment: Theory and Research*. Wiley, New York.

Hammond, K. R., and Summers, D. A. 1972. Cognitive control. *Psychological Review*, *79*, 58–67.

Hammond, K. R., Summers, D. A., and Deane, D. H. 1973. Negative effects of outcome feedback in multiple-cue probability learning. *Organizational Behavior and Human Performance*, *9*, 30–34.

Hammond, K. R., Stewart, T. R., Brehmer, B., and Steinmann, D. O. 1975. Social judgment theory. In: *Human Judgment and Decision Processes: Formal and Mathematical Approaches*. M. F. Kaplan and S. Schwartz (Eds.). Academic Press, New York.

Jenkins, J. 1974. Remember that old theory of memory? Well, forget it! *American Psychologist*, *29*, 785–795.

Krech, D., and Crutchfield, R. S. 1948. *Theory and Problems of Social Psychology*. McGraw-Hill, New York.

Krechevsky, I. 1932. Hypotheses in rats. *Psychological Review*, *39*, 516–532.

Lindell, M. K. 1973. Cognitive and outcome feedback in multiple cue probability learning tasks. Program of Research on Human Judgment and Social Interaction Report No. 157. Institute of Behavioral Science, University of Colorado, Boulder.

Miller, M. J. 1973. Interpersonal understanding: Laboratory and field investigations. In: *Human Judgment and Social Interaction*. L. Rappoport and D. A. Summers (Eds.). Holt, Rinehart and Winston, New York, pp. 267–294.

Slovic, P., Rosov, B., Hoffman, P., Goetsch, J., Earle, T., and Geiseman, R. 1972. Effects of feedback in a multiple-cue learning study. Paper presented at the Fifth Annual Conference on Human Judgment, Boulder, Colorado.

Steinmann, D. O., and Stewart, T. R. 1973. Measuring the relative importance of community goals. Program of Research on Human Judgment and Social Interaction Report No. 156. Institute of Behavioral Science, University of Colorado, Boulder.

Steinmann, D. O., Smith, T. H., and Jurdem, L. 1975. Social judgment theory applied to the formulation of land use policy. Program of Research on Human Judgment and Social Interaction Report No. 174. Institute of Behavioral Science, University of Colorado, Boulder.

Stewart, T. R., and Gelberd, L. 1972. Capturing judgment policy: A new approach for citizen participation in planning. Program of Research on Human Judgment and Social Interaction Report No. 151. Institute of Behavioral Science, University of Colorado, Boulder.

Stewart, T. R., West, R. E., Hammond, K. R., and Kreith, F. 1975*a*. Improving human judgment in technology assessment. *Journal of the International Society for Technology Assessment*, *2*(*4*), 37–43.

Stewart, T. R., Joyce, C. R. B., and Lindell, M. K. 1975*b*. The application of judgment theory to clinical trials In: *Psychoactive Drugs and Social Judgment: Theory and Research*. Wiley, New York.

Summers, D. A., Taliaferro, J. D., and Fletcher, D. J. 1970. Judgment policy and interpersonal learning. *Behavioral Science*, *15*, 514–521.

Todd, F. J., and Hammond, K. R. 1965. Differential feedback in multiple-cue probability learning tasks. *Behavioral Science*, *10*, 429–435.

Tolman, E. C. 1948. Cognitive maps in rats and men. *Psychological Review*, *55*, 189–208.

Webster's Third New International Dictionary (unabridged). 1971. G. and C. Merriam, Springfield, Mass.

Jane W. Torrey

THE PSYCHOLOGY OF LINGUISTIC KNOWLEDGE

In most areas of psychology, methodological decisions are made on the basis of psychological theory. Appropriate units of analysis, causal factors, and types of data are suggested or limited by the theoretical orientation of the researcher and data are selected or interpreted to fit that framework. In the psychology of language, however, more than in other areas, the data themselves have clear characteristics which limit the range of theoretical orientations that can be usefully employed. For example, in speech some units of analysis appropriate for scientific study, such as sentences, phrases, words, and phonemes, are quite easily discernible even to the layman. Furthermore, it is apparent that among the units of language the larger ones are as real and valid as the smaller ones, that is, that sentences cannot be understood exclusively in terms of the words that make them up or words in terms of phonemes. Another obvious fact about linguistic utterances is that they are not something imposed upon the speaker by external influence. Speech is always creative in the sense that the particular utterances emitted are controlled by the speaker and created on the spur of the moment for her (or his) own purposes. The stream of linguistic behavior is largely independent of external events, either simultaneous or in the past. If it were not so, speakers could only say what they had been conditioned to say, and their speech would not serve the purpose of communication. A third elementary observation is that language is the exclusive property of only one species of

Jane W. Torrey • Department of Psychology, Connecticut College, New London, Connecticut.

organisms. It follows that whatever principles are to be used in understanding its nature they must be related to inherited, biological structures. Furthermore, recent findings (Brown and Hanlon, 1970) have shown that environmental "reinforcement" does not occur in a way that could account for language acquisition by human beings, and it is generally agreed that experiences with well-formed language are also inadequate to explain it. The process, then, must be guided by innate properties of the human organism. A further fact that is not so obvious to the layman, but is nevertheless today accepted by many linguists, is that language depends on a highly abstract and covert system of control which is not at all discernible on the surface or in observable sequences of speech. Both the production and the understanding of sentences depend on an elaborate kind of "knowledge" of which only the rare speaker-hearer who has studied linguistics has much explicit awareness.

These characteristics of the behavior we call speech, its molar units, its creativity, its innate basis, and its dependence on an abstract mental system, pose serious problems for behavioristically oriented psychologists because they are firmly wedded to a philosophical tradition in science whose assumptions are inimical or even irreconcilable to these facts of language. Reflexes or simple sensory-motor responses were the chosen units of behavioral analysis partly because the tradition started with the assumption that science was primarily an analytical enterprise, that the smallest molecules of behavior were always the most appropriate unit. The discovery of the conditioned reflex made it possible to imagine that all synthesis into more complex forms of behavior was based on this same "learning" principle. The notion that long sequences of tiny acts could be fastened together in an automatic chain by repeated application of one or another "reinforcing" circumstance during practice gave confidence to these psychologists that all behavior including speech would ultimately be explainable through the same mechanisms. Larger units would be merely complexes of smaller ones glued together by conditioning. Each stimulus or response unit in the sequence would determine the following unit with greater or less probability. The idea is tempting for its simplicity, but unfortunately it will not work for language. Both Lashley (1951) and Chomsky (1957) have argued conclusively that no such model could account for the grammatical structure of speech behavior.

The model of a "response" to an external stimulus has also imposed upon S-R behaviorism a peculiar form of determinism which says that the causes of behavior originate outside the organism in environmental circumstances. This assumption implies that behavior is potentially entirely controllable by manipulation of the environment. The technology of such control has been developed to a considerable degree in the case of subhuman organisms by the Skinnerian school. Skinner (1953) himself has carried it so far as to identify science with technological control, which leaves the organism completely passive at the mercy of chance events, or of other people who are able to manipulate the environment. This leaves very little theoretical framework for dealing with language, which is preeminently creative. With the exception of formulas, such as "Fine, how are you?" or ". . . hallowed be thy name," few utterances are predictable from the stimulus conditions past or present. Utterances are only infrequently "responses" to questions and even then the particular speech uttered is mainly determined by factors inside the responder. Rarely does anyone say anything exactly the same as what anyone else has said before and no genius is required to say something entirely new. In speech, the speaker is usually in control and is never said to "know" the language unless she (or he) is able to say whatever comes to mind.

Closely allied with the assumption of external determinism in this psychological tradition is a profound faith in a radical form of empiricism which maintains that all behavior is a product of conditioning. Many behaviorists regard this assumption as part and parcel of scientific determinism, so much so that they fail to realize that if it were applied consistently it would preclude any behavioral differences between species since such differences must by definition be due to innate factors. Confronted with that implication, they may retreat to the extent of admitting that there are unconditioned responses and other biological differences, but conditioning remains for them the only interesting way in which responses are determined in the development of behavior. The proposal of linguists that humans are equipped with an innate "language acquisition device" (Chomsky, 1965) without which experience would be helpless to teach language comes to these psychologists as an incredible heresy, a betrayal of the most fundamental assumptions of their science. Yet the evidence for this hypothesis of innate determination is both obvious and overwhelming in the simple fact that all except severely damaged human beings learn the language they are exposed to, and no other species, no matter how much exposure or how much carefully contrived training, learns anything that would be worthy of the name of speech in any human. Because of their disposition to assume that all behavior including perception is learned by conditioning, the S-R behaviorists have provided themselves with little or no theoretical framework for understanding the interaction of species-specific patterns with environmental influences. Nature has been so ignored in favor of nurture in S-R theory that there is almost no way to handle its effects. The typical way of treating unavoidable intrusions of nature has been to regard them as uninteresting or not part of the psychological enterprise.

External determinism and radical empiricism have also implied for the scientific researcher a policy of physicalism or operationism whereby stimuli and responses visible both to the psychologist and to his research assistant were treated as the only legitimate fields in which might be found the causes of behavior. Behavior, or visible response, has been treated as the subject matter of psychology, even to the point of renaming the field as "behavioral science." When the facts demanded a retreat from visible explanations, imaginary or "covert" stimuli and responses were invented which were assumed to be of the same nature as their overt equivalents, only too small or too incipient to be seen. Furthermore, it was explicitly assumed that the phenomena to be explained were always overt behavior. Mental events were nonevents; speech might be admitted as behavior, but never its content or meaning. "Verbal behavior" in psychological experiments is rarely if ever a normal use of language to communicate. Memorizing or imitating is as close as most such research comes to the study of "language." These policies and assumptions almost preclude the study of language learning, however, since language competence is not behavior and is not even a set of more or less probable dispositions to respond in any particular way. Language is a highly abstract psychological system; in other words, it is a mental fact. Unless this mental nature is recognized and the explanatory concepts are removed from the time sequence of stimuli and responses, no adequate theoretical treatment is possible. In the case of language, behavior is not what is to be explained; behavior is not what is learned. Focus on behavior makes it impossible to distinguish between competence and performance and thus to isolate the key subject matter of study, namely language itself. Behavior, that is, the performance of particular utterances, will never be explained until the psychology of language is understood. This psychology is not a "behavioral" science, but, in Miller's words, a "science of mental life" (1962).

Behaviorists are a peculiarly imperialistic lot. Not only did they rename psychology in their own terms, they also commonly refer to "learning theory," meaning stimulus-response learning theory, as though it were the only one in psychology. It is a myopic view when the large areas such as social and personality psychology are considered, which also deal with learning and which are largely shaped by other theoretical viewpoints. Among those other perspectives of psychological thought, the Gestalt tradition, to which Krech belongs, provides a theoretical framework which I believe is more compatible with the facts of language and more potentially productive of useful hypotheses in psycholinguistics (see also Neisser, 1967). I would like to try, therefore, to explore systematically the findings and methods associated with the Gestalt-cognitive tradition for their possible value in approaching some of the psychological aspects of language.

The molar units of language present no fundamental theoretical problem for the kind of thinking represented in Krech and Crutchfield's *Theory and Problems of Social Psychology* (1948). Their basic propositions of general psychology included that "the dynamics of molar behavior result from properties of the immediate psychological field" (p. 33), that "the perceptual and cognitive field in its natural state is organized and meaningful" (p. 84), and that "properties of a substructure are determined . . . by properties of the structure of which it is a part" (p. 94).

The Gestalt tradition also involves the ready acceptance of causal determination from within the organism which interacts with external stimuli in shaping mental and behavioral outcomes. The idea that "perception is functionally selective" (p. 87) means that perception must be explained in part by the wishes and purposes of the organism, not exclusively by external conditions past or present. As in utterances, the dynamic properties of the individual participate importantly. Spontaneous dynamic properties of the mind also have their influence when "as long as there is a blockage to a goal, cognitive reorganization tends to take place" (p. 112), and "the cognitive reorganization process typically consists of a hierarchically related series of organizations" (p. 117). The Gestalt concept of "insight" or spontaneous cognitive reorganization in problem solving gives room for creativity, another necessary characteristic of language use. Some such notion of a spontaneous putting together of elements into a new structure according to an abstract rule to conform to an intended meaning must be provided by any psychological theory if it is to deal with language.

The interaction of innate with external influences is also given a clearer framework in Gestalt psychology. Although the Gestalt approach is a long way from simple "nativism," it incorporates the idea that some of the internal organizing principles of perception and cognition are attributable to the given structure of the nervous system rather than to any conceivable combination of past experiences or conditionings. It need not be surprising, for example, if the structure and physiology of the eye, the optic nerve, and the visual cortex are invoked in explanation of the characteristics of the visual field. That experiences with language should also be apprehended by innate mental dispositions to certain hypotheses rather than others evokes no sense of shock or scientific heresy.

The most obvious way in which the Gestalt tradition is hospitable to the facts of language is that it is a cognitive tradition. "Mentalism" has never been anathema on either philosophical or methodological grounds. The necessity for abstracting from larger patterns of behavior the characteristics of underlying mental structure or of assuming the existence of thought from the occurrence of speech has always been accepted without resistance. Köhler (1938) pointed out that such larger patterns were used in other sciences without apology. For example, such things as gravitational forces are not directly observable and do not resemble the traits of anything that is observable.

Although the Gestalt tradition has these general characteristics that seem suited to explanation in psycholinguistics, it has not by any means provided a psychology of language or of linguistic knowledge. This chapter will be an attempt to expand the theory of psychology within the Gestalt-cognitive tradition in directions indicated by linguistic problems. It will try to give some answer to these questions about the psychology of knowledge: What is knowledge? What kinds of knowledge are there? Is linguistic competence a form of knowledge? If so, how does it differ from other knowledge?

Is Linguistic Competence a Form of Knowledge?

The question of whether linguistic competence is knowledge will seem to some to have the obvious answer "yes." We speak of "knowing" a language, or at very least of "knowing how" to speak it, and linguists use words like "knowledge" in describing what they mean by "competence" (Chomsky, 1966). However, if we rephrase the question to "Does a child (or anyone else) know the grammar of the language she speaks?" we will often find ourselves answering "no," because we find that most people of any age know little and care less about the subject of grammar. As psychologists trying to understand the basis of linguistic competence and the processes by which it is acquired, we are confronted with a paradox because linguists tell us that an elaborate and as yet incompletely known structure of interlocking rules is necessary to generate sentences, while at the same time we know that speakers whose performance conforms to those rules with incredible speed and accuracy may have almost no idea what the rules are. We also know that linguists or beginning students of foreign languages may know a good many of the rules without having much competence to speak the language. Linguists may pass off the problem by saying that the grammar "generates" only in a mathematical sense, but psychologists have as one of their tasks to explain how language is "generated" in a more concrete sense by speakers.

To answer the question, we must first start with an adequate psychological statement of what "knowledge" is and then compare that with what we know of linguistic competence. Psychological conceptions of knowledge are directly rooted in dualistic philosophy, which distinguishes sharply between mental and physical. Although the awareness of two such realms is an everyday human experience, and the naive observer usually supposes causal relationships in both directions between the two, the philosophers who have tried to identify the nature of both realms and their potential relationship have not been so successful in understanding how events could shape ideas or especially how ideas could move physical objects. Especially in the framework of a mechanical conception of the physical universe, it has seemed impossible to conceive of material substance being moved by immaterial. Where physical contact is necessary for a cause to produce an effect, it has seemed impossible to locate the point in space where such contact could occur. Descartes supposed that there was a single very small point of contact such as the pineal gland. Berkeley chose an even less plausible solution by supposing that the physical world might have no real existence but consist only of mental representations. Behaviorism took a similar but opposite position in supposing that the mental realm was at most a functionless epiphenomenon whose existence could be ignored in the study of behavior. The scientist who chooses not to take any explicit stand on the matter still implicitly regards knowledge as a clearly mental structure which may parallel the physical because it was acquired from it through the experience of the senses, but is nevertheless clearly separate from it.

Knowledge belongs to this mental realm. "Mental" somehow implies "conscious," since it is only because of our awareness of our own minds as distinguishable experiences that we believe in the separate realms at all. Knowledge, as a mental fact, is something we think of as being conscious. We think of it also as being related somehow to brain events or states about which we, however, know very little.

According to the empiricist tradition, there is nothing in the mind, no knowledge, except what has come in through the senses. Although many philosophers and psychologists have deviated from a strict adherence to this view, it is generally accepted that "knowledge" depends on some input from the environment by way of the senses. From the concrete facts of experience, we abstract concepts and propositions that organize and help to preserve those facts in memory and also generate even more abstract concepts and propositions that unite into extended cognitive structures such as scholarship and science.

Knowledge can also be conceived from the "outside" as if it were a property of the organism which could explain its complex behavior patterns. Tolman's "cognitive maps" (1949) served to explain the search behavior of simpler organisms than humans. Certain rat behavior could best be explained by supposing a simple kind of knowledge on the part of the rat. The same may be said of the "hypotheses" formed by Krech's rats (Krechevsky, 1932). These cognitions, like those of humans, are abstractions since they do not coincide with any particular overt action or object, but rather with certain sets of potential alternative actions in different situations, several of which have to be observed before there is evidence of "knowledge."

Most of us are aware that knowledge is organized into hierarchies of concepts arising from particular concrete experiences. Relatively concrete concepts are organized and interpreted into a pattern of more abstract superordinate concepts by which the experiences are explained or understood, that is, conceptually related to structures deriving in the same way from other experiences. Propositions organize concepts at all levels of abstraction into a variety of structures including causal relationships, logical inferences, deductions, and so forth. The hierarchical-conceptual order of knowledge gives it the property of independence from the sequence of time. The making of generalizations creates an order which transcends the sequence of concrete events, including the stimulus-response chain. The use of the concept of knowledge to explain behavior makes possible the whole abstract realm of explanatory principles from cognitive maps on up to technological know-how and moral laws.

A final most important property of conceptual knowledge is the fact that in the process of forming concepts and propositions the human mind can select from a large variety of properties of concrete experiences and lower-order concepts in the formation of the higher-order ones. Furthermore, any one lower-order concept can be organized simultaneously or successively on the basis of many different properties. In this way, cogitation or cognitive reorganization can be endlessly creative. The structures of knowledge are not rigidly determined by the input of experience, but can vary tremendously among individuals over time. Krech and Crutchfield (1948) formulated propositions stating some of the principles of organization and reorganization, making it clear that the individual with all her existing knowledge, her needs and personality, has an influence on the kinds of cognitive structures that are formed and re-formed. The person, as an individual different from all others, has a positive effect on her own knowledge and thus her own behavior. She is not a passive pawn of outside influences, even where those influences also strongly shape the kinds of mental structures she can have.

Knowledge of Language

Probably the most basic structure of human knowledge is knowledge of language. Linguists distinguish between performance, meaning roughly speech behavior, and competence, meaning the underlying mental structure. Competence is usually described as a speaker's "knowledge" of a language, or as the basis of the capacity to speak and understand the language. Yet this "knowledge" only partially resembles the notion of knowledge that is accepted in other contexts. It is similar in that language does seem to be a conceptual hierarchy and thus to organize behavior from outside the stimulus-response sequence of performance. Further, it is obviously and necessarily creative, so that performance in accord with it is controlled by the speaker as a person, not ingrained exclusively by outside influences. However, in other seemingly important ways, linguistic competence is not like other knowledge. First, it is not normally a conscious process. Awareness of the linguistic rules of grammar is neither necessary nor sufficient for the use of language. Speech performance conforms to elaborate grammatical rules without the speaker being at all conscious of them. Even speakers with some knowledge of grammar are not attending to its rules while they use their language. They are indeed often violating some of the rules they think they know. Second, the system of language as so far understood by linguists is clearly too abstract and complex for the 5-year-old user of the language to grasp; yet her language conforms to it. Linguistic competence seems to have very little relation to intellectual capacity since not only very young children but also most retardates acquire the basic rules of their language. A third fact about language is that we do not understand much about how it is learned. Teaching of any formal kind is obviously not necessary. Young children learn their native tongue in about 2 years with little or no formal instruction. Although second languages are often acquired through teaching, it is not clear what the relation is between the instruction and the acquisition of competence. Certainly it is quite different from the way in which mathematics or history is learned. In mathematics, rules are explicitly stated and consciously applied in problem solving, and the learner who cannot put the rule into words or other symbolic form has not learned the lesson. In language, rules may or may not be part of the instruction, and it is clear that they are neither necessary nor sufficient. The speaker's ability to put the rules into words has little relation to her competence with putting them into practice. A student of history can find most of the content of what she has to learn summarized in print, whereas the student of a language who could say everything that was printed in the text would have failed the course unless she could also generate entirely new sentences about content never mentioned in a text. Language teachers argue endlessly about methods of teaching, and we know little more than we do in the case of children about what experiences are necessary for the adult language learning process. The experiences children or adults seem to have in learning languages are not adequate to account for their success. Children hear and emit pedagogically random and often defective samples of the language they are learning, and students learn from a wide variety of different experiences, few of which closely match behaviorally the performances made possible by them. Linguists have suggested that experience of language impinges, not upon a blank slate or a set of conditionable reflexes, but upon an elaborately programmed "language acquisition device" (Chomsky, 1965) which guides the learner in the formation of appropriate hypotheses, which are then tested against the available linguistic data and rejected or selected within quite a narrow range of possibilities. This raises the question for psychologists of the detailed nature of this innate system and the laws of its operation in language acquisition. What kinds of innate structures or functions can we suppose and how can the processes of "learning" be understood in the presence of them? The notion that "learning" processes can be in any way "innate" seems at first to be a contradiction in itself.

Linguistic Knowledge and Visual Perception

To help in resolving this and other problems about linguistic competence and knowledge, it may help to compare language with another capacity in which we find similar paradoxes. Visual perception is also based on innate structures which must interact with continuing outside stimulation to provide a series of experiences which are simultaneously the product of internal and external factors. If we accept the fact that perceptual processes can be innately organized, it will seem less paradoxical to find that the same is true of learning. Visual perception also shares with speech perception the seemingly impossible fact that the physical stimulus impinging upon the sense organ has a different structure from the perception derived from it. To use Brunswik's (1938) terminology, the proximal stimulus or pattern of light that strikes the retina and the peripheral response processes in the retina itself must be conceived of as being a mosaic of separate points varying individually along the dimensions of color. Visual perception, however, is organized into three-dimensional space and into objects within that space which appear to remain constant in shape, size, and color despite radical changes in the mosaic pattern of retinal stimulation which makes it possible. Brunswik called perception a "central" process, implying that some reorganization of received stimulation was occurring in the central nervous system. The fact that the central perception corresponded quite closely to our conception of the distal objects reflecting the pattern of light into the eye made him believe that the central organization was entirely attributable to learning of some sort. However, although there is some evidence to show that perception can be influenced by experience, the interpretations of these findings are always forced to start with the assumption of some elementary spatial organization in orginal perception. Spatial organization and object perception *as such*, apart from their specific structure, must be made possible by innately determined processes in the visual system. Although it is not possible to specify the exact contributions of innate structures and experience in visual perception, it is at least safe to say that both must participate. As Neisser (1967) points out, it is true for both language and visual perception that the evidence for the role of innate processes is almost entirely deduced from the cognitive processes observed and hardly any evidence exists about them from the physiological side. This is not to say that physiological observations would be better evidence. Since the functions of these processes are largely in the cognitive world, it seems likely that the principal evidence will always come from cognitive data rather than from physiological observation. (This parallels the situation with nearly all theories of learning. Conditioning, for example, has been mainly researched in terms of behavior and much less by means of its physiological correlates.) At any rate, it is clear that our knowledge of the physiological processes that may underlie cognition or behavior should not be allowed to distort or explain away our direct observations of the latter events in themselves.

This suggests another kind of comparison between visual and language processes which can be made if we confine ourselves exclusively to the cognitive side: an exercise in what Köhler (1938) called "the phenomenological method." This means examination which takes the phenomena of vision (or language) as data in themselves without regard to whether or not we think we know anything about the physiological processes which we assume to underlie them. In everyday use of both vision and language, we feel ourselves to be dealing with events and objects which are outside ourselves and independent of our own psychological processes. Although we may as philosophers realize that our perceptions belong to us, are products of the interaction of the environment and our own nervous systems and are thus in some sense entirely private, this solipsist view is not our normal everyday impression of how things are. We see our own body side by side with other visual objects outside it, we act according to this impression, and we find nothing in the results that suggests we were wrong. Similarly with language, words and their meanings seem to belong to the community including other people even when they refer to ideas that we think of as subjective. Sounds appear to emanate from other people's mouths, and therefore, like people's visual shapes, they seem part of the outside world. However, it is not only the physical forms that seem to have external reality, but also the meanings. When other people talk, we have the impression that we are perceiving what they mean and that we are looking into, or rather listening to, their minds. Our perceptions are sometimes inaccurate with respect to what they really are thinking, but if they were not usually correct we would find it hard to conduct social relations. Lies and delusions are thought of as exceptional, irregular forms of communication. In the same way, we perceive meanings behind our visual perceptions. We see that a child has chicken pox, not just that she has spots on her face; we see that a man is rich, not just that he rides in a new Cadillac. In our memory we often forget the literal visual cues by which we reached our knowledge. Indeed, sometimes we do not even know what they are. We also perceive affective qualities and emotions outside ourselves. Facial expressions and tones of voice, sometimes almost unnoticed in themselves, seem to tell us directly some of the most intimate feelings of others even when the individuals are trying to mislead us or when the "person" involved is a work of fiction, as in a painting or a drama. We rely on our perceptions of things, and the objectivity of all these assessments is demonstrated by their correlation with data received from other things and other people. Thus, although in terms of the traditional division between mental and material realms, thoughts, meanings, and feelings and even perceptions belong to the former, a phenomenological description localizes many of them in the external world, and their intercorrelation with other data confirms their reality.

The phenomenal self is also a part of both the visual world and the world of language as one of the set of persons being perceived. Although most of the body is always peripheral to the visual field, it is always present and at the center of the perceived environment. Spoken language is also located in the self and generated by it. In speech or conversation, the self is the most important participant and can partly determine the subject of discourse. As a listener, it plays often a very active role in cogitating about what is being said by someone else or covertly responding. The self appears as the agent of many events in the visual and language worlds. It moves about and does things to other objects at its own will. It can give out orders and requests and see them executed. There is often a sense of voluntary control of events. The self appears phenomenally to be the cause of many events. This impression is what we refer to when we speak naively, at least, of "free will."

In a phenomenological description, we purposely try to ignore everything we might think we know about the genesis of our impressions. The questions of whether feelings exist outside the mind of the persons doing the feeling, or whether the particular perceptual organization comes about partly because of memories of past experience and the question of what physiological processes can account for perceptual qualities—these issues belong to another level of discourse. Among the phenomena to be accounted for by whatever theory are all the consistent patterns of perception and language regardless of how well they can be explained by any limited knowledge of their functional basis. We need, in other words, to know *how* feelings and thoughts are *perceived* in other people, even though we know that the perceptual processes must be different from those involved in perceiving feelings in ourselves. However, our theories about the causes are not themselves part of the phenomenal world. Phenomena like objects and words go their merry way regardless of what we think about their basis. We have only recently known enough about anatomy to realize that there are a retina, an optic nerve, and a brain, yet people could see just as well without such knowledge. The retina is not a visual phenomenon except to the anatomist or physician. The mosaic of points received by it from outside stimulation is never seen by anyone; it is only conceptualized by scientists. The only time an individual even attends to his eyes is when something goes wrong with them. Seeing double makes her realize she has two eyes; blindness, distortion, fuzziness in the visual field make her think about how her eyes work, but nobody would pretend that inability to describe in words how the visual apparatus functions had anything to do with ability to see. Seeing processes are unconscious. Visual organization, although it may be influenced by conscious intention or training, is usually tacit. Attention is normally focused on what is seen rather than on how seeing is done.

These things may also be said of language. Competence functions like the visual system, unconsciously, tacitly. We usually perceive the meaning of what we hear rather than the words as such. We are not aware of any interpretive process in reaching for this meaning, except in unusual circumstances. Just as few people know much about the anatomy of the visual system, so few have any knowledge of the grammatical rules they follow. Vision and speech are little influenced one way or the other by knowledge of the underlying processes and rules. Awareness of grammatical rules occurs only when there is a problem with these processes, as when something is said that we do not understand, or that seems not quite right, or we encounter speech defects and aphasias. These difficulties raise questions in our minds, we turn our attention to forms that we never noticed before and ask questions we never thought of as long as we dealt with normal language functioning.

The comparison between linguistic competence and visual processes is not meant to suggest any conclusion regarding the extent to which innately determined processes are involved in either one. It may be assumed in each case that innate structures play some role and that experience influences or modifies innate functioning. The fact that we refer to linguistic competence as "knowledge" more often than we do visual processes may reflect our greater knowledge of the anatomical basis of the latter or a belief that experience participates more in the former. It is not important here which is more a product of experience. The point is that we can conceptualize tacit mental processes that underlie visual perception or language without having to assume that the seer or speaker is aware of these processes or can use explicit knowledge of them in seeing or speaking.

Two Kinds of Knowledge

We will now return to the question of what kind of "knowledge" it is that can exist and influence mental processes but be unknown to the knower. The seeming contradiction in the concept of unknown knowledge may be resolved if we identify it as a distinct sense or level of knowledge which we may call "intuition." Among the definitions of *intuition* in Webster's *New Third International Dictionary* (1961) are the following:

> 2a: the act or process of coming to direct knowledge or certainty without reasoning or inferring; immediate cognizance or conviction without rational thought; revelation by insight or innate knowledge; immediate apprehension or cognition . . . . c: the power or faculty of attaining to direct knowledge or cognition without rational thought and inference. d *in Bergsonism:* a form of knowing that is akin to instinct or a divining empathy and that gives direct insight into reality as it is in itself and absolutely. e: quick and ready insight . . . . (p. 1187)

The notion of intuition has three characteristics that recommend it for purposes of describing linguistic competence. First, it is immediate. Intuition is generally considered to be natural, to have properties that are innate or "akin to instinct." No preliminary cogitation leads up to an intuition. Instead, it appears to be given from outside sources much in the way that perception does. The intuiter has no sense of having created her intuitions by her own mental efforts and may even be surprised at their content, as in a sudden cognitive reorganization known as "insight" that may occur in problem solving. People often have a similar reaction of surprise when their own linguistic intuitions are elicited. A second characteristic of intuition may be another way of stating the first, namely that the source of intuitions in the mind is unconcious. It is as though there is tacit "knowledge" which comes to consciousness only under special circumstances and normally remains outside of our awareness. We form our own utterances and understand those of other people by means of this knowledge, and we use it to make judgments of correctness of grammar, but only rare individuals (mostly linguists) try to identify the rules and principles of which that knowledge consists. A third characteristic of intuition is that it is typically, if not exclusively, concerned with concrete things and events. Its objects are phenomenally outside the individual, like most of the objects of perception. It consists of specifics rather than generalities, examples rather than words. Words represent concepts, which are to some extent abstracted from concrete experiences. Intuitions deal more directly with concrete reality in either perception or memory.

Intuition is different from another level of knowledge which can be called "reflection." *The Third International's* (1961) definition of *reflection* which is relevant for our purposes reads, "7b: introspective contemplation of the contents or qualities of one's own thoughts or remembered experiences" (p. 1908). The quotation used to illustrate this meaning is from Husserl: "Reflection can be practiced on every experience." Reflection contrasts with intuition in all the characteristics of the latter mentioned above. First, reflection involves inferences, reasoning, or other cogitation. It goes beyond mere classification by similarity of perceptual characteristics. If new ideas result from reflection, they seem to be products of preliminary thinking, of the thinker's own mental efforts. The processes that give birth to them are slow, purposeful, and methodical. They seem to come from within, not from without. Related to this is the second characteristic of reflection, which also gives it its name. Reflection always involves self-awareness. The subject matter of the thought is actually thought itself, usually expressed in words. The reflecting individual knows that she knows. She controls and directs the thinking process purposively and voluntarily. Often techniques of thought are consciously followed, such as scientific methods or mathematical procedures. A third characteristic of reflection is that it always involves symbols, verbal or otherwise. This is necessary because the subject matter of reflection is thought or language, which are themselves abstractions. Since the meanings of verbal symbols are always abstract and sometimes very abstract, reflection is not limited to concrete experiences and images. It is also more closely related to the nature of the symbolic system than is intuition. Thus the effects of language on thought are more evident in reflection. Because of the infinite possibilities for different conceptualizations along different dimensions of experience, reflection is a creative intellectual process, only loosely determined by the data from outside. Teilhard de Chardin (1965) argues that this kind of knowledge is central to the definition of humanity. He attributes to it the possibility of culture and progress.

Comparing intuitive with reflective knowledge, intuition could be said to be closer to perception in that its contents are phenomenally more like objects, more concrete and more directly experienced without intervention of conscious cognitive processes. Table 1 summarizes the general characteristics of perception, intuition, and reflection together with examples of each from visual and verbal material. Perception is already a step removed from peripheral sensory processes in that it is meaningfully organized in ways that stem at least in part from past experiences. However, it also covers organization

Table 1. Kinds of Awareness

	Perception	Intuition	Reflection
General characteristics of contents	Percepts	Concrete concepts	Abstract concepts Deductions Conclusions
Examples of visual cognitions	Objects Space Shapes	Identities Cognitive maps	Judgments Geometry
Examples of verbal cognitions	Phones Intonations Words Sentences	Meanings Understanding Competence	Interpretations Linguistic rules

into spatial objects, shapes, phones, and intonations that probably occur because of innate capacities. We usually speak of perception as a conscious process that takes place in the immediate presence of sensory input. Intuitions, on the other hand, although they may be about immediate perception, also refer to remembered or imagined objects, events, or words. We have characterized intuitions as being about relatively concrete ideas, but it is probably true that some intuitions refer to abstractions which are metaphorically represented in concrete symbols, such as visual patterns. In vision I have assigned to the intuitive level such things as the recognized identities of objects and remembered patterns such as cognitive maps, which serve as guides toward expected goals. Linguistic intuitions include awareness of lexical and grammatical meanings—in other words, language competence, the basis for most production and understanding of language. They would also include those intuitions which a linguist uses as data about the conformity of an utterance to the rules of a language or idiolect.

When we reflect, as opposed to intuit, we are thinking about thought itself or its tool, language. Thus the objects of reflection are necessarily abstractions which we must represent in symbols, mostly linguistic ones. They may be concepts or propositions such as deductions and conclusions. Reflective thought stemming from visual experience would include judgments of space or shape and geometrical reasoning. Reflection about language would include interpretation of meaning, that is, translation of meaning into other terms. It would also include abstract grammatical knowledge, such as knowledge of linguistics or of more simplified grammatical rules such as we learn in school. It would include any kind of ideas an individual might have about language, whether or not correct and whether or not they were descriptive of her own grammatical competence.

To examine further the usefulness of the proposed distinction between intuition and reflection in showing the difference between linguistic competence and abstract knowledge of grammar, let us look at the different characteristics of the two basic kinds of knowledge. First, we said that intuition gives a direct and immediate understanding. When a speaker chooses a word or a hearer understands a sentence, there is no mental reference to a rule of grammar to judge grammatical fitness. No proof or argument is required to determine grammaticality if the individual is a native speaker. Judgments based on grammatical competence seem to carry their own assurance of validity as a given. A linguist, on the other hand, making a similar judgment on the basis of abstract grammatical knowledge rather than on native language competence, must go through an inferential process of first determining which rules are relevant and then systematically comparing them with a given utterance to determine whether it is generated by those rules. Linguists accept the subjective appearance of validity in the native speakers' intuitions by treating them as data (givens) of the science rather than as fallible opinions. Also of an intuitive nature is a speaker's knowledge of meanings of words. These often carry the subjective impression of validity so that the naive speaker may act as though there were some necessary or logical connection between the word and its meaning.

Linguistic competence also resembles intuition in that its basis in the mind is largely unconscious. Children may have learned to speak and still be largely unaware of language as such, so that they cannot imitate exactly or answer questions about it. It is reported that very young bilingual children sometimes cannot understand an instruction to translate from one of the languages they know to another, as though they were not fully aware of the two languages as alternative ways of saying the same things. Similarly in the native language, young children seem unaware of language as such. The following conversation occurred between me and John (age 5) as I tried to elicit from him his preferred way of forming a question:

J. T.: I'm going to ask a question, and you're going to tell me the answer, and then you ask me the same question. All right? Here's a question: "Is John home?"
John: Yeh.

J. T.: And you say "Yes, John is home." "John is home."
John: John is home.

J. T.: All right. Now you ask me the question.
John: (Silence.)

J. T.: You ask me. "Is John home–"
John: Yeh.

J. T.: Um, but you ask me whether John is home.
John: (Silence while he plays with blocks.)

J. T.: You ask me the same question, and see if I can answer it.
John: (More blocks.)

J. T.: You say "Is John home–" to me.
John: Yeh.

J. T.: You say it to me. You ask me.
John: "John is home to me."

J. T.: No. Repeat after me, "Is John home–"
John: Yeh.

J. T.: No repeat. "Is John home–"
John: Yeh.

J. T.: Is . . . John . . . home?
John: Yeh.

J. T.: You ask me.

John: (Very softly) "John is home."

J. T.: No. "Is John home?"
John: Yeh.

John was never able to focus on the question as an example of language. He responded only to its meaning, and therefore answered it "Yeh" or "John is home." Roger Brown's famous attempt to get Adam to judge which of two utterances he considered correct elicited only an irrelevant and perhaps derisive comment to the effect that "Pop goes the weasel." Labov (1972) reports what may be the same phenomenon with teenage boys who were asked to repeat the exact words of an interviewer, "I asked Alvin if he knows how to play basketball." They frequently responded with "I aks Alvin do he know how to pay basketball," as though they had been able to perceive only the meaning of the model, but not the (to them) peculiar way in which it was phrased. Perhaps the all but universal attitude that grammar is a dull subject stems from the fact that very few people attend to the form of language as they use it. Language is the medium, but normally not the message. To think of language as an object is to reflect upon it, using language as a tool to study itself, using words to make explicit rules about the use of words, and using grammatical sentences to explain how sentences are generated. The intuitive or implicit knowledge of grammar shared by every native speaker is directed at questions of meaning, what things mean and whether they mean anything (i.e., whether they are acceptable sentences). It is only by reflection that we can answer the more abstract questions about the structure of utterances and how they are generated.

A third way to express the difference between linguistic intuition and reflective knowledge of language is in terms of concreteness. Intuitions always refer to specific instances. We judge intuitively whether this particular phrase means anything and if so what, but to make a general statement about a class of instances we are forced to use symbols which represent abstractions. As soon as that is done, we lose the ability to judge directly whether the grammatical pattern is acceptable. Intuition works only with the concrete instances. It works whether or not we are even able to make an abstract rule, and the formulation of the rule does not help the judgment at all—in fact, it prevents it from being made directly.

The phenomenological examination of linguistic intuition, then, yields a description of direct and seemingly valid impressions about concrete instances of language with no conscious reference to any store of known abstract rules. It is worthwhile now to describe phenomenologically the kind of knowledge we have called reflection. Like intuitive knowledge, it may also be treated as data about conscious processes. We can ask under what conditions reflection is likely to take place, what linguistic objects are most likely to be reflected upon, and how the tendency to engage in reflection about language is related to other psychological characteristics of the knower.

Reflection about language, as about anything else, tends to occur when and where it is useful. Raise the subject of language in any company of non-linguists and the first aspect of it to be discussed will be word meanings. People use meanings to communicate and they are the linguistic subject matter which is closest to our everyday awareness. Another aspect of language that attracts everyday interest is those variations in language use that have social implications, such as social class or regional marks. It is useful to many people to be aware of social class markers because control of their use may be a way of climbing the social ladder and awareness of their social meaning is a way of judging other people. Another condition for awareness of language as such, that is, for the start of reflective thought about language, is the appearance of a problem involving language. When we do not understand or are not understood, we sometimes focus our attention on the words through which we are supposed to be communicating meaning. When we hear what we think are errors in the use of language or when we disagree with someone about how a thing should be expressed, we may talk about language and linguistic rules in order to justify our judgments. When we are learning a new language, we are often inclined to wonder about the rules of that language because under these conditions nearly every utterance presents serious problems to be solved. Even language teachers who want to develop an intuitive grasp of the system find that students spontaneously either invent or seek information about rules to guide their understanding and production. The most persistent users of reflective thought about language are linguists, who, we might say, have invented problems for themselves about language by giving themselves the task of understanding its structure as such.

Those aspects of language most likely to be thought about are the most concrete, the most easily perceived as objects. Among the social markers of which people are most likely to be aware, the so-called stereotypes, are usages that consist of particular separate words like "ain't" or the "no" in double negatives. Inflections and word order are harder to perceive. I have explored the grammatical knowledge of young children by asking them questions about the meaning of grammatical forms (Torrey, 1972). Those grammatical questions most likely to be answered correctly are the ones that deal with forms that refer directly to concrete meaning. For example, second-graders were asked the meanings of the "s" on the ends of the words in the following sentences. "The dogs eat the cat's food. The cat says it's hers." The question as to the meaning of the "s" on "says" drew no responses that could be considered correct. This inflection is generated by a rule of grammatical agreement with a singular subject, and thus a correct answer would require a subtle abstract knowledge of sentence construction. The "s" on "dogs" was correctly interpreted by 84% of the subjects. It has a clear concrete meaning which is understandable even to young children. Reflective knowledge of language, then, is not the exclusive property of adults who are linguists, but awareness of and interest in the more abstract concepts of grammar are usually limited to special circumstances.

Unlike linguistic competence, any very extensive reflection on grammar depends on a certain level of intellectual maturity and intelligence that would permit abstract thinking. Linguistic competence or an intuitive grasp of grammar is highly developed in very young and even retarded humans, but grammatical reflection depends on a subtle intellect that is capable of understanding abstract rules.

My thesis, then, is that linguistic competence is knowledge of an intuitive sort which is quite distinct from a more sophisticated type of knowledge which I have called reflection. Before concluding I will try to follow the implications of this distinction in understanding the process of learning in the special case of language learning.

The Cultivation of Intuition: Language Learning

It is generally agreed that the goal of language learning is the ability to speak and understand the language, whether it be a first language learned at mother's knee or a second learned in a college classroom. In other words, learning a language is developing a competence, an intuitive form of knowledge, rather than a reflective knowledge of linguistic structure. Theorists of language teaching are very much aware of this distinction. Politzer (1960) says, for example, "linguists distinguish rather unanimously the learning of language (performing in the language) from the learning of rules and grammatical terminology" (p. 2). "Language is an intricate system of patterns. We can communicate in our native language without having the slightest awareness of the nature of these patterns . . . . We manipulate the structures mechanically, unconsciously, automatically. The goal of all language instruction is to achieve precisely the same kind of automatic control in the foreign language" (p. 14). The pedagogical policies recommended by Politzer and others in cultivating linguistic competence conform to the notion that they are aimed at cultivating a mental process that resembles intuition more than reflective knowledge. The first character of intuitive knowledge, moving immediately from idea to behavior without reflection, suggests two quite opposite psychological bases: learned habit and native perceptual organization. Politzer calls it a basic fact that language is a habit, and goes on to say that "This implies that it must be taught by producing the appropriate reactions to external stimuli and responses, until the pattern is learned without our being aware of it" (p. 14). Even while describing this process in terms of stimuli and responses, however, he recognizes that what is learned this way is not particular responses, but rather a pattern—in other words, an abstraction the perception of which requires assuming something other than practice. He goes on, "the stimuli and responses should be arranged in such a way that they make the patterns of language clearly apparent to the student. This does not mean that the student needs to be able to 'verbalize' about the patterns . . . . Language learning becomes the perception of a 'gestalt' " (p. 15). "While transformation and substitution exercises operate on a stimulus-response basis, the very fact that we arrange them according to patterns indicates an appeal to the student's ability to perceive these patterns" (p. 15). There is a clear expectation here that the student will have the capacity to recognize the appropriate grammatical pattern with or without having rules pointed out explicitly. Thus even while promoting the need for habit formation, Politzer recognizes the dependence of language learning on an existing capacity to perceive the system directly. Either psychological process, habit or pattern perception, tends to produce the kind of direct, immediate response that characterizes intuition. Other theorists of this process, such as Fodor (1966), point out that patterned presentation of stimuli is not necessary for the native language acquisition device to discover patterns. Even a random sample of utterance patterns, such as a child hears, will be organized by her perceptual processes so as to reveal to native intuition all the patterns of the language.

Politzer's account of the language learning process also uses the word "unconscious" to describe the kind of automatic process that language competence makes possible. He advocates taking steps to divert attention from conscious, explicitly formulated rules on grounds that the language student will be tempted to use a rule in a conscious, reflective fashion, which is irrelevant and, he believes, even damaging to the acquisition of an automatic (or intuitive) grasp. Exercises are designed to focus attention on the meaning of what is being said so as to divert attention from the forms as such, thus avoiding reflective consideration of language. Repetitive practice with linguistic forms has been described as a means of forming automatic habits, but it can also be interpreted as being a way of increasing exposure to concrete instances. A pattern drill can be thought of as a grammatical rule expressed entirely in terms of concrete examples, without any abstract terms or formulas. Thus the content of the lesson is on the same low level of abstraction as the utterances which will be produced when competence is acquired and about which intuitive judgments must be made. It is possible to believe that pattern drills in artificial languages might not produce pattern learning because the language acquistion device would not entertain the hypothesis that they exemplified linguistic rules.

My experiment (Torrey, 1969) with the learning of simple patterns of Russian grammar by English-speaking students showed that pattern drills materially enhanced the speed and accuracy of translation from English to Russian over what was possible with only an explicit understanding of grammatical rules. The patterns were shown to be acquired by means other than sequential associations between particular word responses, but subjects exposed to them were able to produce Russian sentences with something like the unhesitating efficiency of well-practiced habit or of normal use of language to communicate. Subjects who had only vocabulary training plus an abstract verbal understanding of the syntactic rule were much slower and less accurate because they were applying their explicit knowledge more consciously.

Conclusion

The view of language learning which emerges from this analysis of linguistic knowledge would characterize the language-learning process as a "cultivation of intuition." It can be thought of as the acquisition of a special kind of habit: a habit, not of response, but of conformity to an elaborate abstract system which is, like instinct, partly built into human nature, but also partly "imprinted" through appropriate exposure to the right stimuli. The learning process can also be thought of as developing an ability to perceive the particular patterned manifestations of linguistic universals that characterize the particular language. These particular ways of perceiving are learned in that the perceptions are shaped by the residues of organized experience, but they are also innate in that they depend on the nature of that original organizing process which gives both form and meaning to the experience. Because of two characteristics of language pointed out by Hockett (1960), "interchangeability" and "total feedback," the perceptual organization and habit-formation aspects of language acquisition cannot be separated from one another. "Interchangeability" refers to the fact that anything a person can understand she can also produce. "Total feedback" means that anything she produces she can hear simultaneously. Thus production and perception are learned together as part of one process, and the resulting knowledge we can refer to by one word: language. Similarly, the innate factors in language acquisition cannot be separated from the acquired. The detailed contribution of each kind of factor cannot be known in advance either from physical structure or from theoretical assumption, but must be derived point by point from a study of the cognitive and behavioral properties of language. The result is that in the study of language more than in most other fields of psychology we are building up rather than merely building upon our knowledge of basic human nature.

References

Brown, R., and Hanlon, C. 1970. Derivational complexity and order of acquisition in child speech. In: *Cognition and the Development of Language*. J. R. Hayes (Ed.). Wiley, New York, pp. 155–207.

Brunswik, E. 1938. The conceptual framework of psychology. In: *International Encyclopedia of Unified Science*, Vol. 1, Part 2. O. Neurath, R. Carnap, and C. Morris (Eds.). University of Chicago Press, Chicago, pp. 657–760.

Chomsky, N. 1957. *Syntactic Structures*. Mouton, the Hague.

Chomsky, N. 1965. *Aspects of the Theory of Syntax*. M.I.T. Press, Cambridge, Mass.

Chomsky, N. 1966. *Cartesian Linguistics*. Harper and Row, New York.

Fodor, J. 1966. How to learn to talk: Some simple ways. In: *The Genesis of Language*. F. Smith and G. A. Miller (Eds.). M.I.T. Press, Cambridge, Mass., pp. 105–122.

Hockett, C. D. 1960. The origin of speech. *Scientific American, 203*, 88–96.

Köhler, W. 1938. *The Place of Value in a World of Facts*. Liveright, New York.

Krech, D., and Crutchfield, R. S. 1948. *Theory and Problems of Social Psychology*. McGraw-Hill, New York.

Krechevsky, I. 1932. Hypotheses in rats. *Psychological Review*, *6*, 516–532.

Labov, W. 1972. *Language in the Inner City*. University of Pennsylvania Press, Philadelphia.

Lashley, K. S. 1951. The problem of serial order in behavior. In: *Cerebral Mechanisms in Behavior*. L. A. Jeffress (Ed.). Wiley, New York, pp. 180–198.

Miller, G. A. 1962. *Psychology: The Science of Mental Life*. Harper and Row, New York.

Neisser, U. 1967. *Cognitive Psychology*. Appleton-Century-Crofts, New York.

Politzer, R. I. 1960. *Teaching French: An Introduction to Applied Linguistics*. Ginn, New York.

Skinner, B. F. 1953. *Science and Human Behavior*. Macmillan, New York.

Teilhard de Chardin, P. 1965. *The Phenomenon of Man*. Harper and Row, New York.

Tolman, E. C. 1949. *Purposive Behavior in Animals and Men*. University of California Press, Berkeley.

Torrey, J. W. 1969. The learning of grammatical patterns. *Journal of Verbal Learning and Verbal Behavior*, *8*, 360–368.

Torrey, J. W. 1972. *The Language of Black Children in the Early Grades*. A Report from the Department of Psychology, Connecticut College, New London, Conn.

Webster's Third New International Dictionary of the English Language Unabridged. 1961. P. B. Gove (Ed.). Merriam, Springfield, Mass.

11

George Stone

ON THE CIRCUMSPECT POOLING OF REACTION TIMES

Since Krech never wrote a paper in which reaction times were used as a dependent variable, some brief explanation as to why I include a chapter on this topic in his Festschrift is in order. I find that three of the themes that Krech stressed during the period of my graduate education in the 1950s have been cornerstones of my thinking as a psychologist ever since. Although the subjects in my experiments have shifted twice from animals to humans, and although the substance of my research has varied over a range of biological, pharmacological, educational and even social topics, these three themes have provided a continuity which is visible to me, if to no one else.

The first of these themes was an emphasis on individual differences. In an era when most students of learning and associated phenomena were focusing on "crucial" experiments, Krech's work emphasized differences among subjects, whether rats or human, as not only being interesting in their own right but also offering a source of information about the substrates of the observed behavior.

A second pervasive theme in Krech's work was that of the indivisibility of the mental apparatus. In a period when learning psychologists rarely countenanced any discussion of motivation beyond a statement of the "hours of deprivation," and when neither motivational psychologists nor learning psychologists were inclined to acknowledge the validity of the studies carried on by students of perception, Krech displayed on the wall of

---

George Stone • Langley Porter Neuropsychiatric Institute, University of California, San Francisco, California.

his office the slogan "PERFINK," as a constant reminder to himself and his students that perception, feeling, and thinking were inextricably intertwined, were in fact aspects of the same unitary activity of the brain.

Both of these themes are crucially important for this presentation, but the third theme is the one that inspires the title and carries the greatest burden in my argument. From a very early point in his career, Krech repeatedly insisted that it was dangerous, foolhardy, and in fact nearly immoral to pool data over subjects without having first looked at them carefully, individual by individual. I well remember his diatribes against the learning curve, which he held to be almost entirely an artifact that arose from averaging performances over rats which differed in their time of arrival at insight into their laboratory problems.

Thus Krech taught us to be aware of and concerned with the differences among individuals in our samples, to acknowledge their holism as dynamic, open systems, and to study our data carefully before we began to merge them, to average them, and to perform statistical tests on differences between groups. My aim in this chapter is to demonstrate the relevance of his precepts in the study of response latencies, the dependent variables so dear to contemporary, cognitive psychologists.

Chronometric Study of Human Information Processing

Fortunately, there is no need for me to attempt to capture in a brief summary the current status of a field that has been growing so explosively as has the chronometric study of human thought processes. Excellent reviews are available to the reader who wishes to gain an understanding of substantive issues (e.g., Smith, 1968; many chapters in Kornblum, 1973*a*). I shall present only what is necessary as a background for my methodological concerns.

The chronometric endeavor, originated just over 100 years ago by the Dutch physiologist Donders, attracted a considerable amount of interest during the last quarter of the nineteenth century and the first years of the twentieth. By 1915 attempts to penetrate the nature of mental acts by measuring the time required to perform them had largely been abandoned because of the critiques of the Würzburg psychologists, who demonstrated the indeterminacies introduced by variations in "set" (cf. Woodworth, 1938). Only occasional studies of the physiological and psychophysical factors in reaction time appeared during the next 30 years. Woodworth cites a handful of studies scattered through the years from 1895 to 1928 which provided some information about the shape of distributions of reaction times, and quotes a surprisingly prescient interpretation by Johnson (1923) as to the source of the apparent multiple modes in these distributions. I shall have more to say of this later. In the late 1920s and early 1930s, the impact of discovery by psychologists of the statistical techniques of correlation was demonstrated in a number of studies investigating the generality of response speed over variations in task. The same stimulus gave rise to investigations of the relationships of speed to other characteristics of subjects—age, intelligence, and the like. The prematurity of such questions, on account of inadequate methods for multivariate analysis and inadequate conception of the processes involved, is evident in Woodworth's casual words:

> The correlations lead to the conclusion that speed of action depends on no one factor such as speed of nerve conduction or synapse latency. According to the requirements of any performance, different factors must play a part in securing speed. (Woodworth, 1938, p. 338)

The excellent summary of reaction time studies incorporated in Woodworth's 1938 textbook was not paralleled in other presentations of the period, and reaction time, or response latency, was infrequently used as a dependent variable during the second quarter of this century. A major rejuvenation of the chronometric method was inaugurated by the papers of Hick (1952) and Hyman (1953). Cognitive psychology, largely abandoned by experimental psychologists during the ascendance of the great behaviorists, began its renaissance with the entry of mathematicians and engineers into the fields of information processing during World War II. Operations research, game theory, statistical decision making, the mathematical theory of information transmission, and the development of digital computers with stored programs all demonstrated the feasibility of the rigorous and quantitative analysis of the *substance* of human thought, and offered tempting analogies for exploration regarding its *processes*.

Several fundamental problems have occupied the attention of chronometric experimenters during the past three decades. The first question raised was whether the human nervous system could be considered as an information channel, like those of the telephone engineers, which would demonstrate the characteristic of "limited channel capacity." Quite early in the study of this matter it became clear that the amount of information that could be transmitted, by machines as well as by humans, could not be specified without consideration of the efficiency of the *coding* scheme. "Hick's law," that reaction time was proportional to the logarithm of the number of stimulus-response pairings ("messages") that could possibly occur in a situation, was seen to be an oversimplified description of experimental results, which provided almost no information about the processes by which the transmission of information from stimulus to response took place. The resulting shift in emphasis to studies of coding and representation might well have occurred sooner had not the quest for simple principles led to unwarranted averaging of data.

A second major topic of investigation deriving from the conception of humans as information-transmitting devices was the question of whether there was a single, limited channel through which all information must flow. The emphasis here was not on the rate of processing information originating in a single source, but on the competition between sources. Studies of *selection* of messages coming to different ears, or to ears and eyes, addressed this issue of competition by asking "Which message will gain access to the limited channel?" Another source of competition was cotemporality. Here the question had to do with the delay in processing of that member of a pair of stimuli which came second by virtue of its delayed onset, lesser intensity, or lower priority. It was initially presumed that during the "refractory period" of the single information channel, the second message simply waited in some kind of short-term store.

Coordinated with and related to the investigation of the single-channel hypothesis was that of a second major conjecture—the hypothesis of "central intermittency" (Bertelson, 1966). The idea can be traced at least as far back as William James (1890), but its investigation by experimental means is usually dated to Craik (1947) and Stroud (1949, 1955). By this time, many psychologists were working with digital computers and had learned to be concerned with the "cycle time" of these devices. The suggestion that the human nervous system might incorporate some sort of similar periodicity as a mechanism to prevent "smearing" of incoming information (Lindsley, 1952), or as a gating mechanism in admitting information from multiple sensory channels to a single, decision-making channel (Kristoffersen, 1963), was not unreasonable. Callaway and his associates are mong those who have studied relationships between the alpha rhythm (Callaway and Yeager, 1960), the cardiac or respiratory cycles (Callaway and Buchsbaum, 1965), and simple reaction time.

In addition to the traditional experimental psychologists who studied information transmission, coding, filtering, and the like, and the physiological psychologists who studied cyclical fluctuations in readiness to respond, a growing group of mathematical psychologists were attracted to the rediscovered variable of reaction time. After the early paper by Christie and Luce (1956), a number of authors have investigated the kinds of distributions of response latencies that would be observed under various assumptions about the nature of the processes giving rise to them. These models have emphasized two levels of explanation; at the most elementary level is a statistical decision-making device that monitors a stream (discrete or continuous) of information coming in from a sensory channel. Different elementary distributions are generated depending on specific assumptions about the process, ranging from the simplest case of an exponential distribution (Christie and Luce, 1956) to convolutions of incomplete beta functions (LaBerge, 1962; Vickers, 1970; Luce and Green, 1972). It is generally recognized that in addition to the basic decision-making process there are other stages in the total sequence of events from stimulus to response. These other stages are generally grouped together as a "residual" of unknown form, sometimes assumed to be normal (e.g., Hohle, 1967) or high-order gamma functions that approximate the normal (Taylor, 1965).

This brief résumé of chronometric psychology may be concluded with mention of the neo-Donderians, whose writings began to appear about 10 years ago. Turning from the functional equations of the communications engineer and from models of statistical decision making, these psychologists came under the dominant theoretical influence of the process models or "flow diagrams," which arose by analogy from the complex artificial information-processing systems of computing centers. For them, critical questions were, first, whether a complex process was performed in serial or parallel stages (Egeth, 1966), and, later, which stages could be treated as independently additive and which interacted (Sternberg, 1969). Most recently, models have often embodied the property of modifiable allocations of limited "processing energies" (Atkinson *et al.*, 1969) or "attention" (Kahneman, 1973) to various components of an information-processing task in such a way as to generate fluctuating functional patterns of mixed serial and parallel or independent and interacting components.

The flurry of activity that has appeared with each new focus of interest demonstrates a repeated tendency to start with relatively simple generalizations of wide scope and gradually to introduce increasing qualifications and complications as we are forced to by really critical examination of the fit of our data to the theories. While this process may sound reasonable and efficient, and while it may seem to be in accord with Morgan's principle (Morgan, 1894) of never adopting a complex explanation until the simpler ones have been ruled out, I hold that it is really a false economy. The initial skeleton of our theory should be sufficient to accommodate the full complexity that our data will manifest. As Krech taught us, this complexity arises in part because not all individuals do the same thing in a standardized environment and in part because multiple aspects of the individuals interact in determining momentary performance (they "perfink"). As a result of the complexities, we must develop theories only from data which have been highly purified by critical inspection. I shall develop this argument first by demonstrating the properties of reaction time distributions as they are collected in our laboratory and then by showing what happens if we ignore the knowledge that we could acquire about their nonhomogeneity. Finally, I shall propose a strategy by which we can proceed to develop sound theory.

On Distributions of Reaction Times

Figure 1 is a reproduction of a figure from Woodworth's text (Woodworth, 1938, p. 337) of two reaction time distributions originally presented by Jenkins (1926). These distributions must look familiar to every psychologist who collects sizable numbers of responses from individual subjects and displays them as frequency histograms. They show the characteristic skewness and the tantalizing suggestion of multimodality, which is so difficult to establish as having statistical validity. In commenting on them, Woodworth remarked that

> The skewness admits of an easy interpretation: the quickest reaction depends upon a perfect adjustment in every respect, and the factors that make for imperfect adjustment can delay the reaction greatly and give a few very large RTs.

This interpretation points, albeit somewhat vaguely, to the principal thesis of this presentation: that RT distributions frequently—even charac-

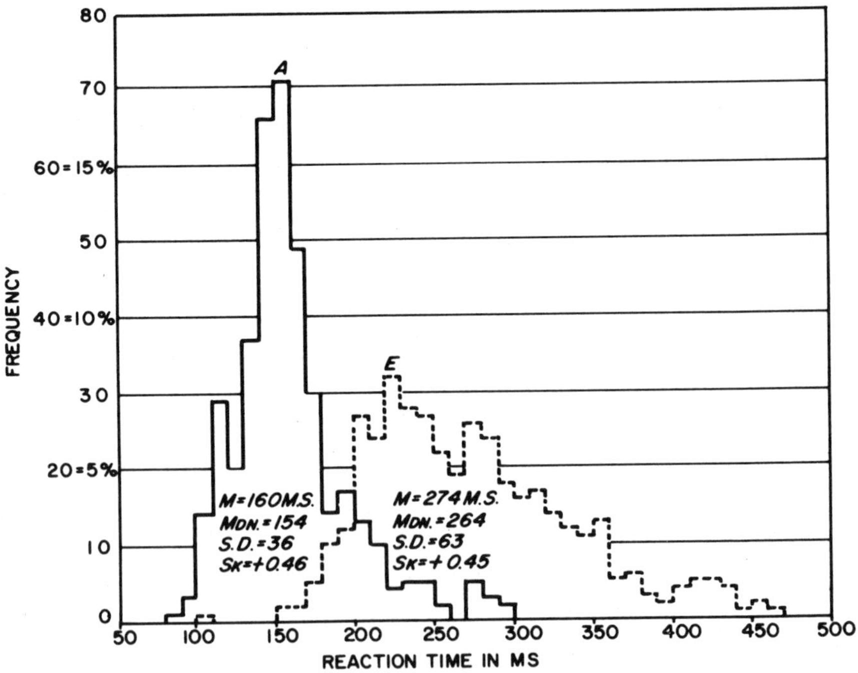

Figure 1. Representative distributions of simple reaction times. Each of two subjects made 400 simple reactions to the offset of a light. "A" was experienced; "E" was not. Data from Jenkins (1926), reprinted in Woodworth (1938).

teristically—consist of mixtures of different kinds of events. The point is made more explicitly in an earlier paper, which Woodworth quotes:

> There are a limited number of reactive mechanisms, having different latent times; those having the shorter times are the harder to excite and hence are less frequently excited under unfavorable conditions . . . the effect of training in reaction time work consists largely in increased frequency of use of the more quickly acting mechanisms. (Johnson, 1923, p. 582)

While I think Johnson's argument errs in important details, he did point to a major difficulty for both those who model means and those who model distributions of RTs. With very few exceptions, they start from the assumption that all or all but a very few of the trials whose latencies they collect represent repeated occurrences of a *single* brain process.

The notion that the variance of reaction time distributions is due in part to their arising from mixtures of *different* events appears from time to time in various contexts, but it has rarely been faced squarely. Instead, experimenters are advised to use catch trials to prevent "premature" responding; elaborate methods are developed for eliminating the influence of "fast guesses" from a distribution (Yellott, 1971); or the psychologist is advised that "the use of a logarithmic time scale will often correct the skewness of a distribution . . ." (Woodworth and Schlosberg, 1954, p. 39).

Let us acknowledge the logical possibility that a collection of reaction times may be based on two or more subsets of trials in which different brain events determined the response latency. I will refer to situations in which such multiplicity exists as "multiple process" (MP) systems. We must recognize that the obtained frequency distributions of RTs in MP systems would be shaped by two conceptually distinct kinds of variables: one is the moment-generating function of each component distribution arising from a homogeneous set of brain events; the second is the relative frequency of each class of events in the total population of reaction times. Differences between distributions obtained under different experimental conditions, from different subjects, or from the same subject as a result of practice, administration of drugs, fatigue, etc., may be due to changes in parameters of constituent distributions or to the proportions of different constituents that compose the total set of RTs.

This multiplicity of origin has been put forward as a theoretical possibility by a number of writers. Experimental and analytic procedures often attempt to reduce the impact of the problem. For example, in a number of studies in which multiple response alternatives were offered the critical analyses have been performed on only those data which were derived from a single response. This practice has not been nearly so common as it would be, however, if the implications of mixed distributions were fully appreciated. Much less common is the practice of isolating trials made in response to individual stimuli. The implicit justification for ignoring this source of variance is the assumption that differences that arise in processing different stimuli do not involve the basic process used by the subject(s) and can be left to the residual error variance so long as stimuli are distributed properly over conditions.

A simple thought experiment of the kind Krech used to offer us with such good effect will demonstrate the absurdity of attempting to build a theory of a process from data in which subsidiary processes are not distinguished. Suppose a Martian professor of social technology is interested in the means by which earthlings travel from one place to another. He cannot actually observe what goes on, but he has established a method for initiating trips between two points on Earth from his Martian laboratory and recording the exact time when the traveler arrives at the specified destination. He locates sites that are at distances of 50, 100, 200, and 400 miles from a convenient terminus, and causes 100 travelers from each city to report to his terminal data facility. He studies the function generated by the mean interval between message and arrival of the traveler at the final destination and finds that the square roots of the trip times are a linear function of the distances. The professor proposes that earthlings travel in a device that accelerates at a uniform rate of 0.022 miles per minute for exactly half the distance, and then decelerates at the same rate.

I generated the thought data for the Martian professor by positing four modes of transportation: local buses that run every 15 min, express buses that run once an hour, private cars that go to the nearest freeway as expeditiously as possible, and airplanes whose terminals are at various distances from the airports in the four cities. I made plausible though crude estimates of the average time required for each mode of travel and the proportions of travelers that would use each as the length of the trip increased, and I multiplied these estimates to get averaged trip time. The fit to the square root function was purely fortuitous, noted by me after rejecting a linear and log function, but with no adjustment of my initial "data."

How can we guard ourselves against committing follies as egregious as that of our fictional Martian colleague? One way is to try to think of every possible type of subprocess that might be involved in producing our data. This is the approach that leads to the concern with "premature" responses, "fast guesses," and strategies that are contingent on payoffs (Swensson and Edwards, 1971). A more empirical approach that is less dependent on the limitations of our imagination is to attend to the details of the latency distributions, emphasizing particularly the observed variance. If we can develop an estimate of the variance to be found in pure populations of uniform neural events, then we can use that estimate to guide us in our evaluation of the purity of the process underlying an obtained distribution. A second approach might lie in the recording of some aspect of neural function that could be used to classify events independent of the response latencies that they yield. Each of these approaches will be explored in light of preliminary data that are available. Before looking at the data, however, it will be well to give some further consideration to the concept of a "homogeneous set of neural events."

Neural Events and Reaction Times

Once we admit the possibility that, even though reaction times have been collected under standardized conditions, they may be the result of a mixture of events, a pair of related concerns is thrust upon us. First, we must consider what a single homogeneous process would be like. Is it the kind of event described by McGill and Gibbon (1965), in which "There is no feedback, no parallel processing, no branching, no backward motion of any kind"? The second question, which cannot be completely separated from the first, has to do with the sources of variance in reaction times of homogeneous processes. Essentially, we will define a "pure process" as one in which there is no "between-process" component of the variance.

We know very well that there is a series of occurrences that intervenes between the physical event (relay closure, transistor switching, etc.) that initiates the stimulus and the comparable physical event that signals the execution of the response. We can trace the sequence for some distance into the organism and pick it up again, if we take sufficient pains, some time before the customary termination with a switch closure. Although the portion of the total "latent period" that can be brought under detailed scrutiny is relatively small, we can observe variation from trial to trial even in that observable part. Leaving aside the variation in the performance of our physical apparatus (which may be considerable if we are using some of the common devices, such as visual patterns illuminated by incandescent bulbs), we encounter on each trial the operation of a sensory transducer which gives rise to modulations of frequency in the firing of a number of individual sensory neurons. Scott (Brink, 1951) has reported the events shown in Figure 2 as a result of stimulating a Pacinian capsule. Clearly, the pattern of impulses even in a single fiber will not be identical from trial to trial. Similar variability at the level of individual neurons on the response side has been reported (Calvin and Stevens, 1968). Thus our classification of two neural events as belonging to the same homogeneous class can only be a quantitative judgment. We must attempt to give meaning to the judgment by attending to those cases in which we conclude that they do not belong to the same class.

Let me propose some pairs of neural events that ought to be kept conceptually distinct: responses made by different fingers; trials with stimuli

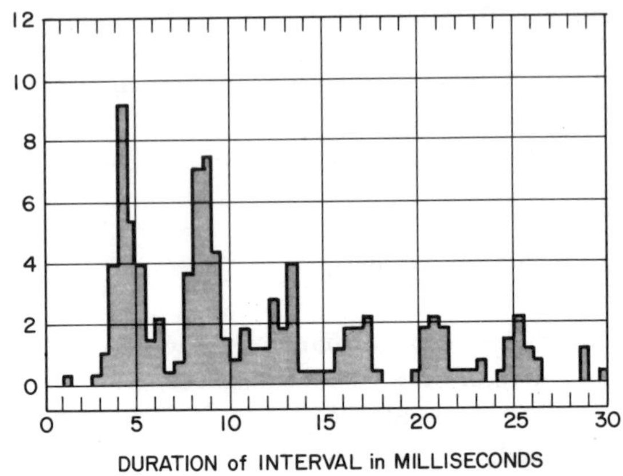

Figure 2. Distribution of interpulse times from single axon of a Pacinian corpuscle, chemically stimulated. Data from unpublished records of D. Scott, Jr., Johnson Foundation, University of Pennsylvania (1948); reprinted in Brink (1951).

projected on different sides of the retina; trials in which the sets of possible response altenatives have different measures. The first two of these examples involve demonstrably different populations of neurons, while the third is concerned with hypothesized populations involved in the representation of possible stimuli that were not actually given on a particular trial (Stone and Solem, 1970). For present purposes, this basis of distinction will have to suffice: I will mean by "different neural events" those which are determined by the action of populations of neurons which can be separated by some objective manipulation so that separate variance estimates can be obtained. I will also argue that when tasks yield large variances they should be suspected of arising from MP systems. The variation that arises due to sampling from the possible configurations of activity states *within* a population will be treated as parametric variance within a homogeneous or pure process (pp).

This formulation might also be considered in terms of levels of organization within a hierarchical system. Conceptually, the situation can be viewed as shown in Figure 3. In this directed graph, the nodes are to be interpreted as critical information states (CIS) which must be achieved before stimulus-based constraints can be imposed upon the activity of the later connected sections. If we could repeatedly measure the time interval between the appearance of activity at any two nodes, we would, as mentioned earlier, obtain a distribution determined by two kinds of variables: the time required to traverse each alternative path between the nodes multiplied by the second variable, the probability that that path will, on a given trial, yield the shortest interval. Conceptually, the single line connecting two adjacent nodes can always be decomposed into a graph with multiple nodes and multiple paths, down to the level of subatomic quantum events. In practice, we are limited in the resolution we can attain by our capacity to influence the probabilities associated with the various alternative pathways, or to identify those trials on which one or another of them was traversed by the information that triggered the observable response.

In the simplest MP system, we might think of a stimulus giving rise to activity in one or both of two alternative pathways, both of which converge on a single response (path A and B in Figure 3). If the two paths are *independent*, we have the "horse race" or "deadline" model, one variation of which has been investigated by Ollman and Billington (1972). Here the distribution of response times arises from the minimum of pairs of independent events. It can be calculated if we know the distributions of times to traverse each of the two alternative paths. We can then estimate the mean and variance of the distribution of reaction times that would result from such an arrangement. Some efforts have been made to apply such a model (e.g., Stone, 1971*a*) but have generally not been found to provide satisfying fits to empirical data (Rabbitt, 1971).

It ought perhaps not to surprise us too much if a model that assumes independence between competing organizations of neural activity falls short of the mark. From the level of single cells to as high a level as we are able to study systematically, the nervous system appears to be organized on a principle of reciprocal inhibition between competing systems (Eccles, 1953). Shallice (1972) and Walley and Weiden (1973) have offered specific psychological models that make use of this principle to account for properties of human information processing. The physiological processes that give rise to such inhibitory mechanisms can hardly be guided by a fine discrimination

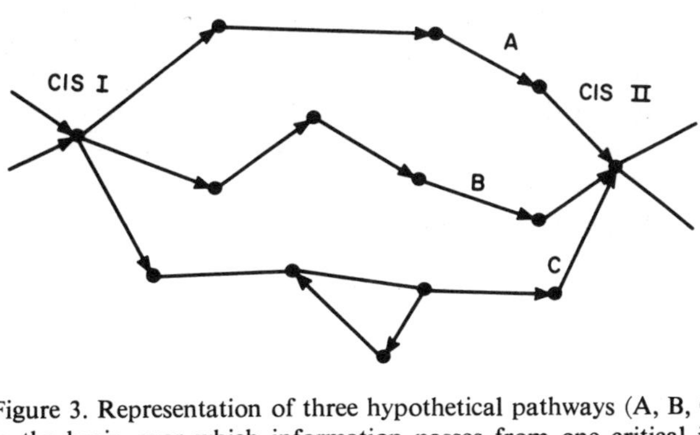

Figure 3. Representation of three hypothetical pathways (A, B, C) in the brain over which information passes from one critical information state (CIS) to the next.

of what is competitive and what is logically an alternative (converges at some CIS prior to the terminal state). Therefore, it would seem biologically appropriate, even though mathematically unfortunate, to suppose that alternative pathways do exert some measure of reciprocal inhibition upon each other. To extend the horse race analogy, it may be as though the steed that gains a temporary advantage scatters tacks in the path of its competitors. Perhaps this kind of obstruction, rather than a division of necessary processing energies (Atkinson *et al.*, 1969), may be the source of at least some of the phenomena of divided attention.

Now consider what might happen if the activity in paths A and B were struggling for advantage. If the situation were such that the first momentary edge for one pathway totally or at least decisively inhibited activity in the second, our distribution of observed outcome times would be a simple mixture of trials. Given the proportion of trials in which one or the other pathway gets the edge, and the means and variances of the two elementary distributions, the mean and variance of the mixture would be readily calculated. Naus (Naus *et al.*, 1972; Naus, 1974) has attempted, with modest success, to apply such a model to data from memory search for target words among two categories. More likely than immediate dominance of the competition by one of the contenders is a period of struggle which impedes progress in both pathways before one or the other wins out. This competition would increase the time required by the winner for completion of the process; and the variance of completion times would be increased for each of the constituent elementary distributions, since the amount of slowing would vary from trial to trial.

Until now, we have been considering only two pathways, each of which proceeds without feedback to the terminal state. However, some trials have such long RTs that it seems unlikely that they are completed with a single, uninterrupted traversal of a path. In fact, our experience when we serve as subjects supports the notion that reversions such as that depicted in path C of Figure 3 sometimes occur. Such events could occur only if the other entrants in the race had dropped out or been forced out, leaving the field to the faulty but restartable process. Our investigation of the processes of information processing will clearly be facilitated if we can exclude such deviants. Many investigators use some procedure for eliminating statistical outliers. Use of the median or some other percentile of the distribution greatly reduces the effects of any small proportion of such deviant trials on our estimate of the *location* of a distribution. But if MP systems are the rule in the operation of the brain, then we must be vitally concerned with variances as well as averages; and outliers which cannot be detected by the usual statistical procedures will grossly distort our estimates of variance. At this point, we must turn our attention to some discussion of the variance of RT distributions in order to see how we can interpret the variances we obtain in our experiments.

On the Variance of Distributions of Reaction Times

It is traditional to remark that the mean and variance of RT distributions are correlated. Two reasons are advanced for the correlation. On the one hand, as Woodworth and Schlosberg (1954) observed, it occurs because of the laggard RTs that are also supposed by these writers to produce the characteristic skewness. "The closer the reaction time approaches the [physiologically determined] minimum, the harder it is to shorten it further" (p. 39). This "explanation" begs major questions about RT distributions—what sets the minimum, what causes the laggards. Also, this rationale is applicable only to those situations in which a single process can be reasonably supposed to give rise to a large proportion of the RTs. The earlier tendency to "correct" for the correlation of mean and variance by using the logarithms or, occasionally, square roots of RTs was not appropriate to this source of correlation and has now been largely superseded by the more appropriate use of medians to define locations of distributions. A corresponding approach to the estimation of variability would be the use of the semi-interquartile range, or of the time interval between two percentiles on the left of the distributions, such as the difference between the tenth and fiftieth percentiles (Stone, 1971*b*).

The second, and psychologically more interesting, basis for the correlation of mean and standard deviation arises from the now commonly postulated "stages" of information processing (Sternberg, 1969; Smith, 1968). Complex tasks may require more stages of processing than simple ones: for example, the simple RT requires only that the stimulus be detected and the response made, while a choice reaction time requires that it be detected and coded and the response be selected and then executed. Each of these stages is expected to take time to perform, and variability is presumed to be associated with each stage. This presumption is sometimes used to test whether an information-processing stage is added by certain experimental manipulations, or whether mixed strategies are being employed (e.g., Naus *et al.*, 1972; Stone and Peeke, 1974; Warren and Lasher, 1974). Our lack of clarity regarding the definition of stages becomes evident when we ask ourselves how much variance ought to increase when we add an additional stage in processing. Our first reaction to this question may be that it probably depends on the complexity of the added process—thus on its addition to mean reaction time. Then we may visualize a hierarchical decomposition of stages into substages, and these into subsubstages, until eventually we are left with atoms of processing which have predictable mean durations and predictable variance. Such a conception would lead to an expectation that variance would increase in a constant proportion to the mean reaction time, an expectation that is a stronger version of the belief that mean and variance are correlated.

What do we actually know about the relationships between mean and variance of RT distributions of pure, homogeneous processes? Here we come face to face with the issue of circumspection in pooling data. Clearly, if we are looking at choice reaction time, same-difference judgments, or the widely used memory search task (Sternberg, 1966), the overall distribution of reaction times has trials that include a number of subsets that can be readily isolated. In choice RT, there are multiple stimuli and responses between which variance is likely to exist. In same-difference judgments, substantial differences between judgments of "same" and "different" are usually found, and data are rarely pooled over these conditions. But there may be differences between the speed of responding to different stimuli within the sets of "same" trials, for example, and these are almost never isolated. There may also be differences in the speed of repeating a judgment on successive trials, as opposed to changing one's judgment. There surely are large differences from this source demonstrable in classification tasks (e.g., Hyman, 1953; Peeke and Stone, 1972; Kornblum, 1973*b*). The point at issue here is that before we contrast variances of reaction time between two types of task we must be sure that we are comparing similarly purified sets of trials. In examining the variability of RTs, we will be most influenced by the lowest SDs that can be found, since there are many ways for extraneous variance to creep into a study, but few ways for an estimate to be spuriously low.

I cannot give here the results of any exhaustive survey of the literature with regard to variability of RTs, but a sampling of data will pose the issues. The simplest behavior that has often engaged the attention of psychologists is the "simple reaction time," the indication by the press or release of a key that a stimulus has been detected. Reaction times of highly practiced subjects usually have means in the range of 100–200 msec, depending on modality and intensity of the stimulus. The reported standard deviations of such reaction times are rarely over 30 msec and range down toward about 18 msec (Stroud, 1955). When the mean value of the simple RT is increased by diminishing the intensity of the stimulus, the standard deviation increases in proportion to the mean at a rate of 10–13% (Chocholle, 1940). When, however, the mean value is changed by instructing subjects to concentrate their responses in a particular "payoff band," results have been equivocal.

Snodgrass *et al.* (1967) obtained increases in standard deviations from about 20 msec, when means near 140 were obtained using a "payoff band" between 100 and 200 msec, to about 40 msec when means of about 240 were obtained from a payoff band of 200–300 msec. Thus the SD remained approximately 15% of the mean. Saslow (1974) used an easier payoff criterion in her fast band (175–225 msec), and obtained means close to 200 and SDs mostly in the range of 20–30 msec. From her payoff band of 300–350, she obtained means that ranged from 304 to 340, while standard deviations were still predominantly in the range of 20–30 msec. There was certainly not a proportionate increase of the SD at the longer RTs. One way of explaining the difference is to note that the fast payoff band of Snodgrass and colleagues required extremely fast responses, placing a pressure on their subjects which led to low variance. Their wide and easily satisfied payoff band between 200 and 300 msec did not press for precision, and precision was not obtained. However, in Saslow's study the narrower payoff band at the longer response time made an issue of precision and was able to exact it.

RTs from more complex tasks such as classification, memory search, and "same-difference" judgments usually yield SDs in the range of 40–60 msec when practiced subjects are used. (It is distressing that so few authors report the within-subject variability of RTs in their experiments.) Here again, the SD is very often close to 10–12% of the mean, particularly at the lower end of the range of observed mean values. For example, Swensson's (1972) very highly motivated subjects, making rather difficult discriminations after 20 or more sessions of practice, had means around 400 msec and SDs of 40–60 msec.

It would truly be convenient if we could adopt a figure, such as 10–12%, to represent the relation between the SD and the mean, for we could then recognize immediately those experiments where an excessive variance warned of a substantial mixture of events. The figure of 10–12% appears in many places. For example, an estimate of the SD taken from the distributions of interpulse times in the firing of sensory neurons presented in Brink's classic chapter (Brink, 1951) comes out very close to this value. Thus we might envision a scheme in which increasingly complex neural systems could be described in terms of the minimum number (r) of neural pulses necessary for them to perform their function, regardless of what those pulses did within the system. Then at the limit, when the system functioned flawlessly, the distribution of times for the system to do its work would be the convolution of r interpulse times. Similar proposals have been made by a number of authors. One very explicit suggestion was made by Restle (1961), who used Chocholle's (1940) data to estimate that about 100 stages were required to produce a simple reaction to sound. An implicit consequence of Restle's formulation was that each stage varied from 1 to 3 msec in duration depend-

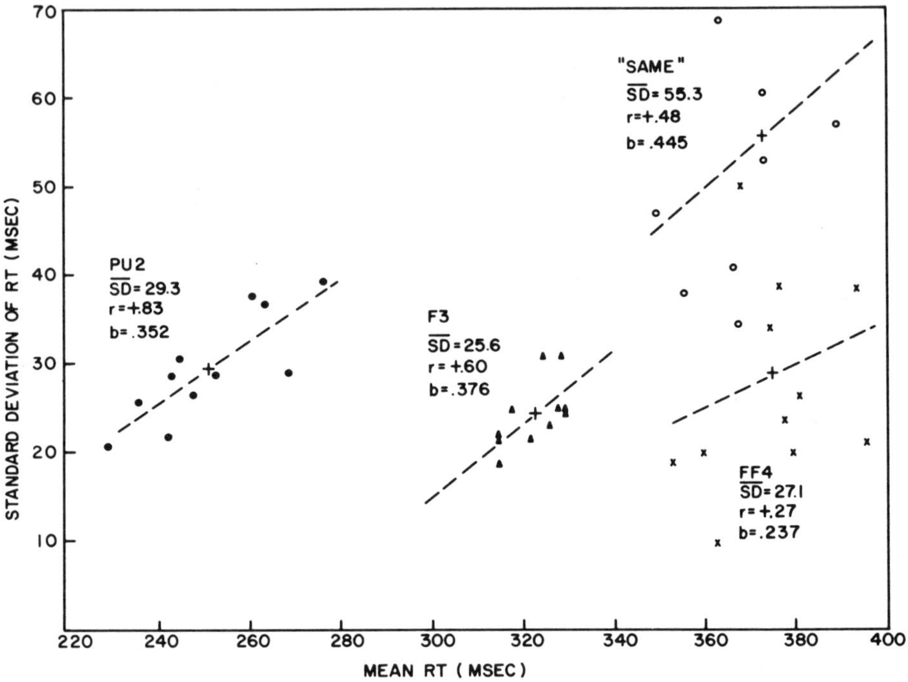

Figure 4. Plot of mean vs. standard deviation from 11 sessions for four different tasks (see text for explanation of tasks). Crosses on regression lines indicate the mean values of main and SD over all sessions.

ing on the intensity of the tone. The coefficient of variation, 10%, came directly from a property of the gamma function, which Restle took to be the form of an RT distribution, namely $\mu^2/\sigma^2 = r$.

Unfortunately, there appear to be some obstacles to the quick acceptance of this scheme. In the first place, coefficients of variation of even such elementary measures as interneural pulse times may vary widely—at least from 0.05 to 0.6 (Jansen and Walle, 1970)—depending on whether the neuron is idling or receiving steady input. If there is such a range *within* a single neuron, one can hardly hold to the assumption that distributions of intervals between two relatively "distant" CIS will be adequately described by the gamma function.

A second difficulty is that while there are good demonstrations of a linear relation between mean and standard deviation over a range of variations in the same task, equally convincing evidence does not exist for consistency over tasks. I shall now present some data from our laboratory that indicate that such consistency does not always prevail.

Figure 4 is a plot of the means and standard deviations of data from 11 sessions, in each of which a single, very experienced subject performed different tasks. These sessions, each about 45 min in duration, were control sessions spread out over a period of 6 months as part of a study of the effect of abstinence from alcohol on the acute impact of that drug. The data shown are from responses made on a single panel in four tasks selected to represent the range of demands. The tasks are described fully elsewhere (Stone, 1970; Peeke and Stone, 1973). The simplest task was to press on one of two panels when it was illuminated by a visual display. This task, indicated by the circles in the figure, produced a mean RT of 252 msec and a standard deviation of 29 msec, based on the pooling of values of means and standard deviations from individual sessions after first eliminating statistical outliers (Grubbs, 1969). There was a statistically significant correlation (+0.83) between means and SDs of individual sessions, to which skewing contributed only modestly. Most of the sessions yielded unskewed distributions of RT, with mean and median separated by no more than 2 msec. The SD is almost exactly 12% of the mean.

The next simplest task, as indicated by the mean RT, was to locate a target stimulus, presented briefly at the left of a display, from among a set of three test stimuli presented 200 msec later and to report its location by pressing on a panel overlying it. The stimuli were four simple forms, circle, triangle, square, and plus sign. The mean RT for this task, represented by triangles in the figure, was 323 msec, approximately 70 msec greater than that of task 1; but the pooled SD was only 26 msec, actually less than that in the first task, and only 8% of the mean. The correlation of means and standard deviations was +0.60.

Squares are used to represent data from a very similar matching task which was made more time consuming by using two superimposed forms as stimuli and a test display containing four such stimuli. These changes increased the mean RT by another 52 msec, to 375 msec, but left the SD essentially unchanged at 27 msec, and only 7% of the mean.

Finally, a "same-different" judgment was required, based on pairs of compound forms presented sequentially. The interstimulus interval was 300 msec, and the subject pressed the same panel whose data we have been examining to record his judgment that the paired stimuli were the same. The plus signs in the figure show a mean RT of 375 msec on this task, the same as that of the last task described, but here the SD is 55 msec, which amounts to 15% of the mean. Here again, the mean and SD are correlated, +0.45; and the correlation is not due entirely to skewing since the differences between mean and median correlate only +0.24 with the SDs.

What are we to make of these data? Clearly, it is possible to obtain standard deviations in some tasks that are substantially less than 10%, and to show progressions of mean RTs across tasks that are not accompanied by corresponding increases in SD. But low variability cannot be achieved simply by practice or by motivation, since we have here tasks performed by a single subject in the same test sessions with identical means, but the SD of one task is twice that of the other.

It should be noted that the (discredited) gamma function hypothesis of Restle, mentioned earlier, would imply that as r (the number of stages) increased, the coefficient of variation (CV) would decrease ($CV = 100/\sqrt{r}$). It seems likely that a similar relationship would prevail in the more appropriate, generalized gamma function (McGill and Gibbon, 1965).

We really cannot know how to interpret the relationships between tasks until we have in some way identified any subpopulations that exist in them. In the data just presented, for example, the different stimuli have not been segregated, nor have trials in which the stimulus or reponse was repeated. Suppose, for example, that repetitions of a "same" judgment cause a greater reduction of RT than do repetitions of a matching response, thereby introducing a greater variance between repetitions and nonrepetitions. I ruled out this possibility in the data cited above when I found that, in both tasks 3 and 4, repetitions of response actually produced longer RTs than changes, but that the differences were comparable for the two tasks. Other possibilities obviously exist to account for the different variances, but the point should be clear that we cannot at this time rely on a "figure of merit" for the CV that will apprise us of the adequacy or the inadequacy of our experimental control.

A Possible Method for Dealing with Nonhomogeneous Trials

If the considerations presented above are accepted as a valid critique of the current applications of the chronometric method, must we conclude that it should once again be shelved, as it was by the criticisms of Ach and Watt? One alternative to abandoning the chronometric approach has already been mentioned: we could insist that it be applied only in those situations where the variance of the RT distributions has been shown to be of a size consistent with the interpretation that a pure process underlies the observed latencies. But we do not now know what variance to use; and this occurrence may be so rare as to limit very severely the utility of the method. In this section, I will outline an alternative approach and present some very preliminary data relative to evaluating its promise.

The problem that I have claimed we face is that of distinguishing among trials on which qualitatively different events occur, even though the distributions of associated reaction times overlap substantially. The proposal is to use information from the electrical potentials available at the scalp to aid classification. The enormous literature on evoked responses provides ample evidence that events produced by different stimuli give rise to distinguishable averaged evoked responses (John *et al.*, 1967; Regan, 1972). More recently, Vidal (1974) and Pinneo *et al.* (1973) have reported techniques that permit them to distinguish with considerable accuracy which of a small set of possible stimuli occurred on a given, single trial. Might it not be possible to carry this process a step further, and identify those trials on which a fixed stimulus was handled in one or another way by the brain?

Considering the possibility from another vantage point, we also have evidence that the averaged evoked responses associated with fast and slow reaction times are not the same (Donchin and Lindsley, 1966; Morrell and Morrell, 1966; Bostock and Jarvis, 1970). These results suggest that there could be sufficient information available in the evoked responses from individual trials to classify the trials into pure populations of brain events.

I have done some investigations of responses evoked by auditory stimuli when two subjects performed a binary classification task. The subjects were required to judge as quickly as possible whether a tone was "high" or "low" in frequency. These data were collected as part of extensive studies of the effects of alcohol and marijuana on human cognition, which are being done at Langley Porter Institute by research teams headed by Enoch Callaway and Reese T. Jones. Full reports of the experiments from which I took these data will be published elsewhere. Very briefly: The subjects (both male) sat in a comfortable chair in a dim, sound-deadened room. A loudspeaker in the room presented, at intervals of 2.0 or 2.8 sec (randomly mixed), tones at 70 ± 2 dB intensity, and frequencies of 890 and about 900 Hz. The exact frequency of the higher tone was set to produce about 10% errors in classification. The tone persisted until the subject pressed one of two microswitches, under his right index finger or his left, to indicate whether the tone was "high" or "low." We recorded reaction time to the nearest 4 msec and two channels of EEG amplitude data for a 1-sec epoch beginning with the onset of the stimulus. The EEG recordings were taken between locations C3 and C4, and the vertex (C2). These locations are approximately over the central sulcus of the brain, on left and right sides, respectively.

I first sought a discriminant function that would predict which segment of the distribution of reaction times would be occupied by the latency on a given trial. Only the data from those trials of a single session in which the subject responded correctly to the low tone have been analyzed. Subject D had 247 such trials; subject B had 334. The 500 data points from the two channels of EEG (based on a 4-msec sampling of a 1-sec epoch) were reduced to 60 by pooling pairs of points in a 58–290 msec "window," then smoothed with a digital filter (Kaiser, 1966) in such a way as to greatly reduce the effect of frequency components below 4 and above 50 Hz. Reaction times less than

350 msec were rare, so the "window" of EEG data was relatively free from contamination by phasic motor potentials (Vaughan *et al.*, 1968; Kornhuber, 1974).

I first grouped the data approximately into quartiles, making use of nearby low points in the frequency distribution for the actual placing of the splits. In the case of subject B, the responses in the 10-sec interval where the split was made were removed from the analysis. For each subject, the data were randomly divided into halves; one half was used for the criterion groups and the other half was reserved for cross-validating the discriminant functions. In the analysis for both subjects, a few of the data points yielded significant *F* values in the stepwise program for multiple discriminant function (BMD 07M). However, in neither case was the classification of the reserved test cases better than chance. There are three possible interpretations to be placed on this outcome: (1) the EEG data did not contain information that would permit classification of the response; (2) the selection and smoothing procedures eliminated the information that existed; (3) the quartiles did not provide a sound basis for partitioning the trials.

The third possibility seemed most interesting to explore first, since it implied that even more than four kinds of processes might be present. It was evaluated in two different ways. First, cluster analysis was used to separate trials into groups in the hope that these groups would be homogeneous with respect to reaction time. Because of the inefficiency of available computer programs for cluster analysis, it was necessary to reduce the number of variables greatly. Two approaches were taken to this reduction: we obtained ten orthogonal factor scores by Varimax factor analysis; and we used the first seven variables selected in the initial multiple discriminations. Neither of these approaches yielded clusters of trials which had small variances of RTs. When the cluster analysis of all cases failed, discriminant analysis was done on narrow groupings of RTs. In the case of subject D, we chose 84 trials falling into three groups of RTs, each having a range of 40 msec and separated from the other groups by 10 msec or more. Multiple discriminant analysis still failed to produce accurate classifications, and cluster analysis of these selected cases did not reveal good associations of like RTs. As a last step before abandoning alternative 3, above, and returning to the first or second alternative, RTs from subject B were subjected to a somewhat Byzantine analysis. The primary mode of the data was located as a 30-msec strip which held 39 trials. These trials were partitioned into two "criterion" groups, following the rationale depicted in Figure 5. The region of the criterion groups is labeled *C*. I reasoned that if this mode actually represented an overlap of two closely approximated populations, as suggested by the dotted curves, the trials in the test intervals (*T*) on either side ought to be differentially represented in the classes that resulted from the partitioning

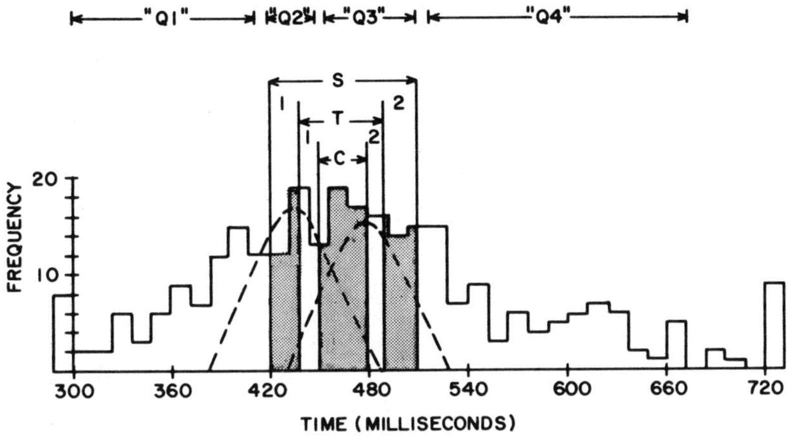

Figure 5. Approach to isolating subpopulations of evoked responses on the basis of RT distributions. The total distribution of RTs is shown by solid lines. Two hypothetical subpopulations are shown with dashed lines. The trials in the shaded areas, S_1 and S_2, were used to select seven variables by a stepwise multiple discriminant function. These variables were used in a partition of the trials in the shaded central region, *C*. Two resulting groups were called criterion groups for a final discriminant function analysis that classified trials in the unshaded regions, T_1 and T_2.

of the central group of trials. But what data ought to be the basis for the partitioning? Attempts to use variables derived from factor analysis or discriminant analysis of all trials had been signally unsuccessful in forming clusters. I decided to use the trials that lay just to the left and right of my test trials to select variables. These occupy the regions designated *S* in Figure 5. A multiple discriminant analysis was therefore performed on the EEG data using the 25 trials with RTs between 420 and 439 as one criterion group and the 29 trials with RTs between 490 and 509 as the other. The seven variables that yielded the best classification of these trials were next used in a cluster analysis program (IBMCLS) which finds the best partition of a group into a specified number of groups by maximizing the ratio of covariance within groups to that between groups.

When instructed to form two groups, the program returned groups containing 3 and 36 trials. The program was run again, therefore, with three groups requested. The same three trials, which interestingly were the first three trials of the session whose RTs fell into the specified range, again formed a group. Each of the other two groups contained 18 trials. These larger groups were then used as criterion groups in a multiple discriminant analysis, and the discriminant functions obtained were used to classify the test trials. The results of this analysis are shown in Table 1. The first thing

Table 1. Classification by Multiple Discriminant Function of Four Sets of Trials, with Associated Posterior Probabilities (P) [a]

Group C_1				Group C_2				Group T_1				Group T_2			
Trial No.	RT	Classification	P	Trial No.	RT	Classification	P	Trial No.	RT	Classification	P	Trial No.	RT	Classification	P
46	460	One	0.99	31	468	Two	0.99	6	448	Two	0.99	55	480	One	0.69
71	472	One	1.00	34	460	Two	0.98	40	440	One	1.00	63	484	One	0.51
92	464	One	0.92	72	476	Two	1.00	59	448	One	1.00	76	484	Two	1.00
102	460	One	0.99	82	464	Two	1.00	101	444	Two	0.41	138	484	One	0.83
105	452	One	1.00	93	472	Two	1.00	104	440	One	0.99	143	484	One	0.99
112	464	One	1.00	142	476	Two	1.00	106	440	One	1.00	150	484	Two	0.66
113	456	One	0.99	149	468	Two	1.00	114	440	One	0.91	155	484	One	1.00
133	460	One	1.00	169	460	Two	0.81	127	444	One	0.99	158	484	One	1.00
141	460	One	0.98	170	476	Two	1.00	153	448	One	1.00	185	484	One	1.00
154	472	Two	0.89	173	464	Two	1.00	156	440	One	1.00	191	488	Two	0.97
178	460	One	1.00	200	460	Two	0.99	165	448	Two	0.98	197	488	Two	0.71
213	468	One	0.99	219	472	Two	0.99	177	444	Two	0.84	204	484	One	0.83
272	468	One	0.93	220	452	Two	1.00	212	440	One	0.97	214	488	One	0.83
312	464	One	0.99	234	476	Two	0.95	238	448	Two	0.79	218	484	Two	0.97
315	464	One	1.00	249	252	Two	1.00	258	440	Two	1.00	248	480	One	0.99
330	468	One	0.82	252	476	Two	0.99	265	440	Two	0.58	267	488	Two	0.59
332	472	One	0.99	275	464	Two	0.97	299	448	One	0.99	274	488	Two	1.00
333	456	One	1.00	305	464	Two	1.00	306	448	Two	1.00	280	488	Two	0.75

[a] Criterion groups (C_1 and C_2) were established by prior partitioning of a single group of trials, using the same seven variables as were used in the present analysis. The two test groups (T_1 and T_2) had not been used previously in this analysis.

to be noted is that the hoped-for separation of the two test groups did not occur. The next thing to be noted is that many of the test cases were classified with posterior probabilities of essentially 1.0, which indicates that the selected aspects of their evoked responses conformed very precisely to those of one or the other of the criterion groups. Therefore, it seems reasonable to believe that there really were two well-defined groups of brain events associated with reaction times in the range of 440–489 msec. However, these two sets of events were not associated with discriminable RTs.

To examine the location of trials representing the two EEG groups within the total distribution of RTs, I pooled members of both the partitioned group and test groups whose posterior probabilities exceeded 0.90 and used these as two new criterion groups against which all other trials were classified. The result of this analysis was puzzling; 240 of the 278 trials in the test group were assigned with probabilities of 0.9 or better to one of the two criterion groups, and there was still no differentiation with respect to RT. To help clarify matters, I obtained the average EEGs of the two groups. Figure 6 shows these averages. Practitioners of evoked response technology who have looked at these curves have offered a variety of comments as to their possible significance. One possibility is that they may represent a kind of phase-locking of the alpha cycle. Whatever their electrophysiological meaning, it is clear that these classes of events are not distorting the RT distributions, since they have virtually identical means and SDs.

It still seemed possible that with this dominating component removed the approach might yet work. The process was therefore repeated separately for the two groups identified on the first iteration. Test groups were not formed, in the interest of bringing the selection groups closer to the trials to be partitioned. Once again, groups were identified to which most trials could be assigned with very high probabilities by the multiple discriminant function

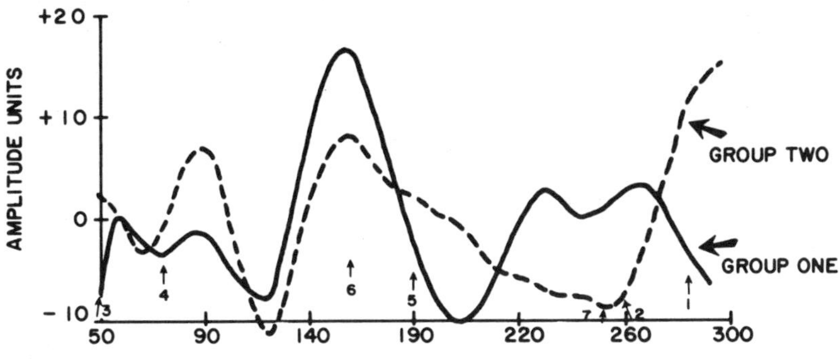

Figure 6. Portions of averaged evoked responses for two groups of trials that could be classified with posterior probabilities of 0.90 in the analysis depicted in Figure 5.

program. Once more the distributions of RTs associated with the groups were the same.

A similar analysis was carried out with data from subject B, with similar results. I conclude that there are subgroups of trials identifiable by their EEG events but that the data I chose for analysis did not include any that would permit the identification of subpopulations having different RT distributions. The problem could be in the smoothing operation, in the window selected; or it could be that the variables that affect RTs of complex tasks are not mirrored in the EEG (Morris, 1971). This conclusion should be reached only with additional data, however, in view of reports of significant differences in studies of the simple reaction, cited earlier.

Conclusions

Let me review the arguments and the empirical propositions that I have advanced, and then outline the strategies for chronometric studies of cognition that I believe to be recommended by them. The fundamental proposition was that quantitative properties of cognitive models cannot be deduced from data which unwittingly merge trials in which different brain events occur. A conceptual distinction between homogeneous and nonhomogeneous sets of events was proposed on the basis of whether or not objectively distinguishable groups of neurons were involved. Two possible approaches to the empirical classification of trials were considered. Some review of the literature and of data from my laboratory suggested that the variance of RT distributions offered a criterion that could sometimes lead to reasonable assurance of homogeneity, or could raise serious questions about it. However, some distributions cannot now be evaluated entirely by the criterion of variance, since we lack sufficient information as to what to expect in variances of "pure process" distributions. Preliminary attempts to use evoked cortical potentials as an external means for classifying events indicated that heavy investment of resources might be necessary before we could evaluate the potential of this approach.

Even though the first efforts were not very promising, it seems to me strategic at this time to pursue the possibility of a solution, *deus ex machina*, from the evoked response. Although this method may be difficult and costly, the value of such a technique would be so great as to warrant considerable expenditure in prospecting. Imagine that there existed a procedure whereby individual trials could be classified with respect to their conformance to certain prototypical patterns of brain activity. We could then trace the trial-by-trial development of the mature patterns during learning, and study the impact of instructions, sets, divided attention, drugs, etc., upon them.

The hope that we can ever achieve such analyses of our data, using the EEG or some other means to purify mixtures of events that generate overlapping distributions of reaction time, is certainly unsupported at this time. But I maintain that the evidence is plain in the standard deviations of our RT distributions that such mixtures exist. While we wait for the outcome of efforts toward the development of extrinsic classification systems, we should endeavor to isolate pure populations of trials by experimental means. This endeavor must proceed through the study of data most circumspectly pooled, while we observe at each step the effect of the pooling on the distribution of RTs. As we pursue this path, we will, *ipso facto*, uncover many of the sources of variance in our data. And we can proceed with the development of our models using lightly pooled data, for the halving of the standard deviation gains as much precision as increasing the number of trials fourfold. With a standard deviation of 25 msec, only 25 trials are needed to estimate a mean with confidence limits of ± 10 msec. This level of precision may be sufficient to let us proceed with the chronometric enterprise. The implication for research strategy is that we should not undertake model building until we have determined what the minimum variance in RT for a particular task should be; and we should then use the attainment of that degree of precision in our data as the criterion for proceeding to draw theoretical implications. It should go without saying that much greater stress should be placed on the inclusion of information on intrasubject variability in our reports of experiments.

I cannot close more fittingly than with a quote from the delightful polemic remarks made by Krech to his colleagues Egon Brunswik and Leo Postman, in a discussion of strategies for psychologists:

> I am convinced that it is in the microscopic world that one will most readily find uniform laws. And so Brunswik is eminently right when he argues that psychology becomes more and more probabilistic as it becomes more and more molar . . . . But if that is so, then if we are ever to build *theory* in behavior, we must, as Feigl has expressed it several times, stop being "psychologists" (again read "molar psychologists") . . . let us seek really to become unified scientists by consciously espousing the "microscopic" approach. (Krech, 1955, pp. 230–231)

Acknowledgments

The original results reported here were obtained with the support of U.S. Army Medical Research and Development Command Contract No. DADA-73-C-3146 and U.S. Public Health Service National Institutes of Health General Research Support Grant No. FR05550.

References

Atkinson, R. C., Holmgren, J. E., and Juola, J. F. 1969. Processing time as influenced by the number of elements in a visual display. *Perception and Psychophysics*, *6*, 321–326.

Bertelson, P. 1966. Central intermittency twenty years later. *Quarterly Journal of Experimental Psychology*, *18*, 153–163.

Bostock, H., and Jarvis, M. J. 1970. Changes in the form of the cerebral evoked response related to the speed of simple reaction time. *Electroencephalography and Clinical Neurophysiology*, *29*, 137–145.

Brink, F., Jr. 1951. Excitation and conduction in the neuron. In: *Handbook of Experimental Psychology*. S. S. Stevens (Ed.). Wiley, New York.

Callaway, E., and Buchsbaum, M. 1965. Effects of cardiac and respiratory cycles on averaged visual evoked responses. *Electroencephalography and Clinical Neurophysiology*, *19*, 476–480.

Callaway, E., and Yeager, C. L. 1960. Relationship between reaction time and electroencephalographic alpha phase. *Science*, *132*, 1765–1766.

Calvin, W. H., and Stevens, C. F. 1968. Synaptic noise and other sources of randomness in motoneuron interspike intervals. *Journal of Neurophysiology*, *31*, 574–587.

Chocholle, R. 1940. Variation des temps de réaction auditifs en fonction de l'intensité à diverses fréquences. *L'Annee Psychologique*, *41*, 65–124.

Christie, L. S., and Luce, R. D. 1956. Decision structure and time relations in simple choice behavior. *Bulletin of Mathematical Biophysics*, *18*, 89–112.

Craik, K. W. J. 1947. Theory of the human operator in control systems: The operator as an engineering system. *British Journal of Psychology*, *38*, 56–61.

Donchin, E., and Lindsley, D. B. 1966. Average evoked potentials and reaction times to visual stimuli. *Electroencephalography and Clinical Neurophysiology*, *20*, 217–223.

Donders, F. C. [On the speed of mental processes.] In: *Attention and Performance II*. W. G. Koster (Ed. and trans.). North-Holland, Amsterdam. (Reprinted from *Acta Psychologica*, 1969, *30*.)

Eccles, J. C. 1953. *The Neurophysiological Basis of Mind*. Clarendon Press, Oxford.

Egeth, H. E. 1966. Parallel versus serial processes in multi-dimensional stimulus discrimination. *Perception and Psychophysics*, *1*, 242–252.

Grubbs, F. E. 1969. Procedures for detecting outlying observations in samples. *Technometrics*, *11*, 1–20.

Hick, W. E. 1952. On the rate of gain of information. *Quarterly Journal of Experimental Psychology 4*, 11–26.

Hohle, R. H. 1967. Component process latencies in reaction times of children and adults. In: *Advances in Child Development and Behavior*, Vol. 3. L. P. Lipsett and C. C. Spiker (Eds.). Academic Press, New York.

Hyman, R. 1953. Stimulus Information as a determinant of reaction time. *Journal of Experimental Psychology 45*, 188–189.

James, W. 1890. *Principles of Psychology*. Holt, New York.

Jansen, J. K. S., and Walle, L. 1970. Signal transmission between successive neurons in the dorsal spinocerebellum pathway. In: *The Neuroscience Second Study Program*. F. O. Schmitt (Ed.). Rockefeller University Press, New York.

Jenkins, T. N. 1926. Facilitation and inhibition. *Archives of Psychology*, *14(86)*, 1–56.

John, E. R., Herrington, R. N., and Sutton, S. 1967. Effects of visual form on the evoked response. *Science*, *155*, 1439–1442.

Johnson, H. M. 1923. Reaction time measurements. *Psychological Bulletin*, *20*, 562–589.

Kahneman, D. 1973. *Attention and Effort*. Prentice-Hall, Englewood Cliffs, N.J.

Kaiser, J. F. 1966. Digital filters. In: *System Analysis by Digital Computers.* F. F. Kuo and J. F. Kaiser (Eds.). Wiley, New York.

Konorski, J. 1948. *Conditioned Reflexes and Neuron Organization.* Cambridge University Press, Cambridge.

Kornblum, S. (Ed.) 1973*a*. *Attention and Performance IV.* Academic Press, New York.

Kornblum, S. 1973*b*. Sequential effects in reaction time and absolute judgments. In: *Attention and Performance IV.* S. Kornblum (Ed.). Academic Press, New York.

Kornhuber, H. H. 1974. Cerebral cortex, cerebellum and basal ganglia: An introduction to their motor functions. In: *The Neurosciences Third Study Program.* F. O. Schmitt and F. G. Worden (Eds.). M.I.T. Press, Cambridge, Mass.

Krech, D. 1955. Discussion: Theory and reductionism. *Psychological Review, 62,* 229–231.

Kristoffersen, A. B. 1963. Discrimination of successiveness: A test of a model of attention. *Science, 139,* 112–113.

LaBerge, D. 1962. A recruitment theory of simple behavior. *Psychometrika, 27,* 375–396.

Lindsley, D. B. 1952. Psychological phenomena and the electroencephalogram. *Electroencephalography and Clinical Neurophysiology, 4,* 413.

Luce, D. R., and Green, D. M. 1972. A neural timing theory for response times and the psychophysics of intensity. *Psychological Review, 79,* 14–57.

McGill, W. J., and Gibbon, J. 1965. The general-gamma distribution and reaction times. *Journal of Mathematical Psychology, 2,* 1–18.

Morgan, C. L. 1894. *An Introduction to Comparative Psychology.* Scott, London.

Morrell, L. 1965. EEG correlates of reaction time: A study of background and light-evoked potentials. *Electroencephalography and Clinical Neurophysiology, 18,* 523.

Morrell, L. K., and Morrell, F. 1966. Evoked potentials and reaction times: A study of intra-individual variability. *Electroencephalography and Clinical Neurophysiology, 20,* 567–575.

Morris, C. J. 1971. Electroencephalographic and evoked potential correlates of reaction time and visual discrimination performance. *Psychonomic Science, 23,* 193–195.

Naus, M. J. 1974. Memory search of categorized lists: A consideration of alternative, self-terminating strategies. *Journal of Experimental Psychology, 102,* 992–1000.

Naus, M. J., Glucksberg, S., and Ornstein, P. 1972. Taxonomic word categories and memory search. *Cognitive Psychology, 3,* 643–654.

Ollman, R. T., and Billington, M. J. 1972. The deadline model for simple reaction times. *Cognitive Psychology, 3,* 311–336.

Peeke, S. C., and Stone, G. C. 1972. Sequential effects in two- and four-choice tasks. *Journal of Experimental Psychology, 92,* 111–116.

Peeke, S. C., and Stone, G. C. 1973. Focal and nonfocal processing of color and form. *Perception and Psychophysics, 14,* 71–80.

Pinneo, L. R., Johnson, P. A., Herron, J., and Wolf, D. E. 1973. Feasibility study for design of a biocybernetic communication system. *Third Semi-annual Technical Progress Report.* Stanford Research Institute, Menlo Park, Calif., September.

Rabbitt, P. M. A. 1971. Times for the analysis of stimuli and for the selection of responses. *British Medical Bulletin, 27.* 259–265.

Regan, D. 1972. *Evoked Potentials in Psychology, Sensory Physiology and Clinical Medicine.* Wiley, New York.

Restle, F. 1961. *The Psychology of Judgment and Choice.* Wiley, New York.

Saslow, C. A. 1974. Dual payoff band control of reaction time. *Perception and Psychophysics, 15,* 108–114.

Shallice, T. 1972. Dual function of consciousness. *Psychological Review, 79,* 383–393.

Smith, E. E. 1968. Choice reaction time: An analysis of the major theoretical positions. *Psychological Bulletin, 69,* 77–110.

Snodgrass, J. G., Luce, R. D., and Galanter, E. 1967. Some experiments on simple and choice reaction. *Journal of Experimental Psychology*, *75*, 1–17.

Sternberg, S. 1966. High-speed scanning in human memory. *Science*, *153*, 652–654.

Sternberg, S. 1969. The discovery of processing stages: Extension of Donders' method. In: *Attention and Performance II*. W. G. Koster (Ed.). North-Holland, Amsterdam, pp. 276–315.

Stone, G. C. 1970. Response latencies in human matching-to-sample. *Perception and Psychophysics*, *7*, 197–205.

Stone, G. C. 1971*a*. Response latencies in visual search involving redundant or irrelevant information. *Perception and Psychophysics*, *9*, 9–14.

Stone, G. C. 1971*b*. Individual differences in information processing comparison of simple visual stimuli. *Perceptual and Motor Skills*, *33*, 395–414.

Stone, G. C., and Callaway, E. 1964. Effects of stimulus probability on reaction time in number naming task. *Quarterly Journal of Experimental Psychology*, *16*, 47–55.

Stone, G. C., and Peeke, S. C. 1974. Relative frequency of attribute relevance and response times in visual search. *Memory and Cognition*, *2*, 453–462.

Stone, G. C., and Solem, R. A. 1970 Size of stimulus set and response latency in visual search. *Psychonomic Science*, *20*, 88–89.

Stroud, J. M. 1949. The moment function hypothesis. M.S. thesis, Stanford University.

Stroud, J. M. 1955. The fine structure of psychological time. In: *Information Theory in Psychology*. H. Quastler (Ed.). Free Press, Glencoe, Ill.

Swensson, R. G. 1972. The elusive tradeoff: Speed vs. accuracy in visual discrimination tasks. *Perception and Psychophysics*, *12*, 16–32.

Swensson, R. G., and Edwards, W. 1971. Response strategies in a two-choice reaction task with a continuous cost for time. *Journal of Experimental Psychology*, *88*, 67–81.

Taylor, D. H. 1965. Latency models for reaction time distributions. *Psychometrika*, *30*, 157–163.

Vaughan, H. G., Jr., Costa, L. D., and Ritter, W. 1968. Topography of the human motor potential. *Electroencephalography and Clinical Neurophysiology*, *25*, 1–10.

Vickers, D. 1970. Evidence for an accumulator model of psychophysical discrimination. *Ergonomics*, *13*, 37–58.

Vidal, J. 1974. Personal communication.

Walley, R. E., and Weiden T. D. 1973. Lateral inhibition and cognitive masking. *Psychological Review*, *80*, 284–302.

Warren, R. E., and Lasher, M. D. 1974. Interference in a type face variant of the Stroop test. *Perception and Psychophysics*, *15*, 128–130.

Woodworth, R. S. 1938. *Experimental Psychology*. Holt, New York.

Woodworth, R. S., and Schlosberg, H. 1954. *Experimental Psychology*. Holt, New York.

Yellott, J. I., Jr. 1971. Correction for fast guessing and the speed-accuracy tradeoff in choice reaction time. *Journal of Mathematical Psychology*, **8**, **159**–199.

INDEX